DISCOURSES
and
ESSAY ON THE
ORIGIN OF LANGUAGES

JEAN-JACQUES ROUSSEAU

THE FIRST AND SECOND DISCOURSES
together with the Replies to Critics

and

ESSAY ON THE ORIGIN OF LANGUAGES

Edited, translated, and annotated by
Victor Gourevitch

Harper Torchbooks

Harper & Row, Publishers, New York
Grand Rapids, Philadelphia, St. Louis, San Francisco
London, Singapore, Sydney, Tokyo, Toronto

These essays were published separately in French under the titles *Discours sur les sciences et les arts, Discours sur l'origine et les fondements de l'inégalité parmi les hommes,* and *Essai sur l'origine des langues.*

First TORCHBOOK edition published 1990.

Designer: C. Linda Dingler
Photograph on p. 116 by Joseph Szaszfai

The Library of Congress has catalogued the first edition as follows:

Rousseau, Jean-Jacques, 1712–1778.
    The first and the second discourses together with
the replies to critics and the essay on the origin of
languages.

    Includes index.
    1. Philosophy—Addresses, essays, lectures.
2. Language and languages—Origin—Addresses, essays,
lectures. I. Gourevitch, Victor. II. Title
B2132.E5   1986   844'.5   85-45226
ISBN 0-06-015538-8
ISBN 0-06-096029-9 (pbk.)

ISBN 0-06-132083-8 (torchbook)
90 91 92 93 94 MPC 10 9 8 7 6 5 4 3

Contents

Editor's Preface

This volume brings together Rousseau's major early theoretical writings: the First and Second *Discourses,* the extensive Replies to various critics of the *Discourses,* and the *Essay on the Origin of Languages.* These are Rousseau's great diagnostic and critical works. They are more exploratory, and they are more radical than his great constructive or reconstructive works, *Of the Social Contract* and the *Emile.* Although they differ in form and emphasis, these works form a remarkably comprehensive and coherent whole. The problems they explore are the abiding problems of moral and political life: what are the relations between knowledge, morals, and happiness; hence: what is our moral psychology, what are the bases of the various forms of social life, what would constitute a just order; does, or can, nature, in any of its senses, provide guides or norms for it?

These writings speak to us with great immediacy. My aim throughout the translations has been to preserve that immediacy. At the same time, I have tried to make them sufficiently accurate to permit close, even minute study of Rousseau's text. I have therefore adhered as closely as I could both to what he said and to how he said it. I did not attempt to dissolve difficulties which he chose to let stand, I did not paraphrase or transpose his vocabulary into ours, and as far as possible I even followed his punctuation and use of capitals. The text may therefore at times look slightly unfamiliar. But that should prove no more disturbing to the reader of the translation than it does to readers of the original, or than it does to us when we read Locke, or Fielding, or Gibbon. Attentive readers may at times find it helpful. An honest translation first and foremost respects the surface of the text and attempts to reproduce it, much as an honest performance does a score or a script. If it is successful, it also reveals what lies beyond that surface. But nothing can be revealed by distorting the surface.

The aim of the Notes and of the Index is much the same as that of the translations: to help make the texts as directly accessible as possible. The Notes have been relegated to the end of the volume in order to keep them from intruding between text and reader. They identify persons, events, places, texts, and sometimes doctrines which Rousseau mentions or alludes to; very occasionally they point out parallels with what he says in other writings. They remain at or very near the surface of the texts. They do not analyze or interpret. A full commentary and interpretation of the texts here translated will be offered in a separate volume. In the meantime, interested readers may consult my "Rousseau on the Arts and Sciences," *The Journal of Philosophy* 69 (1972): 737–754, for a preliminary reading of the *First Discourse* and of the discussion surrounding it.

I am indebted to many of the scholars who have written on these texts and on the issues which they raise.

I owe thanks to the Zentrum für interdisziplinäre Forschung of the University of Bielefeld for a Senior Fellowship which permitted me to complete some of the work on this volume.

I wish to thank the reference staff of Wesleyan University's Olin Library, and in particular the ever-resourceful Steven Lebergott, for their assistance. I also wish to thank my production editor, Diane Conley, who has been exceptionally patient and understanding, and my copy editor, Dorian Hastings, who has saved me from numerous minor and several major errors. Hugh Van Dusen and Janet Goldstein have been the most helpful of editors at every stage of this project.

I welcome the opportunity to express my gratitude to the colleagues and friends who have most generously encouraged or in other ways helped me at different stages of this work: Warren Anderson, Shlomo Avineri, Jon Barlow, Bob Burns, Stanley Cavell, George McFadden, Shirley Robin Letwin, Reinhart Koselleck, Joseph Hamburger, Donald Moon, Charles Sherover, Carl Viggiani, and Robert Whitman.

It gives me particular pleasure also to express my gratitude to my sons Philip and Marc for their advice and critical reading of successive versions of these translations.

To my wife's judgment, tact, and example I owe far more than I can adequately acknowledge.

VICTOR GOUREVITCH

March 1985

A Note on the Text
of the Translation

All additions to Rousseau's text are enclosed in square brackets: the occasional word that is implied in the original but has to be made explicit in the translation; the paragraph numberings; the italic numerals that refer to the pagination of the Pléiade edition, now generally accepted as the standard Rousseau edition, and that have been inserted in the translations of all the texts so far published in that edition in order to help readers who might wish to consult the original: thus *[202]* means that what follows translates page 202 of the indicated Pléiade volume of Rousseau's *Oeuvres complètes*.

As a rule, every word Rousseau capitalizes is capitalized in the translation. However, I have not used a capital every time Rousseau does so following a semicolon, and sometimes I have capitalized adjectives which Rousseau did not capitalize: for example, Greek music, or Middle East.

Satyr, you do not know it. See p. 14.

Jaequet Sculp.

DISCOURSE

which won the prize
OF THE ACADEMY
OF DIJON
In the year 1750
On this Question proposed by the Academy:
*Whether the restoration of the Sciences and Arts
has contributed to the purification of morals*

By a Citizen of Geneva

*Here I am the barbarian because
they do not understand me.*—Ovid

GENEVA
Barillot & Son

PREFACE

[1] *Here is one of the grand and finest questions ever raised. This Discourse is not concerned with those metaphysical subtleties that have spread to all departments of Literature, and of which the Programs of Academies are not always free: it is concerned, rather, with one of those truths that affect the happiness of mankind.*

[2] *I expect that I shall not easily be forgiven for the side I have dared to choose. Clashing head on with all that is today admired by men, I can only expect universal blame: and to have been honored by the approbation of a few Wise men ought not to lead me to expect that of the Public. Hence my decision is made. I do not care whether I please Wits or the Fashionable. There will always be men destined to be subjugated by the opinions of their century, of their Country, of their Society: Some men today act the part of the Freethinker and the Philosopher who, for the same reason, would have been but fanatics at the time of the League. One ought not to write for such Readers when one wants to live beyond one's century.*

[3] *One word more, and I have done. Little expecting the honor bestowed on me, I had, after sending off this Discourse, recast and expanded it to the point of making it, as it were, into another Work; I believed myself obliged to restore it today to the state in which it was awarded the prize. I have only thrown in some notes and let stand two additions easy to recognize and of which the Academy might perhaps not have approved. I thought that equity, respect, and gratitude required this notice of me.*

DISCOURSE

We are deceived by the appearance of right.

[4] Has the restoration of the Sciences and Arts contributed to the purification of Morals, or to their corruption? That is what has to be examined. Which side ought I to take in this question? The side, Gentlemen, which becomes an honest man who knows nothing and esteems himself no less for it.

[5] I am sensible to the difficulty of conforming what I have to say to the Tribunal before which I appear. How shall I dare to blame the Sciences before one of the most learned Associations of Europe, praise ignorance in a celebrated Academy, and reconcile contempt for study with respect for the truly Learned? I have seen these contradictions, and they have not deterred me. It is not, so I have told myself, Science I abuse; it is Virtue I defend before virtuous men. Probity is even dearer to Good Men than erudition is to the Learned. What, then, have I to fear? The enlightenment of the Assembly listening to me? I acknowledge it; but only with regard to the composition of the discourse, not to the Speaker's sentiment. Equitable Sovereigns have never hesitated to pass judgment against themselves in debates of doubtful issue; and the most advantageous position in a just cause is to have to defend oneself against a Party of integrity and enlightenment judging in his own case.

[6] To this motive which emboldens me, is joined another which decides me: namely that, having by my natural light upheld the side of truth, there is one Prize which cannot fail me whatever my success: I shall find it in the depths of my heart.

PART I

[7] It is a grand and fine spectacle to see man go forth as it were out of nothing by his own efforts; to dispel by the lights of his reason the darkness in which nature had enveloped him; to raise himself above himself; to soar by the mind to the celestial realms; to traverse the vast expanse of the Universe with Giant strides, like to the Sun; and, what is grander and more difficult still, to return into himself, there to study man and to know his nature, his duties, and his end. All these wonders have occurred anew in the past few Generations.

[8] Europe had relapsed into the Barbarism of the first ages. A few centuries ago the Peoples of this Part of the World, which is today so enlightened, lived in a state worse than ignorance. I know not what scientific jargon more contemptible still than ignorance had usurped the name of knowledge, and stood as an almost insurmountable obstacle in the path of its return. A revolution was required to return men to common sense; it finally came from the quarter from which it was least to be expected. The stupid Muslim, the eternal scourge of Letters, caused them to be reborn among us. The fall of the Throne of Constantine carried the wreckage of ancient Greece into Italy. France, in turn, was enriched by these precious spoils. Soon the sciences followed Letters; the Art of writing was joined by the Art of thinking, a sequence which appears strange but is perhaps only too natural; and the major advantage of commerce with the muses began to be felt, namely of rendering men more sociable by inspiring in them the desire to please one another with works worthy of their mutual approval.

[9] The mind has its needs, as has the body. The latter make up the foundations of society, the former make for its being agreeable. While the Government and the Laws see to the *[7]* safety and the well-being of men assembled, the Sciences, Letters, and Arts, less despotic and perhaps more powerful, spread garlands of flowers over the iron chains with which they

are laden, throttle in them the sentiment of that original freedom for which they seemed born, make them love their slavery, and fashion them into what is called civilized Peoples. Need raised up Thrones; the Sciences and Arts have made them strong. Earthly Powers, love talents and protect those who cultivate them!* Civilized peoples, cultivate them: Happy slaves, you owe them the delicate and refined taste on which you pride yourselves; the sweet character and urbane morals which make for such engaging and easy relations among you; in a word, the appearances of all the virtues without having a one.

[10] This is the kind of politeness, the more endearing as it affects to show itself less, that formerly distinguished Athens and Rome in the so much vaunted days of their magnificence and splendor; by it, no doubt, our century and our Nation shall surpass all times and all Peoples. A philosophic tone devoid of pedantry, manners natural yet engaging, as far removed from Teutonic rusticity as from Italian Pantomime: Such are the fruits of taste acquired by good education and perfected in dealings with the World.

[11] How sweet it would be to live among us if the outward countenance were always the image of the heart's dispositions; if decency were virtue; if our maxims were our rules; if genuine Philosophy were inseparable from the title of Philosopher! But so many qualities [8] all too seldom go together, and virtue hardly goes forth with so much pomp. Rich finery may herald a man of wealth, and elegant attire a man of taste; the healthy and robust man is recognized by other signs: strength and vigor of body will be found under the rustic habit of a Plowman, and not under the gilding of a Courtier. Finery is no less alien to virtue, which is the strength and vigor of the soul. The good

* Princes always view with pleasure the dissemination among their subjects of a taste for the agreeable Arts and for superfluities which entail no export of monies. For besides thus nurturing in them that pettiness of soul so suited to servitude, they well know that all the needs which a People imposes on itself are so many chains which it assumes. Alexander, wishing to keep the Ichthyophagi dependent on him, compelled them to give up fishing and to eat the foods common to other Peoples; and the Savages of America who go about altogether naked and who live entirely off the products of their hunt, have proved impossible to tame. Indeed, what yoke could be imposed upon men who need nothing?

man is an Athlete who delights in fighting naked. He despises all those vile ornaments which would hinder his use of his strength, and most of which were invented only to conceal some deformity.

[12] Before Art had fashioned our manners and taught our passions to speak in ready-made terms, our morals were rustic but natural; and differences in conduct conveyed differences of character at first glance. Human nature was, at bottom, no better; but men found their security in how easily they saw through one another, and this advantage, to the value of which we are no longer sensible, spared them a good many vices.

[13] Today, when subtler inquiries and a more refined taste have reduced the Art of pleasing to principles, a vile and deceiving uniformity reigns in our morals, and all minds seem to have been cast in the same mold: constantly politeness demands, propriety commands; constantly one follows custom, never one's own genius. One no longer dares to appear what one is; and under this perpetual constraint, the men who make up the herd that is called society will, when placed in similar circumstances, all act in similar ways unless more powerful motives incline them differently. One will thus never really know with whom one is dealing: in order to know one's friend one will therefore have to wait for great occasions, that is, to wait until it is too late, since it is for these very occasions that it would have been essential to know him.

[14] What a train of vices must attend upon such uncertainty. No more sincere friendships; no more real esteem; no more well-founded trust. Suspicions, offenses, fears, coolness, reserve, hatred, betrayal, will constantly hide beneath this uniform and deceitful veil of politeness, beneath this so much vaunted urbanity which we *[9]* owe to the enlightenment of our century. One will no longer profane the name of the Lord of the Universe with oaths, but insult it with blasphemies that pass our scrupulous ears without offending them. One will not vaunt one's own desert, but disparage that of others. One will not crudely offend one's enemy, but malign him artfully. National hatreds will die out, but so will the love of Fatherland. Scorned ignorance will be replaced by a dangerous Pyrrhonism. Some excesses will be

proscribed, some vices held in dishonor, but others will be emblazoned with the name of virtues; one will either have to have them or to affect them. Let those who wish to do so, extol the sobriety of the Wise men of the age, but for myself, I see in it but a refinement of intemperance as unworthy of my praise as is their artful simplicity.*

[15] Such is the purity our morals have acquired, this is how we have become good Men. Let Letters, the Sciences, and the Arts each claim their share in such a salutary achievement. I shall add but one reflection: that if an Inhabitant of some distant region, seeking to form an idea of European morals from the state of the Sciences among us, the perfection of our Arts, the propriety of our Theater, the politeness of our manners, the affability of our discourse, our incessant professions of goodwill, and this bustling race of men of all ages and conditions who, from early Dawn until the setting of the Sun, seem at pains to oblige one another; this Stranger, I say, would guess our morals to be precisely the opposite of what they are.

[16] Where there is no effect, no cause need be sought; but here the effect is certain, the depravation real, and our souls have become corrupted in proportion as our Sciences and our Arts have advanced toward perfection. Shall it be said that this is a misfortune peculiar to our age? No, Gentlemen, the ills caused by our vain curiosity are as old [10] as the world. The daily rise and fall of the Ocean's waters have not been more strictly subjected to the course of the Star that illumines us by night, than has the fate of morals and probity to the progress of the Sciences and Arts. Virtue has been seen fleeing in proportion as their light rose on our horizon, and the same phenomenon has been observed at all times and in all places.

[17] Consider Egypt, that first school of the Universe, that fertile climate beneath a brazen sky, that famous land from which Sesostris long ago set out to conquer the World. She became the mother of Philosophy and the fine Arts, and soon

---

* *I like*, says Montaigne, *to argue and discuss, but only with but a few men and for my own sake. For I find it to be a most unbecoming profession for a man of honor to serve as a Spectacle to the Great and wantonly to display one's mind and one's prattling.* It is the profession of all our wits save one.

thereafter was conquered by Cambyses, then by the Greeks, by the Romans, the Arabs, and finally the Turks.

[18] Consider Greece, formerly peopled by Heroes who twice vanquished Asia, once before Troy, and once by their own hearths. Nascent Letters had not yet carried corruption into the hearts of its Inhabitants; but the progress of the Arts, the disintegration of morals, and the Macedonian's yoke closely followed one another; and Greece, ever learned, ever voluptuous, and ever enslaved, thereafter experienced, throughout its revolutions, nothing but a change of masters. All of Demosthenes's eloquence never succeeded in revivifying a body which luxury and the Arts had enervated.

[19] It is at the time of Ennius and of Terence that Rome, founded by a Shepherd and rendered illustrious by Tillers of the soil, begins to degenerate. But after the Ovids, the Catulluses, the Martials, and that host of obscene Writers whose very names offend modesty, Rome, formerly the Temple of Virtue, becomes the Theater of crime, the scandal of Nations, and the sport of barbarians. This Capital of the World finally succumbs to the yoke it had imposed on so many Peoples, and the day of its fall was the eve of the day on which one of its Citizens was given the title of Arbiter of good taste.

[20] What shall I say of the Capital of the Eastern Empire which, by its location, seemed destined to be that of the entire World, that refuge of the Sciences and the Arts banned from the rest of Europe perhaps due more to wisdom than to barbarism. All that is most shameful in debauchery and corruption; blackest in betrayals, assassinations and poisons; most atrocious in the combination of crimes of every kind; *[11]* that is what makes up the fabric of the History of Constantinople; that is the pure source from which the Enlightenment in which our century glories has come to us.

[21] But why seek in remote times proofs of a truth for which we have abiding testimony before our own eyes. There is in Asia an immense land where Letters are honored and lead to the foremost dignities of State. If the Sciences purified morals, if they taught men to shed their blood for the Fatherland, if they

animated courage, then the Peoples of China should be wise, free, and invincible. But if there is not a single vice that does not rule them; not a single crime that is unfamiliar to them; if neither the enlightenment of the Ministers, nor the presumed wisdom of the Laws, nor the large number of Inhabitants of that vast Empire have been able to protect it from the yoke of the ignorant and coarse Tartar, of what use have all its Scholars been? What benefits has China derived from all the honors bestowed upon them? To be peopled by slaves and evil-doers?

[22] Let us contrast these scenes with that of the morals of the small number of Peoples who, protected against this contamination of vain knowledge, have by their virtues wrought their own happiness and the model for all other Nations. Such were the first Persians, a singular Nation where virtue was learned as Science is learned among us; which so easily mastered Asia, and is the only Nation to enjoy the glory of having the history of its institutions mistaken for a Philosophical Romance. Such were the Scythians of whom such magnificent praise has come down to us: Such were the Germans, whose simplicity, innocence and virtues a pen weary of tracing the crimes and blackness of an educated, opulent, and voluptuous People, took relief in depicting. Such had been Rome itself in the times of its poverty and ignorance. Such, finally, has shown itself to be down to our own day the rustic nation so vaunted for its courage which adversity could not subdue, and its faithfulness which example could not corrupt.*[12]

[23] It was not owing to stupidity that they preferred other forms of exercise to those of the mind. They were not ignorant of the fact that in other lands idle men spent their lives arguing about the sovereign good, [and] vice and virtue, or that prideful ratiocinators heaped the greatest praise upon themselves while

* I dare not speak of those happy Nations which do not know even by name the vices we have so much difficulty in repressing, those savages of America whose simple and natural polity Montaigne unhesitatingly prefers not only to Plato's *Laws, [13]* but even to everything that Philosophy could ever imagine as most perfect for the government of Peoples. He cites numerous examples striking to those able to admire them: "But then," says he, "they wear no breeches!"

assimilating all other Peoples under the contemptuous name of barbarians; but they considered their morals and learned to disdain their teaching.*

[24] Can I forget that it was in the very lap of Greece that was seen to arise the City equally famed for its happy ignorance and for the wisdom of its Laws, that Republic of demi-Gods rather than of men, so much superior to humanity did their virtues appear? O Sparta! eternal shame to a vain teaching! While the vices, led by the fine Arts, together insinuated themselves into Athens, while a Tyrant was there so carefully assembling the works of the Prince of Poets, you expelled the Arts and Artists, the Sciences and Scientists from your walls.

[25] The event confirmed this difference. Athens became the home of sophistication and of taste, the country of Orators and Philosophers. The elegance of its Buildings matched that of the language. Marble and canvas enlivened by the hands of the most skillful Masters could be seen everywhere. From Athens issued those astounding works that will stand as models in every corrupt age. The Picture of Lacedaemon is less brilliant. *There,* the other Peoples used to say, *[13] men are born virtuous, and the very air of the Country seems to inspire virtue.* All that is left us of its Inhabitants is the memory of their heroic deeds. Are such monuments worth less to us than the quaint marbles left us by Athens?

[26] Some few wise men did, it is true, withstand the general tide, and guard against vice in the midst of the Muses. But listen to the indictment by the foremost and the most wretched of them, of the Learned and the Artists of his time.

[27] "I have," he says, "examined the Poets, and I consider them to be people whose talent impresses themselves and

---

* I should honestly like to be told what must have been the Athenians' own opinion about eloquence, when they so carefully excluded it from that upright Tribunal whose Judgments the Gods themselves did not appeal? What did the Romans think of medicine when they banished it from their Republic? And when a residue of humanity led the Spaniards to forbid their Lawyers entry into America, what must have been their idea of Jurisprudence? Do they not appear to have believed that with this one Edict they could make up for all the evils they had inflicted on those wretched Indians?

others, who claim to be wise men, who are taken to be such, and who are anything but that."

[28] "From the Poets," Socrates continues, "I went on to the Artists. No one was more ignorant of the Arts than I; no one was more convinced that the Artists possessed some very fine secrets. Yet I perceived that their condition is no better than the Poets', and that they both labor under the same prejudice. Because the most skilled among them excel in their particular Field, they look upon themselves as the wisest of men. In my eyes this presumption has completely tarnished their knowledge: So that, putting myself in the place of the Oracle, and asking myself what I would prefer, to be what I am or what they are, to know what they have learned or to know that I know nothing, I answered myself and the God: I want to remain what I am.

[29] "We do not know, neither the Sophists nor the Poets, nor the Orators, nor the Artists, nor I, what is the true, the good, and the beautiful: But there is this difference between us that, although these people know nothing, they all believe themselves to know something: Whereas I, while I know nothing, am at least not in any doubt about that. So that the whole superiority in wisdom which the Oracle attributes to me reduces to this, that I am fully convinced that I am ignorant of what I do not know."

[30] Here, then, is the Wisest of men in the Judgment of the Gods, and the most learned of Athenians according to the sense of all Greece, Socrates, speaking in Praise of ignorance! Does anyone believe that, if he were to be reborn among us, our *[14]* Learned and our Artists would make him change his mind? No, Gentlemen, this just man would continue to despise our vain Sciences; he would not help swell the mass of books that flood in on us from all sides, and the only precept which he would leave is the precept which he did leave to his disciples and to our Descendents, the example and the memory of his virtue. It is fine thus to teach men!

[31] Socrates had begun in Athens, the elder Cato continued in Rome to inveigh against those artful and subtle Greeks who seduced virtue and enervated the courage of his fellow-citizens.

But the Sciences, the Arts, and dialectics once again prevailed. Rome filled up with Philosophers and Orators; military discipline came to be neglected, agriculture despised; Sects joined, and the Fatherland forgotten. The sacred names of liberty, disinterestedness, obedience to the Laws, were replaced by the names of Epicurus, Zeno, Arcesilaus. *Ever since the Learned have begun to appear among us,* so their own Philosophers themselves said, *good Men have been in eclipse.* Until then the Romans had been content to practice virtue; all was lost when they began to study it.

[32] O Fabricius! What would your great soul have thought if, unhappily recalled to life, you had seen the pompous countenance of that Rome which your arm rescued and your good name adorned more than did all of her conquests? "Gods!" you would have said, "what has become of the thatch roofs and the rustic hearths where moderation and virtue used to dwell? What fatal splendor has replaced Roman simplicity? What is this alien speech? What are these effeminate morals? What is the meaning of these statues, these Paintings, these buildings? Fools, what have you done? You, the Masters of Nations, made yourselves the slaves of the frivolous men you vanquished? Do Rhetoricians govern you? Was it in order to enrich Architects, Painters, Sculptors, and Thespians that you spilled your blood in Greece and in Asia? Have the spoils of Carthage become the prey of a flute-player? Romans, hasten to overturn these Amphitheaters; smash these marbles; burn these paintings; drive out these slaves who *[15]* subjugate you and whose fatal arts corrupt you. Let other hands acquire fame for vain talents; the only talent worthy of Rome is that of conquering the world and making virtue reign in it. When Cineas took our Senate for an Assembly of Kings he was not dazzled by vain pomp or studied elegance. He did not, in that Senate, hear the frivolous eloquence that is the object of study and delight of futile men. What, then, did Cineas see that was so majestic? O Citizens! He saw a spectacle which neither your riches nor all your arts shall ever succeed in exhibiting; the finest spectacle ever to appear under heaven, the Assembly of two hundred virtuous men worthy of commanding in Rome, and of governing the earth."

[33] But let us cross the distance of place and time, and see what has occurred in our lands and before our own eyes; or rather, let us set aside repugnant depictions that would offend our delicacy, and spare ourselves the trouble of repeating the same thing with different names. My invoking Fabricius's shade was not haphazard; and what did I have this great man say that I could not have put into the mouth of Louis XII or of Henry IV? Among us, it is true, Socrates would not have drunk the hemlock; but he would have drunk from a cup more bitter still, the insulting jeers and the scorn that are a hundred times worse than death.

[34] That is how luxury, dissoluteness, and slavery have at all times been the punishment visited upon our prideful efforts to leave the happy ignorance in which eternal wisdom had placed us. The heavy veil it had drawn over all of its operations seemed sufficiently to warn us that it had not destined us for vain inquiries. But is there even one of its lessons from which we have known how to profit, or which we have neglected with impunity? Peoples, know, then, once and for all, that nature wanted to preserve you from science as a mother snatches a dangerous weapon from the hands of her child; that all the secrets she hides from you are so many evils from which she protects you, and that the difficulty you have in learning is not the least of her favors. Men are perverse; they would be worse still if they had had the misfortune of being born learned.

[35] How humiliating to humanity such reflections are! *[16]* How greatly mortified our pride must be by them! What! probity the daughter of ignorance? Science and virtue incompatible? What conclusions might not be drawn from such prejudices? But in order to resolve these apparent contradictions one need only examine closely the vanity and vacuousness of those proud titles which dazzle us and which we so gratuitously bestow on human knowledge. Let us, therefore, consider the Sciences and the Arts in themselves. Let us see what must result from their progress; and let us no longer hesitate to grant all the points where our reasoning shall be found to agree with the historical inferences.

[17]

PART II

[36] According to an ancient tradition passed on from Egypt to Greece, a God inimical to men's repose was the inventor of the sciences.* What, then, must the Egyptians themselves, among whom the sciences were born, have thought of them! It is that they saw near at hand the sources that had brought them forth. Indeed, whether one consults the annals of the world, or supplements uncertain chronicles with philosophical inquiries, one will not find an origin of human knowledge that corresponds to the idea one would like to hold regarding it. Astronomy was born of superstition; Eloquence of ambition, hatred, flattery, lying; Geometry of avarice; Physics of a vain curiosity; all of them, even Ethics, of human pride. The Sciences and the Arts thus owe their birth to our vices; we should be less in doubt regarding their advantages if they owed it to our virtues.

[37] Their flawed origin is all too clearly mirrored for us in their objects. What would we do with the Arts without luxury to sustain them? Without men's injustices, of what use would Jurisprudence be? What would become of History if there were neither Tyrants, nor Wars, nor Conspirators? In short, who would want to spend his life in barren thoughts if everyone consulted only man's duties and nature's needs, and had time only for the Fatherland, for the unfortunate, and for his *[18]* friends? Are we, then, destined to die tied to the edge of the well to which truth has withdrawn? This reflection alone should from the very outset deter anyone seriously trying to educate himself by studying Philosophy.

[38] How many dangers! How many wrong roads in the investigation of the Sciences! How many errors a thousand times

---

* It is easy to see the allegory of the Prometheus fable; and it does not appear that the Greeks who nailed him to Mount Caucasus thought any more favorably of him than did the Egyptians of their God Theuth. "The satyr," says an ancient fable, "wanted to kiss and embrace fire the first time he saw it; but Prometheus cried out to him: 'Satyr, you will weep the loss of the beard on your chin, for it burns when you touch it.' " That is the subject of the frontispiece.

more dangerous than the truth is useful, have to be overcome in order to reach it? The drawbacks are manifest: for falsehood admits of an infinite number of combinations; but truth has only one mode of being. Besides, who seeks it altogether sincerely? But even with the best will, by what indices is one sure to recognize it? Amid this host of different sentiments, what shall be our criterion for it?* And, most difficult of all, if we should have the good fortune of finally finding it, who of us will know how to use it well?

[39] While our sciences are vain with respect to the objects they pursue, they are even more dangerous in the effects they produce. Born in idleness, they nourish it in turn; and the irreparable loss of time is the first injury they necessarily inflict on society. In politics, as in ethics, not to do good is a great evil, and every useless citizen may be looked upon as a pernicious man. Answer me then, illustrious Philosophers, you to whom we owe it to know in what ratios bodies attract one another in a vacuum; the proportions between areas swept in equal times by the revolutions of the planets; which curves have conjugate points, which have inflection points, and which cusps; how man sees everything in God; how the soul and the body correspond to one another without communicating, like two clocks; what stars may be inhabited; what insects reproduce in some extraordinary fashion. *[19]* Answer me, I say, you from whom we have received so much sublime knowledge; if you had never taught us any of these things, would we have been any the less numerous for it, any the less well governed, the less formidable, the less flourishing, or the more perverse? Reconsider the importance of your achievements, then; and if the labors of our most enlightened learned men and our best Citizens provide us with so little that is useful, tell us what we are to think of that host of obscure Writers and idle Literati who devour the State's substance at a pure loss.

* The less one knows, the more one believes oneself to know. Did the Peripatetics doubt anything? Did not Descartes construct the Universe with cubes and vortices? Is there even nowadays in Europe a Physicist, however paltry, who would not make bold to explain the profound mystery of electricity, which will perhaps forever remain the despair of true Philosophers?

[40] Did I say idle? Would to God they indeed were! Morals would be the healthier and society more peaceful. But these vain and futile declaimers go off in all directions, armed with their deadly paradoxes, undermining the foundations of faith and annihilating virtue. They smile disdainfully at such old-fashioned words as Fatherland and Religion, and dedicate their talents and their Philosophy to destroying and degrading all that is sacred among men. Not that they at bottom hate either virtue or our dogmas; rather, they are the enemies of public opinion; and in order to bring them back to the feet of the altars, one would only have to banish them among Atheists. O rage for distinction, what will you not do?

[41] The abuse of time is a great evil. Other, even worse evils follow in the wake of the Letters and Arts. One of these is luxury, born, like they, of men's idleness and vanity. Luxury is seldom found without the sciences and the arts, and they are never found without it. I know that our Philosophy, ever fertile in singular maxims, contends, in the face of the experience of all centuries, that luxury makes for the splendor of States; but after forgetting the necessity of sumptuary laws, will it also dare deny that good morals are essential if Empires are to endure, and that luxury is diametrically opposed to good morals? Granting that luxury is a certain sign of riches; that, if you like, it even serves to increase them; what conclusion is to be drawn from this paradox so worthy of being born in our time; and what will become of virtue when one has to get rich at all cost? The ancient political Thinkers forever spoke of morals and of virtue; ours speak only of commerce and of money. One will tell you that in a given [20] land a man is worth the sum for which he would be sold in Algiers; another, pursuing this calculation, will find countries where a man is worth nothing, and others where he is worth less than nothing. They appraise men like herds of cattle. According to them a man is worth to the State only what he consumes in it. By that token one Sybarite would easily have been worth thirty Lacedaemonians. Try to guess, then, which of the two Republics, Sparta or Sybaris, was subdued by a handful of peasants, and which caused Asia to tremble.

[42] The Monarchy of Cyrus was conquered with thirty thou-

sand men by a Prince poorer than the least Persian Satrap; and the Scythians, the most miserable of all Peoples, resisted the most powerful Monarchs of the Universe. Two famed Republics contended for the Empire of the World; one was very rich and the other had nothing, and it was the latter which destroyed the first. The Roman Empire, having swallowed all the riches of the Universe, in its turn fell prey to men who did not so much as know what riches were. The Franks conquered the Gauls, and the Saxons conquered England with no other treasures than their bravery and their poverty. A band of poor Mountaineers whose entire greed was confined to a few sheepskins, having tamed Austrian pride, went on to crush the opulent and formidable House of Burgundy before which the Potentates of Europe trembled. Finally, all the power and wisdom of Charles the Fifth's heir, backed by all the treasures of the Indies, were beaten by a handful of herring fishers. Let our political thinkers deign to suspend their calculations in order to reflect on these examples, and learn once and for all that with money one has everything except morals and Citizens.

[43] What, then, precisely is at issue in this question of luxury? To know what matters most to Empires, to be brilliant and short-lived, or virtuous and long-lasting. I say brilliant, but by what luster? A taste for ostentation is scarcely ever combined in one soul with a taste for the honest. No, Minds debased by a host of futile cares cannot possibly ever rise to anything great; and even if they had the requisite strength, they would lack the courage. *[21]*

[44] Every Artist wants to be applauded. His contemporaries' praise is the most precious portion of his reward. What, then, will he do to obtain it, if he has the misfortune to be born among a People and at a time when the Learned, having become fashionable, have placed frivolous youths in the position of setting the tone; when men have sacrificed their taste to the Tyrants of their freedom;* when masterpieces of dramatic Poetry

* I am far from thinking that this ascendancy of women is in itself an evil. It is a gift bestowed upon them by nature for the happiness of Mankind: better directed, it might produce as much good as it nowadays does harm. We are not sufficiently sensible to the benefits that would accrue to society if the half of

are dropped [from repertories] and wonders of harmony rejected because one of the sexes dares to approve only of what suits the other's pusillanimity? What will he do, Gentlemen? He will lower his genius to the level of his century, and compose popular works that are admired during his lifetime rather than marvels that would be admired only long after his death. Tell us, famed Arouet, how many manly and strong beauties you have sacrificed to our false delicacy, and how many great things the spirit of gallantry, so prolific in small things, has cost you?

[45] That is how the dissolution of morals, the necessary consequence of luxury, in turn leads to the corruption of taste. If, by chance, someone among the men of extraordinary talents were steadfast of soul, and refused to yield to the genius of his century and to debase himself by puerile productions, woe betide him! He will die in poverty and oblivion. Would that I were making a prediction and not reporting an experience! Carle, Pierre; the time has come when the brush intended to enhance the majesty of our Temples with sublime and holy images will either fall from your hands or be prostituted to decorate the panels of a carriage with lascivious pictures. And you, the rival *[22]* of the likes of Praxiteles and of Phidias, you whose chisel the ancients would have employed to make them such Gods as would have excused their idolatry in our eyes, inimitable Pigal, either your hand will consent to burnish the belly of some grotesque figurine, or it will have to remain idle.

[46] One cannot reflect on morals, without taking delight in recalling the image of the simplicity of the first times. It is a fair shore, adorned by the hands of nature alone, toward which one forever turns one's eyes, and from which one feels oneself moving away with regret. When innocent and virtuous men liked to have the Gods for witnesses of their deeds, they lived together in the same huts; but soon, having become wicked,

---

Mankind which governs the other were given a better education. Men will always be what it pleases women that they be: so that if you want them to become great and virtuous, teach women what greatness of soul and virtue is. The reflections to which this subject lends itself, and which Plato made in former times, amply deserve to be more fully detailed by a pen worthy of modeling itself on such a master and of defending so grand a cause.

they wearied of these inconvenient onlookers and banished them to magnificent Temples. At last they drove them out of the Temples in order to settle in them themselves, or at least the Temples of the Gods became indistinguishable from the homes of the citizens. That was the period of the utmost depravation; and the vices were never carried to a greater pitch than when they were, so to speak, seen borne up on columns of marble and carved on Corinthian capitals at the entrance to the Palaces of the Great.

[47] While the conveniences of life increase, the arts improve, and luxury spreads, true courage is enervated, the military virtues vanish, and this too is the work of the sciences and of all the arts that are practiced in the closeness of the study. When the Goths ravaged Greece, the Libraries were saved from fire only because of the opinion, spread by one of them, that the enemy should be left furnishings so well suited to distract them from military exercise and to keep them amused with idle and sedentary occupations. Charles the Eighth found himself master of Tuscany and of the Kingdom of Naples almost without having drawn sword; and his entire Court attributed this unexpected ease to the fact that the Italian Princes and Nobility amused themselves more trying to become ingenious and learned, than they exerted themselves trying to become vigorous and warlike. Indeed, says the sensible man who reports these two episodes, all examples teach us that in this martial polity as well as in all others like it, the study of the sciences is much more apt to soften and effeminate men's courage than to strengthen and animate it. *[23]*

[48] The Romans admitted that military virtue died out among them in proportion as they began to be knowledgeable about Paintings, Etchings, Goldsmiths' vessels, and to cultivate the fine arts; and as if that famous land had been destined forever to serve as an example to other peoples, the rise of the Medicis and the restoration of Letters destroyed once more and perhaps forever the martial reputation which, a few centuries ago, Italy seemed to have recovered.

[49] The ancient Republics of Greece, with the wisdom that was so conspicuous in most of their institutions, had forbidden

their Citizens the exercise of all those quiet and sedentary occupations which, by allowing the body to grow slack and corrupted, soon enervate the vigor of the soul. How, indeed, can men overwhelmed by the least need and repelled by the least pain, be expected to face up to hunger, thirst, fatigues, dangers, and death. With what courage will soldiers bear up under extreme labors to which they are in no way accustomed? With what spirit will they go on forced marches under Officers who have not even the strength to travel on horseback? Do not cite the renowned valor of all these scientifically trained modern warriors as an objection against me. I hear praised their bravery on a day of battle, but I am not told how they bear up under extreme labors, how they withstand the harshness of the seasons and the inclemency of the weather. A little sunshine or a little snow, the want of a few superfluities, is enough to melt and destroy the best of our armies in a few days. Intrepid warriors, suffer, for once, the truth which you so rarely hear; you are brave, I know; you would have triumphed with Hannibal at Cannae and at Trasimene; with you Caesar would have crossed the Rubicon and reduced his country to servitude; but it is not with you that the one would have crossed the Alps, and the other vanquished your ancestors.

[50] Success in battles does not always make for success in war, and there is for Generals an art higher than that of winning battles. A man may boldly run into the line of fire, and yet be a very bad officer; even a [common] soldier may need a little more strength and vigor than all that bravery [24] which does not protect him from death; and what difference does it make to the State whether its troops die by fever and cold, or by the enemy's sword?

[51] While the cultivation of the sciences is harmful to the martial qualities, it is even more so to the moral qualities. From our very first years a senseless education adorns our mind and corrupts our judgment. Everywhere I see huge establishments in which young people are brought up at great expense to learn everything except their duties. Your children will not know their own language, but they will speak others which are

nowhere in use; they will be able to compose Verses which they will hardly be able to understand; without being able to disentangle error from truth, they will possess the art of making them unrecognizable to others by specious arguments; but they will not know the meaning of the words magnanimity, equity, temperance, humanity, courage; the sweet name Fatherland will never strike their ear; and if they hear God spoken of at all, it will be less to be in awe than to be in fear of him.* I would as soon, said a Wise man, that my pupil had spent his time on the Tennis Court, at least his body would have been fitter for it. I know that children have to be kept busy, and that idleness is the danger most to be feared for them. What then should they learn? That is certainly a fine question! Let them learn what they ought to do when they are men,** and not what they ought to forget. *[25]*

[52] Our gardens are decorated with statues and our Galleries with pictures. What would you think these masterpieces of art, exhibited for public admiration, represent? The defenders of the Fatherland or those still greater men who enriched it with their virtues? No. They are images of all the aberrations of the heart and of the reason, carefully culled from ancient Mythology, and presented to our children's curiosity at an early age,

---

* Pens[ées] Philosoph[iques].

** Such was the education of the Spartans according to the greatest of their Kings. It is well worth considering, says Montaigne, that in that excellent and indeed truly monstrously perfect polity of Lycurgus, although it was so very attentive to the nurture of children, whom it regarded as its main responsibility, and although it was situated in the very seat of the Muses, so little mention should be made of doctrine: as if those magnanimous youths, disdainful of every other yoke, required only Teachers of valor, prudence, and justice, instead of our Teachers of science.

Let us now see what the same Author says about the ancient Persians. Plato, he says, tells that the eldest son in their Royal line was brought up as follows. After his birth he was handed over not to women, but to Eunuchs who, because of their virtue, enjoyed the greatest authority with the King. They took charge of making his body fair and healthy, and after seven years they taught him to ride and to hunt. When he reached his fourteenth year, they placed him in the hands of four persons: the wisest, the most just, the most temperate, and the most valiant in the Nation. The first taught him Religion, the second always to be true, the third to conquer his appetites, the fourth to fear nothing. All, I would add, to make him good, none to make him learned.

doubtless so that they may have models of bad deeds in front of their eyes even before they can read.

[53] Where do all these abuses arise, if not in the fatal inequality introduced among men by the distinction of talents and the disparagement of the virtues? That is the most obvious effect of all our studies, and the most dangerous of all their consequences. People no longer ask whether a man has probity, but whether he has talents; nor whether a Book is useful, but whether it is well-written. Rewards are lavished upon wits, and virtue remains without honors. There are a thousand prizes for fine discourses, none for fine deeds. And yet I should like to be told whether the glory attaching to the best of the discourses that will be crowned by this Academy is comparable to the merit of having established the prize? *[26]*

[54] The wise man does not run after fortune; but he is not insensitive to glory; and when he sees it so badly distributed, his virtue, which a little emulation would have animated and turned to the advantage of society, languishes and dies in misery and oblivion. This is what, in the long run, the preference for the agreeable over the useful talents must everywhere bring about, and what experience has only all too fully confirmed since the revival of the sciences and arts. We have Physicists, Geometricians, Chemists, Astronomers, Poets, Musicians, Painters; we no longer have citizens; or, if we still have some, dispersed in our abandoned rural areas, they waste away indigent and despised. Such is the condition to which those who give us bread and our children milk are reduced, and such are the sentiments they get from us.

Astyages, in Xenophon, asks Cyrus for an account of his last Lesson: It was this, said he, that in our school a big boy who had a small coat gave it to one of his companions who was smaller than himself, and took from him his coat, which was larger. Our Preceptor, having appointed me judge of this difference, I judged that matters should be left in this state, and that in this respect they each seemed better suited. Whereupon he remonstrated with me, saying that I had acted wrongly, for I had paused to consider what was fitting; and one ought in the first place to have heeded justice, which requires that no one be forced in what belongs to him. And he said that he was punished as we were punished in our villages for having forgotten the first aorist of τύπτω. My Schoolmaster would have to deliver me a fine harangue in *genere demonstrativo* to persuade me that his school is as good as that one.

[55] I nevertheless admit that the evil is not as great as it might have become. Eternal foresight, by placing medicinal herbs next to various noxious plants and the antidote into the very substance of the bites of a number of injurious animals, has taught Sovereigns, who are its ministers, to imitate its wisdom. By following its example, the great Monarch, whose glory will only acquire greater luster with every succeeding age, drew from the very bosom of the sciences and arts, the sources of a thousand aberrations, those famous societies that are charged with the dangerous trust of human knowledge at the same time as they are charged with the sacred trust of morals, by the care they take to preserve them in all their purity in their own midst, as well as to require them from the members they admit.

[56] These wise institutions, strengthened by his august successor and imitated by all the Kings of Europe, will at least act as checks on men of letters who, since they all aspire to the honor of being admitted to the Academies, will watch themselves and strive to make themselves worthy of it by useful works and irreproachable morals. Those among these Associations that will select for prize competitions honoring literary merit, topics apt to revive the love of virtue in Citizens' hearts, will show that such love reigns among them, and give Peoples the altogether rare and sweet pleasure of seeing learned societies dedicated to disseminating among Mankind not only *[27]* agreeable enlightenment, but also salutary teachings.

[57] Do not, therefore, urge as an objection against me what I regard as but one more proof. So many precautions all too clearly show the need for them, and no one looks for remedies to nonexistent evils. Why should the fact that they are inadequate stamp them as also common remedies? So many organizations established for the benefit of the learned, are all the more apt to make the objects of the sciences appear impressive and to direct men's minds to their cultivation. To judge by the precautions being taken, it would appear that there is a surplus of Ploughmen and fear of a shortage of Philosophers. I do not wish here to venture a comparison between agriculture and philosophy, it would not be tolerated. I will only ask, what is Philosophy? What do the writings of the best-known philosophers contain?

What are the Lessons of these lovers of wisdom? To listen to
them, might they not be taken for a troop of charlatans, each
hawking from his own stand on a public square: come to me, I
am the only one who does not deceive? One claims that there
are no bodies and that everything is in idea. Another that there
is no substance other than matter, and no God other than the
world. This one urges that there are neither virtues nor vices,
and that moral good and evil are chimeras. That other, that men
are wolves and may devour one another in good conscience. O
great Philosophers! why do you not reserve these profitable
Lessons for your friends and your children; you would soon reap
the reward for them, and we would not have to fear finding one
of your followers among our own friends and children.

[58] These, then, are the wonderful men on whom the esteem
of their contemporaries was lavished during their lifetimes, and
for whom immortality was reserved after their deaths! These are
the wise maxims we have received from them and which we
will transmit from age to age to our descendants. Has Paganism,
given to all the aberrations of human reason, left to posterity
anything comparable to the shameful memorials of reason made
by Printing during the reign of the Gospel? The impious writings
of such men as Leucippus and Diagoras perished with them.
The art of immortalizing [28] the extravagances of the human
mind had not yet been invented. But thanks to Typography* and
to the use we make of it, the dangerous reveries of such men as
Hobbes and Spinoza will last forever. Go, famed writings of

---

* Considering the frightful disorders Printing has already caused in Europe,
and judging of the future by the progress this evil daily makes, it is easy to
foresee that before long sovereigns will take as many pains to banish this terrible
art from their States as they took to establish it in them. Sultan Achmed, yielding
to the importunings of some supposed men of taste, had consented to establish
a Printing Shop in Constantinople. But the press had hardly begun to run when
it had to be destroyed and the equipment to be thrown into a well. It is said
that the Calif Omar, when asked what should be done with the library of
Alexandria, answered in these terms: "If the Books in this library contain things
contrary to the Koran they are bad and ought to be burned. If they contain
nothing but the doctrine of the Koran, burn them still: they are superfluous."
Our Learned men have cited this reasoning as the height of absurdity. Yet
suppose Gregory the Great in the place of Omar and the Gospel in the place of
the Koran, the Library would still have been burned, and it might perhaps be
the finest episode in that Illustrious Pontiff's life.

which our Forefathers' ignorance and rusticity would have been incapable; go to our descendants in company with those still more dangerous works that exude the corruption of our century's morals, and together transmit to future centuries a faithful history of the progress and the benefits of our sciences and our arts. If they read you, you will leave them in no doubt regarding the question we are examining today; and unless they are more devoid of sense than are we, they will raise their hands to Heaven and say with a bitter heart: "Almighty God, you who hold all Minds in your hands, deliver us from the Enlightenment and the fatal arts of our Forefathers, and restore us to ignorance, innocence, and poverty, the only goods that can make for our happiness and that are precious in your sight."

[59] But if the progress of the sciences and the arts has added nothing to our genuine felicity; if it has corrupted our morals, and if the corruption of morals has injured the purity of taste, what are we to think of that crowd of Popularizers who have removed the difficulties which protected the approaches to the Temple of [29] the Muses and which nature had placed there as a trial of the strength of those who might be tempted to know? What are we to think of those Anthologizers of works which have indiscreetly broken down the gate of the Sciences and introduced into their Sanctuary a populace unworthy of coming near it; whereas what would have been desirable is to have had all those who could not go far in a career in Letters deterred from the outset, and become involved in Arts useful to society? Someone who his whole life long will remain a bad versifier or an inferior Geometer, might perhaps have become a great clothier. Those whom nature intended as her disciples had no need of masters. Such men as Verulam, Descartes and Newton, these Preceptors of Mankind, had none themselves, and indeed what guides could have led them as far as their own vast genius carried them? Ordinary Masters could only have cramped their understanding by confining it within the narrow scope of their own: The first obstacles taught them to exert themselves and to practice covering the immense distance which they traveled. If a few men are to be allowed to devote themselves to the study of the Sciences and the Arts, it must be only those who feel the

strength to go forth alone in their footsteps, and to overtake them: It belongs to this small number to raise monuments to the glory of the human mind. But if nothing is to be beyond their genius, nothing must be beyond their hopes. That is the only encouragement they need. The soul insensibly proportions itself to the objects that occupy it, and it is great occasions that make great men. The Prince of Eloquence was Consul of Rome, and perhaps the greatest of Philosophers was Lord Chancellor of England. Is it likely that if the one had merely occupied a chair in some University and the other received a modest pension from an Academy, is it likely, I say, that their works would not have smacked of their condition? Let Kings, therefore, not disdain admitting into their councils the people most capable of counseling them well: let them reject the old prejudice invented by the pride of the Great, that the art of leading Peoples is more difficult than that of enlightening them; as if *[30]* it were easier to move men to act well of their own accord than to compel them to do so by force. Let learned men of the first rank find honorable asylum in their courts. Let them there receive the only reward worthy of them; by the credit they enjoy, to contribute to the happiness of the Peoples to whom they have taught wisdom. Only then will it be possible to see what virtue, science, and authority, animated by a noble emulation and working in concert for the felicity of Mankind, can do. But as long as power remains by itself on one side, [and] enlightenment and wisdom by themselves on the other, the learned will rarely think great things, Princes will more rarely still perform fine ones, and Peoples will continue to be base, corrupt, and wretched.

[60] As for ourselves, common men, to whom Heaven has not vouchsafed such great talents and whom it does not destine for so much glory, let us remain in our obscurity. Let us not run after a reputation which would escape us and which, in the present state of things, would never restore what it would have cost us, even if we had every title to obtain it. What good is it to seek our happiness in the opinion of another if we can find it within ourselves? Let us leave to others the care of instructing Peoples in their duties, and confine ourselves to fulfilling our

own duties well, we have no need of knowing more.

[61] O virtue! Sublime science of simple souls, are so many efforts and so much equipment really required to know you? Are not your principles engraved in all hearts, and is it not enough, in order to learn your Laws, to return into oneself and, in the silence of the passions, to listen to the voice of one's conscience? That is true Philosophy, let us know how to rest content with it; and without envying the glory of those famous men who render themselves immortal in the Republic of Letters, let us try to place between them and ourselves the glorious distinction formerly seen between two great Peoples: that the one knew how to speak well, and the other to act well.

LETTER
to Monsieur L'ABBÉ RAYNAL
Writer for the *Mercure de France*

[1] I owe thanks, sir, to the persons who relayed to you the observations which you have the goodness of conveying to me, and I shall try to profit from them; I must, however, confess to you that I find my Censors a little harsh on my logic, and I suspect that they would have proven less punctilious if I had shared their views. It at least seems to me that if they themselves had displayed some of the rigorous precision which they demand of me, I would not need the clarifications for which I am about to ask them.

[2] *The Writer,* they say, *seems to prefer the condition of Europe prior to the restoration of the Sciences; a state worse than ignorance because of the false knowledge or of the jargon that prevailed.* The Writer of this remark seems to make me say that false knowledge or scholastic jargon is preferable to Science, whereas I myself said that it is worse than ignorance; but how does he understand the word *condition*? Is he referring to enlightenment or to morals, or does he confuse two things I took such pains to distinguish? However, since this is the heart of the matter, I admit that it is most awkward of me to have only appeared to take a stand on this issue.

[3] They add that *the Writer prefers rusticity to politeness.*

[4] It is true that the Writer prefers rusticity to the prideful and false politeness of our century, and he has stated the reason for his preference. *And that he seeks to do away with all Learned men and Artists.* Very well, since you insist, I agree to eliminate all the distinctions I had drawn.

[5] *He should,* they further say, *have indicated the point with reference to which he [32] speaks of a period of decadence.* I did more; I cast my thesis in the form of a general proposition: I assigned this first stage in the decadence of morals to the first moment at which Letters came to be cultivated in any country of the world, and I found the progress of these two things always to be directly proportional. *And by going back to that*

first period, to compare the morals of those times with ours.
I would have done so in still greater detail in a full-length book.

[6] *Short of that, we do not see how far back one would
have to go, lest it be to the time of the Apostles.* I do not,
myself, see any objection to doing so, if that should, in fact, be
the case. But I ask my Censor in all fairness: Would he have had
me say that the time of the deepest ignorance was the time of
the Apostles?

[7] They add that, *regarding luxury, it is known that sound
policy calls for it to be prohibited in small States, but that
the case of a kingdom such as, for example, France, is
altogether different. The reasons why it is so, are well known.*
Have I not here, once again, cause for complaint? These reasons
are the very reasons to which I tried to address myself. Well or
ill, I did address myself to them. Now, one can scarcely show
greater contempt for a Writer than to urge nothing more in
reply to him than the very arguments he has refuted. Does the
difficulty they have to resolve nevertheless have to be pointed
out to them? It is this: *What will become of virtue when one
has to become rich at all cost?** That is what I asked them, and
what I ask them still.

[8] As for the two subsequent observations, the first of which
begins with the words: *Finally, the objection is,* and the other
of which begins: *but what more directly concerns;* I beg the
Reader to spare me the trouble of transcribing them. The
Academy had asked me whether the restoration of the Sciences
and Arts had contributed to the purification of morals. That was
the problem I had to solve: yet here I am being charged with
not having solved a different problem. Surely that is, to say the
least, a very odd criticism. Yet I am almost in the position of
having to beg the Reader's pardon for having anticipated it, as
that is what he might believe happened when he reads the last
five or six pages of my discourse. *[33]*

[9] Besides, if my Censors continue to insist on practical
conclusions, I promise them very clearly spelled-out ones in my
first reply.

* *Disc[ourse]*, p. 16.

[10] Regarding the uselessness of sumptuary Laws in uprooting luxury once it has taken a firm hold, they say that *the Writer is not unaware of what can be said on the subject*. Indeed not. I am not unaware of the fact that once a man is dead one does not call the Doctor.

[11] *It is impossible to be too emphatic about truths* that *clash* so *head-on with the general taste, and it is important to deny chicanery every possible hold*. I am not altogether of the same opinion, and I believe that children should be left some playthings.

[12] *Many Readers would also prefer them presented in a plain style rather than in the formal dress called for in Academy Discourses*. I very much share those Readers' taste. This, then, is a point on which I can agree with my Censors' sentiment, and I do so forthwith.

[13] I do not know who the opponent is whom I am threatened with in the *Postscript*. Whoever he might be, I cannot bring myself to reply to a work before I have read it, nor to consider myself defeated before I have been attacked.

[14] Besides, regardless of whether I answer the criticisms I am told are forthcoming, or leave it at publishing the expanded work that is requested of me, I warn my Censors that they might not find in them the changes they hope for. I anticipate that when it comes to having to defend myself, I will not hesitate to accept all the consequences that follow from my principles.

[15] I know in advance with what great words I will be attacked. Enlightenment, knowledge, laws, morality, reason, propriety, considerateness, gentleness, amenity, politeness, education, etc. To all of this I will only answer with two other words which ring even more loudly in my ear. Virtue, truth! I will call out incessantly; truth, virtue! If anyone sees no more than words in that, I have nothing further to say to him.

OBSERVATIONS
By Jean-Jacques ROUSSEAU of Geneva
On the Answer to his Discourse

[1] I owe thanks rather than a reply to the Anonymous Writer who has just honored my Discourse with an Answer. But the claims of gratitude will not cause me to forget the claims of truth; nor will I forget that whenever reason is at issue, men are restored to the right of Nature and recover their original equality.

[2] The Discourse to which I have to reply is full of very true and very well-proved things, to which I have nothing to answer: for although in it I am called Doctor, I should be very sorry to be one of those who have an answer to everything.

[3] My defense will be no less easy. It will be restricted to a comparison between my sentiment and the truths urged against me; for if I prove that they do not affect it, I will, I believe, have defended it adequately.

[4] I can reduce all the Propositions established by my Adversary to two principal points; one involves the praise of the Sciences; the other deals with their abuse. I shall examine them separately.

[5] The tone of the Answer suggests a wish to have had me speak far worse of the Sciences than I in fact did. It assumes that the praise of them found at the beginning of my Discourse, must have cost me a great *[36]* deal; it is, according to the Writer, an acknowledgment wrested from me by the truth, and which I was not slow in retracting.

[6] If that acknowledgment is praise wrested from me by the truth, then it would seem that I did think as well of the Sciences as I said I did; the good the Writer himself says of them is, then, not at odds with my sentiment. The admission is, he says, wrested from me by force: so much the better for my cause, since it shows that with me truth has greater force than has inclination. But on what grounds is this praise judged to be forced? Is it for being badly done? To judge a Writer's sincerity by this novel principle would be to put it to a terrifying test. Is it for being too short? It seems to me that I might easily have

31

said less in more pages. It is, he says, because I retracted; I do not know where I committed that fault; and all I can answer is that it was not my intention to do so.

[7] Science in itself is very good, that is obvious: and one would have to have taken leave of one's good sense, to maintain the contrary. The Author of all things is the fountain of truth; omniscience is one of his divine attributes. To acquire knowledge and to extend one's enlightenment is, then, in a way to participate in the supreme intelligence. It is in this sense that I praised knowledge, and this is the sense in which my Adversary praises it. He goes on to speak at length about the various kinds of utility Man can derive from the Sciences and Arts; and I should readily have said as much if that had been my topic. We are thus perfectly agreed on this point.

[8] But how does it happen that the Sciences, so pure in their source and so praiseworthy in their end, give rise to so many impieties, so many heresies, so many errors, so many absurd systems, so many vexations, so much foolishness, so many bitter Satires, so many wretched Romances, so many licentious Poems, so many obscene Books; and in those who cultivate them, so much pride, so much avarice, so much malice, so many intrigues, so many jealousies, so many lies, so many evil deeds, so many calumnies, so many cowardly and shameful flatteries? I had said that it is because Science, however beautiful, however sublime, is not made for man; that his mind is too limited to make much progress in it, and his heart too full of passions to keep him from putting it to bad use; *[37]* that it is sufficient for him to study his duties well, and that everyone has received all the light he needs for such study. My Adversary, for his part, admits that the Sciences become harmful when they are abused and that many do, indeed, abuse them. In all this we are not, I believe, saying such very different things; I do, it is true, add that they are much abused, and that they are always abused, and it does not seem to me that the contrary had been upheld in the Answer.

[9] I am therefore confident that our principles, and hence all the propositions that can be deduced from them, do not in any way conflict, and that is what I had to prove. Yet when it

comes to drawing conclusions, our conclusions are at odds. Mine was that, since the Sciences harm morals more than they benefit society, it would be preferable to have men pursue them less eagerly. My Adversary's is that, although the Sciences do much harm, they ought nevertheless to be cultivated because of the good they do. I leave it, not to the Public, but to the small number of true Philosophers, to decide which of these two conclusions ought to be preferred.

[10] It remains for me to make a few slight Observations on some passages in the Answer which seemed to me to be somewhat lacking in the precision I readily admire in the rest, and which may thereby have contributed to the erroneous conclusion the Writer draws from them.

[11] The work begins with some personal remarks to which I shall refer only in so far as they bear on the question. The Writer honors me with a good deal of praise, and so certainly gives me a ready opening. But there is too little common measure in such matters: a respectful silence about the objects of our admiration is often more becoming than is indiscreet praise.*[38]

[12] My Discourse is said to be somewhat surprising;** the remark seems to me to call for elucidation. Surprise is also expressed at seeing it crowned; yet it is not so very extraordinary to see mediocre writings crowned. Taken in any other sense,

---

* All Princes, good and bad ones alike, will always be obsequiously and indiscriminately praised as long as there are Courtiers and Men of Letters. As for Princes who are great Men, they require more moderate and judicious praise. Flattery offends their virtue, and even praise may tarnish their glory. I, in any event, know that Trajan would be much greater in my eyes if Pliny had never written. If Alexander had really been what he affected to appear, he would have given no thought to his portrait [38] or Statue; rather, he would have allowed none but a Lacedaemonian to deliver his Panegyric, even at the risk of remaining without one. The only praise worthy of a King is that heard, not from the mercenary mouth of an Orator, but from the voice of a free People.

** The question itself might surprise: a great and fine question if ever there was one, and which might not soon be raised again. The French Academy has just proposed a very similar subject for the prize in eloquence for the year 1752: to be affirmed that *The Love of Letters Inspires the Love of Virtue*. The Academy did not see fit to leave such a subject in the form of a problem; and for the occasion this wise Company doubled the time it used to allow Writers for even the most difficult subjects.

this surprise would do the Academy of Dijon as much honor as it would prove insulting to the integrity of Academies in general; and the advantage I might derive from it for my cause is readily apparent.

[13] In most agreeably turned Phrases I am taxed with a contradiction between my conduct and my doctrine; I am reproached with myself having cultivated studies which I condemn;* since Science and Virtue are incompatible, as I am supposed to be at pains to prove, I am asked in a somewhat insistent tone, how I dare use the one in speaking on behalf of the other.

[14] It is clever to involve me in the issue in this way; such a personal reference cannot fail to embarrass me in my Answer, or rather Answers; for, unfortunately I have more than one. Let us at least try to have them make up in precision what they lack in elegance. *[39]*

[15] 1. The cultivation of the Sciences corrupts a nation's morals, that is what I dared to maintain, that is what I dare believe I have proved. But how could I have said that Science and Virtue are incompatible in every Individual, I, who exhorted Princes to invite the truly Learned to their Court and to place their trust in them so that we might for once see what Science and Virtue combined can do for the happiness of mankind? These truly Learned men are few in number, I admit it; for it takes a combination of great talents and great Virtues to put Science to good use; and that can barely be hoped for in few privileged souls, but it cannot be expected from an entire people. One can therefore not conclude from my principles that a man cannot be both learned and virtuous.

[16] 2. One can even less [plausibly] charge me personally with this supposed contradiction, even if it really did exist. I adore Virtue, my heart bears me witness of it; it also tells me

---

* Unlike many others, I cannot justify myself by maintaining that our education does not depend on ourselves, and that we are not consulted about being poisoned: I threw myself into study most willingly; and I gave it up even more wholeheartedly when I realized into what turmoil it threw my soul without any profit to my reason. I want nothing more to do with a deceitful profession in which one believes one is doing much for wisdom while doing everything for vanity.

all too clearly how great the distance is between this love and
the conduct that makes for a virtuous man; besides, I am very
far from possessing Science, and farther still from pretending
that I do. I should have thought that my candid admission at
the beginning of my Discourse would have protected me against
this imputation; I feared, rather, that I would be accused of
passing judgment on things I do not know. It is readily enough
evident that I could not possibly avoid both reproaches. Who
knows whether someone might not even decide to combine
them, if I do not promptly refute this one, however undeserved
it may be.

[17] 3. I might, in this connection, refer to what the Church
Fathers used to say regarding the worldly Sciences which they
despised and nevertheless employed to combat the Heathen
Philosophers. I could appeal to the comparison they drew
between them and the Egyptians' vessels stolen by the Israelites;
but as a final Answer I will leave it at submitting the following
question: if someone came to kill me and I had the good fortune
to seize his weapon, would I be forbidden to use it to drive
him off, before I threw it away?

[18] If the contradiction I am reproached with does not exist,
[40] then it is not necessary to suppose that I simply sought to
amuse myself with a frivolous paradox; and it seems to me all
the less necessary to do so as the tone I took, bad as it may have
been, is at least not the tone of witticisms.

[19] It is time to have done with what pertains to me: to
speak of oneself never profits a man; and it is an indiscretion
which, even when it is forced on one, the Public does not
readily forgive. Truth is so independent of those who attack and
defend it, that Writers who argue about it should altogether
forget one another; it would save a great deal of ink and paper.
But this rule, so easy to follow with respect to myself, is not at
all easy to follow with respect to my Adversary; and this
difference does not redound to the advantage of my reply.

[20] The Writer, noting that I attack the Sciences and Arts in
terms of their effect on morals, answers me with an inventory
of the uses to which they are put in all states; which is as if, in
order to justify an accused person, all one did was to prove that

he is quite well, most skillful, or very rich. As long as it is granted me that the Arts and Sciences make us bad people, I shall not deny that they also greatly contribute to our convenience; that is one more respect in which they are like most vices.

[21] The Writer goes further, and also claims that we have to study in order to admire the beauties of the universe, and that even the spectacle of nature, exhibited, it would seem, to the eyes of all for the instruction of simple men, can be apprehended only by Observers who have had a great deal of instruction. I must admit that that proposition surprises me: is it that all men are required to be Philosophers, or that only Philosophers are required to believe in God? Scripture in a thousand places exhorts us to revere the greatness and goodness of God in the wonders of His works; I do not think that it has anywhere prescribed to us the study of Physics, nor that the Author of Nature is less well adored by me, who know nothing, than by him who knows and the cedar, and the hyssop, and the trunk of the fly, and that of the Elephant.

[22] One always believes one has said what the Sciences do *[41]* when one has said what they should do. Yet the two seem to me quite different: the study of the Universe should elevate man to his Creator, I know; but it only elevates human vanity. The Philosopher, flattering himself that he fathoms God's secrets, dares to liken his supposed wisdom with eternal wisdom: he approves, he blames, he corrects, he prescribes laws to nature and limits to Divinity; and while he is busy with his vain systems and takes endless pains to arrange the machine of the world, the Ploughman who sees the rain and sun by turns fertilize his field, admires, praises and blesses the hand from which he receives these graces without troubling himself about how they reach him. He does not seek to justify his ignorance or his vices by his incredulity. He does not censure God's works, nor challenge his master in order to display his self-importance. Never will the impious remark of Alfonse X occur to one of the vulgar: that blasphemy was reserved for a learned mouth.

[23] *Man's natural curiosity,* they go on, *inspires him with the desire to learn*. He should therefore endeavor to curb it, like all his natural inclinations. *His needs make him feel the*

necessity of doing so. In a good many respects, knowledge is useful; yet savages are men, and they do not feel this necessity. *His occupations oblige him to do so.* They far more often oblige him to give up study in order to attend to his duties.* *His progress lets him taste its pleasure.* He should, for that very reason, be suspicious of it. *His first discoveries increase his greed for knowledge.* That does, indeed, happen to those who have talent. *The more he knows, the more aware he is of having to acquire knowledge;* that is to say that the time he loses only serves to excite him to lose more: only in a very few men of genius does insight into their own ignorance grow as they learn, and they are the only ones for whom study may be good; almost as soon as small minds have learned something, they believe they know everything, *[42]* and there is no sort of foolishness which this conviction will not make them say or do. *The more knowledge a man has acquired, the easier it is for him to do well.* It is evident that in saying this, the Writer has consulted his heart far more than he has observed men.

[24] He further says that it is good to know evil, so as to learn to shun it; and he implies that one can be assured of one's virtue only after having put it to trial. These maxims are, at the very least, doubtful, and open to much discussion. It is not certain that in order to learn to do good [or well] one has to know how many ways there are of doing evil [or ill]. We have a guide within, much more infallible than all the books, and which never forsakes us when we are in need. It would suffice to guide us in innocence if we were willing always to heed it; and besides, how can we be obliged to test our strength in order to be assured of our virtue, when one way to practice virtue is to shun occasions for vice?

[25] The wise man is ever on his guard, and always suspicious of his own strength: he keeps all his courage in reserve for times of need, and never runs unnecessary risks. The swaggerer is the one who forever boasts of more than he can do and who, after having stood up to and insulted everybody, allows himself

---

* It is a bad mark against a society that those who lead it need so much Science; if men were what they ought to be, they would hardly need to study in order to learn the things they have to do.

to be defeated in the first encounter. I should like to know which of these two portraits best resembles a Philosopher at grips with his passions.

[26] I am reproached with consistently having chosen my examples of virtue from among the ancients. I could probably have found many more if I could have reached still farther back: I also mentioned one modern people, and it is not my fault that I found only one. Further, I am, in a general maxim, reproached with drawing abhorrent comparisons prompted, it is said, less by enthusiasm and fair-mindedness than by envy of my countrymen and ill-humor toward my contemporaries. Yet perhaps no one loves his country and his compatriots as much as I do. Beyond that, I have only one word to say in reply. I have stated my arguments, and they are what has to be weighed. As for my motives, they must be left to be judged by him who alone may judge of them.

[27] I ought not here pass over in silence a weighty objection *[43]* that had already been addressed to me by a Philosopher:* *Is not,* I am asked here, *the difference that is sometimes observed between the morals of different countries and different times, due to climate, temperament, the lack of opportunity, the want of an object, the economy of the government, the Customs, the Laws, to any cause other than the Sciences?*

[28] The question implies large views, and it would require more extensive clarification than is appropriate in the present writing. Besides, the very hidden but very real relations between the nature of government on the one hand, and the genius, morals, and knowledge of the citizens on the other, would have to be examined; and this would involve me in delicate discussions that might lead me too far. Moreover, it would be difficult for me to speak about government without giving my Adversary an undue advantage; and, all things considered, these are inquiries best pursued in Geneva and under different circumstances.

[29] I go on to an accusation that is far more serious than the preceding objection. I shall transcribe it literally; for it is important to place it faithfully before the Reader's eyes.

---

* Pref[ace] to the *Encycl[opedia]*.

[30] *The more a Christian examines the authenticity of his Titles, the more secure is he in the possession of his belief; the more he studies revelation, the more strengthened is he in his faith: He discovers its origin and excellence in the divine Scriptures; he follows its development from one century to the next in the learned writings of the Church Fathers; he finds examples and models of it in the Books of ethics and the sacred chronicles.*

[31] *What! shall ignorance deprive Religion and virtue of such powerful supports! and shall a Doctor from Geneva openly teach that it is responsible for the wantonness of morals! Such a strange paradox would cause even greater consternation if it were not well known that for those who have no other rule than their individual mind, the singularity of a system, however dangerous, is but one more reason* [in its favor].

[32] I dare ask the Writer; how could he ever have placed such an interpretation on the principles I established? How could he accuse me of blaming the study of Religion, when I blame the study of our vain Sciences chiefly because it turns us away from the study *[44]* of our duties? And what is the study of a Christian's duties if not the study of his Religion?

[33] I should probably have blamed explicitly all the childish subtleties of Scholasticism by which the spirit of Religion only gets destroyed on the pretext of elucidating its principles, by substituting scientific pride for christian humility. I should have spoken out more forcefully against the rash Ministers who first dared to lay a hand on the Ark in order with their feeble learning to bolster a structure that is upheld by the hand of God. I should have waxed indignant against those frivolous men who, with their wretched hair-splitting, have degraded the sublime simplicity of the Gospel and reduced the doctrine of Jesus Christ to syllogisms. But my present concern is to defend myself, not to attack.

[34] I see that the best way to put an end to this disputation is with history and facts. If I could show in a few words what the relations between the Sciences and Religion have been from the very first, it might help settle the point at issue.

[35] The People God chose for himself never cultivated the Sciences, and were never advised to study them; yet if such study had served a useful purpose, they would have needed it more than any other. On the contrary, their Leaders always bent all their efforts on keeping them as separate as possible from the idolatrous and learned neighboring Nations. A precaution which, in their case, was less necessary with regard to Nations of the first than of the second kind: for this weak and crude People was far more liable to be seduced by the impostures of the Priests of Baal, than by the Sophisms of the Philosophers.

[36] Even after their frequent dispersion amongst the Egyptians and the Greeks, Science had a very difficult time taking root in the Hebrews' heads. Josephus and Philo who, anywhere else, would have been but mediocre men, were prodigies among them. The Sadducees, recognizable by their irreligiousness, were the Philosophers of Jerusalem; the Pharisees, great hypocrites, * were its *[45]* Doctors. Although they more or less restricted their Science to the study of the Law, they pursued this study with typically dogmatic ostentation and self-importance; they also observed all the practices of Religion with the utmost care; but the Gospel acquaints us with the spirit of that exactitude and how it is to be judged: moreover, they all had very little Science and a great deal of pride, and it is not in this respect that they most differed from our Doctors today.

[37] In establishing the new Law, Jesus Christ did not wish to entrust his doctrine and ministry to scholars. In making his choice he followed the preference he on all occasions showed for the lowly and simple. And in his teaching of his disciples there are no learned or scientific words to be found, lest it be to indicate his contempt for everything of that kind.

* The same hatred and mutual contempt was seen to reign between these two parties, that has at all times reigned between the Doctors and the Philosophers; that is to say between those who use their heads as a storehouse for other people's Science and those who lay claim to a head of their *[45]* own. Pit the music master and the dancing master of the *Bourgeois Gentilhomme* against one another, you will have the antiquarian and the wit; the Chemist and the Man of Letters; the Jurist and the Physician; the Geometer and the Versifier; the Theologian and the Philosopher; to judge soundly of all these People, one need only consult them, and listen to what each one tells you, not about himself, but about the others.

[38] After the death of Jesus Christ twelve poor fishermen and artisans undertook to instruct and convert the world. Their method was simple; they preached artlessly but with utter conviction, and of all the miracles with which God honored their faith, the most striking was the saintliness of their lives; the disciples followed this example, and their success was prodigious. Alarmed, the Pagan Priests gave Princes to understand that the state was lost because donations were dwindling. Persecutions arose, and the persecutors only hastened the progress of the Religion they sought to stifle. All Christians rushed to martyrdom, all Peoples rushed to Baptism: the history of these first times is a continual marvel.

[39] However, the Priests of the idols, not content with persecuting Christians, began to calumny them; the Philosophers, finding a Religion that preached humility unrewarding, joined their Priests. Ridicule and insults were showered [46] on the new Sect from all sides. They had to take up the pen to defend themselves. Saint Justin Martyr* was the first to write [47] an

---

* These first writers, who sealed the testimony of their pen with their blood, would today be very scandalous Writers; for they upheld exactly the same sentiment I uphold. In his exchange with Tripho, Saint Justin reviews the various Sects of Philosophers he had formerly tried, and makes them appear so ridiculous that one might believe oneself to be reading a Dialogue of Lucian: and Tertullian's Apology shows how offended the first Christians were to be taken for Philosophers.

Indeed, it would be rather discreditable to Philosophy to have the pernicious maxims and the impious dogmas of its various Sects exposed. The Epicureans denied all providence, the Academics doubted the existence of the Divinity, and the Stoics the immortality of the soul. The sentiments entertained by the less famous Sects were no better; here is a sample of those of Theodorus, the head of one of the two branches of the Cyrenaics, as reported by Diogenes Laertius. "He discarded friendship because it was without advantage to the ignorant or to the learned. . . . He said that it was reasonable for a prudent man not to risk his life for his fatherland, and indeed that prudence should not be cast aside for the benefit of the ignorant. . . . He held that the wise man might steal and commit adultery and sacrilege when it was opportune for him to do so. None of these are shameful by nature. They should be freed of the opinion of the vulgar which is due to fools and ignoramuses. . . . The wise man can, publicly, without shame, and without becoming an object of reproach, go to prostitutes."

These are one man's opinions, I know; but is there a single one of all the Sects that did not fall into some dangerous error; and what are we to say about the distinction between two doctrines so eagerly embraced by all Philosophers

Apology of his faith. The Pagans were attacked in turn; to attack
them was to defeat them; the first successes encouraged new
writers: on the pretext of exposing the depravity of Paganism,
they threw themselves into mythology and erudition;* they
wanted to display Science and wit; large numbers of Books were
published, and morals began to relax.

[40] Soon they ceased to be satisfied with the simplicity of
the Gospel and the faith of the Apostles, they constantly wanted
to prove themselves cleverer than their predecessors. Every
dogma became an occasion for hair-splitting; everyone wanted
to uphold his opinion, no one wanted to yield. The ambition to
be the Chief of a Sect arose, heresies proliferated on all sides.

[41] Before long ill-temper and violence accompanied the
quarrel. Those ever so gentle Christians who had only known
how to yield their throat to the knife, became one another's
frenzied persecutors, worse than the idolators: everyone partook
in the same excesses, and the party of truth was upheld no more
moderately than was the party of error.

[42] Another, even more dangerous evil, arose from the same
source. It was the introduction of ancient Philosophy into
Christian doctrine. The more they studied the Greek Philosophers, the more connections did they believe they saw with

---

and in accordance with which they in secret professed sentiments that were the
opposite of those which they professed in public? Pythagoras was the first to
resort to the internal doctrine; he disclosed it to his disciples only after long
trials and with the greatest mystery; he gave them secret lessons in Atheism
while solemnly offering Sacrifices to Jupiter. The Philosophers found that this
proceeding suited them so well that it spread rapidly throughout Greece, and
from Greece to Rome, as appears from the works of Cicero who in the company
of his friend laughed at the immortal Gods to which he so emphatically appealed
from the Rostrum. The internal doctrine was not transmitted from Europe to
China; but, there too, it was born together with Philosophy; and to it the
Chinese owe the great number of Atheists or Philosophers in their midst. The
History of this fatal doctrine, written by a learned and sincere man, would prove
a terrible blow to ancient as well as to modern Philosophy. But Philosophy will
always defy reason, truth, and time itself, because it has its source in man's
pride, more powerful than all these things.
    * Clement of Alexandria has been justly blamed for displaying in his writings
a profane erudition that ill-becomes a Christian. Yet it would seem that at that
time it was excusable to acquaint oneself with the teaching against which one
had to defend oneself. But who can help laughing at all the trouble our Scholars
nowadays take to elucidate the reveries of mythology.

Christianity. They dared to believe that Religion would become more respectable if it were clothed in the authority of Philosophy; there was a time when, to be Orthodox, one had to be a Platonist; and first Plato, and later Aristotle very nearly came to be placed on the Altar alongside of Jesus Christ.

[43] The Church more than once rose up against these excesses. Its most illustrious defenders frequently deplored them in forceful and energetic terms: frequently they attempted to expel from it all the worldly Science that soiled its [48] purity. One of the most illustrious Popes carried zeal to such an extreme as to maintain that it is shameful to subject the word of God to the rules of Grammar.

[44] But they cried out to no avail; swept along by the torrent, they were compelled to conform to the practice they condemned; and it was in a most learned fashion that most of them inveighed against the progress of the Sciences.

[45] After prolonged turmoil, things finally settled down. In about the tenth century, the torch of the Sciences ceased to light the earth; the Clergy remained plunged in an ignorance I do not wish to justify since it affected things they ought to know no less than things that are of no use to them, but due to which the Church at least achieved a little more quiet than it had experienced until then.

[46] After the revival of Letters, divisions soon arose anew, which were more terrible than ever. Learned Men stirred up the quarrel, learned Men kept it alive, and the most able always proved to be the most stubborn. Conferences between the Doctors of the different parties proved to be of no avail: no one brought to them a love of reconciliation or perhaps even of the truth; all brought to them only the desire to shine at their Adversary's expense; everyone wanted to prevail, no one wanted to learn; the stronger silenced the weaker; disputation always ended in insults, and persecution was its invariable consequence. God only knows when all these evils will cease.

[47] Today the Sciences flourish, Literature and the Arts shine brightly among us; what has it benefited Religion? Let us ask the many Philosophers who pride themselves on not having any. Our Libraries overflow with Books on Theology; and Casuists

abound among us. In the past we had Saints and no Casuists. Science spreads, and faith vanishes. Everyone wants to teach how to do the good, and no one wants to learn it; we have all become Doctors, and have ceased to be Christians.

[48] No, it is not with so much Art and circumstance that the Gospel spread through the Universe, and that its touching beauty entered men's hearts. One only has to meditate on that divine Book, *[49]* the only book a Christian needs and the most useful of all books even for those who might not be Christians, and it suffuses the soul with love for its Author, and the will to carry out his precepts. Never did virtue speak in such gentle terms; never did the deepest wisdom express itself with such energy and simplicity. One never leaves off reading it without feeling better than before. O you, Ministers of the Law that is there proclaimed to me, take fewer pains to teach me so many useless things. Give up all those Learned Books that can neither convince nor move me. Prostrate yourselves at the feet of the God of mercy you are charged with making me know and love; ask him to give you the profound humility which you must preach to me. Do not spread before my eyes the prideful Science or the indecent pomp that dishonor you and disgust me; be moved yourselves, if you would have me be moved; and above all, show to me by your conduct the practice of the Law which you claim to teach me. You need know or teach me nothing more, and your ministry is accomplished. None of this involves Letters or Philosophy. That is how the Gospel should be practiced and preached, and how its first defenders made it triumph in all the Nations, *not in the manner of Aristotle,* the Church Fathers used to say, *but in the Fisherman's.*

[49] I sense I grow prolix, but I believed I could not avoid going into some detail on an issue as important as this. Besides, impatient Readers must recognize that there are great advantages to being the critic: for while one can attack with a single word, it takes pages to defend oneself.

[50] I proceed to the second part of the Answer, about which I shall try to be briefer, although I find that there are hardly fewer observations to be made regarding it.

[51] *It is not from the Sciences,* I am told, *but from the lap*

of riches, that softness and luxury have at all times been born. I had also not said that luxury was born of the Sciences; I had said, rather, that both were born together and that one hardly ever goes without the other. Here is how I would arrange that genealogy. The first source of evil is inequality; from inequality arose riches; for the words poor *[50]* and rich are relative, and wherever men are equal there is neither rich nor poor. From riches are born luxury and idleness; from luxury arose the fine Arts, and from idleness the Sciences. *At no time have riches been the portion of the Learned.* Which makes for an even greater evil, as the rich and the learned only serve to corrupt one another. If the rich were more learned or the learned more rich, these would be less pusillanimous flatterers, the others would love base flattery less, and everyone would be better for it. So much is evident from the small number of persons who have the good fortune to be both learned and rich. *For every Plato who is wealthy, for every Aristippus who is respected at Court, how many Philosophers are reduced to beggary, wrapped in their virtue and ignored in their solitude?* I do not deny that a great many Philosophers are very poor, and certainly very annoyed to be so; nor do I doubt that most of them owe their Philosophy solely to their poverty; but, even if I were ready to assume that the Philosophers are virtuous, can their morals—which the people do not see—teach the people to reform their own? *The Learned have neither the taste nor the leisure to amass great wealth.* I am ready to believe that they have not the necessary leisure. *They love study.* Whoever did not love his profession would be either mad or miserable. *They live in modest circumstances;* one has to be extremely well disposed toward them to give them credit for it. *An industrious and moderate life, spent in silent retreat, devoted to reading and work, is surely not a voluptuous and criminal life.* At least not in men's eyes: everything depends on the inside. A man may be constrained to lead such a life and yet have a very corrupt soul; besides, what does it matter whether he himself is virtuous and modest if his labors nourish the idleness and spoil the minds of his fellow-citizens? *Although the conveniences of life are often the products of the Arts, the Artists do not enjoy a greater share of them*. They hardly seem to me to be the kind of people who would deprive themselves of them; especially those who, by devoting themselves to altogether useless and therefore very lucrative Arts, are in a better position to acquire whatever they desire. *They only work for the rich.* *[51]* The way things are going, I would not be surprised to see the rich work for them some day. *And it is the idle rich who profit from the fruits of their labor, and who misuse them.* Once again, I do not see that our Artists are such simple and modest folk; luxury cannot prevail among one order of Citizens without soon insinuating itself under various guises into all the others, and everywhere it causes the same ravages.

[52] Luxury corrupts everything, the rich who enjoy it, and the wretched who covet it. To wear lace ruffles, an embroidered coat, and carry an enameled snuffbox, cannot be said to be an evil in itself. But it is a very great evil to put any stock by such trifles, to regard as happy the people that wears them, and to devote to the acquisition of such things the time and effort which every human being owes to nobler objects. I do not need to know the profession of the person absorbed in such pursuits, in order to know what to think of him.

[53] I have omitted the fine portrait of the Learned which we are here offered, and I believe myself entitled to some credit for being so considerate. My Adversary is not so indulgent: not only does he not grant me anything he can deny me; but, rather than condemn my thinking ill of our vain and false politeness, he prefers to justify hypocrisy. He asks me whether I would wish vice to show itself openly? Certainly I would. Confidence and esteem would be reborn among the good, men would learn to distrust the wicked, and as a result society would be more secure. I prefer to have my enemy attack me openly than to come and strike me treacherously from behind. What then! Should scandal be added to crime? I do not know; but I would prefer it if imposture were not added to it. Vicious people are perfectly comfortable with all these maxims about scandal that have been doled out to us for so long: if one were to adhere to them strictly, one would have to let oneself be robbed, betrayed, killed with impunity, and never punish anyone; for a knave on

the rack is a most scandalous sight. But is not hypocrisy an homage vice pays to virtue? Yes, like that of Caesar's assassins, who prostrated themselves at his feet the more securely to murder him. The thought may be brilliant, *[52]* the famous name of its Author may give it authority, it is nevertheless not right. Would a thief, dressed up in the livery of the house in order to do his deed more easily, ever be said to be paying homage to the master of the house he robs? No, to cover one's wickedness with the dangerous mantle of hypocrisy is not to honor virtue; it is to offend it by profaning its standards; it is to add cowardice and imposture to all the other vices; it is to make it forever impossible for oneself to return to probity. There are lofty characters who bring even to crime something proud and generous which reveals that they still have left in them some spark of that celestial fire made to animate beautiful souls. But the vile and creeping soul of the hypocrite is like a corpse, without fire, or warmth, or remnant of life. I appeal to experience. Great villains have been known to return into themselves, end their life wholesomely, and die saved. But a hypocrite becoming a good man, that has never been seen; one might reasonably have tried to convert Cartouche, but never would a wise man have undertaken to convert Cromwell.

[54] I have attributed the elegance and politeness of our manners to the restoration of the Letters and Arts; the Writer of the Answer takes issue with me on this point, and it surprises me that he does so: for since he puts so much stock by politeness and so much stock by the Sciences, I do not see what advantage he derives from denying to one the honor of having produced the other. But let us examine his proofs: they come down to this. *The Learned are not found to be more polite than other men: on the contrary, often they are less so; hence our politeness is not the work of the Sciences.*

[55] I should, first of all, like to say that this is not so much a question of the Sciences as it is one of Literature, the fine Arts, and works of taste; and our wits, as deficient in Learning as you please, and yet ever so polite, so worldly, so scintillating, so foppish, will have difficulty recognizing themselves in the sullen and pedantic air the Writer of the Reply attributes to them. But

be that as it may; let us grant, if we must, that the Learned, the
Poets, and the wits are all equally ridiculous; that the Gentlemen
of the Academy of Letters, the Gentlemen of the Academy of
[53] Sciences, and the Gentlemen of the French Academy are
crude folk, who do not know how to speak or behave in the
world, and who are by their state excluded from good company;
the Writer will not gain much from this concession, and it will
not give him a better title to deny that the politeness and the
urbanity that prevail among us are the effect of good taste,
derived originally from the ancients, and disseminated amongst
the peoples of Europe by the agreeable Books that get published
throughout the continent.* Just as the best dancing masters are
not always those who bear themselves best, so it is possible to
give excellent lessons of politeness without being inclined or
able to be polite oneself. The ponderous Commentators who,
we are told, knew everything of the ancients save their grace
and delicacy did, nevertheless, with their useful though despised
works, teach us to be sensible of those beauties, although they
were themselves insensitive to them. The same may be said
regarding the agreeable manners and the elegance of morals
which men substitute for purity of morals, and which have been
in evidence among all peoples among whom Letters have been
held in honor, in Athens, in Rome, in China, everywhere
politeness of language and of manners has consistently been
seen to accompany, not Learned men and Artists, but Learning
and the fine Arts.

[56] The Writer next attacks my praise of ignorance: and

* When such very general objects as the morals and the manners of a people
are at issue, one has to be careful not always to focus too narrowly on particular
examples. For if one did, one would never see the sources of things. To find
out whether I am right to attribute politeness to the cultivation of Letters, one
should not look for whether some Learned person or other is polite; rather, one
should inquire into the possible relations between literature and politeness, and
then see among which peoples these things are found together, and among
which they are found separately. The same has to be done regarding luxury,
liberty and all the other things that influence the morals of a Nation and about
which I daily hear such pitiable arguments: To examine all this narrowly and in
some few individual cases is not to Philosophize, it is to waste one's time and
reflections; for one can know Peter or James thoroughly, and yet have made very
little progress in the knowledge of men.

while taxing me with having spoken more like an Orator than a Philosopher, he depicts ignorance in his turn; as might be suspected, he does not lend it pretty colors.

[57] I do not deny that he is right, but I do not believe *[54]* I am wrong. All that is required to reconcile us, is a single and true distinction.

[58] There is a ferocious* and brutal ignorance, born of a wicked heart and a deceitful mind; a criminal ignorance of even the duties of humanity, which multiplies the vices, degrades reason, depraves the soul, and renders men similar to beasts: this is the ignorance which the Writer attacks and of which he paints a most odious and most faithful portrait. There is another, reasonable sort of ignorance which consists in restricting one's curiosity to the scope of the faculties one has received; a modest ignorance, born of a lively love of virtue, and which inspires nothing but indifference toward all that is unworthy of occupying man's heart and does not contribute to making him better; a gentle and precious ignorance, the treasure of a soul pure and satisfied with itself, that finds all its felicity in retreating into itself, in confirming itself in its innocence, and has no need to seek a false and vain happiness in the opinion others might have of its enlightenment: That is the ignorance I praised and which I ask Heaven to grant me in punishment for the scandal I caused to the learned by my professed contempt for men's Sciences.

[59] *Compare,* says the Writer, *the times of ignorance and barbarism with the happy centuries when the Sciences everywhere disseminated a spirit of order and of justice.* Those happy centuries will be difficult to find; it will be easier to find centuries when, thanks to the Sciences, Order and Justice will be nothing but vain names used to impress the people, and when they will have been carefully preserved in appearance so

---

* I shall be greatly surprised if someone of my critics does not take my praise of several ignorant and virtuous peoples as the occasion to confront me with a list of all the bands of Brigands who have infested the earth, and who are not usually very Learned men. I urge them in advance not to trouble with such inquiries, unless they think them necessary to show me their erudition. If I had said that in order to be virtuous it is enough to be ignorant, it would not be worth bothering to answer me: and for the same reason I shall consider myself free not to answer those who waste their time maintaining the contrary.

that they might be destroyed with greater impunity in fact. *Nowadays wars are found to be less frequent but more just;* how, at any *[55]* time whatsoever, can war be more just on one side without being more unjust on the other? I cannot conceive of it! *Deeds less astounding but more heroic.* Certainly no one will challenge my Adversary's right to judge of heroism; but does he think that what he does not find astounding, is not so for us? *Victories less bloody but more glorious; Conquests less rapid but more certain; warriors less violent but more feared; able to achieve victory with moderation, treating the vanquished humanely; honor is their guide, glory their reward.* I do not gainsay the Writer that there are great men among us, it would be too easy for him to prove that there are; that does not prevent peoples from being deeply corrupted. Besides, all this is so vague that the same could almost be said of every age; and it is impossible to respond to it, because one would have to go through entire Libraries and write large tomes to prove either the affirmative or the negative.

[60] When Socrates dealt harshly with the Sciences he could not, it seems to me, have had reference either to the Stoics' pride, or to the Epicureans' effeminacy, or to the Pyrrhonists' absurd jargon, because none of these folk existed in his time. But this slight anachronism is not unbecoming to my Adversary: he has spent his life better than in checking dates, and is no more obliged to know his Diogenes Laertius by heart than I am to have seen at close quarters what happens in battles.

[61] I grant, then, that Socrates only intended to criticize the vices of the Philosophers of his own time; but I do not know what conclusion to draw from it, other than that even then vices abounded where there were Philosophers. In reply, I am told that this is due to the abuse of Philosophy, and I do not think I said the contrary. What! Are all things that get abused to be eliminated, then? Yes indeed, I will unhesitatingly answer: all those that are useless; all those the abuse of which does more harm than their use does good.

[62] Let us briefly pause at this last conclusion, and let us beware of inferring from it that we should now burn all Libraries and destroy the Universities and Academies. We would only

plunge Europe back into Barbarism, without benefiting morals.*
[56] It is with sorrow that I shall state a great and fatal truth.
From knowledge to ignorance, it is but a single step; and Nations
have frequently gone from one to the other; but never has a
people, once corrupted, been known to return to virtue. You
would in vain aspire to destroy the sources of the evil; in vain
deprive vanity, idleness, and luxury of all sustenance; in vain
even that you would return men to their first equality, the
preserver of innocence and the source of all virtue; their hearts,
once spoiled, will be so forever; no remedy remains, short of
some great revolution almost as much to be feared as the evil it
might cure, and which it is blameworthy to desire and impossible
to foresee.

[63] Let us therefore let the Sciences and the Arts in some
measure temper the ferociousness of the men they have corrupted; let us strive wisely to divert them, and try to baffle their
passions. Let us feed those Tigers something to keep them from
devouring our children. A wicked person's enlightenment is, on
balance, less to be feared than is his brutal stupidity; it at least
causes him to be more circumspect about the harm he might
do, by acquainting him with the harm he himself would suffer.

[64] I have praised Academies and their illustrious founders,
and I am ready to do so again. When the sickness is incurable,
the Physician administers palliatives and adapts his remedies
less to the patient's needs than to his constitution. Wise legislators
ought to imitate his prudence; and since they can no longer
adapt the best policy to a sick People, they ought at least, like
Solon, give it the best which it can tolerate.

[65] There is in Europe a great Prince and, what is far more,
a virtuous Citizen, who recently founded several institutions in
support of Letters in the fatherland he has adopted and renders
happy. In doing so, he has done something eminently worthy
of his wisdom and virtue. With respect to political establishments,
time and *[57]* place are all-important. Princes must always favor

---

* *We would be left the vices,* says the Philosopher I have already mentioned,
and we would have ignorance besides. The few lines that Author has written
on this great subject show that he has turned his gaze in that direction, and has
seen far.

the Sciences and Arts out of self-interest; I have said why; and
in the present state of things, they must now also favor them
even in the People's interest. If there currently were among us
a Monarch so foolish as to think and act differently, his subjects
would stay poor and ignorant, and be no less vicious for it. My
Adversary has failed to take advantage of an example so striking
and apparently so favorable to his cause; perhaps he is the only
person not to know or to think of it. Let him therefore permit
us to remind him of it; let him not deprive great objects of the
praise due them; let him admire them as much as we do, and
not think himself thereby strengthened against the truths which
he attacks.

LETTER
By J. J. ROUSSEAU of Geneva
to M. GRIMM
about the refutation of his Discourse
by M. Gautier
Professor of Mathematics and of History
and Member of the Royal Academy of Letters
at Nancy

[1] I return, Sir, the October issue of the *Mercure* which you were good enough to loan me. I have read with much pleasure the refutation of my Discourse which M. Gautier took the trouble to write; but I do not believe that I am, as you maintain, required to reply to it; and here are my reasons.

[2] 1. I cannot persuade myself that in order to be in the right, one invariably has to have the last word.

[3] 2. The more I reread the refutation, the more convinced I am that I need offer M. Gautier no other rejoinder than the very Discourse to which he replied. Read, if you please, in each of these writings the discussions of luxury, war, Academies, education; read the Prosopopoeia of Louis the Great and that of Fabricius; finally, read M. Gautier's conclusion and mine, and you will understand what I mean.

[4] 3. I think so differently from M. Gautier in everything that, if I had to take up all the passages where our opinions differ, I would have to take issue with him even regarding the points I would have stated as he stated them, and that would give me an air of contrariness which I should rather like to be able to avoid. For example, in speaking of [60] politeness he very clearly implies that in order to become a good man one does well to begin by being a hypocrite, and that falseness is an assured path to virtue. He further says that the vices adorned by politeness are not contagious, as they would be if they showed themselves boorishly head-on; that the art of seeing through men has made as much progress as has the art of dissembling; that everyone is convinced that men cannot be counted on

53

unless one pleases or is useful to them; that everyone knows what store to set by specious professions of politeness; which, I suppose, is to say, that when two men exchange compliments, and in his heart of hearts one of them says to the other *I treat you like a fool and don't give a hang about you,* the other answers him in his heart of hearts *I know that you are lying shamelessly, but I fully reciprocate in kind.* If I had wished to resort to the bitterest irony, I might have said something like that.

[5] 4. It is evident from every page of the refutation that the Author does not understand or does not wish to understand the work he is refuting, which certainly makes it very convenient for him; for by constantly answering his own thought and never mine, he has the best opportunity in the world to say anything he pleases. On the other hand, while that makes it more difficult for me to reply, it also makes it less necessary; for no one has ever claimed that a Painter who exhibits a picture in public has to examine the spectators' eyes, and supply everyone who needs them with glasses.

[6] Besides, it is by no means certain that even if I did reply, I would be understood; for example, I would tell M. Gautier that I know that our soldiers are not Réaumurs and Fontenelles, and that it is so much the worse for them, for us, and especially for the enemy. I know that they know nothing, that they are brutal and coarse, and nevertheless I did say, and I say again that they have been enervated by the Sciences which they despise and by the fine Arts which they do not know. One of the great drawbacks attending the cultivation of Letters is that, for a few men they enlighten, they corrupt an entire nation at a pure loss. Now, you can readily see, Sir, that this would merely be another unintelligible paradox for M. Gautier; for the M. Gautier who proudly asks me what Troops have in common with Academies; whether soldiers will be braver if they are ill *[61]* clad and ill fed; what I mean by maintaining that by dint of honoring talents, virtues suffer neglect; and other similar questions which show that it is impossible to answer them intelligibly to the satisfaction of the person who raises them. I believe you will agree that it is not worth the trouble to explain

my position a second time if I am to be understood no better than the first.

[7] 5. If I wished to reply to the first part of the refutation, there would be no end to it. M. Gautier feels at liberty to tell me which Authors I may cite and which I am to reject. His choice is natural enough; he challenges the authority of those who testify on my behalf, and wishes me to rely on those he believes to be against me. It would be in vain for me to try and make him understand that a single witness in my favor is conclusive, while a hundred witnesses prove nothing against my sentiment, because the witnesses are parties to the trial; in vain for me to request him to draw distinctions in the examples he adduces; in vain for me to point out to him that to be a barbarian is one thing, and to be criminal is another thing entirely, and that truly corrupted peoples are not so much peoples with bad Laws as those with contempt for the Laws; his rejoinder is easy to anticipate: How can one possibly trust shocking Writers who dare to praise barbarians unable to read or write! How can people who go about completely naked possibly be thought modest, and people who eat raw flesh virtuous? There will, then, have to be disputations. Here, then, are Herodotus, Strabo, Pomponius-Mela, grappling with Xenophon, Justin, Quintus Curtius, Tacitus; here we are, then, engaged in Critical studies, Antiquities, erudition. Pamphlets grow into Volumes, Books multiply, and the issue is forgotten: such is the fate of Literary disputations, that after Tomes of elucidation one always ends up not kowing where one is: it is not worth starting in the first place.

[8] If I wished to reply to the second Part, I would soon be done; but I would not be telling anyone anything. In order to refute me, M. Gautier leaves it at saying yes wherever I said no, and no wherever I said yes; so that I need only say no again wherever I had *[62]* said no, yes wherever I had said yes, leave out the proofs, and I shall have answered punctiliously. Thus by following M. Gautier's method, I cannot reply to the two Parts of the refutation without saying either too much or too little: yet I should like not to do either.

[9] 6. I could follow another method, and deal separately

with M. Gautier's argument on the one hand, and the style of his refutation on the other.

[10] If I examined his arguments I could easily show that they are all beside the point, that the Writer failed to grasp the issue, and that he did not understand me.

[11] For example, M. Gautier takes the trouble to inform me that some peoples are vicious without being learned, and it had already occurred to me that the Kalmuks, the Bedouins, and the Kaffirs were not prodigies of virtue or of erudition. If M. Gautier had taken as much care to show me a single learned People that is not vicious, he would have surprised me more. He constantly has me argue as if I had said that Science is the only source of corruption among men; if he sincerely believed that, I admire his being so good as to answer me at all.

[12] He says that experience of the world is all one needs to acquire the politeness a gentleman prides himself in possessing; from which he concludes that to honor the Sciences for it is unjustified; but what, then, shall he allow us to honor for it? As long as men have lived in society, some Peoples have been polite, and others have not. M. Gautier forgot to tell us the reason for this difference.

[13] M. Gautier everywhere expresses admiration for the purity of our present morals. His good opinion of them undoubtedly does great honor to his own; but it does not testify to much experience. To judge by how he speaks of them, he appears to have studied men the way the Peripatetics studied Physics, without leaving his closet. I, on the other hand, closed my Books; and after having listened to men talk, I watched them act. No wonder that, having followed such different methods, we agree so little in our conclusions. I quite see that men could not speak *[63]* with greater propriety than we nowadays do; and that is what strikes M. Gautier; but I also see that there could be no more corrupt morals, and that is what shocks me. Do we really believe we have become good men because by dint of giving our vices decent names, we no longer blush at them?

[14] He further says that even if it could be proven by an appeal to facts that dissoluteness of morals has always prevailed together with the Sciences, it would not follow that the fate of

probity depends on their progress. After having devoted the first Part of my Discourse to proving that these things had always gone together, I spent the second showing that one was indeed dependent on the other. To whom, then, am I to imagine that M. Gautier is here trying to reply?

[15] He appears to me to be above all very much shocked by the way I spoke about College education. He tells me that young people are there taught any number of fine things that might help amuse them when they are grown up, but I must admit that I do not see the connection between these things and the duties of Citizens, which they should be taught in the first place. "We readily inquire 'Does he know Greek and Latin? Does he write verse or prose?' But 'has he become better or more sensible,' which used to be the principal question, is no longer asked. Call out to our People about a Passer-by *Oh, what a learned man!* and about another *Oh, what a good man!* They will not fail to turn their eyes and respect toward the first. A third Caller is needed. *Oh, what blockheads!*"

[16] I said that Nature sought to preserve man from Science as a mother snatches a dangerous weapon from her child's hands, and that the difficulty we have in learning is not the least of its favors. M. Gautier would as soon have had me say: Peoples, recognize once and for all that Nature does not wish you to get your sustenance from the earth's productions; the difficulties with which it has surrounded the cultivation of the earth are a warning to you to let it lie fallow. M. Gautier has not given thought to the fact that with a little work one is certain to make bread; but that with much study it is very doubtful that one succeeds in making a reasonable man. He has also not given thought to the fact that this is just *[64]* one more observation in my favor; for, why has Nature imposed necessary labors on us, if it is not to turn us away from useless occupations? But by the contempt he shows for agriculture it is easy to see that, if it were up to himself alone, all Ploughmen would soon abandon the Countryside in order to go argue in the Schools, an occupation which, according to M. Gautier and, I believe, a good many Professors, is most important for the State's happiness.

[17] In thinking about a passage in Plato, I had concluded

that perhaps the ancient Egyptians did not hold the Sciences in quite as high esteem as might have been believed. The Author of the refutation asks me how that opinion can be reconciled with the inscription Ozymandias had placed on his Library. That might have been a good question to raise during the Prince's lifetime. Now that he is dead, I, in turn, ask, what need there is to look for agreement between King Ozymandias's sentiment and that of Egypt's Wise men? Who can say confidently that if he had counted, and especially if he had weighed opinions, the word *poisons* would not have been substituted for the word *remedies?* But let us pass over that ostentatious Inscription. Such remedies are excellent, I grant it, and I have often repeated it; but is that a reason for administering them indiscriminately and without regard to the sick persons' temperament? A given food may be very good in itself, and only cause indigestion and ill-humors in a weak stomach. What would people say about a Physician who, after speaking well of some hearty meats, concluded that all sick people should gorge on them?

[18] I showed that the Sciences and the Arts enervate courage. M. Gautier calls that an odd way to argue, and does not see the connection between courage and virtue. Yet it is not, it seems to me, particularly difficult to understand. Once a man is accustomed to prefer his life to his duty, he will soon also prefer to it the things that make life easy and agreeable.

[19] I said that Science suits a few great geniuses; but that it is always harmful to the Peoples that cultivate it. M. Gautier says that Socrates and Cato, who censured the Sciences, were nevertheless themselves *[65]* very learned Men: and he calls that refuting me.

[20] I said that Socrates was the most learned of the Athenians, and that that is why I regard his testimony authoritative: none of which prevents M. Gautier from informing me that Socrates was learned.

[21] He blames me for having maintained that Cato despised the Greek Philosophers; and he does so on the grounds that Carneades made a game of upholding and refuting the very same propositions, which unjustifiably prejudiced Cato against the Writings of the Greeks. M. Gautier should really tell us this

Carneades's country and profession.

[22] No doubt Carneades is the only Philosopher or Scholar to have prided himself on upholding both the pro and the con; otherwise everything M. Gautier says here would be entirely irrelevant. I rely on his erudition in this matter.

[23] What the refutation lacks in good arguments it amply makes up for in fine declamations. The Author everywhere substitutes artful embellishments for the solid proofs he had initially promised; and he lavishes oratorical pomp on a Refutation in which he reproves me for having used it in an Academy Discourse.

[24] *To what end, then,* says M. Gautier, *do M. Rousseau's eloquent declamations tend?* To abolish, if possible, the vain declamations of Colleges. *Who would not be moved to indignation at hearing him assert that we have the appearance of all the virtues without possessing a one.* I admit that there is some flattery in saying that we have the appearance of the virtues; but M. Gautier, more than anyone else, should have forgiven me that one. *Well! Why is there no more virtue? Because Letters, the Sciences, and the Arts are cultivated.* For that very reason. *If one were impolite, rustic, ignorant, Goths, Huns, or Vandals, one would be worthy of M. Rousseau's praise.* Why not? Is any one of those names incompatible with virtue? *Will they never weary of inveighing against men?* Will they never weary of being wicked? *Will they keep on believing that they make men more virtuous by telling them that they are without virtue?* Will they believe that they make men better by convincing them that they are good enough? *Is it permissible, on the pretext of purifying morals, to knock down their supports?* [66] Must souls be perverted, on the pretext of enlightening minds? *O sweet bonds of society! amiable virtues, the charm of true Philosophers; it is by your inherent attractiveness that you rule in men's hearts; you owe your sway neither to stoic sternness, nor to barbarous uproars, nor to the counsels of a prideful rusticity.*

[25] First of all, I note a rather amusing fact; that [of] all the Sects of ancient Philosophers I attacked as being useless to virtue, the Stoics are the only ones M. Gautier grants me, and

he even seems to want to put them in my camp. He is right; I
will not be any the prouder for it.

[26] But let us see whether I cannot convey the exact meaning
of this exclamation in different terms: *O amiable virtues! it is
by your inherent attractiveness that you rule in men's souls.
You have no need of all the elaborate trappings of ignorance
and rusticity. You go to the heart by simpler and more
natural paths. It is enough to know Rhetoric, Logic, Physics,
Metaphysics, and Mathematics to acquire the right to possess
you.*

[27] Another example of M. Gautier's style:

[28] *You know that the Sciences taught to young Philosophers in the Universities are Logic, Metaphysics, Ethics, Physics, and elementary Mathematics.* If I did know, I forgot it,
as we all do on reaching the age of reason. *According to you,
then, these are sterile speculations!* sterile according to the
common opinion; but according to me, most fertile in bad
things. *The Universities are much obliged to you for informing
them that the truth of these sciences has withdrawn to the
bottom of a well.* I do not believe I informed anyone of it. I
did not coin the phrase; it is as old as Philosophy. Besides,
I know that the Universities owe me no gratitude; and when I
took up my pen I was not unaware of the fact that I could not
at one and the same time court men and honor the truth. *The
great Philosophers who possess them to an eminent degree
are doubtless rather surprised to learn that they know nothing.*
I believe that these great Philosophers who possess all these
great sciences to an eminent degree, would, indeed, be very
surprised to learn that they know nothing. But I, myself, would
be even more surprised if these men, who know so many things,
ever did know that. *[67]*

[29] I notice that M. Gautier, who, throughout, treats me
with the utmost politeness, does not neglect a single opportunity
to make me enemies; his attentions on this score range all the
way from the College Regents to the sovereign power. M.
Gautier does well to justify the ways of the world; he is clearly
not a stranger to them. But let us return to the refutation.

[30] All these ways of writing and of reasoning, which do not

at all become a man as intelligent as M. Gautier appears to me
to be, have led me to frame a conjecture which you will find
bold, yet I believe reasonable. He accuses me, surely without
himself believing it, of not being persuaded of the sentiments I
uphold. I, on the other hand, on better grounds, suspect him of
secretly agreeing with me. The positions he occupies, the
circumstances in which he finds himself, must have placed him
under a kind of necessity to come out against me. Our century's
propriety has many uses; he will, then, have refuted me out of
propriety; but he will have taken all manner of precautions and
been as artful as possible to do so in a way that will not persuade
anyone.

[31] It is with this end in view that he begins by announcing,
quite irrelevantly, that the cause he defends has a direct bearing
on the happiness of the assembly before which he speaks, and
on the glory of the great Prince under whose laws he has the
pleasure of living. That is as much as to say: Gentlemen, you
cannot avoid deciding in my favor without showing ingratitude
toward your respectable Protector; moreover, I am today pleading
your own cause before you; so that from whatever angle you
examine my arguments, I have the right to expect you not to
prove difficult about their soundness. I say that any man who
speaks this way is more concerned with shutting peoples'
mouths than he is interested in convincing them.

[32] If you read the refutation attentively, you will hardly
find a single line in it that does not seem to be there awaiting
and indicating the answer. One example will suffice to make
myself understood.

[33] *The victories of the Athenians over the Persians and
even the Lacedaemonians, show that the Arts can be combined
with military virtue.* I ask whether that is not a ruse designed
to recall what I said about the *[68]* defeat of Xerxes, and to call
my attention to the outcome of the Peloponnesian War. *Their
government, having become venal under Pericles, assumes a
new complexion: the love of pleasure stifles their bravery, the
most honorable offices are debased, impunity makes for a
growing number of bad Citizens, the funds intended for the
war are used to feed effeminacy and idleness; what relation*

is there between all these causes of corruption and the Sciences?

[34] What is M. Gautier doing here if not recalling the entire second Part of my Discourse where I showed this relation? Note how artfully he presents the effects of corruption as its causes, in order to lead any sensible person to look for the first cause of these supposed causes on his own. Note, further, how, in order to let the Reader make that reflection himself, he pretends not to know what he cannot, in fact, be assumed not to know, and what all Historians unanimously maintain, that the corruption of the Athenians' morals and of their government were due to the Orators. It is therefore obvious that to attack me in this way is very clearly to indicate to me the answers I am supposed to give.

[35] Still, this is merely a conjecture which I do not claim I can confirm. M. Gautier might perhaps not approve of my wishing to vindicate his knowledge at the expense of his good faith: but if, in refuting my Discourse, he did indeed speak sincerely, why was M. Gautier, Professor of History, Professor of Mathematics, Member of the Academy of Nancy, not a little wary of all his titles?

[36] I will therefore not reply to M. Gautier, that is a settled issue. I could never answer seriously, and take up the refutation point by point; you can see why; and to resort to *ridiculum acri,* irony and bitter jest, would be a poor acknowledgment of the praise with which M. Gautier honors me. I am rather afraid that he may already have too much cause to complain of the tone of this Letter: at least he knew, when he wrote his refutation, that he was attacking a man who does not set enough stock by politeness to wish to learn from it how to disguise his sentiment.

[37] Besides, I am ready to do M. Gautier all the justice due him. His Work seems to me that of a gifted man who has a good deal of knowledge. *[69]* Others will perhaps find Philosophy in it; as for myself, I find in it much erudition.

I am wholeheartedly, Sir, etc.

[38] P.S. I have just read in the Utrecht Gazette of October

22 a pompous account of M. Gautier's Work, and that account seems deliberately designed to confirm my suspicions. An Author who is at all confident of the value of his Work lets others praise it, and himself does no more than to prepare a good Summary of it. The Summary of the refutation is done so skillfully that, although it deals solely with trivialities which I had simply used as transitions, there is not one about which a judicious Reader can be of M. Gautier's opinion.

[39] It is, according to him, not true that History is primarily interesting owing to men's vices.

[40] I might set aside proofs based on reasoning; and in order to meet M. Gautier on his own ground, I will refer him to authorities.

[41] *Happy the Peoples whose Kings have caused little stir in History.*

[42] *If ever men became wise, their history will scarcely be entertaining.*

[43] M. Gautier rightly says that even a society made up entirely of just men could not endure without Laws; and from this he concludes that it is not true that, were it not for men's injustices, Jurisprudence would be useless. Would so learned a Writer confuse Jurisprudence with the Laws?

[44] I might, once again, set aside proofs based on reasoning and, in order to meet M. Gautier on his own ground, refer him to facts.

[45] The Lacedaemonians had neither Jurisconsults nor Lawyers; their Laws were not even committed to writing; yet they had Laws. I leave it to M. Gautier's erudition to tell me whether the Laws were less well observed in Lacedaemon than in the Countries teeming with Men of the Law.

[46] I will not take up every one of the trivialities to which M. Gautier refers and upon which he expatiates in the Gazette; instead I will close by submitting the following observation to your examination. *[70]*

[47] Let us concede everything to M. Gautier, and eliminate from my Discourse everything he attacks, my proofs will have lost almost nothing of their force. Let us eliminate from M. Gautier's text everything that does not bear on the heart of the

matter; nothing whatever will be left of it.

[48] I once again conclude that M. Gautier should not be answered.

Paris, November 1, 1751.

LAST REPLY
By J.-J. ROUSSEAU of Geneva

*Let us not appear to remain silent
out of shame but out of discretion.*
—Cyprian, Contra Demet[rianum]

[1] It is with the utmost reluctance that I entertain idle Readers who care very little for the truth with my disputations: but it has just been attacked in a way that forces me once again to take up its defense, lest the many mistake my silence for a concession, or the Philosophers mistake it for indifference.

[2] I have to repeat myself; I realize it, and the public will not forgive me for it. But the wise will say: This man does not constantly have to look for new arguments; which is one proof of how sound his arguments are.* *[72]*

[3] Since those who attack me never fail to stray from the issue and to eliminate the essential distinctions I had introduced, I always have to begin by reintroducing them. Here, then, is a summary of the propositions I upheld and will continue to uphold as long as I shall heed no other interest than that of truth.

[4] The Sciences are the masterpiece of genius and of reason. The spirit of imitation has produced the fine Arts, and experience has perfected them. We are indebted to the mechanical arts for a great many useful inventions that have added to the charms

---

* Some very solid truths appear absurd at first glance, and to the great majority they will always appear to be so. Go tell a man of the People that the sun is closer to us in winter than in summer or that it has set before we cease to see it, and he will laugh at you. The same is true of the sentiment I uphold. The most superficial men have always been readiest to side against me; the true Philosophers are not so hasty, and if I have the glory of having made a few converts, it is only among the latter. Before stating my views, I had meditated on the subject long and thoroughly, and had tried to consider it in all of its aspects. I doubt that any one of my adversaries can say as much. At least I do not find in their writings any of those luminous truths *[72]* that strike by their evidence no less than by their novelty, and that are always both the fruit and the proof of adequate meditation. I daresay that they have never raised against me a single reasonable objection which I had not foreseen and answered in advance. That is why I have no choice but constantly to repeat the same things.

and comforts of life. These are truths which I certainly grant most wholeheartedly. But let us now consider these various kinds of knowledge in their relation to morals.*

[5] If celestial intelligences cultivated the sciences, only good would come of it; I say as much about the great men made to guide others. Socrates, learned and virtuous, did mankind honor; but the vices of vulgar men poison the most *[73]* sublime knowledge and render it pernicious to Nations; the wicked derive much that is harmful from it; the good derive little benefit from it. If none but Socrates had laid claim to Philosophy in Athens, the blood of a just man would not have cried out for vengeance against the fatherland of the Sciences and Arts.**

[6] The question of whether it would be advantageous for men to have science, bears examination, even assuming that what they call by that name does indeed deserve it: but it is folly to pretend that the chimeras of Philosophy, the errors and the lies of the Philosophers can be good for anything. Shall we forever be deceived by words, and never understand that studies, knowledge, learning and Philosophy are but empty shams con-

---

* *Knowledge makes men gentle,* says the famous Philosopher whose always profound and sometimes sublime work everywhere breathes the love of humanity. With these few words he has written and, what is exceptional, he has done so without bombast, the most solid thing ever written on behalf of Letters. True, knowledge makes men gentle: But gentleness, the most amiable of virtues, is also sometimes a weakness of the soul. Virtue is not always gentle; when the occasion requires, it can arm itself with due severity against vice, be fired with indignation against crime.

And the just cannot pardon the wicked

A King of Lacedaemon replied most wisely to those who in his presence praised the extreme goodness of his Colleague Charillus. *How can he be good,* he told them, *if he cannot be terrible to the wicked?* Brutus was not a gentle man; who would be so bold as to say that he was not virtuous? By contrast, there are cowardly and pusillanimous souls, that lack fire or warmth, and are only gentle out of indifference for good and evil. That is the gentleness which the taste for Letters instills in Peoples.

** It cost Socrates his life to have said exactly the same things I am saying. In the trial against him one of his accusers brought charges on behalf of the Artists, another on behalf of the Orators, the third on behalf of the Poets, all of them on behalf of the supposed cause of the Gods. The Poets, the Artists, the Fanatics, the Rhetoricians triumphed; and Socrates perished. I am rather afraid that I did my century too much honor when I asserted that Socrates would not have had to drink the Hemlock now.

jured up by men's pride and altogether unworthy of the pompous names it bestows on them?

[7] As the taste for such foolishness spreads in a nation, it loses its taste for the solid virtues: for it takes less to achieve distinction by chatter than by good morals, once men are exempted from being good if only they are agreeable.

[8] The greater the inner corruption, the greater the external composure:* that is how the cultivation of Letters insensibly engenders politeness. Taste springs from the same source, as well. Since public approval is the first reward of literary labors, it is natural that those who *[74]* pursue such labors should reflect on the means to please; and these reflections eventually shape style, purify taste, and disseminate graciousness and urbanity everywhere. All these things may, perhaps, be regarded as supplements to virtue: but they can never be said to be virtue, and they will rarely be combined with it. There will always be this difference, that he who makes himself useful works for others, whereas he who seeks only to make himself agreeable works solely for himself. For example, the flatterer spares no effort in order to please, and yet he does only harm.

[9] Vanity and idleness, which have given rise to our sciences, have also given rise to luxury. A taste for luxury always accompanies a taste for Letters, and a taste for Letters often accompanies a taste for luxury;** all these things keep each other company

---

* I never attend a performance of one of Molière's Plays without admiring the spectators' delicacy: a single somewhat free word, a single expression that is not so much obscene as crude, everything offends their chaste ears; and I do not doubt that the most corrupt are always the most shocked. Yet is there anyone who believes that if the morals of Molière's century were compared with those of our own, the result would be to the credit of ours? Once the imagination is sullied, it turns everything into an object for scandal; once nothing but one's exterior remains good, one takes twice as much care to preserve it.

** Somewhere someone has sought to refute me with [references to] the luxury of the Asiatics by reasoning in the same way as do those who refer to the vices of ignorant peoples [in order to refute me]. But by a misfortune that keeps pursuing my adversaries, they are mistaken even about facts that prove nothing against me. I know perfectly well that the peoples of the Orient are no less ignorant than ourselves; but that does not prevent their being as vain, and turning out almost as many books as do we. The Turks, who cultivate Letters less than do any others, reckoned that by the middle of the last century they had five hundred and eighty classical Poets.

fairly faithfully, because they are products of the same vices.

[10] If experience did not agree with these demonstrated propositions, then the specific causes of the discrepancy would have to be sought. But the first idea of these propositions was itself born of a long meditation on experience: and in order to see how fully experience confirms them, one need only consult the annals of the world.

[11] The first men were exceedingly ignorant. How could one dare maintain that they were corrupted at a time when the sources of corruption were not yet open.

[12] Beyond the obscurity [that surrounds] ancient times, and beyond the rusticity of ancient Peoples, one discerns in a number of them very considerable virtues, especially a severity of morals that is the unmistakable mark of their purity, good faith, hospitality, justice and, most important, *[75]* a great horror of debauchery,* that teeming lap of all other vices. Virtue is,

---

* I have no intention of courting the favor of women; I accept their honoring me with the epithet Pedant, so dreaded by all our gallant Philosophers. I am crude, sullen, impolite on principle, and I want no one to fawn on me; so I will speak the truth quite unhampered.

Men and women are made to love one another and to unite; but beyond this legitimate union all amorous dealings between them prove a dreadful source of disorders in society and in morals. Certain it is that women alone could restore honor and probity among us; but they spurn from the hands of virtue an empire which they wish to owe solely to their charms; thus they do only harm, and often they themselves suffer the punishment for this preference. It is difficult to understand how in so pure a Religion, chastity could have become a base and monastic virtue which renders ridiculous any man and, I am almost inclined to say, any woman who might dare to claim it; whereas amongst the Pagans this same virtue was universally honored, regarded as becoming to great men, and admired in their most illustrious heroes. I can cite three who yield to none and who, quite independently of Religion, all gave memorable examples of continence: Cyrus, Alexander, and the younger Scipio. Of all the rare objects in the King's Collections, the only one I should like to see is the silver shield given to Scipio by the Peoples of Spain and on which they had etched the triumph of his virtue: that is how it was meet for the Romans to subdue other Peoples, as much by the respect owed to their morals as by the effort of their arms; that is how the city of the Falises was conquered and a victorious Pyrrhus driven out of Italy.

I recall having read somewhere a rather good reply made by the Poet Dryden to a young English Lord who criticized him because in one of his Tragedies Cleomenes spent his time in intimate conversation with his beloved instead of pursuing projects worthy of his love. When I am with a fair lady, the young

LAST REPLY   69

then, not incompatible with ignorance.

[13] Nor is it always its companion: for a number of very ignorant peoples were very vicious. Ignorance is an obstacle neither to good nor to evil; it is merely man's natural state.* *[76]*

[14] The same cannot be said of science. All learned Peoples were corrupted, and that is already a terrible presumption against it. But since comparisons between one People and another are difficult, since a great many factors have to be taken into account in making such comparisons, and since they are always in some respect imprecise, one is far better off tracing the history of one and the same People, and comparing its progress in knowledge with the revolutions in its morals. Now, the result of that inquiry is that the fair time, the time of virtue for every People, was the time of its ignorance; and that in proportion as it became learned, Artistic and Philosophic, it lost its morals and its probity; it, in this respect, reverted to the rank of the ignorant and vicious Nations that are the shame of mankind. If one nevertheless insists on looking for differences between them, I can discern one, and it is this: that all barbarous Peoples, even those that are without virtue, nevertheless always honor it, whereas learned and Philosophic Peoples by dint of progress eventually succeed in turning virtue into an object of derision and to despise it. Once a nation has reached that point, its corruption may be said to have reached its zenith, and it is past remedy.

[15] That is the summary of what I advanced and I believe I proved. Let us now look at the summary of the Doctrine urged against mine.

[16] "Men are naturally wicked; they were so prior to the formation of societies; and wherever the sciences did not carry

---

Lord told him, I put my time to better use: I believe it, Dryden answered, but then, you must allow that you are no Hero.

* I cannot help laughing when I see I know not how many perfectly learned men who honor me with their criticism trying to refute me by forever referring to the vices of a host of ignorant Peoples, as *[76]* if that had any bearing whatever on the issue. From the fact that science necessarily gives rise to vice, does it follow that ignorance necessarily gives rise to virtue? Such ways of arguing may suit Rhetoricians or the children who have been made to refute me in my country; but Philosophers should reason differently.

their torch, Peoples, abandoned to *the faculties of instinct* alone, reduced, like lions and bears, to a purely animal existence, remained immersed in barbarism and misery.

[17] "In ancient times, Greece alone thought, and *by means of the mind raised itself* to all that can make a People [77] worthy of praise. Philosophers fashioned its morals and gave it laws.

[18] "Sparta, it is true, was poor and ignorant by institution as well as by choice; but its laws had great defects, and its Citizens a strong tendency to let themselves be corrupted: its glory was insubstantial, and it soon lost its institutions, its laws, and its morals.

[19] "Athens and Rome also degenerated. The first yielded to Macedonia's [rising] fortune; the other collapsed under its own greatness, because the laws of a small city were not suited to the government of the world. If sometimes the glory of great Empires did not long survive their literary glory, the reason is that the glory of these Empires had reached its zenith by the time letters came to be cultivated in them, and that it is the fate of human things not to endure long in the same state. By thus granting that a change in laws and morals influenced these great events, one is not forced to concede that the Sciences and Arts contributed to them: and it can be seen that, on the contrary, the progress and decay of letters is always directly proportional to the fortune and decline of Empires.

[20] "This truth is confirmed by the experience of recent times where, in a vast and powerful Monarchy, the prosperity of the state, the cultivation of the Sciences and Arts, and of military virtue, can all be seen to contribute to the glory and grandeur of the Empire.

[21] "Our morals are the best that men can have; a number of vices have been banished from among us; those that are left us are inseparable from humanity, and the sciences have no share in them.

[22] "Luxury has nothing to do with them either; hence the disorders which it may occasion must not be attributed to them. Besides, luxury is necessary in large States; it does them more

good than harm: it serves to keep idle Citizens busy, and to provide bread for the poor.

[23] "Politeness ought to be reckoned among the virtues rather than among the vices; it keeps men from showing themselves for what they are, a most necessary precaution if they are to find one another tolerable.

[24] "The Sciences have rarely attained the goal they *[78]* set themselves; but at least they aim at it. Progress in the knowledge of truth proceeds by slow steps; which is not to say that no progress is made in it.

[25] "Finally, even if it were true that the Sciences and Arts weaken courage, would not the endless goods which they do provide us with still be preferable to that barbarous and fierce virtue which causes humanity to tremble?" I omit the useless and pretentious inventory of these goods: and, to begin on this last point with an acknowledgment that should prevent much verbiage, I declare once and for all that, if anything can make up for ruined morals, I am prepared to grant that the Sciences do more good than harm. Let us now proceed to the rest.

[26] I could, without much risk, assume all this to have been proven, because very few of these many, boldly propounded assertions go to the heart of the matter, fewer still allow of a single valid conclusion at odds with my sentiment, and most of them would even provide me with fresh arguments, if my cause were in need of them.

[27] Indeed, 1. If men are by nature wicked, then it is, admittedly, possible that some good might happen to come of the sciences at their hands; but it is perfectly certain that they will lead to far more harm: Madmen should not be given weapons.

[28] 2. If the sciences rarely achieve their goal, it only means that much more time will be wasted than well spent. And even if it were true that we have discovered the best methods, the greater part of our labors would still be just as ridiculous as those of a man who, because he is confident of being able to work exactly to a plumb line, tried to dig a well all the way to the center of the earth.

[29] 3. We should not be made to feel so frightened of a purely animal life, nor to regard it as the worst state we might fall into; for it is still better to resemble a sheep than an evil Angel.

[30] 4. Greece owed its morals and its laws to Philosophers and to Legislators. I quite agree. I have said a hundred times over that it is good that there be Philosophers, provided the People do not pretend to be Philosophers.

[31] 5. Since no one dares to maintain that Sparta did not have good *[79]* laws, her laws are criticized for having been badly flawed: so that, in order to rebut my charge that learned Peoples have always been corrupted, ignorant Peoples are blamed for not having attained perfection.

[32] 6. The progress of letters is always directly proportioned to the greatness of Empires. So be it. I note that I am forever being told about fortune and greatness. I, for my part, was talking about morals and virtue.

[33] 7. Our morals are the best that wicked men like ourselves can have; that may be so. We have banished a number of vices; I do not deny it. I do not accuse the men of this century of having all the vices; they have only the vices of cowardly souls; they are only rogues and knaves. As for the vices requiring courage and fortitude, I believe that they are incapable of them.

[34] 8. Luxury may be needed to provide bread for the poor: but if there were no luxury, there would be no poor.* It keeps idle Citizens busy. And why are there idle Citizens? When agriculture was held in honor there was neither misery nor idleness, and there were far fewer vices.

[35] 9. I see that while they take this issue of luxury very

---

* For every hundred paupers whom luxury feeds in our cities, it causes a hundred thousand to perish in our countryside: the money that passes between the hands of the rich and the Artists to provide for their superfluities, is lost for the Husbandman's subsistence; and he is without a suit of clothing just because they must have piping on theirs. The waste of foodstuffs alone is enough to make luxury abhorrent to mankind. My adversaries are fortunate that the culpable delicacy of our language prevents me from going into details on this score which would make them blush for the cause they dare to defend. Our dishes require gravies; that is why so many sick people lack broth. We have to have liquors on our tables; that is why the peasant drinks only water. We have to have powder for our wigs; that is why so many poor people have no bread.

much to heart, they maintain the pretense of dealing with it independently of the Sciences and Arts. I will grant, then, since they so categorically insist on it, that luxury supports States as Caryatids support the palaces they adorn: or rather, *[80]* as do the beams used to prop up rotting buildings and which often only complete their collapse altogether. Wise and prudent men, abandon any house that is being propped up.

[36] This may show how easily I could turn to my advantage most of what is urged against me: but, frankly speaking, I find none of it sufficiently well-established to venture taking advantage of it.

[37] It is said that the first men were wicked; whence it follows that man is naturally wicked.* That is an assertion of no mean importance: it seems to me that it would have been well worth the trouble to prove it. The Annals of all the peoples which they dare to cite in proof, lend far more support to the contrary assumption; and it would take a great many testimonies to make me believe an absurdity. Before those dreadful words *thine* and *mine* were invented; before the cruel and brutal species of men called masters, and that other knavish and lying species of men called slaves existed; before there were men so abominable as to dare to have superfluities while other men die of hunger; before mutual dependence had forced all of them to become deceitful, jealous, and treacherous; I should like to have it explained to me wherein those vices, those crimes with which they are so insistently being reproached, could have consisted. I am told that men have long since been disabused of the chimera of the golden Age. Why not also add that they have long since been disabused of the chimera of virtue?

[38] I said that, before science corrupted them, the first

* This note is for Philosophers. I advise others to ignore it. If man is by his nature wicked, it is clear that the Sciences will only make him worse; so that their cause is lost on this assumption alone. But note well that, although man is naturally good, as I believe, and as I have the good fortune to feel, it does not follow that the sciences benefit him; for all circumstances that lead a people to cultivate them, necessarily announce a beginning of corruption which they then rapidly accelerate. After this, the vice of the constitution does all the harm which that of nature might have done, and bad prejudices play the part of bad inclinations.

Greeks were virtuous; *[81]* and I do not wish to retract on this point, although, on looking at it more closely, I am not without some misgivings about the solidity of such a chatty people's virtues, or about the justice of the praise they so loved to lavish on themselves, and which I do not find confirmed by any other testimony. What is brought up against me in this connection? That the first Greeks whose virtue I praised were enlightened and learned, since Philosophers formed their morals and gave them laws. But with that way of arguing, who is to keep me from saying as much about all other Nations? Did not the Persians have their Magi, the Assyrians their Chaldeans, the Indians their Gymnosophists, the Celts their Druids? Did not Ochus shine among the Phoenicians, Atlas among the Libyans, Zoroaster among the Persians, Zamolxis among the Thracians? Have not some even claimed that Philosophy was born among the Barbarians? Were all these peoples scholars, then, on this account? *Alongside of a Miltiades and a Themistocles, could be found, I am told, an Aristides and a Socrates.* Alongside of them, if you wish; for what does it matter to me? Still, Miltiades, Aristides, Themistocles, who were Heroes, lived in one age, Socrates and Plato, who were Philosophers, lived in another; and by the time public schools of Philosophy were first opened, a degraded and decadent Greece had already forsaken its virtue and sold its liberty.

[39] *Proud Asia saw its numberless armies shattered by a handful of men led to glory by Philosophy.* It is true: Philosophy in the soul leads to true glory, but that is not the kind that is learned in books. *Such is the effect knowledge invariably has on the mind.* I ask the Reader to note this conclusion. *Morals and laws are the only sources of true heroism.* The Sciences have nothing to do with it, then. *In a word, Greece owed everything to the Sciences, and the rest of the world owed everything to Greece.* Neither Greece nor the world owed anything to the laws or to morals, then. I beg my adversaries' pardon for it; but it is simply not possible to allow them such sophisms.

[40] Let us take a moment longer to examine this preference for Greece above all other peoples, and which seems to have

become a point of major importance. *I will, if you wish, admire peoples that spend their lives at war or in the woods, sleep on the ground, and live off vegetation.* Such admiration is indeed most worthy of a true *[82]* Philosopher: only the blind and stupid people admires those who spend their life not in defending their liberty but in robbing and betraying one another in order to gratify their self-indulgence or their ambition, and who dare support their idleness with the sweat, the blood and the toil of a million wretches. *But is it among these crude people that one would look for happiness?* It would be much more reasonable to look for it among them, than to look for virtue among the others. *What would Mankind look like if it were made up exclusively of ploughmen, soldiers, hunters, and shepherds?* It would look infinitely more beautiful than a Mankind made up of Cooks, Poets, Printers, Silversmiths, Painters and Musicians. The word *soldier* is the only one that has to be erased from the first picture. War is sometimes a duty, it is not made to be a trade. Every man should be a soldier in the defense of his liberty; none to invade another's; and to die in the service of the fatherland is too noble an enterprise to entrust to mercenaries. *Must we live like lions and bears, then, if we are to be worthy of being called men?* If I have the good fortune to find a single Reader who is impartial and a friend of the truth, I beg him to cast a glance at present society and to see who are the ones who live together like lions and bears, tigers and crocodiles. *Are the faculties of the instinct to feed, to perpetuate, and to defend ourselves, to be elevated to the rank of virtues?* They are virtues, let us be in no doubt about that, when they are guided by reason and managed wisely and, above all, they are virtues when they are used to help our fellows. *I see in them nothing but animal virtues which have little in common with the dignity of our being. The body is active, but the soul, enslaved, merely creeps and languishes.* On perusing the pretentious research carried on in our Academies, I am ready to say: "I see in them nothing but ingenious subtleties which have little in common with the dignity of our being. The mind is active, but the soul, enslaved, merely creeps and languishes." *Eliminate the arts from the world,* we are told

elsewhere, *what is left? Bodily activities and the passions.*
Please note how reason and virtue are always forgotten! *The
Arts have brought into being the pleasures of the soul, the
only pleasures worthy of us.* Which is to say that they have
substituted other pleasures for that of acting well, which is far
worthier of *[83]* us still. Attend to the spirit of all this, and you
will see in it, as you will see in the arguments of most of my
adversaries, such a pronounced enthusiasm for the wonders of
the understanding, that this other faculty, which is so infinitely
more sublime and more capable of elevating and ennobling the
soul, is never taken into account. Such is the invariable and
certain effect of cultivating letters. I am sure that there is not,
at present, a single scholar who does not hold Cicero's eloquence
in much higher esteem than he does his civic-spiritedness, and
who would not infinitely prefer to have written the Catilinarians
than to have saved his country.

[41] My adversaries' discomfiture is evident whenever they
have to speak about Sparta. What would they not give for this
fatal Sparta never to have existed; and how dearly would those
who contend that great deeds are good for nothing but to be
celebrated, wish that Sparta's great deeds had never been celebrated! It is really dreadful that at the very center of that famous
Greece which owed its virtue solely to Philosophy, the State
where virtue was purest and where it lasted longest should have
been the very State where there were no Philosophers. Sparta's
morals were always held up as a model to the whole of Greece;
the whole of Greece had become corrupted, yet virtue was still
to be found in Sparta; the whole of Greece was enslaved, Sparta
alone was still free: that is distressing. But at last proud Sparta
lost its morals and its liberty, as learned Athens had lost them;
Sparta came to an end. What can I reply to that?

[42] Two more observations about Sparta and I go on to other
things; here is the first. *After having several times been on the
verge of victory, Athens was, it is true, defeated; and it is
surprising that she was not defeated sooner, since Attica was
entirely open country and could be defended only by over-
whelming successes.* Athens should have been victorious for all
kinds of reasons. It was larger and much more populous than

Lacedaemon; it enjoyed large revenues, and several peoples paid it tribute; none of this was true of Sparta. Athens, mainly because of its location, enjoyed an advantage which Sparta lacked, which enabled it several times to devastate the Peloponnesus and which alone should have assured its Empire over Greece. It had a large and convenient harbor; it had a formidable Navy for which it was indebted to the foresight of that *[84]* boor Themistocles who did not know how to play the flute. One might therefore be surprised that Athens, with all these advantages, nevertheless finally succumbed. But although the Peloponnesian war, which ruined Greece, did not redound to the honor of either Republic, and although it represented, especially on the Lacedaemonians' part, a violation of the maxims of their wise Lawgiver, it is not surprising that eventually true courage prevailed over [material] resources, nor even that Sparta's reputation secured it some resources which made its victory easier. Truly, I am rather ashamed to know these things and to be forced to say them.

[43] The other remark will be no less striking. Here is the text which I believe I should again place before the Reader's eyes.

[44] *Let us suppose that all the states that made up Greece had adhered to the same laws as Sparta, what would have been left us of that famous country? Scarcely its name would have come down to us. It would have scorned to produce historians who might transmit its glory to posterity; the spectacle of its fierce virtues would have been lost to us; it would therefore have been a matter of indifference to us whether they had existed or not. The many systems of Philosophy which have exhausted all the possible combinations of our ideas and which, although they have not greatly extended the limits of our mind, have at least taught us where they are fixed: those masterpieces of eloquence and of poetry that have taught us all the ways of the heart; the useful or the agreeable arts that preserve or embellish life; finally, the invaluable tradition of the thoughts and of the deeds of all the great men who have made for the glory or the happiness of their fellows: all these precious riches of the mind would have been*

lost forever. Centuries would have been added to centuries,
generations of men would have succeeded one another like
those of animals, without any profit to posterity, and have
left behind nothing but a confused memory of their existence:
the world would have grown old, and men have remained in
eternal childhood.

[45] Let us, in turn, suppose that a Lacedaemonian, swayed
by the force of these arguments, wanted to present them to his
compatriots; and let us try to imagine the speech he might have
given in the public square of Sparta.

[46] "Citizens, open your eyes and behold what you have
been blind to. I am pained to see you laboring *[85]* solely in
order to acquire virtue, to exercise your courage, and to preserve
your liberty; yet you forget the more important duty of providing
amusement for the idle of future generations. Tell me; what
good is virtue if it does not cause a stir in the world? What will
it have profited you to have been good men if no one will talk
about you? What will it matter to later centuries that at Thermopylae you sacrificed your lives to save the Athenians, if you
do not, like they, leave systems of Philosophy, or poems, or
comedies, or statues?* Hasten to give up, then, laws that are
good for nothing but to make you happy; think only of being
much talked about when you will be no longer; and never
forget that if great men were not celebrated, it would be useless
to be one."

[47] That, I believe, is more or less what this man might have

---

* Pericles had great talents, much eloquence, grandeur and taste: he embellished
Athens with excellent sculptures, lavish buildings, and masterpieces in all the
arts. And God knows how much he has, as a result, been extolled by the crowd
of writers! Yet it still remains to be seen whether Pericles was a good Magistrate:
for in the management of States, what matters is not to erect statues but to
govern men well. I will not waste my time reviewing the secret causes of the
Peloponnesian war which ruined the Republic; I will not inquire whether
Alcibiades' advice was well- or ill-founded; whether Pericles was justly or
unjustly accused of embezzlement; I will only ask whether the Athenians became
better or worse under his government; I will ask for the name of a single person
among the Citizens, among the Slaves, or even among his own children whom
his attentions made a good man. Yet that, it seems to me, is the Magistrate's and
the Sovereign's foremost task. For the shortest and surest way of making men
happy is not to adorn their cities, nor even to enrich them, but to make them
good.

said, if the Ephors had allowed him to finish.

[48] This is not the only passage where we are warned that virtue is good only to get oneself talked about. In yet another passage we find the Philosopher's thoughts praised, on the grounds that they are immortal and dedicated to the admiration of the ages; *whereas others see their ideas disappear with the day, the occasion, the moment that saw them born. For three-quarters of mankind each new day erases the previous day, leaving not a trace behind.* Ah! *[86]* at least some trace is left behind in the testimony of a good conscience, the unfortunates one has helped, the good deeds performed, and the memory of the beneficient God one will silently have served. Dead or alive, good Socrates used to say, the good man is never forgotten by the Gods. I will perhaps be told that they were not talking about these sorts of thoughts; and I say that all others are not worth talking about.

[49] It is easy to imagine that where so little is made of Sparta, not much more esteem is shown for the ancient Romans. *We are prepared to believe that they were great men, although they did only small things.* On that basis, I will admit that, for a long time now, only great things have been done. The Romans' temperance and courage are taxed with having been not true virtues, but forced qualities;* yet a few pages below, it is acknowledged that Fabricius scorned Pyrrhus's gold, and it is impossible not to know that Roman history is full of instances of how easily those Magistrates, those venerable warriors who

* I see most minds of my time exercise their ingenuity to dim the glory of the fine and generous ancient deeds, placing a base interpretation on them, and contriving vain occasions and causes for them. How subtle! Give me the most excellent and pure deed, I could easily find fifty plausible vicious motives for it. God knows, to one who is inclined to expand on it, what a variety of fancies assault our inmost will. In all their calumny, their ingenuity is not so much malicious as it is clumsy and crude. All the trouble and license they take to demean these great names, I would as soon take to elevate them. These rare personages, selected by the common consent of the wise as examples for the world, I shall not hesitate to add to their honor as much as my powers permit, by construal and favorable circumstances. And it is likely that all the efforts of our ingenuity are far beneath their merit. The task of good men is to portray virtue as as beautiful as possible. And it would not be unseemly if passions carried us away in favor of such saintly forms. It is not Rousseau who says all this, it is Montaigne.

made such a point of their poverty, could have enriched themselves.* As for courage, is it not well-known *[87]* that cowardice is deaf to reason, and that a poltroon continues to flee although he is certain to be killed in flight? *To wish to recall great States to the small virtues of small Republics is,* they say, *like wishing to compel a strong and a sturdy man to babble in a crib.* Now, that is certainly a statement that cannot be unfamiliar at Courts. It would have been worthy of Tiberius or of Catherine de Medici, and I have no doubt that both of them often made ones like it.

[50] It is difficult to imagine that morality should have to be measured with a surveyor's tool. Yet the size of States cannot be said to be altogether unrelated to the Citizens' morals. Some proportion surely obtains between these things; I wonder whether it is not an inverse proportion.** This important question calls for meditation; and I believe that, in spite of the more condescending than philosophic tone in which it is here dismissed with two words, it may properly be regarded as not yet settled.

[51] *It was,* they go on, *Cato's madness: with his family's hereditary temper and prejudices he perorated his whole life long, fought, and died without having done anything useful for his fatherland.* I do not know whether he did anything for his Fatherland; but I do know that he did a great deal for mankind by offering it the spectacle and the model of the purest virtue that ever was: he taught those who sincerely love genuine honor how to resist their century's vices and to loathe the abominable maxim of the fashionable that one ought to do as the others do; a maxim that would, no doubt, carry them far if they had the misfortune of falling in with a band of highwaymen. Someday our descendants will learn that in this century of wise

---

* Curius, refusing the presents of the Samnites, said that he would rather command men who have gold than have any himself. Curius was right. Those who love riches are made *[87]* to serve, and those who despise them, to command. It is not the power of gold that subordinates the poor to the rich, it is that they want to become rich in their turn; otherwise they would necessarily be the masters.

** My adversaries' haughtiness might in the end lead me to be indiscreet if I continued to dispute with them. They believe that they awe me with their contempt for small States: are they not afraid that I might finally ask them whether it is good that there be large ones?

men and of Philosophers, the most virtuous of men was held up to ridicule and called *[88]* a madman for having wished not to sully his great soul with his contemporaries' crimes, for having wished not to be a villain along with Caesar and the other brigands of his time.

[52] We have just seen how our Philosophers speak of Cato. Let us see how the ancient Philosophers spoke of him. *Behold a spectacle worthy of a god intent on his own work, Behold a spectacle of a struggle worthy of a god, a stalwart man grappling with evil fortune. I declare that I can see no fairer spectacle on earth for Jupiter to behold, should he wish to attend to it, than Cato, after his party's repeated defeats, standing upright still amidst his country's ruins.*

[53] Here is what we are elsewhere told about the first Romans: *I admire a Brutus, a Decius, a Lucretia, a Virginius, a Scaevola.* That is something, in the century we are in. *But I would admire even more a powerful and well-governed state.* A powerful state, and well-governed! So would I, truly. *Where the Citizens are not condemned to such cruel virtues.* I understand; it is more comfortable to live where things are so constituted that everyone is exempt from being a good man. But if the Citizens of this admired state were, by some misfortune, reduced to having either to give up virtue or to practice those cruel virtues, and they had the strength to do their duty, would that be a reason to admire them any the less?

[54] Let us take the case which our century finds most revolting and examine the conduct of Brutus who, as sovereign Magistrate, had his children put to death after they had conspired against the State at a critical moment when almost anything might have overthrown it. It is certain that if he had pardoned them, his colleague would inevitably have saved all the other conspirators, and the Republic would have been lost. What does that matter? I will be asked. Since it makes so little difference, let us suppose that the Republic survived, and that Brutus, having condemned some criminal to death, the culprit had spoken as follows: "Consul, why do you cause me to die? Have I done anything worse than to betray my fatherland? and am I not also your child?" I would very much like for someone to

take the trouble to tell me what Brutus could have answered.

[55] Brutus, I will further be told, should have abdicated the Consulship rather than cause his children's death. And I say that a Magistrate who, at such a perilous juncture, *[89]* abandons the care of the fatherland and abdicates the Magistracy, is a traitor who deserves death.

[56] There is no middle ground; the alternative for Brutus was infamy or letting the heads of Titus and Tiberinus fall at his order by the Lictors' axe. I am not saying it follows that many people would have chosen as did he.

[57] Although they do not explicitly opt for Rome's late period, we are clearly enough given to understand their preference for it over Rome's early days; and they are as much at a loss to find great men amidst the simplicity of the early days, as I am to find honest people amidst the pomp of the late period. They contrast Titus with Fabricius; but they overlooked this difference, that in Pyrrhus's time all Romans were like Fabricius, whereas in Titus's reign, he was the only good man.* I am ready to forget the heroic deeds of the first and the crimes of the late Romans: but what I cannot forget is that virtue was honored by the former and despised by the latter; and that when there were crowns for the winners of the Circus games, there no longer were any for the man who saved a Citizen's life. However, it should not be thought that this is peculiar to Rome. There was a time when the Republic of Athens was rich enough to spend huge sums on its spectacles and to pay Authors, Actors, and even Spectators a great deal of money: that was the very same time when no money could be found to defend the State against Philip's stratagems.

[58] Finally they come to [speak of] modern peoples; and I do not propose to take up the arguments they judge relevant to the topic. I only note that the advantage gained in not refuting

---

* If Titus had not been Emperor, we would never have heard of him; for he would have continued to live like everyone else: and he became a good man only once he ceased to follow the example of his century and was free to set it a better example. "As a private person, and even when his father was principex, he did not escape public hatred or even recrimination. But his reputation turned from bad to good and gave way to great praise [when it became evident that he was a good ruler]."

one's adversary's reasons by preventing him from stating them, is not a very honorable one. *[90]*

[59] I will also not take up all their reflections about luxury, politeness, the admirable education of our children,* the best methods to increase our knowledge, the usefulness of the Sciences and the pleasures of the fine Arts, and about many other points, of which a number are of no concern to me, several refute themselves, and the rest have already been refuted. I will leave it at citing a few more passages selected at random and which seem to me in need of elucidation. I have no choice but to restrict myself to [single] sentences, since I cannot take up arguments the thread of which I could not grasp.

[60] It is claimed that the ignorant Nations that had *ideas of glory and of virtue are individual exceptions which do not justify a presumption against the sciences.* Very well; but all learned Nations, with their fine ideas of glory and virtue, have always lost their love and practice of both. That is so without exception: let us go on to the proof. *In order to convince ourselves of it, let us look at the immense continent of Africa,* [to the interior of] *which no mortal is bold enough to penetrate or lucky enough to have been successful in the attempt.* Thus, on the grounds that we have been unable to penetrate the continent of Africa, that we are ignorant of what goes on there, we are made to conclude that its peoples are laden with vices: that would indeed have been the conclusion to draw if we had found a way of introducing our vices there. If I were the chief of one of the people of Niger, I declare that I would have a gallows erected at the country's border, where I would cause to be hanged without appeal the first European who dared to penetrate into it, and the first *[91]* Citizen who tried to leave

* There is no need to wonder whether fathers and teachers will take care to keep my dangerous writings out of their children's and pupils' sight. Indeed, what frightful confusion, what indecency would ensue if these well-brought-up children were to scorn so many pretty things, and seriously to prefer virtue to knowledge? That reminds me of a Lacedaemonian preceptor's reply when he was mockingly asked what he would teach his student. *I will teach him,* he said, *to love all that is honest.* If I met such a man among us, I would whisper in his ear, "Beware of speaking like that; for you will never have any students; say, instead, that you will teach them to chatter pleasantly, and I answer for your fortune."

it.* *America offers us spectacles that are no less shameful for mankind.* Especially since the Europeans are there. *For every ignorant people that is virtuous, one finds a hundred that are barbarous or savage.* So be it; at least one is found: but a people that is both virtuous and cultivates the sciences, has never been seen. *The earth, when left uncultivated, is not idle; it produces poisons, it breeds monsters.* That is what it begins to do wherever the taste for the frivolous Arts has caused the taste for agriculture to be forsaken. *Our soul,* one might also say, *is not idle when virtue forsakes it. It produces fictions, Romances, Satires, Verse; it feeds vice.*

[61] *Barbarians have conquered only because they were most unjust.* What, pray, were we during our so greatly admired conquest of America? But then, how could people with artillery, naval charts, and compasses, commit injustices? Will it be said that the outcome proves the Conquerors' valor? It proves only their cunning and their skill; it proves that an adroit and clever man can owe to his industry the success which a brave man expects only from his valor. Let us speak impartially. Whom shall we judge more courageous, the odious Cortés subjugating Mexico with powder, treachery and betrayal, or the unfortunate Guatimozin stretched by honest Europeans on a bed of burning coals to get his treasures, chiding one of his Officers when the same treatment wrests some moans from him, and proudly saying, what of me, am I on a bed of roses?

[62] *To say that the sciences were born of idleness is a manifest abuse of terms; they are born of leisure, but they protect against idleness.* I do not understand this distinction between idleness and leisure. But I do for a certainty know that no honest man can ever boast of leisure as long as good remains to be done, a fatherland to be served, unfortunates to be relieved; and *[92]* I challenge anyone to show me how, on my principles, the word leisure can mean anything honest. *The Citizen whose needs tie him to the plow is not more occupied*

---

* I may be asked what harm is done the state by a Citizen who leaves it never to return. He harms the rest by the bad example he sets, and himself by the vices he seeks. In either case it is up to the law to prevent it, and it is preferable that he be hanged than that he be wicked.

than is the Geometer or the Anatomist. Nor than the child building a house of cards, but more usefully. *Must everyone till the ground, just because bread is necessary?* Why not? Let them even graze, if need be. I would still rather see men eat grass in the fields than devour one another in the cities: It is true that if they were such as I call for, they would be very like beasts; and that being such as they are, they are very like men.

[63] *The state of ignorance is a state of fear and of need. Everything is then a danger to our frailty. Death thunders overhead; it lurks in the grass underfoot: When one fears everything and needs everything, what could be a more reasonable attitude than to want to know everything?* One only has to consider the constant worries of Doctors and Anatomists about their life and health, to decide whether knowledge helps to reassure us regarding the dangers we face. Since it always reveals many more dangers to us than it reveals means to guard against them, it is no wonder that it only increases our worries and makes us pusillanimous. In all these respects, animals live in profound security without being any the worse off for it. A Heifer need not study botany to learn to pick over its hay, and the wolf devours its prey without thinking about indigestion. Will anyone meet these objections by daring to take the side of instinct against reason? That is precisely what I call for.

[64] *It would appear,* we are told, *that there is an excess of ploughmen and fear of a shortage of Philosophers. I, in turn, ask whether there is fear of a shortage of people going into the lucrative professions. That is surely to underestimate the empire of covetousness. From childhood on, everything drives us toward the useful stations. And how many prejudices one has to overcome, how much courage one has to muster, just to dare to be a Descartes, a Newton, a Locke.*

[65] Leibniz and Newton died laden with goods and honors, and they deserved even more. Are we to say that it was out of moderation that they did not *[93]* raise themselves to the station of farmers? I know the empire of covetousness well enough to know that everything drives us toward the lucrative professions; that is why I say that everything drives us away from the useful

professions. Men like Hebert, Lafrenaye, Dulac, Martin, earn more money in one day than all the ploughmen of a Province could make in a month. I might suggest a somewhat odd puzzle in connection with the passage I am just now discussing; leaving out the first two lines, and reading it out of context, to guess whether it is taken from my writings or from my adversaries'.

[66] *Good books are the only protection of weak minds, that is to say of three-quarters of mankind, against infection by example.* In the first place, the Learned will never write as many good books as they set bad examples. In the second place, there will always be more bad books than good. In the third place, the best guides which honest men can have, are reason and conscience: *A good mind needs little learning.* As for those whose mind is unsound or conscience hardened, reading cannot ever do them any good. Finally, for anyone whatsoever, the only books needed are the books of Religion, the only ones I have never condemned.

[67] *We are told to mourn the education of the Persians.* Note that it is Plato who says so. I had thought to make myself a shield of that Philosopher's authority; but I see that nothing can protect me against my adversaries' animus: *Be he Trojan or Rutulian;* they prefer to stab one another than to give me any quarter, and they hurt themselves more than they do me.* *That education was,* they say, *founded on barbarous principles; for there was a different master for the exercise of each virtue, although virtue is indivisible; for what matters, is to inspire virtue, not to teach it; to instill love for its practice, not to demonstrate its Theory.* There is much I should *[94]* like to say in reply to this; but one should not insult one's Readers by telling them everything. I shall limit myself to the following two remarks. The first, that a person who wants to raise a child does not begin by telling him that he should practice virtue; for he would not be understood: rather, he begins by teaching him

---

* A new scheme for my defense occurs to me, and I am not sure that I may not some day have the weakness to carry it out. That defense will be made up exclusively of arguments drawn from the Philosophers; from which it would follow that they have all been chatterboxes as I maintain, if their arguments are found to be bad; or that I have won my case, if they are found to be good.

to be true, then to be temperate, then courageous, etc., and finally he tells him that all of these things together are called virtue. The second, that it is we who leave it at demonstrating Theory; but the Persians taught practice. See my discourse, p. 21.

[68] *All the criticisms leveled at Philosophy attack the human mind.* I concede it. *Or rather, the author of nature, who made us as we are.* If he made us Philosophers, what is the good of going to so much trouble trying to become one? *The Philosophers were men; they erred; is that to be wondered at?* It is when they no longer err, that there will be cause for wonder. *Let us be sorry for them, profit from their mistakes, and correct ourselves.* Yes, let us correct ourselves, and not philosophize any more. . . . *A thousand roads lead to error, and only one to the truth?* That is precisely what I said. *Is it surprising that truth should so often have been mistaken, and been discovered so late?* Ah! So we have found it at last!

[69] *An opinion of Socrates's is urged against us, which dealt not with the Learned but with the Sophists, not with the sciences but with their possible abuse.* Can anyone who holds that all our sciences are nothing but abuse and all our Learned men nothing but true Sophists, ask for more? *Socrates was the leader of a sect that taught doubt.* My veneration for Socrates would greatly diminish if I believed that he had had the silly vanity of wishing to be the leader of a sect. *And he justly censured the pride of anyone who claimed to know everything.* That is to say the pride of all Learned men. *True science is very far from such affectation.* Truly: but I am talking about ours. *Socrates here bears witness against himself.* I find that difficult to understand. *The most learned of Greeks did not blush at his own ignorance.* By his own admission, the most learned of Greeks knew nothing; draw your own conclusion about everyone else. *Hence the sciences do not arise from our vices.* Hence the sciences arise from our vices. *They are therefore not all born of human pride.* I have already stated my sentiment *[95]* in the matter. *Vain declamations which can delude only informed minds.* I don't know how to reply to that.

[70] With respect to the limits of luxury, we are told that

that is presumably not something regarding which one should reason about the present on the basis of the past. *When men walked about completely naked, the one to whom it first occurred to wear clogs was deemed a sensualist; every century has been denounced for corruption, without its being clear what was meant.*

[71] It is true that until the present time, luxury, although often prevalent, had at least always been viewed as the fatal source of infinitely many evils. It was left for M. Melon to be the first to publish the poisonous doctrine whose novelty brought him more followers than did the soundness of his reasoning. I am not afraid to be alone in my century to fight those odious maxims which only tend to destroy and debase virtue, and to make for rich people and wretches, that is to say only for wicked men.

[72] I am expected to be greatly embarrassed to be asked at what point limits should be placed on luxury. My sentiment is that there should be none at all. Everything beyond the physically necessary is a source of evil. Nature gives us quite enough needs; and it is at the very least exceedingly imprudent to multiply them unnecessarily, and thereby to place one's soul in greater dependence. It was not without reason that Socrates, seeing the display in a shop, congratulated himself on having no use for any of those things. The odds are a hundred to one that he who first wore clogs was punishable, unless his feet hurt. As for ourselves, we are too much in need of having shoes to be exempt from having virtue.

[73] I have already said elsewhere that I did not suggest overthrowing existing society, burning Libraries and all books, destroying Colleges and Academies: and I must here add that I also do not suggest reducing men to make do with the bare necessities. I am quite sensible of the fact that one ought not entertain the chimerical project of making honest men of them; but I believed myself obliged to state plainly the truth I was asked for. I have seen the evil and have tried to discover its causes: Others, more daring or more foolish, may seek the cure. *[96]*

[74] I grow weary, and I lay down my pen, resolved not to

take it up again in this excessively drawn-out dispute. I hear that a great many Authors* have sought to refute me. I am very sorry not to be able to answer them all. But I believe that my choice of those I have answered shows that it is not fear that keeps me from answering the others.

[75] I have tried to erect a monument that owed nothing of its strength and solidity to Art: truth alone, to which I have dedicated it, has the right to make it unassailable: And if I once again repulse the blows struck against it, it is more in order to do myself honor by defending it, than to lend it an assistance which it does not need.

[76] Let me be permitted to conclude by stating emphatically that the love of humanity and of virtue alone made me break my silence; and that the bitterness of my invectives against the vices I witness arises solely from the pain they cause me, and from my intense desire to see men happier and especially worthier of being so.

* Even small critical sheets put out for the amusement of young people have done me the honor of remembering me. I have not read them, and I most certainly shall not read them; but nothing prevents me from taking notice of them as they deserve, and I have no doubt that all this is most amusing.

I am told that M. Gautier has done me the honor of a rebuttal although I have not answered him and have even stated my reasons for not doing so. Evidently M. Gautier does not think them good reasons, since he takes the trouble to refute them. I see that I must yield to M. Gautier; and I wholeheartedly acknowledge my wrong in not having answered him; we are in agreement, then. I regret I cannot redress my fault. For unfortunately it is too late, and no one would know what I was talking about.

LETTER
By Jean-Jacques ROUSSEAU of Geneva
About a New Refutation of his Discourse
by a Member of the Academy of Dijon

[1] I have just seen, Sir, a Pamphlet entitled *Discourse which won the prize of the Academy of Dijon in 1750, together with the refutation of that Discourse by a Member of the Academy of Dijon who denied it his vote;* and while perusing this Writing, it occurred to me that, instead of lowering himself to the point of editing my Discourse, the Academician who denied it his vote should really have published the work for which he did vote: that would have been an excellent way to refute mine.

[2] Here, then, is one of my Judges who does not hesitate to become one of my adversaries, and who finds it thoroughly objectionable that his colleagues should have honored me with the Prize: I confess that I was very surprised by it myself; I had tried to deserve it, but had done nothing to obtain it. Besides, although I know that Academies do not endorse the sentiments of the Writers they crown, and that the Prize is awarded not to the one who is believed to have defended the better cause but to the one who has spoken best; even assuming that I had done so, I was far from expecting an Academy to display an impartiality which the learned do not by any means always observe when their self-interest is involved.

[3] But while I was surprised by my Judges' equity, I must confess that I am no less surprised by my adversaries' indiscreetness: how dare they so publicly vent their ill-humor at the honor done me? *[98]* How can they fail to perceive the irreparable harm they thereby do their own cause? Let them not imagine that anyone will be deceived about the reason for their vexation: it is not because it is badly done that they are annoyed to see my Discourse awarded a prize; equally bad ones are daily awarded prizes, and they do not say a word; it is for another reason, which bears much more directly on their profession,

and which is not difficult to perceive. I knew that the sciences corrupt morals, render men unjust and jealous, and cause them to sacrifice everything to their self-interest and vainglory; but it seemed to me that this was done a little more decently and skillfully: I saw men of letters constantly talk about equity, moderation, virtue and behind the sacred shield of these fine words give their passions and vices free rein with impunity; but I would never have believed they had the effrontery publicly to censure their Colleagues' impartiality. Everywhere else, to reach an equitable verdict at odds with his self-interest is a Judge's title to glory; only the sciences hold it against their practitioners to exhibit integrity: truly a fine prerogative, that.

[4] I dare say that, by greatly contributing to my glory, the Academy of Dijon greatly contributed to its own: the day will come when the adversaries of my cause will take advantage of that Judgment to prove that the cultivation of Letters is compatible with equity and disinterestedness. Whereupon the Partisans of truth will answer them: that particular case does seem to tell against us; but remember the scandal the Judgment caused in Literary circles at the time, and the manner in which they complained about it, and draw the correct conclusion about their maxims from that [episode].

[5] It seems to me no less unwise to complain about the Academy's stating its topic in the form of a question: I leave aside how unlikely it was that, in the universal enthusiasm which today prevails, anyone would have had the courage willingly to forgo the Prize by announcing for the negative; but I cannot understand how Philosophers dare find it objectionable to be offered opportunities for discussion: /99/ what a fine love of truth, that is frightened at having the pro and con examined! In Philosophical inquiries the best way to render a sentiment suspect is to deny the opposite sentiment a hearing: whoever goes about it that way rather gives the impression of being in bad faith and of not trusting the goodness of his cause. The whole of France eagerly awaits the Entry that will win the French Academy Prize this year; not only will it most certainly eclipse my Discourse, which will not be very difficult, but it will undoubtedly be a masterpiece. Yet how will that help solve

the question? not at all; for after having read it, everyone will say: *This discourse is very fine; but if the Writer had been free to defend the opposite sentiment, he might well have written an even finer one.*

[6] I have perused this new refutation; for it is yet another refutation, and I cannot fathom why the Writings by my adversaries which bear this peremptory title are forever fated to be the ones in which I am the most inadequately refuted. I did peruse it, then, this refutation, without the least regret at having resolved not to answer anyone anymore: I will quote just one passage, and from it the Reader may judge whether I am right or wrong: here it is.

[7] *I will admit that it is possible to be an honest man without being talented; but does society require no more of us than to be an honest man? And what does an honest man who is ignorant and untalented amount to? a useless weight, a burden to the earth itself,* etc. I will certainly not reply to an Author capable of writing this way; but I believe that he can thank me for it.

[8] Nor could I, without being as diffuse as the Author, reply to the extensive collection of Latin texts, verses by La Fontaine, Boileau, Molière, Voiture, Regnard, M. Gresset, the story of Nimrod, or that of the Peasants from Picardy; for what is one to say to a Philosopher who assures us that he is ill-disposed toward the ignorant because his Farmer in Picardy, who is not a Doctor, does, it is true, pay him exactly what he owes him, but does not give him enough money for his land? The Author is so preoccupied with his land holdings, that he even speaks about mine. Land of my own! Jean-Jacques Rousseau's land! *[100]* I really advise him to slander* me more skillfully than that.

[9] If I were to reply to any portion of the refutation, it would be to the personal remarks that abound in it; but as they do not bear on the question, I will not deviate from the steady maxim to which I have always adhered, to confine myself to the subject

---

* If the Author does me the honor of refuting this Letter, he will no doubt prove by means of an elegant and learned argument supported by the weightiest authorities, that it is not a crime to own land: for others it may indeed not be one, but it would be one for me.

at hand without letting any personal considerations intrude: the genuine respect one owes the Public consists not in sparing it sad truths which it might find useful, but all the petty Authors' squabbles* that fill polemical Writings and serve no other purpose than to indulge a shameful animus. I am charged with having drawn from Clenard** a word used by Cicero; so be it; that I have committed *[101]* solecisms; so much the better; that I pursue Literature and Music in spite of my low opinion of them; I will acknowledge it, if I must, I will have to pay at a more reasonable age the penalty for the amusements of my youth; but what difference does all this after all make to the public or to the cause of the Sciences? Rousseau may speak French badly, and yet Grammar be none the more useful to virtue. Jean-Jacques may behave badly, and the Learned behave none the better for it; that is all I shall and, I believe, all I need say in reply to this new refutation.

[10] I will conclude this Letter as well as what I have to say

---

* The Lyon Discourse serves as an excellent example of how Philosophers should attack and fight without resorting to personalities or invectives. I flatter myself that my reply, which is in press, also provides an example of how one can defend what one believes to be true with all the strength at one's disposal, without bitterness against those who attack it.

** If I said that such a recondite reference surely comes from someone more familiar with Clenard's *Greek Primer* than with Cicero's *On Duties,* and who therefore seems to rush to the defense of Literature without much justification; if I added that there are professions, such as, for example, Surgery, where so many terms derived from the Greek are used that anyone practicing them has to acquire some rudimentary notions of that Language, I would be assuming the tone of my new adversary and answering as he might have done in my place. I can, however, answer that when I suggested the word *Investigation,* I sought to be of use to the Language by trying to introduce a gentle, harmonious, intelligible term which has no French synonym. These, I believe, are the only conditions necessary to justify the exercise of this salutary freedom:

Why should I be denied this privilege if it can achieve some small benefit;
When Cato's and Ennius's speech have enriched the language of the fatherland?

Above all, I wanted to convey my idea accurately; I do, it is true, know that the first rule of all our Writers is to write cor*[101]*rectly and idiomatically; but then they have pretensions, and want to be considered correct and elegant. The first rule I follow, who do not in the least care about what may be thought of my style, is to make myself understood: any time I can make my point more forcefully or clearly with ten solecisms, I will never hesitate to do so. As long as Philosophers understand me clearly, I am ready to let purists go chasing after words.

on a subject that has been discussed at such length, with a caution to my adversaries which they will surely disregard, although it would benefit the side they wish to defend more than they might think; namely, not to heed their zeal to the point of neglecting to consult their strength and *what their shoulders can carry.* They will probably tell me that I should have followed that advice myself, and that may be true; but there is at least this difference, that I was alone of my party, whereas theirs is the party of the multitude, and latecomers are therefore either excused from joining the fray or obliged to do better than the others.

[11] Lest this appear a rash or presumptuous piece of advice, I here add one sample of my adversaries' reasoning, on the basis of which the relevance and force of their criticism may be judged. *A few centuries ago,* I had said, *the Peoples of Europe lived in a state worse than ignorance; I know not what scientific jargon more contemptible still than ignorance had usurped the name of knowledge and stood as an almost insuperable obstacle in the path of its return: it took a revolution to bring men back to common sense.* Peoples had lost common sense not because they were ignorant but because they were *[102]* foolish enough to believe that with Aristotle's big words and Raymond Lulle's pretentious doctrine they knew something; it took a revolution to teach them that they knew nothing, and another is badly needed to teach us the same truth. Here is my adversaries' argument on this point: *That revolution was brought about by Letters; as the Author himself admits; they restored common sense, yet according to him they also corrupted morals: it follows that a People must give up common sense for the sake of good morals.* Three Writers in succession have repeated this fine argument: I now ask them, what would they rather I blamed, their minds for failing to grasp the perfectly clear meaning of this passage, or their bad faith for pretending not to understand it? Since they are men of Letters, there can be no doubt about which they will choose. But what are we to say about the silly interpretations this latest adversary sees fit to give of my Frontispiece? I should have thought I was insulting Readers and treating them like children,

if I had interpreted such an obvious allegory for them; if I had told them that Prometheus's torch is the torch of the Sciences made to quicken great geniuses; that the Satyr who, seeing fire for the first time, runs toward it and wants to embrace it, represents the vulgar who, seduced by the brilliance of Letters, indiscreetly give themselves over to study; that the Prometheus who cries out and warns them of the danger is the Citizen of Geneva. This allegory is apt, fine, I dare believe it is sublime. What is one to think of a Writer who has meditated on it, and could not succeed in understanding it? Surely he would not have been a great Doctor among his friends, the Egyptians.

[12] I therefore take the liberty of recommending to my adversaries, and especially to the latest one among them, the following wise lesson formulated by a Philosopher in connection with another subject: recognize that no one's objections can injure your party as much as can your own bad rejoinders; recognize that if you have not said anything worthwhile, people will disparage your cause by doing you the honor of believing that nothing better could have been said on its behalf.

I am, etc.

PREFACE
to *NARCISSUS*

[1] I wrote this Play at the age of eighteen, and refrained from showing it as long as I at all cared about my reputation as an Author. I finally felt bold enough to publish it, but I shall never feel so bold as to say anything about it. So that what is at issue here is not my play, but myself.

[2] I have to speak about myself in spite of my reluctance to do so; I either have to acknowledge the wrongs ascribed to me, or to vindicate myself. I realize that it will not be an even match. For I will be attacked with witticisms, and defend myself with nothing but arguments: but provided I convince my adversaries, I do not much care whether I persuade them; in striving to deserve my self-esteem, I have learned to do without the esteem of others, who, after all, for the most part do without mine. But while it does not matter to me whether I am thought of well or ill, it does matter to me that no one have the right to think ill of me, and it matters to the truth I have upheld that its defender not be justly accused of having lent it his assistance on a mere whim or out of vanity, without loving or knowing it.

[3] The side I chose in the question I was investigating some years ago did not fail to make me a host of adversaries,* who

---

* I am told that a number of people object to my calling my adversaries my adversaries, and I am quite prepared to believe it, in a century in which people no longer dare to call anything by its name. I also hear that everyone of my adversaries complains when I answer objections other than his own, that I am wasting my time fighting chimeras; which confirms something I had rather suspected, namely that they do not waste their time reading or listening to one another. I, on the other hand, thought it incumbent on me to take that trouble, *[960]* and I have read the numerous writings against me which they have published, from the first reply with which I was honored, to the four German sermons of which one begins more or less as follows: *My brethren, if Socrates were to return among us and to see the thriving state of the sciences in Europe; what am I saying, in Europe? in Germany; what am I saying, in Germany? in Saxony; what am I saying, in Saxony? in Leipzig; what am I saying, in Leipzig? in this University; then, struck with astonishment and filled with respect, Socrates would modestly take his place among our pupils and, humbly absorbing our teaching, he would, under our tutelage, soon be rid of the ignorance of which he so justifiably complained.* I read all this and made only a few replies. Perhaps that was still too many. But I am pleased that

perhaps cared more about the interests *[960]* of men of letters than about the honor of literature. I had anticipated as much, and I rather suspected that their behavior in these circumstances would do more for my cause than would all my discourses. Indeed, they did not hide their astonishment and vexation that an Academy should so ill-advisedly have acted with integrity. In their effort to undermine the authority of its judgment, they did not spare it insults or even falsehoods.* Nor was I forgotten in their tirades. Some undertook to refute me directly: the wise could see how cogently, and the public how successfully they did so. Others, more skillful, knowing the danger of attacking established truths head-on, adroitly deflected attention on my person when it should have been focused exclusively on my arguments, and their accusations against me set off debates that caused my more serious accusations against them to be forgotten. *[961]* They are, therefore, the ones who have to be answered once and for all.

[4] They contend that I do not believe a word of the truths I upheld, and that while I was proving one proposition, I continued to believe its opposite. That is tantamount to saying that I proved such outlandish things that people can claim I could have upheld them only in jest. What a fine tribute they thereby pay to the science that serves as the foundation of all the other sciences; and to see the art of reasoning so successfully used to

---

these Gentlemen should have liked them enough to be jealous of those who were favored with them. As for the people who are shocked by the word *adversaries,* I will gladly give it up if they will kindly show me another with which to refer not only to all those who have attacked my sentiment either in writing or, more cautiously and safely, at gatherings of ladies and wits where they were sure I would not go to defend myself, but also to those who now pretend to believe that I have no adversaries, but who at first found my adversaries' replies irrefutable and who, once I had refuted them, blamed me for having done so because, according to them, I had not been attacked. Meanwhile I trust that they will permit me to call my adversaries my adversaries, for in spite of the politeness of my century, I am as crude as Philip's Macedonians.

* In the *Mercure* for August 1752 will be found a disclaimer by the Academy of Dijon of I know not what writing which its Author had falsely attributed to one of the members of that Academy.

prove absurdities, certainly leads one to believe that it is most helpful in the discovery of truth!

[5] They contend that I do not believe a word of the truths I upheld; that is evidently a new and convenient way of theirs to assail unassailable arguments, to refute the proofs even of Euclid, and all demonstrated truths in the universe. Now it seems to me that those who so rashly accuse me of speaking in contradiction with my thought, have, themselves, few scruples about speaking in contradiction with theirs: for, as I shall soon prove, they have surely not found anything in my Writings or in my conduct that could have given them this idea; and they must know that a man who speaks seriously must be thought to believe what he says, unless either his deeds or his discourses belie it; and even that is not always enough to be sure that he does not believe it.

[6] They may therefore proclaim as loudly as they please that when I came out against the sciences, I spoke in contradiction with my sentiment; I know of only one reply to a claim so rash and so devoid of proof or plausibility; it is short, vigorous, and I ask them to consider it delivered.

[7] They also contend that my conduct contradicts my principles, and they undoubtedly rely on this second charge to establish the first; for there are many people who can discover proofs for what is not [so]. Thus they will say that it is unbecoming for someone who writes music and poetry to denigrate the fine arts, and that literature, which I profess to despise, can, after all, be pursued in a thousand more praiseworthy ways than by writing Plays. This accusation, too, has to be answered. [962]

[8] First of all; even if it were strictly granted, I say that it would prove that I behave badly, but not that I fail to speak in good faith. If it were permissible to derive proofs about men's sentiments from their actions, we would have to say that the love of justice has been banished from all hearts, and that there is not a single Christian on earth. Show me men who always act in conformity with their maxims, and I will condemn my own. It is mankind's fate that reason shows us the goal, and the passions divert us from it. Hence even if it were true that I do

not act according to my principles, that, by itself alone, would not be reason enough to accuse me of speaking in contradiction with my sentiment, or to accuse my principles of falseness.

[9] But if I wished to concede the point, all I would have to do, in order to reconcile matters, is to contrast the [different] times [involved]. I have not always had the good fortune to think as I do now. For a long time seduced by the prejudices of my century, I took study to be the only occupation worthy of a wise man, I looked upon the sciences with nothing but respect, and upon the learned with nothing but admiration.* I did not understand that one can go astray while forever proving things, or do evil while forever talking about wisdom. Only after I had seen things from close up did I learn to assess them at their true worth; and although I had, in my inquiries, always found *glibness enough, not enough wisdom,* it took me much reflection, much observation, and much time to rid myself of my illusions about all this vain scientific pomp. It is not surprising that during those times of prejudice and error, when I held being an Author in such high regard, I occasionally aspired to be one myself. That is when I wrote the Poems and most of the other Pieces that have issued from my pen, and, among others, this little Play. It might be rather *[963]* harsh to reproach me now for these amusements of my youth, and it would, to say the least, be wrong to accuse me on their account of having contradicted principles I did not yet hold. I long ago ceased to set any stock whatsoever by any of these things; and to venture to offer them to the Public under these circumstances, after having had the sense to keep them this long, is to indicate clearly enough that I am equally indifferent to the praise and to the blame they may deserve; for I no longer think as did the Author whose work they are. They are illegitimate children one still fondles with pleasure while blushing to be their father, of

* Whenever I recall my former simplicity I cannot help laughing. In every book of Ethics or of Philosophy I read, I believed I saw the Author's soul and principles. I looked upon all these grave Writers as modest, wise, virtuous, irreproachable men. I entertained angelic notions about what it would be like to have dealings with them, and I would only have approached the house of anyone of them, as if it were a sanctuary. Finally I saw them; this childish prejudice vanished, and it is the only error of which they have cured me.

whom one takes one's final leave, and whom one sends off to seek their fortune without greatly worrying about what will become of them.

[10] But all this is to argue at excessive length on the basis of chimerical assumptions. If the accusation that I cultivate letters when I despise them is unfounded, then my defense against that accusation is unnecessary; for even if it were in fact true, it would not involve an inconsistency: that is what it remains for me to prove.

[11] To this end I will, as is my wont, follow the simple and easy method that suits the truth. I will once again set forth the problem, I will once again state my sentiment, and I will await to be shown how, in terms of this account, my deeds belie my speeches. My adversaries will, for their part, not be at a loss for a reply, since they have mastered the wonderful art of arguing pro and con on all manner of subjects. They will begin, as is their wont, by setting forth an altogether different question according to their fancy; they will have me resolve it to suit themselves: in order to attack me more easily they will have me arguing not in my own way, but in theirs; they will skillfully shift the Reader's eyes from the primary object and fix them to the right or to the left; they will fight a specter and claim to have defeated me: but I will have done what I must do, and I begin.

[12] "Science is good for nothing, and it never does anything but harm, because it is by its very nature bad. It is as inseparable from vice as ignorance is from virtue. All lettered peoples have at all times been corrupt; all ignorant peoples have been virtuous: in a word, only among the learned are there vices, only a man who knows nothing is virtuous. There is a way, then, *[964]* for us to become honest folk again: forthwith to banish science and the learned, burn our libraries, close our Academies, our Colleges, our Universities, and plunge back into the full barbarism of the first centuries."

[13] This much my adversaries have thoroughly refuted; but then I never said or thought a single word of any of it, and it is impossible to imagine anything more contrary to my system than this absurd doctrine they have the goodness to attribute to me.

Here is what I did say, and what has not been refuted.

[14] The issue was whether the restoration of the arts and sciences had contributed to the purification of our morals.

[15] By showing, as I did, that our morals were not purified,* the question was more or less resolved.

[16] But it implicitly raised another, more *[965]* general and more important question, about what must be the influence of the pursuit of the sciences on the morals of peoples under any circumstances. It is this question, of which the first is but a corollary, that I undertook to examine with care.

[17] I began with the facts, and showed that in all peoples of the world, morals have deteriorated in proportion as a taste for study and letters has spread among them.

[18] That was not all; for although it was impossible to deny that these things always occurred together, it was possible to deny that one brought about the other: I therefore endeavored to establish this necessary connection. I showed that the source of our errors on this point comes from our mistaking our vain and deceptive knowledge for the sovereign intelligence that sees the truth of all things at one glance. Science, taken

* When I said that our morals had been corrupted, I did not mean to say that our ancestors' morals were good, but only that ours were even worse. There are a thousand sources of corruption among men; and although the sciences may be the most profuse and rapid of them, they are far from being the only one. The destruction of the Roman Empire, the invasions by hosts of Barbarians, resulted in a mixing of all peoples that must inevitably have destroyed each one's morals and customs. The crusades, commerce, the discovery of the Indies, navigation, farflung journeys, and still other causes which I do not wish to mention, have perpetuated and increased this disarray. Everything that facilitates communication between nations, transmits not the virtues, but the crimes of each to the others, and in each one of them it alters the morals appropriate to its climate and the constitution of its government. So that the sciences have not done all of the harm; they have only had a considerable share in it; and the harm most specifically due to them is that they have given our vices a pleasing appearance, an air of honesty that keeps us from abominating them. When *The Villain* was first performed, I recall that people did not think that the play's title really fit the main character. Cleon seemed to be simply an ordinary man; he was, they said, like everyone else. This frightful scoundrel whose character is so thoroughly laid bare that everyone who has the misfortune of resembling him should have been made to shudder at himself, was judged to be an altogether unsuccessfully drawn character, and his darkest deeds were thought charming because men who looked upon themselves as very honest folk recognized themselves in him feature by feature.

abstractly, deserves all our admiration. The foolish science of men deserves nothing but derision and contempt.

[19] A taste for letters always heralds a beginning of corruption in a people, which it very rapidly accelerates. For, in an entire nation this taste can only arise from two sources, both of them bad, and both of which study in turn perpetuates and increases, namely idleness and a craving for distinction. In a well-constituted State, every citizen has his duties to fulfill; and he holds these important cares too dear to find leisure for frivolous speculations. In a well-constituted State all citizens are so thoroughly equal that none may enjoy precedence over others for being the most learned or even the most skilled, but at most for being the best: though this last distinction is often dangerous; for it makes for scoundrels and hypocrites.

[20] A taste for letters born of a craving for distinction necessarily engenders evils infinitely more dangerous than all the good they do is useful, in that those who yield to it eventually become quite unscrupulous about the means of success. The first Philosophers earned great renown by teaching men to perform their duties and the principles of virtue. But before long these precepts had become commonplaces, and in order to achieve distinction men had to strike out in opposite directions. Such is the origin of the absurd systems of men like Leucippus, Diogenes, Pyrrho, Protagoras, Lucretius. Men like Hobbes, *[966]* Mandeville and a thousand others have chosen to achieve distinction among us in the same way; and their dangerous teaching has borne so much fruit that, although we still have some true Philosophers eager to recall to our hearts the laws of humanity and of virtue, one is horrified to see how far the maxims of our ratiocinating century have carried the contempt for the duties of man and citizen.

[21] A taste for letters, philosophy, and the fine arts destroys the love of our primary duties and of true glory. Once talents preempt the honors owed to virtue, everyone wants to be an agreeable man, and no one cares to be a good man. This gives rise to the further inconsistency, that men are rewarded only for qualities which do not depend on them: for we are born with our talents, only our virtues belong to us.

[22] The first and almost the only care taken for our education is both the fruit and the seed of these ridiculous prejudices. For the sake of teaching us letters, we are made to suffer torments throughout our unhappy youth: we know all the rules of grammar before we ever hear any mention of man's duties: we know everything that has been done up to now before being told anything about what we should do; and as long as we are trained to prattle, nobody cares whether we know how to act or think. In a word, we are required to be learned only in things that can be of no use to us; and our children are brought up exactly like the athletes of the ancient public games who, because they dedicated their sturdy limbs to a useless and superfluous exercise, carefully avoided ever using them for any kind of productive work.

[23] A taste for letters, philosophy and the fine arts enervates bodies and souls. Work in the study causes men to grow frail, it weakens their temperament, and the soul's vigor is difficult to preserve once the body's vigor is lost. Study uses up the machine, exhausts minds, destroys strength, enervates courage, and this alone shows us clearly enough that it is not made for us: that is how men grow cowardly and pusillanimous, equally incapable of withstanding pain and the passions. Everyone knows how unfit city dwellers are to endure the toils of war, and the reputation of *[967]* men of letters as regards bravery is familiar enough.* And nothing is more justly suspect than an arrant coward's honor.

[24] So many reflections on the weakness of our nature often do no more than divert us from generous enterprises. The more we think about the miseries of mankind, the more our imagination oppresses us with their weight, and too much foresight deprives us of courage by depriving us of confidence. It is quite in vain that we strive to provide against unforeseen accidents "if science, trying to arm us with new defenses against natural discomforts,

---

* Here is a modern example for the benefit of those who accuse me of mentioning only ancient examples. The Republic of Genoa, looking for a way to subjugate the Corsicans more fully, found none more effective than to establish an Academy among them. I would have no difficulty expanding this Note, but to do so would be to insult the intelligence of the only Readers about whom I care.

has impressed our imagination more deeply with their magnitude and weight than with its own reasons or with the vain subtleties that lead us to seek cover behind it.''

[25] A taste for philosophy loosens all the bonds of esteem and benevolence that tie men to society, and this is perhaps the most dangerous of the evils it engenders. The charm of study soon dulls all other attachments. What is more, continued reflection about mankind, continued observation of men, teach the Philosopher to judge them at their worth, and it is difficult to be particularly fond of what one holds in contempt. Before long he comes to focus on himself alone all the interest which virtuous men share with their fellows; his contempt for others heightens his pride: his vanity grows in direct proportion with his indifference to the rest of the universe. Family, fatherland, become for him words devoid of meaning: he is neither parent, nor citizen, nor man; he is a philosopher.

[26] At the same time, as the pursuit of the sciences as it were withdraws the philosopher's heart from the throng, it in other ways entangles the man of letters' heart in the throng, and in both cases it does so with equal prejudice to virtue. Anyone who cultivates the agreeable talents wants to please, to be admired, and indeed wants to be admired more than anyone else. Public applause is to be his alone: I *[968]* would say that he does everything to obtain it, if he did not do more to deprive his competitors of it. Hence arise, on the one hand, those refinements of taste and politeness, that vile and obsequious flattery, those seductive, insidious, puerile attentions which in time make for a petty soul and a corrupt heart; and, on the other hand, the jealousies, the rivalries, the well-known hatred of artists for one another, sly slander, deceit, treachery, and all the most cowardly and revolting aspects of vice. If the philosopher holds men in contempt, the artist soon causes them to hold him in contempt, and in the end both conspire to render them contemptible.

[27] There is more; and of all the truths I submitted to the judgment of the wise, this is the most arresting and the most cruel. All our Writers regard the crowning achievement of our century's politics to be the sciences, the arts, luxury, commerce,

laws, and all the other bonds which, by tightening the knots of society* among men through self-interest, place them all in a position of mutual dependence, impose on them mutual needs and common interests, and oblige everyone to contribute to everyone else's happiness in order to secure his own. These are certainly fine ideas, and they are presented in a favorable light. But when they are examined carefully and impartially, the advantages which they seem at first to hold out prove to be open to considerable criticism.

[28] It is quite a wonderful thing, then, to have placed men in a position where they cannot possibly live together without obstructing, supplanting, deceiving, betraying, destroying one another! From now on we must take care never to let ourselves be seen such as we are: because for every two men whose interests coincide, perhaps a hundred thousand oppose them, and the only way to succeed is either to deceive or to ruin all those people. That is the fatal source of the violence, the betrayals, the deceits and all the horrors necessarily required by a state of [969] affairs in which everyone pretends to be working for the others' profit or reputation, while only seeking to raise his own above them and at their expense.

[29] What have we gained from all this? Much babbling, rich people, and arguers, that is to say enemies of virtue and of common sense. In return we have lost innocence and morals. The multitude grovels in poverty; all are the slaves of vice. As yet uncommitted crimes already dwell deep inside men's hearts, and all that keeps them from being carried out is the promise of impunity.

[30] What a strange and ruinous constitution, where to have wealth always makes it easier to acquire more, and where he who has nothing finds it impossible to acquire something; where a good man has no way out of his misery; where the most knavish are the most honored, and where one necessarily has to

* I complain that Philosophy loosens the bonds of society formed by mutual esteem and goodwill, and I complain that the sciences, the arts and all the other objects of commerce tighten the bonds of society through self-interest. For it is indeed impossible to tighten one of these bonds without having the other relax by as much. There is therefore no contradiction here.

renounce virtue in order to become an honest man! I know that sermonizers have said all this a hundred times; but they were delivering sermons, whereas I give reasons; they perceived the evil, and I lay bare its causes and, above all, by showing that all these vices belong not so much to man, as to man badly governed, I point out something that is both most consoling and most useful.* *[970]*

[31] These are the truths I have expounded and tried to prove in the various Writings I have published on this subject. Here, now, are the conclusions I have drawn from them.

* I have noticed that at present a great many petty maxims hold sway in the world which seduce simple minds with a sham semblance of philosophy and are, besides, very handy for cutting off discussions in an authoritative and peremptory tone without having to consider the issue. One of them is: "Men are everywhere subject to the same passions; everywhere vanity and interest guide them; hence they are everywhere the same." When Geometricians make an assumption which, argument by argument, leads them to an absurd conclusion, they retrace their steps, and so prove the assumption false. The same method, applied to the maxim in question, would readily show its absurdity. But let us argue differently. A Savage is a man, and a European is a man. The half-philosopher immediately concludes that the one is no better than the other; but the philosopher says: in Europe the government, the laws, the customs, self-interest, everything places individuals under the necessity of deceiving one another, and of doing so incessantly; everything conspires to make vice a duty for them; they have to be wicked if they are to be wise, since there is no greater folly than to provide for the happiness of scoundrels at the expense of one's own. Among Savages self-interest speaks as insistently as it does among us, but it does not say the same things: love of society and care for their *[970]* common defense are the only bonds that unite them: the word *property*, that causes so many crimes among our honest folk, is, for them, almost devoid of meaning; discussions about a clash of interests simply do not arise among them; nothing leads them to deceive one another; public esteem is the only good to which everyone aspires and which they all deserve. It is perfectly possible that a Savage might commit a bad deed, but it is not possible that he will acquire the habit of doing evil, because to do so would profit him nothing. I believe that men's morals can be very accurately gauged by how much business they have with one another: the more dealings they have, the more they admire their talents and their industry, the more decorously and cunningly are they villains, and the more contemptible they are. I say it reluctantly: the good man is he who has no need to deceive anyone, and the Savage is that man.

> He is not moved by the people's fasces, nor by the King's purple,
> Nor by the discord that pits faithless brothers against one another;
> Nor by Rome's affairs, nor by kingdoms doomed to fall. Neither does he
> In his misery pity the poor, or envy the rich.

[32] Science is not suited to man in general. He forever goes astray in his quest for it; and if he sometimes does attain it, he almost always does so to his detriment. He is born to act and to think, not to reflect. Reflection only makes him unhappy without making him better or wiser: it causes him to regret past benefits and keeps him from enjoying the present: it shows him a happy future, so that his imagination might seduce and his desires torment him, and it shows him an unhappy future so that he might experience it ahead of time. Study corrupts his morals, affects his health, ruins his temperament, and often spoils his reason: even if it did teach him something, I would find that a rather poor compensation.

[33] I acknowledge that there are a few sublime geniuses capable of piercing the veils in which the truth wraps itself, a few privileged souls able to withstand the folly of vanity, base jealousy, and the other passions to which a taste for letters gives rise. The small number of those who have the good fortune of combining these qualities are the beacon and the honor of mankind; only they should properly engage in study for the good of all *[971]*, and this very exception confirms the rule; for if all men were Socrates, science would not harm them, but neither would they need it.

[34] Any people that has morals, and hence is respectful of its laws and free of any desire to improve on its traditional ways, must carefully guard against the sciences, and above all against men of science and learning whose sententious and dogmatic maxims would soon teach it to despise its ways and laws; which is something a nation can never do without being corrupted. The slightest change in customs, even if it is in some respects advantageous, invariably proves prejudicial to morals. For customs are the morality of the people; and as soon as it ceases to respect them, it is left with no rule but its passions, and no curb but the laws, which can sometimes keep the wicked in check, but can never make them good. Besides, once philosophy has taught the people to despise its customs, it soon learns to circumvent its laws. I therefore say that a people's morals are like a man's honor; they are a treasure to be preserved but

which, once lost, cannot be recovered.*

[35] But once a people is to a certain extent corrupted, should the sciences—regardless of whether they did or did not contribute to its corruption—be banished, or the people be shielded from them, either in order to improve it, or to keep it from becoming worse? This is another question about which I positively declared for the negative. For, in the first place, since *[972]* a vicious people never returns to virtue, the problem is not how to make good those who no longer are so, but how to keep good those who are fortunate enough to be so. In the second place, the same causes that have corrupted peoples, sometimes help prevent a greater corruption; thus, a man who has ruined his temperament by an injudicious use of medicines, is forced to continue to rely on doctors in order to stay alive; and that is how the arts and sciences, after fostering the vices, become necessary in order to keep them from turning into crimes; they at least coat them with a varnish which prevents the poison from being exuded quite so freely. They destroy virtue, but preserve its public semblance,** and that is at least a fine thing to do. They introduce politeness and propriety in its stead, and for the fear of appearing wicked they substitute the fear of appearing ridiculous.

* I find in history a single, but a striking example that seems to contradict this maxim: the founding of Rome by a troop of bandits whose descendants within a few generations became the most virtuous people that ever was. I would have no difficulty explaining this fact if this were the place to do so; but I will leave it at pointing out that the founders of Rome were not so much men whose morals were corrupt as men whose morals had not yet been formed: they did not despise virtue, rather, they did not yet know it; for the words *virtues* and *vices* are collective notions which arise only in the intercourse between men. Besides, the example of Rome lends no support to the case for the sciences: for the two first Kings of Rome, who gave the Republic form and instituted its customs and morals, were concerned, the one with nothing but wars, the other with nothing but sacred rites; the two things in the world that are at the farthest remove from philosophy.
** This semblance consists in a certain gentleness of morals which sometimes makes up for their lack of purity, a certain appearance of order which averts frightful confusion, a certain admiration for fine things which prevents good things from being entirely forgotten. Vice here puts on the mask of virtue not as hypocrisy does, in order to deceive and to betray, but rather in order to escape, behind this pleasing and sacred effigy, its horror at itself when it sees itself naked.

[36] My opinion, as I have already said more than once, therefore is to keep and even carefully to support Academies, Colleges, Universities, Libraries, Spectacles and all the other amusements that might to some extent distract men's wickedness, and prevent them from spending their idleness in more dangerous pursuits. For in a land where honest folk and good morals no longer count, it would still be preferable to live among scoundrels than among bandits.

[37] Now I ask, where is the contradiction, when I cultivate tastes the progress of which I approve? It is no longer a matter of getting people to do good, but only of distracting them from doing evil; they have to be kept busy with trifles to keep them from evil deeds; they have to be entertained rather than sermonized. If my Writings have edified the few good [people], then I have done them all the good it was in my power to do, and perhaps it is further useful to them to have the other people provided with objects that distract and *[973]* keep them from thinking about them. I would count myself most happy to have a Play a day hissed, if at that price I could keep the evil intentions of but a single one of its Spectators in check for two hours, and save the honor of his friend's daughter or wife, the secret of those who have confided in him, or the fortune of his creditor. When morals are no more, one has to think exclusively in terms of the polity; and it is well enough known that Music and Theater are among its most important concerns.

[38] If my justification leaves some difficulties unresolved, I frankly dare say that it does so not with regard to the public or to my adversaries, but with regard to myself alone: for only by examining myself can I decide whether I belong among the few, and whether my soul can bear the burden of literary pursuits. I have sensed their danger more than once; I have more than once given them up with the intention of never taking them up again, and in renouncing their seductive charm, I sacrificed to my peace of heart the only pleasures that could still delight it. If in the weariness that overcomes me, if at the end of a difficult and painful life, I have dared to take them up again for a few more moments in order to relieve my suffering, I at least believe that I have not become so interested or involved

in them as to deserve on their account the just reproofs I have
leveled at men of letters.

[39] I needed a test in order to achieve full self-knowledge,
and I did not hesitate to perform that test. Once I knew how
my soul reacted to literary success, it remained for me to see
how it would react to setbacks. I now know, and I can openly
state the worst. My Play suffered the fate which it deserved and
which I anticipated; but except for its boring me, I left the
performance much more satisfied with myself, and with better
reason to be so, than if it had succeeded.

[40] I therefore advise those who are so eager to find things
to reproach me with, to be prepared to study my principles and
to observe my conduct more carefully before they tax them
with contradiction and incoherence. If they ever see that I start
currying the public's favor, or that it flatters my vanity to have
composed pretty songs, or that I blush to have written poor
Plays, or that I seek to undermine my rivals' fame, or that I
come to speak ill of the great [974] men of the age in order to
raise myself to their level by lowering them to mine, or that I
aspire to positions in Academies, or that I dance attendance on
the women who set the tone, or that I fawn on the foolishness
of the Great, or that, no longer wishing to live by the work of
my hands, I become contemptuous of the craft I have chosen
and strike out in quest of wealth, in a word if they notice that
the love of reputation causes me to forget the love of virtue, I
beg them to warn me, even publicly, and I promise instantly to
commit my Writings and my Books to the flames, and to concede
all the errors they may wish to reproach me with.

[41] In the meantime I shall write Books, compose Poems
and Music, if I have the talent, the time, the strength and the
will to do so: I shall continue to state openly the bad opinion
in which I hold letters and those who practice them,* and to

* I am amazed at how confused most men of letters have been in this affair.
When they saw the sciences and arts under attack, they took it personally,
whereas all of them could, without any self-contradiction, hold the same view
I do, that while these things have done society great harm, it is now essential
to use them against the harm they have done, as one does a medication or those
noxious insects that have to be crushed on their bite. In a word, there is not a

believe that I am not worth any the less for it. True, people may some day say: This avowed enemy of the sciences and arts nevertheless wrote and published Plays; and I admit that that discourse will be a most bitter satire, not on myself, but on my century.

---

single man of letters who, if his conduct can pass the test in the preceding paragraph, could not say on his own behalf what I say on mine; and it seems to me that an argument along these lines suits them particularly since, between us, they care very little about the sciences as long as they continue to cause scholars to be honored. They are like pagan priests, who valued religion only as long as it caused them to be respected.

PREFACE
of a Second Letter to BORDES

[1] Forced by renewed attacks to break the silence I had vowed in this drawn-out dispute, I do not scruple once again to take up the pen I had abandoned. If, in the judgment of the Wise, I can shed some new light on the important maxims I established, it does not matter to me that the Public grows bored with seeing the same question discussed for such a long time: for even if the responsibility for it were not the attackers', I am not inclined to sacrifice my enthusiasm for truth to a solicitude for my reputation, and I do not see why I should be so much afraid of boring Readers whom I am so little afraid of displeasing.

[2] I believe I have discovered great things, and have stated them with a frankness that is rather dangerous, and none of this is particularly praiseworthy; for my independence is all my courage, and long meditations have stood me in the stead of Genius. A solitary who enjoys living by himself, naturally acquires a taste for reflection, and a man who takes a lively interest in the happiness of others without being in need of them for his own, does not have to spare their false delicacy by telling them what is useful. As such a condition is exceptional and as I have the good fortune to find myself in it, I feel obliged to put it to use on behalf of the truth, and to state it without reservations whenever it will appear to me to bear on men's innocence or happiness. If it was a mistake on my part to pledge myself to silence when I should not have done so, I must not commit a greater mistake by stubbornly keeping my word in the face of my duty, and it is in order to remain faithful to my principles that I wish to give up my errors as soon as I notice them. *[104]*

[3] I will pick up the thread of my ideas, then, and continue to write as I always have, like an isolated Being who neither desires nor fears anything from anyone, who speaks to others for their sakes rather than for his own, like a man too fond of his brethren not to hate their vices, and who would like them to learn for once to see themselves as wicked as they are, so that they might at least wish to become as good as they could be.

[4] I know very well that the trouble I go to is useless, and my

exhortations do not give me the chimerical pleasure of hoping for men's reformation: I know that they will ridicule my person because I love them, and my maxims because they are useful to them: I know that they will be no less eager for Glory and money after I have convinced them that these two passions are the sources of all their ills, and that they are wicked because of the one and miserable because of the other: I am sure that they will tax as folly my scorn for these objects of their admiration and labors: But I would rather be the butt of their ridicule than a party to their errors, and regardless of what their duties may be, mine is to tell them the truth or what I take to be the truth; a more powerful voice will have to make them love it.

[5] I have quietly borne the abuse from a host of authors to whom I have never done any other harm than to exhort them to be good men. They have had their amusement at my expense unhindered; they have made me out as ridiculous as they pleased; they have publicly lashed out at my writings and even at my person without my ever having been tempted to repulse their excesses otherwise than by my conduct. If I had deserved them, then the only way I could have taken my revenge would have been to try to reply in kind, whereas I am so far from enjoying this hateful war that the more truths I would have found to tell them, the more it would have saddened my heart. If I do not deserve their insults, then they have leveled them exclusively at themselves: Perhaps their rancor will not even have the effect on the Public which they had hoped for and which does not in the least concern me; extreme passion is often inept and alerts one to be mistrustful of it. Perhaps their own writings shall cause the public to judge me better than I in fact am, [especially] once it realizes that for all their eagerness to blacken me, the greatest crime they could find to *[105]* hold against me is that I let a famous artist paint my portrait.

[6] I find it much more difficult to maintain the same Equanimity toward those who leave my person out of account, and more or less adroitly attack the truths I have established. This sad and great System, the product of a sincere study of man's nature, of his faculties and of his destination, is dear to me in spite of the fact that it humbles me; for I am sensible to how important it is that pride not deceive us regarding what ought

to make for our genuine greatness, and how much it is to be feared that by dint of trying to raise ourselves above our nature, we may relapse beneath it. In any case it is useful for men, if not to know the truth, at least not to be in error, and it is an error, the most dangerous of all, to fear error less than ignorance and to prefer, when forced to choose, to be vicious and miserable than poor and crude.

[7] My sentiment has been hotly contested by a host of Writers, as I had anticipated that it would be; up to now I have replied to all those who seemed to me worth the trouble, and I am determined to do the same in the future, not for the sake of my own glory, for it is not J. J. Rousseau I wish to defend; he must have erred frequently: whenever he will seem to me to do so I will abandon him without scruple and without sorrow, even if he should be in the right, provided only his person is at issue. So that as long as I am only reproached with having published bad books, or reasoning badly, or committing mistakes of usage, or historical errors, or writing badly, or being ill-humored, I will not greatly mind all these criticisms, I will not be surprised by them, and I will never reply to them. But as for the System I upheld, I will defend it with all my strength as long as I remain convinced that it is the system of truth and of virtue, and that because they ill-advisedly abandoned it, most men have degenerated from their primitive goodness, [and] lapsed into all the errors that blind and all the miseries that oppress them.

[8] With so many interests to combat, so many prejudices to overcome, and so many harsh things to proclaim, I thought that in my Readers' own interest I should as it were make some allowance *[106]* for their pusillanimity and only successively let them perceive what I had to tell them. If the mere Dijon *Discourse* aroused so much grumbling and caused such scandal, what would have happened if I had, from the first, unfolded the full extent of a true but distressing System, of which the question dealt with in that *Discourse* is but a Corollary? I, who am the declared enemy of the violence of the wicked, would, at the very least, have been taken for an enemy of the public peace, and if the zealots of the opposing party had not charitably labored for the greater glory of philosophy to ruin me, but had set out to do so to an unknown, they would without a doubt

easily have succeeded in making both the work and the author appear ridiculous; and if they had begun by making fun of my System, that so frequently used method would have spared them the troublesome effort of examining my proofs.

[9] Hence I had to take some precautions at first, and I did not want to say everything in order to make sure that everything got a hearing. I unfolded my ideas only successively and always to only a small number of Readers. I spared not myself, but the truth, in order to have it pass more readily, and make it more useful. Often I went to great trouble to try and condense into a single Sentence, a single line, a single word tossed off as if by chance, the result of a long chain of reflections. The majority of my Readers must often have found my discourses poorly structured and almost entirely disjointed for want of perceiving the trunk of which I only showed them the branches. But that was enough for those capable of understanding, and I never wanted to speak to the others.

[10] This method put me in a position of frequently having to reply to my adversaries, either in order to meet objections, or to expand and elucidate ideas that required it, or to unfold fully all the parts of my System in proportion as the approbation of the Wise secured me the attention of the public. I did, it is true, believe I had attended to all these matters adequately with my earlier replies, at least in so far as the Readers I had in mind were concerned: But as I see from the Lyon Academician's second *Discourse* that he has still not understood me, I prefer to accuse myself of ineptness *[107]* than him of a lack of goodwill. I will therefore try to state my position better, and since the time has come to speak openly, I will overcome my distaste and for once write for the People.

[11] The work I propose to examine is full of agreeable sophisms, more sparkling than subtle, and which, because they seduce with a certain vividness of style as well as with the ruses of a cunning logic, are doubly dangerous to the multitude. I will proceed in this analysis in an utterly different way and, by following the Author's arguments step by step as accurately as I can, I will, in this discussion, rely solely on the directness and the zeal of a friend of the truth and of humanity, who seeks glory solely in honoring the one, and happiness solely in being useful to the other.

J.M. Moreau le J.ᵉ del.

N. De Launay Sculp

He returns to his equals. See p. 229.

DISCOURSE

on
THE ORIGIN
and the
FOUNDATIONS OF INEQUALITY
AMONG MEN

By
Jean Jacques Rousseau
Citizen of Geneva

*What is natural must be investigated not
in beings that are depraved, but in
those that are good according to nature.*
Aristot[le]. Politic[s] Bk. 2

AMSTERDAM
Marc Michel Rey

MDCCLV

A

LA REPUBLIQUE

DE GENÉVE.

MAGNIFIQUES, TRÈS HONORÉS,
ET SOUVERAINS SEIGNEURS,

TO
THE REPUBLIC
OF GENEVA
MAGNIFICENT, MOST HONORED,
AND SOVEREIGN LORDS,

[1] Convinced that only the virtuous Citizen may fittingly
present to his Fatherland honors it may acknowledge, I have for

118

thirty years been working to deserve to offer you some public homage; and this happy occasion partly making up for what my efforts have not been able to do, I believed that I might here be permitted to heed the zeal which animates me more than right which should authorize me. Having had the good fortune to be born among you, how could I meditate about the equality nature established among men and the inequality they have instituted, without thinking about the deep wisdom with which both, happily combined in this State, contribute in the manner most closely approximating natural law and most favorable to society, to the preservation of public order, and to the happiness of individuals? In looking for the best maxims which good sense might dictate regarding the constitution of a government, I was so struck to see them all implemented in yours that, even if I had not been born within your walls, I would have believed myself unable to refrain from offering this picture of human society to the one People which seems to me to possess its greatest advantages and to have best forestalled its abuses.

[2] If I had had to choose my place of birth, I should have chosen a society of a size confined to the range of human faculties, that is to say to the possibility *[112]* of being well governed, and where, everyone being equal to his task, no one would have been compelled to commit to others the functions with which he was himself entrusted: a State where, since all individuals know one another, neither the shady stratagems of vice nor the modesty of virtue could have escaped the Public's gaze and judgment, and where this gentle habit of seeing and knowing one another would have made the love of one's Fatherland a love of the Citizens rather than of the soil.

[3] I should have wished to be born in a country where the Sovereign and the people could have had only one and the same interest, so that all the motions of the machine might always tend only to the common happiness; since that is impossible unless the People and the Sovereign are the same person, it follows that I should have wished to be born under a democratic government wisely tempered.

[4] I should have wished to live and die free, that is to say so far subject to the laws that neither I nor anyone else could

shake off their honorable yoke; the salutary and gentle yoke
which the proudest heads bear with all the more docility as
they are made to bear none other.

[5] I should have wished, then, that no one inside the State
could have declared himself to be above the law, and No one
outside it could have imposed any [law] which it was obliged
to recognize. For regardless of how a government is constituted,
if there is a single person in it who is not subject to the law, all
the others are necessarily at his discretion (I)*; and if there is
one national Chief, and another foreign Chief, then regardless
of the division of authority they may establish, it is impossible
that both be obeyed well and the State well governed.

[6] I should not have wished to live in a newly established
Republic, regardless of how good its laws might be, for fear
that, if the government were perhaps constituted differently than
it should have been under the circumstances, either by being
ill-suited to the new Citizens or by the Citizens' being ill-suited
to the new government, the State might be liable to be upset
and destroyed almost from birth. For freedom is like the solid
and hearty foods or the full-bodied wines fit to sustain and
strengthen the robust temperaments used to them, but *[113]*
which overwhelm, ruin and intoxicate weak and delicate ones
that are not up to them. Once Peoples are accustomed to
Masters, they can no longer do without them. If they attempt to
shake off the yoke, they move all the farther away from freedom
because, as they mistake unbridled license for freedom, which
is its very opposite, their revolutions almost always deliver them
up to seducers who only increase their chains. Even the Roman
People, that model of all free Peoples, could not govern itself
on emerging from the Tarquins' oppression. Degraded by the
slavery and the ignominious labors which the Tarquins had
imposed upon it, it was at first but a stupid Populace that had
to be handled with care and governed with the utmost wisdom;
so that these souls, enervated, or rather numbed under the
tyranny, as they little by little grew accustomed to breathe the
salutary air of freedom, might gradually acquire that severity of

* [Rousseau's notes, numbered (I) through (XIX), begin on p. 200.]

morals and that proud courage which eventually made of them the most respectable of all Peoples. I should, then, have sought out as my Fatherland a happy and quiet Republic of an antiquity that lost itself, as it were, in the night of the ages; which had been subject only to such attacks as are apt to stimulate and to strengthen its inhabitants' courage and love of Fatherland, and whose Citizens, accustomed by long experience to a wise independence, not only were free, but were worthy of being so.

[7] I should have wished to choose a Fatherland diverted from the ferocious love of Conquest by a fortunate powerlessness, and protected against the fear of itself becoming the Conquest of some other State by an even more fortunate location: A free City, situated amidst a number of Peoples of which none had any interest in invading it, but each had an interest in preventing the others from invading it: In a word, a Republic which did not tempt the ambition of its neighbors, and might reasonably count on their help in case of need. It follows that, being so fortunately located, it would have had nothing to fear but from itself alone; and that if its Citizens had military training, it would have been more in order to keep alive in them that martial spirit and proud courage which so becomes freedom and maintains the taste for it, than from the necessity to provide for their own defense.

[8] I should have sought out a Country where the right of legislation *[114]* was common to all Citizens; for who could know better than they, the conditions under which it suits them to live together in one society? But I should not have approved of Plebiscites like those of the Romans, where the Chiefs of the State and those most interested in its preservation were excluded from the deliberations on which its security often depended, and where, by an absurd inconsistency, the Magistrates were deprived of rights enjoyed by ordinary Citizens.

[9] On the contrary, I should have wished, in order to forestall the self-seeking and ill-conceived projects and the dangerous innovations which finally ruined the Athenians, that not everyone have the power to propose new Laws according to his fancy; that this right belong to the Magistrates alone; that they even exercise it so circumspectly, that the People, for their part, be

so guarded in granting their consent to these Laws, and that their promulgation require so much solemnity that, before the constitution could be disturbed, everyone had had the time to realize that it is above all the great antiquity of the Laws that renders them holy and venerable, that the People soon scorn those they see change every day, and that by growing used to neglecting ancient ways on the pretext of doing better, great evils are often introduced to correct lesser ones.

[10] I should above all have fled as necessarily ill-governed, a Republic where the People, believing that they could do without their Magistrates or allow them no more than a precarious authority, had imprudently retained in their own hands the administration of Civil affairs and the execution of their own Laws; such must have been the rude constitution of the first governments arising immediately from the state of Nature, and it still was one of the Vices that ruined the Republic of Athens.

[11] Rather, I should have chosen one where private persons, content to ratify the Laws and decide the most important public business in a Body and on the recommendation of the Chiefs, established respected tribunals, carefully distinguished their several departments, yearly elected the most capable and the most upright among their Fellow-Citizens to administer Justice and to govern the State; and where the Virtue of the Magistrates thus bearing witness to the wisdom of the People, *[115]* each would do the other honor. So that if ever fatal misunderstandings arose to disturb the public harmony, even those times of blindness and errors might be marked by evidences of moderation, mutual esteem, and a shared respect for the Laws; harbingers and guarantees of a sincere and everlasting reconciliation.

[12] Such, MAGNIFICENT, MOST HONORED AND SOVEREIGN LORDS, are the advantages I should have sought in the Fatherland I would have chosen. If, to these, providence had added a lovely location, a temperate Climate, a fertile soil, and the most delightful vistas under Heaven, I should only have wished, in order to complete my happiness, to enjoy all of these goods in the bosom of this happy Fatherland, living peacefully in the sweet society of my Fellow-Citizens, practicing toward them,

and at their example, humanity, friendship, and all the virtues, and leaving behind the honorable memory of a good man and an honest and virtuous Patriot.

[13] If, less happy or too late grown wise, I saw myself reduced to ending a lame and languishing career in other Climes, bootlessly regretting the quiet and the Peace of which a youthful want of prudence would have deprived me, I would at least have nurtured in my soul the very same sentiments, though I could not use them in my country, and imbued with tender and selfless affection for my distant Fellow-Citizens, I would from the bottom of my heart have addressed to them approximately the following discourse.

[14] My dear Fellow-Citizens, or rather, my brothers, since ties of blood as well as the Laws unite almost all of us, it pleases me that I cannot think of you without at the same time thinking of all the goods you enjoy and of which perhaps none of you feels the value better than I, who have lost them. The more I reflect on your Political and Civil situation, the less can I imagine that the nature of human things could admit of a better. In all other Governments, when it is a question of providing for the greatest good of the State, everything always remains [at the stage of] ideas for projects, and at most [of] simple possibilities. Whereas for you, your happiness is complete, you have only to enjoy it; and all you need in order to become perfectly happy is [116] to know how to be content with being so. Your Sovereignty, acquired or recovered at sword's point, and maintained for two centuries by dint of valor and wisdom, is at last fully and universally recognized. Honorable Treaties fix your boundaries, insure your rights, and confirm your security. Your constitution is excellent, dictated by the most sublime reason and guaranteed by friendly and respectable Powers; your State enjoys tranquility, you have neither wars nor conquerors to fear; you have no other masters than wise laws, made by yourselves, administered by upright Magistrates of your own choosing; you are neither so rich as to become enervated by softness and lose the taste for true happiness and solid virtues in vain delights, nor so poor as to need more foreign assistance than your industry

provides; and it costs you almost nothing to preserve the precious freedom which great Nations can maintain only by means of exorbitant Taxes.

[15] May a Republic so wisely and so happily constituted last forever, both for its Citizens' happiness, and as an example to all Peoples! That is the only wish it remains for you to make, and the only care it remains for you to take. Henceforth it is up to yourselves alone not, indeed, to provide for your happiness, your Ancestors have spared you that trouble, but to make it long-lasting by the wisdom of using it well. Your preservation depends on your everlasting union, your obedience to the laws, your respect for their Ministers. If there remains among you the least germ of bitterness or of mistrust, hasten to destroy it as a fatal leaven which would sooner or later bring about your miseries and the State's ruin: I implore all of you to return to the depths of your Heart and consult the secret voice of your conscience. Does anyone of you know anywhere in the universe a more upright, more enlightened, or more respectable Body than your Magistrature? Do not all of its members offer you an example of moderation, of simplicity of morals, of respect for the laws, and of the most sincere reconciliation: then grant without reservations to these wise Chiefs the salutary confidence which reason owes to virtue; remember that you have chosen them, that they justify your choice, and that the honors owed to those whom you have [117] made dignitaries, necessarily redound upon yourselves. None of you is so unenlightened as not to know that where the laws lose their vigor and its defenders their authority, there can be neither security nor freedom for anyone. What else, then, is at issue between you, than that you wholeheartedly and with justified confidence do what you would in any event have to do out of true interest, duty, and reason? May a guilty and fatal indifference to the preservation of the constitution never cause you to neglect in case of need the wise opinions of the most enlightened and zealous among you: Rather, may equity, moderation, and the most respectful firmness continue to regulate all your undertakings and through you exhibit to the entire universe the example of a proud and modest People as jealous of its glory as of its

freedom. Above all, and this will be my last Advice, beware of ever heeding sinister interpretations and venomous discourses, the secret motives of which are often more dangerous than are the actions they are about. An entire household is awake and on the lookout at the first calls of a good and loyal Guardian who barks only when Thieves draw near; but people hate the importunity of those noisy animals that continually disturb the public repose, and their constant and misplaced warnings are not even heeded at the moment when they are needed.

[16] And you, MAGNIFICENT AND MOST HONORED LORDS, you worthy and respectable Magistrates of a free People; allow me to offer my homage and respects to you in particular. If there is in the world a rank suited to confer distinction on those who occupy it, it is without a doubt the rank bestowed by talents and virtue, the rank of which you have proved yourselves worthy, and to which your Fellow-Citizens have raised you. Their own merit adds further luster to yours, and I find that for having been chosen to govern them by men capable of governing others, you are as much superior to all other Magistrates as a free People, and particularly the free people you have the honor of leading, is, by its enlightenment and reason, superior to the populace of other States.

[17] May I be allowed to cite an example of which there should be better records, and which will always be present to my Heart. I never recall without the *[118]* sweetest emotion the memory of the virtuous Citizen to whom I owe my life, and who often in my childhood impressed on me the respect due you. I see him still, living from the work of his hands and sustaining his soul with the most sublime Truths. I see Tacitus, Plutarch, and Grotius before him amidst the tools of his trade. I see at his side a beloved son receiving with too little profit the tender teachings of the best of Fathers. But if the excesses of a foolish youth caused me to forget such wise lessons for a time, I have the happiness of at last experiencing that, whatever may be one's inclination to vice, an education in which the heart has a share is unlikely to be lost forever.

[18] Such are, MAGNIFICENT AND MOST HONORED LORDS, the Citizens and even the mere residents born in the State you

govern; such are the educated and sensible men about whom, under the name of Workers and the People, they have such low and false ideas in other Nations. My Father, I gladly admit it, was not outstanding among his fellow-citizens; he was but what they all are, and such as he was, there is no Country where his society would not have been sought after, cultivated, and even profitably so, by the most honest people. It is not for me, and thank Heaven it is not necessary, to tell you how much regard men of such mettle can expect from you, your equals by education as well as by the rights of nature and of birth; your inferiors by their own will, by the preference which they owe to your merit, which they have granted to it, and for which you, in turn, owe them a kind of gratitude. I learn with lively satisfaction how much you, in your dealings with them, temper the gravity behooving the ministers of the Laws with gentleness and condescension, how much you reciprocate in esteem and attentions what they owe you by way of obedience and respect; such conduct full of justice and of wisdom is apt to put increasingly far behind the memory of the unhappy events which must be forgotten if they are never to recur: such conduct is all the more judicious as this equitable and generous People makes a pleasure of its duty, as it naturally loves to honor you, and as those who are most intent on upholding their rights are the ones who are most inclined to respect yours. *[119]*

[19] It should not be surprising that the Chiefs of a Civil Society love its glory and happiness, but it is altogether too surprising for men's peace of mind that those who look upon themselves as the Magistrates, or rather as the masters of a Fatherland more holy and more sublime, should exhibit any love for the earthly Fatherland that sustains them. How pleased I am to be able to make such a rare exception in our favor, and to rank among our best Citizens those zealous trustees of the sacred dogmas authorized by the laws, those venerable Pastors of souls whose lively and sweet eloquence carries the maxims of the Gospel into men's Hearts all the more effectively as they themselves are always the first to practice them! Everybody knows how successfully the great art of the Pulpit is cultivated in Geneva; But as they are too accustomed to see things said

one way and done another, few People know to what an extent the spirit of Christianity, holiness of morals, severity toward oneself and gentleness toward others, prevail in the Body of our Ministers. Perhaps it falls to the City of Geneva alone to provide the edifying example of such a perfect union between a Society of Theologians and of Men of Letters. It is in large measure on their acknowledged wisdom and moderation, it is on their zeal for the State's prosperity that I base the hope for its eternal tranquility; and I note with a mixture of pleasure, surprise, and respect, how much they abhor the frightful maxims of those holy and barbarous men of whom History provides more than one example and who, in order to uphold the supposed rights of God, that is to say their own interests, were all the less sparing of human blood as they flattered themselves that their own would always be respected.

[20] Could I forget that precious half of the Republic which causes the other's happiness, and whose gentleness and wisdom preserve its peace and good morals in it? Amiable and virtuous Citizen-women, it will always be the lot of your sex to govern ours. How fortunate when your chaste power, exercised in conjugal union alone, makes itself felt solely for the State's glory and the public happiness: That is how women commanded in Sparta, and that is how you deserve to command in Geneva. What man would be so barbarous *[120]* as to resist the voice of honor and reason from the mouth of a tender wife; and who would not despise vain luxury upon seeing your simple and modest attire which, by the radiance it owes to you, seems to complement beauty most? It is up to you, by your amiable and innocent dominion and your winning wit, always to preserve the love of the laws in the State and Concord among the Citizens; by happy marriages to reunite divided families; and above all, by the persuasive gentleness of your lessons and the modest graces of your conversation, to correct the misconceptions which our young Men acquire in other countries from which, instead of the many useful things that could profit them, they only bring back, together with a childish tone and ridiculous airs adopted among lost women, an admiration for I know not what presumed grandeurs, the frivolous compensations for ser-

vitude which will never match the value of noble freedom. Therefore always be what you are, the chaste guardians of morals and the gentle bonds of peace, and continue at every opportunity to assert the rights of the Heart and of Nature on behalf of duty and of virtue.

[21] I flatter myself that, in the event, I shall not be proven wrong when I base the hope for the Citizens' common happiness and the Republic's glory on such guarantors. I admit that, for all of these advantages, it will not glitter with the brilliance by which most eyes are dazzled, and the childish and fatal taste for which is the deadliest enemy of happiness and of freedom. Let dissolute youths go elsewhere in search of easy pleasures and lasting remorse. Let supposed men of taste admire elsewhere the grandeur of Palaces, the beauty of carriages, the sumptuous furnishings, the pomp of spectacles, and all the refinements of softness and luxury. In Geneva will be found only men, yet such a spectacle has its own value, and those who will seek it out will certainly be worth as much as those who admire the rest.

[22] Deign, MAGNIFICENT, MOST HONORED AND SOVER-EIGN LORDS, to accept, all of you with equal goodness, the respectful testimonies of the interest I take in your common prosperity. If, in this lively outpouring of my Heart, I were so unfortunate as to be guilty of some indiscreet transport, I beseech you to pardon it as due to the tender affection of a [121] true Patriot, and the ardent and legitimate zeal of a man who envisages no greater happiness for himself than that of seeing all of you happy.

I am with the deepest respect

MAGNIFICENT, MOST HONORED

AND SOVEREIGN LORDS

Your most humble and most obedient
servant and Fellow-Citizen

JEAN JACQUES ROUSSEAU

At Chamberi, June 12, 1754

PREFACE

[1] The most useful and the least advanced of all human knowledge seems to me to be that of man (II); and I dare say that the inscription on the Temple at Delphi alone, contained a more important and more difficult Precept than all the big Books of the Moralists. I therefore consider the subject of this Discourse to be one of the most interesting questions Philosophy might raise and, unfortunately for us, one of the thorniest Philosophers might have to resolve: For how can the source of inequality among men be known without first knowing men themselves? And how will man ever succeed in seeing himself as Nature formed him, through all the changes which the succession of times and of things must have wrought in his original constitution, and to disentangle what he owes to his own stock from what circumstances and his progress have added to or changed in his primitive state? Like the statue of Glaucus which time, sea, and storms had so disfigured that it less resembled a God than a ferocious Beast, the human soul, altered in the lap of society by a thousand forever recurring causes, by the acquisition of a mass of knowledge and errors, by the changes that have taken place in the constitution of Bodies, and by the continual impact of the passions, has, so to speak, changed in appearance to the point of being almost unrecognizable; and instead of a being always acting on certain and unvarying Principles, instead of the Celestial and majestic simplicity with which it had been endowed by its Author, all one still finds is the disfiguring contrast of passion that believes it reasons and the understanding that hallucinates.

[2] What is more cruel still is that, since every progress of the human Species removes it ever farther from *[123]* its primitive state, the more new knowledge we accumulate the more we deprive ourselves of the means of acquiring the most important knowledge of all, and that, in a sense, it is by dint of studying man that we have made it impossible for us to know him.

[3] It is easy to see that it is in these successive changes of
man's constitution that one must seek the first origin of the
differences that distinguish men who, by common consent, are
naturally as equal among themselves as were the animals of
every species before various Physical causes introduced in some
species the varieties which we observe among them. Indeed, it
is not conceivable that these first changes, however they may
have come about, altered all the Individuals of the species at
once and in the same way; rather, while some were perfected
or deteriorated and acquired various good or bad qualities which
were not inherent in their Nature, the others remained in their
original state for a longer time; and such was, among men, the
first source of inequality, which it is easier to establish thus in
general, than it is to assign its genuine causes with precision.

[4] Let my Readers therefore not imagine that I dare flatter
myself with having seen what seems to me so difficult to see. I
have initiated some arguments; I have hazarded some conjectures,
less in the hope of resolving the question than with the intention
of elucidating it and reducing it to its true state. Others will
easily be able to go farther along the same road, though it will
not be easy for anyone to reach the end. For it is no light
undertaking to disentangle what is original from what is artificial
in man's present Nature, and to know accurately a state which
no longer exists, which perhaps never did exist, which probably
never will exist, and about which it is nevertheless necessary to
have exact Notions in order accurately to judge of our present
state. Whoever might undertake to ascertain exactly the precautions required to make solid observations on this subject would
need even more Philosophy than might be thought; and a good
solution of the following Problem does not seem to me unworthy
of the Aristotles and the Plinys of our century: *What experiments
would be needed in order to come [124] to know natural
man; and by what means can these experiments be performed
within society?* Far from undertaking to solve this Problem, I
believe that I have meditated upon the Subject sufficiently to
dare answer in advance that the greatest Philosophers will not
be too good to direct these experiments, nor the most powerful
sovereigns to perform them; a collaboration which it is scarcely

reasonable to expect, especially in conjunction with the sustained or rather the successive enlightenment and goodwill needed by both parties in order to succeed.

[5] Yet these investigations, so difficult to carry out and to which so little thought has been devoted until now, are the only means left us by which to remove a host of difficulties that deprive us of the knowledge of the real foundations of human society. It is this ignorance of the nature of man that casts such uncertainty and obscurity on the true definition of natural right: for the idea of right, says Mr. Burlamaqui, and still more that of natural right, are manifestly ideas relative to the Nature of man. Hence it is from this very Nature of man, he goes on, from his constitution and his state, that the principles of this science must be deduced.

[6] It is not without surprise and scandal that one observes how little agreement prevails about this important matter among the various Authors who have dealt with it. Among the most serious Writers, scarcely two can be found who are of the same opinion on this point. To say nothing of the Ancient Philosophers, who seem deliberately to have set out to contradict one another on the most fundamental principles, the Roman Jurists indiscriminately subject man and all other animals to the same natural Law, because they consider under that name the Law which Nature imposes upon itself rather than that which it prescribes; or rather, because of the particular sense in which these Jurists understand the word Law, which they seem on this occasion to have taken only for the expression of the general relations established by nature among all animate beings for their common preservation. The Moderns, since they allow the name of Law only for a rule prescribed to a moral being, that is to say to a being that is intelligent, free, and considered in its relations with other beings, restrict the province of natural Law to the only animal endowed with reason, that is to say to man; [125] but while each one of them defines this Law in his own fashion, all of them base it on such metaphysical principles that, even among us, there are very few people capable of understanding these principles, let alone capable of discovering them on their own. So that all the definitions by these learned men, which in

every other respect constantly contradict one another, agree only in this, that it is impossible to understand the Law of Nature, and hence to obey it, without being a very great reasoner and a profound Metaphysician. Which precisely means that in order to establish society men must have employed an enlightenment which develops only with much difficulty and among very few people within society itself.

[7] Knowing Nature so little, and agreeing so poorly about the meaning of the word *Law,* it would be most difficult to agree on a good definition of natural Law. Indeed, all those that are found in Books, besides not being uniform, have the further defect of being derived from a range of Knowledge which men do not naturally have, and from advantages the idea of which they can conceive of only once they have left the state of Nature. One begins by looking for the rules on which it would be appropriate for men to agree among themselves for the sake of the common utility; and then gives the name natural Law to the collection of these rules, with no further proof than the good which, in one's view, would result from universal compliance with them. That is certainly a very convenient way of framing definitions and of explaining the nature of things by almost arbitrary appropriatenesses.

[8] But as long as we do not know natural man we shall in vain try to ascertain either the Law he has received or that which best suits his condition. All we can very clearly see about this Law is that not only, for it to be law, the will of him whom it obligates must be able to submit to it knowingly; but also, for it to be natural, it must speak immediately with the voice of Nature.

[9] Hence, disregarding all the scientific books that only teach us to see men as they have made themselves, and meditating on the first and simplest operations of the human Soul, I believe I perceive in it two *[126]* principles prior to reason, of which one interests us intensely in our well-being and our self-preservation, and the other inspires in us a natural repugnance at seeing any sentient Being, and especially any being like ourselves, perish or suffer. It is from the association and combination which our mind is capable of making between these two Principles, without

it being necessary to introduce into it that of sociability, that all the rules of natural right seem to me to flow; rules which reason is subsequently forced to reestablish on different foundations when, by its successive developments, it has succeeded in smothering Nature.

[10] This way one is not obliged to make a Philosopher of man before making a man of him; his duties toward others are not dictated to him exclusively by the belated lessons of Wisdom; and as long as he does not resist the internal impulsion of commiseration, he will never harm another man or even any sentient being, except in the legitimate case when, his preservation being involved, he is obliged to give himself preference. By this means the ancient disputes about whether animals participate in the natural Law are also brought to an end: For it is clear that, since they are deprived of enlightenment and of freedom, they cannot recognize that Law; but since they in some measure partake in our nature through the sentience with which they are endowed, it will be judged that they must also participate in natural right, and that man is subject to some kind of duties toward them. Indeed, it would seem that if I am obliged not to harm another being like myself, it is less because that being is rational than because it is sentient; a quality which, since it is common to beast and man, must at least give the beast the right not to be uselessly maltreated by man.

[11] This same study of original man, of his true needs and of the fundamental principles of his duties is, moreover, the only effective means available to dispel the numerous difficulties surrounding the origin of moral inequality, the true foundations of the Body politic, the reciprocal rights of its members, and a thousand similar questions, as important as they are badly elucidated.

[12] Human society viewed with a calm [127] and disinterested gaze seems at first to exhibit only the violence of powerful men and the oppression of the weak; the mind rebels at the harshness of the first; one is inclined to deplore the blindness of the others; and since nothing is less stable among men than those external relationships that are more often the product of chance than of wisdom, and that are called weakness or power, wealth

or poverty, human establishments seem at first glance to be founded on piles of quicksand; it is only by examining them closely, only after setting aside the dust and sand that surround the Edifice, that one perceives the unshakable base on which it is raised, and learns to respect its foundations. Now, without the serious study of man, of his natural faculties and their successive developments, one will never succeed in drawing these distinctions and in separating what, in the present constitution of things, divine will has done, from what human art has pretended to do. The Political and moral investigations occasioned by the important question I am examining are, therefore, in every way useful, and the hypothetical history of governments is in all respects an instructive lesson for man. By considering what we would have become if we had been abandoned to ourselves, we must learn to bless him whose beneficent hand, correcting our institutions and grounding them unshakably, forestalled the disorders that have resulted from them, and caused our happiness to be born from the very means that seemed bound to complete our misery.

Learn what the God ordered you to be,
And what your place is in the human world.

A NOTE ABOUT THE NOTES

I have added some notes to this work after my lazy practice of working in fits and starts. These notes sometimes stray so wide of the subject that they are not good to read together with the text. I therefore cast them to the end of the Discourse, in which I tried my best to follow the straightest road. Those who will have the courage to start over again can amuse themselves the second time with beating the bushes and trying to go through the notes; there will be no harm in the others' not reading them at all.

QUESTION
Proposed by the Academy of Dijon

What is the origin of inequality among
men, and whether it is authorized
by the natural Law

DISCOURSE

ON THE ORIGIN
AND THE
FOUNDATIONS OF INEQUALITY
· AMONG MEN

[1] It is of man that I am to speak, and the question I examine tells me that I shall be speaking to men, for one does not propose such questions if one is afraid of honoring the truth. I shall therefore confidently uphold the cause of humanity before the wise men who invite me to do so, and I shall not be dissatisfied with myself if I prove worthy of my subject and my judges.

[2] I conceive of two sorts of inequality in the human Species: one, which I call natural or Physical, because it is established by Nature, and which consists in differences of age, health, strengths of Body, and qualities of Mind or of Soul; the other, which may be called moral, or political inequality because it depends on a sort of convention and is established, or at least authorized by Men's consent. It consists in the different Privileges which some enjoy to the prejudice of the others, such as to be more wealthy, more honored, more Powerful than they, or even to get themselves obeyed by them.

[3] It makes no sense to ask what the source of Natural inequality is, because the answer would be given by the simple definition of the word: Still less does it make sense to inquire whether there might not be some essential connection between the two inequalities; for that would be to ask in different terms whether those who command are necessarily better than those who obey, and whether individuals always possess strength of Body or of Mind, wisdom, or virtue, [*132*] in proportion to their Power or their Wealth: A question which it may perhaps be good for Slaves to debate within hearing of their Masters, but not befitting rational and free Men who seek the truth.

[4] What, precisely, then, is at issue in this Discourse? To mark, in the progress of things, the moment when, Right

138

replacing Violence, Nature was subjected to Law; to explain by what succession of wonders the strong could resolve to serve the weak, and the People to purchase the idea of repose at the price of real felicity.

[5] The Philosophers who have examined the foundations of society have all felt the necessity of going back as far as the state of Nature, but none of them has reached it. Some have not hesitated to ascribe to Man in that state the notion of the Just and the Unjust, without bothering to show that he had to have that notion, or even that it would have been useful to him; Others have spoken of everyone's Natural Right to keep what belongs to him, without explaining what they understood by belong; Others still, after first granting to the stronger authority over the weaker, had Government arise straightway, without giving thought to the time that must have elapsed before the language of authority and of government could have meaning among Men: Finally, all of them, continually speaking of need, greed, oppression, desires, and pride transferred to the state of Nature ideas they had taken from society; they spoke of Savage Man and depicted Civil man. It did not even enter the mind of most of our philosophers to doubt that the state of Nature had existed, whereas it is evident, from reading the Holy Scriptures, that the first Man, having received some lights and Precepts immediately from God, was not himself in that state, and that, if the Writings of Moses are granted the credence owed them by every Christian Philosopher, it has to be denied that, even before the Flood, Men were ever in the pure state of Nature, unless they by some extraordinary Occurrence relapsed into it: a Paradox most embarrassing to defend, and altogether impossible to prove.

[6] Let us therefore begin by setting aside all the facts, for they do not affect the question. *[133]* The Inquiries that may be pursued regarding this Subject ought not be taken for historical truths, but only for hypothetical and conditional reasonings; better suited to elucidate the Nature of things than to show their genuine origin, and comparable to those our Physicists daily make regarding the formation of the World. Religion commands us to believe that since God himself drew Men out

of the state of Nature immediately after the creation, they are unequal because he wanted them to be so; but it does not forbid us to frame conjectures based solely on the nature of man and of the Beings that surround him, about what Mankind might have become if it had remained abandoned to itself. That is what I am asked, and what I propose to examine in this Discourse. Since my subject concerns man in general, I shall try to speak in a language suited to all Nations, or rather, forgetting times and Places in order to think only about the Men to whom I speak, I shall suppose myself in the Lyceum of Athens, repeating the Lessons of my Masters, with such men as Plato and Xenocrates for Judges, and Mankind for an Audience.

[7] O Man, whatever Land you may be from, whatever may be your opinions, listen; Here is your history such as I believed I read it, not in the Books by your kind, who are liars, but in Nature, which never lies. Everything that will have come from it will be true: Nothing will be false but what I will unintentionally have introduced of my own. The times of which I will speak are very remote: How much you have changed from what you were! It is, so to speak, the life of your species that I will describe to you in terms of the qualities you received, which your education and your habits could deprave, but which they could not destroy. There is, I sense, an age at which the individual human being would want to stop; you will seek the age at which you would wish your Species had stopped. Discontent with your present state for reasons that herald even greater discontents for your unhappy Posterity, you might perhaps wish to be able to go back; And this sentiment must serve as the Praise of your first ancestors, the criticism of your contemporaries, and the dread of those who will have the misfortune to live after you.

[*134*]

PART I

[1] However important it may be, in order to judge soundly regarding Man's natural state, to consider him from his origin, and to examine him, so to speak, in the first Embryo of the species, I shall not follow the successive developments of his organization; I shall not pause to search in the animal System what he may have been at the beginning if he was eventually to become what he now is; I shall not examine whether, as Aristotle thinks, his elongated nails were at first hooked claws; whether he was as hairy as a bear, and whether, walking on all fours (III), his gaze directed to the Earth and confined to a horizon of but a few paces, determined both the character and the limits of his ideas. I could frame only vague and almost imaginary conjectures on this subject: Comparative Anatomy has as yet made too little progress, the observations of Naturalists are as yet too uncertain to permit establishing the basis of a solid argument on such foundations; so that without invoking the supernatural knowledge we have on this point, and without taking into account the changes that must have occurred in man's internal and the external conformation in proportion as he put his limbs to new uses and took up new foods, I shall assume that he was always conformed as I see him today, walking on two feet, using his hands as we do ours, directing his gaze over the whole of Nature, and with his eyes surveying the vast expanse of Heaven.

[2] By stripping the Being, so constituted, of all the supernatural gifts he may have received, and of all the artificial faculties he could only have acquired by prolonged progress; by considering him, in a word, such as he must have issued from the hands of Nature, I see an animal *[135]* less strong than some, less agile than others, but, all things considered, the most advantageously organized of all: I see him sating his hunger beneath an oak, slaking his thirst at the first Stream, finding his

bed at the foot of the same tree that supplied his meal, and
with that his needs are satisfied.

[3] The Earth, abandoned to its natural fertility (IV) and
covered by immense forests which no Axe ever mutilated, at
every step offers Storage and shelter to the animals of every
species. Men, dispersed among them, observe, imitate their
industry, and so raise themselves to the level of the Beasts'
instinct, with this advantage, that each species has but its own
instinct, while man, perhaps having none that belongs to him,
appropriates them all, feeds indifferently on most of the various
foods (V) which the other animals divide among themselves,
and as a result finds his subsistence more easily than can any
one of them.

[4] Accustomed from childhood to the inclemencies of the
weather and the rigor of the seasons, hardened to fatigue, and
forced to defend naked and unarmed their life and their Prey
against the other ferocious Beasts or to escape them by running,
Men develop a robust and almost unalterable temperament; the
Children, since they come into the world with their Fathers'
excellent constitution and strengthen it by the same activities
that produced it, acquire all the vigor of which the human
species is capable. Nature deals with them exactly as the Law
of Sparta did with the Children of Citizens; it makes those who
have a good constitution strong and robust, and causes all the
others to perish; differing, in this, from our societies, where the
State kills Children indiscriminately before their birth by making
them a burden to their Fathers.

[5] Since his body is the only tool which savage man knows,
he puts it to various uses of which our bodies are incapable for
want of practice; our industry deprives us of the strength and
the agility which necessity obliges him to acquire. If he had
had an axe, could he break such solid branches by hand? If
he had had a sling, would he throw a stone as hard by hand? If
he had had a Horse, would he run as fast? Give civilized man
[136] the time to gather all his machines around him, and he
will without a doubt easily overcome Savage man; but if you
want to see an even more unequal combat, have them confront
each other naked and unarmed, and you will soon recognize

the advantage of constantly having all one's strength at one's disposal, of being ever ready for every eventuality and of, so to speak, always carrying all of oneself along with one (VI).

[6] Hobbes contends that man is naturally intrepid, and seeks only to attack and to fight. An illustrious Philosopher thinks, on the contrary, and Cumberland and Pufendorf also maintain, that nothing is as timid as man in the state of Nature, and that he is forever trembling and ready to flee at the least noise that strikes him or the least movement he notices. That may be so with regard to objects he does not know, and I do not doubt that he is frightened by all new Sights that present themselves to him when he cannot tell whether to expect Physical good or evil from them, or when he cannot compare his strength with the dangers he runs; such circumstances are rare in the state of Nature where everything proceeds in such a uniform fashion, and where the face of the Earth is not subject to the sudden and constant changes caused by the passions and the inconstancy of Peoples assembled. But Savage man, living dispersed amongst the animals and early finding himself in the position of having to measure himself against them, soon makes the comparison and, feeling that he surpasses them in skill more than they do him in strength, learns to fear them no more. Set a bear or a wolf against a Savage who is sturdy, agile and courageous, as they all are, armed with stones and a good stick, and you will see that the danger will at the very least be mutual, and that after several such experiences, ferocious Beasts, disinclined as they are to attack one another, will not readily attack man, whom they will have found to be just as ferocious as themselves. As for the animals that really do have more strength than he has skill, he is in the same position with regard to them as are the other weaker species which none the less continue to subsist; with this advantage on man's side that, since he runs just as well as they and can find almost certain refuge in trees, he has the initiative in any encounter, as well as the choice of *[137]* fleeing or fighting. Let us add that it does not seem that any animal naturally wars against man except in the case of self-defense or of extreme hunger, or that any bears him those violent antipathies that seem to announce that one species is

destined by Nature to serve as food for another.

[7] These are undoubtedly the reasons why Negroes and Savages worry so little about the ferocious beasts they might meet up with in the woods. In this respect the Caribs of Venezuela, among others, live in the most profound security and without the slightest problem. Although they are almost naked, says François Corréal, they do not hesitate boldly to take their chances in the woods armed only with bow and arrow; yet nobody has ever heard of a single one of them being devoured by beasts.

[8] Other, more formidable, enemies against which man has not the same means of defense, are the natural infirmities, childhood, old age, and illnesses of every kind: melancholy signs of our weakness, of which the first two are common to all animals, and the last belongs primarily to man living in Society. As regards Childhood, I even note that, since the Mother carries her child with her everywhere, she can feed it much more readily than can the females of a number of animals, forced as they are to wear themselves out going back and forth, in one direction to find their food, in the other to suckle or feed their young. It is true that if the woman happens to perish, the child runs a considerable risk of perishing with her; but that danger is common to a hundred other species whose young are for a long time not in a condition to forage for themselves; and while Childhood lasts longer among us, life also does, so that everything remains more or less equal in this respect (VII); although there are other rules regarding the duration of the first period of life and the number of young (VIII) which do not pertain to my Subject. Among Old people, who act and perspire little, the need for food diminishes together with the capacity to provide it; and since Savage life keeps gout and rheumatism from them, and old age is of all ills that which human assistance can least alleviate, they eventually die without anyone's noticing that they cease to be, and almost without noticing it themselves. *[138]*

[9] Regarding illnesses, I shall not repeat the vain and false declamations against Medicine by most healthy people; but I shall ask whether there is any solid evidence to conclude that

in Countries where this art is most neglected the average life span is shorter than in those where it is cultivated with the greatest care; how could it be, if we inflict more ills on ourselves than Medicine can provide Remedies! The extreme inequality in ways of life, the excess of idleness among some, the excess of work among others, the ease with which our appetites and our sensuality are aroused and satisfied, the excessively exotic dishes of the rich which fill them with inflammatory humors and wrack them with indigestion, the bad food of the Poor which most of the time they do not even have and the want of which leads them greedily to overburden their stomachs when they get the chance, the late nights, the excesses of every kind, the immoderate transports of all the Passions, the fatigues and exhaustion of the Mind, the innumerable sorrows and pains that are experienced in every station of life and that constantly gnaw away at men's souls; such are the fatal guaranties that most of our ills are of our own making, and that we would have avoided almost all of them if we had retained the simple, uniform and solitary way of life prescribed to us by Nature. If it destined us to be healthy then, I almost dare assert, the state of reflection is a state against Nature, and the man who meditates a depraved animal. When one considers the good constitution of Savages, at least of those we have not ruined with our strong liquors, when one realizes that they know almost no other illnesses than wounds and old age, one is strongly inclined to believe that the history of human diseases could easily be written by following that of civil Societies. Such at least is the opinion of Plato who, on the basis of certain Remedies used or approved by Podalirius and Machaon at the siege of Troy, judges that various diseases which these remedies should have brought on were not yet known among men. And Celsus reports that dieting, which is nowadays so necessary, was only invented by Hippocrates. *[139]*

[10] With so few sources of illness, man in the state of Nature scarcely needs remedies, and Doctors even less so; in this respect too, the human species is no worse off than all the others, and one can easily find out from Hunters whether they come across many unhealthy animals in their expeditions. They do find some with massive, very well-healed wounds, with broken bones and

even limbs that knit with no other Surgeon than time, no other regimen than their ordinary life, and are no less perfectly cured for not having been tormented by incisions, poisoned by Drugs, or exhausted by fasts. In short, however useful well-administered medicine may be among us, it is in any event certain that if the sick Savage abandoned to himself alone has nothing to hope for but from Nature, he in return has nothing to fear but from his illness, and this often makes his situation preferable to ours.

[11] Let us therefore beware of confusing Savage man with the men we have before our eyes. Nature treats all animals abandoned to its care with a partiality that seems to indicate how jealous it is of this right. The Horse, the Cat, the Bull, even the Ass for the most part have a higher stature and always have a more robust constitution, more vigor, strength and courage in the forests than in our homes; they lose half of these advantages when they are Domesticated, and it would seem that all our care to treat and to feed these animals well only succeeds in bastardizing them. The same is true of man himself: As he becomes sociable and a Slave, he becomes weak, timorous, groveling, and his soft and effeminate way of life completes the enervation of both his strength and his courage. Let us add that the difference between man and man in the Savage and in the Domesticated conditions must be still greater than that between beast and beast in the two conditions; for since animal and man were treated alike by Nature, all the conveniences which man gives himself above and beyond those he gives to the animals he tames, are so many particular causes that lead him to degenerate more appreciably.

[12] To go naked, to be without habitation, and to be deprived of all the useless things we believe so necessary is, then, not such a great misfortune for these first men nor, above all, is it such a great obstacle to their preservation. *[140]* While their skin is not very hairy, they do not need it to be in warm Countries, and in cold Countries they soon learn to appropriate the skins of the Beasts they have overcome; though they have only two feet for running, they have two arms to provide for their defense and for their needs; their Children may walk late and with difficulty, but the Mothers carry them with ease: an

advantage not enjoyed by the other species where the mother, when pursued, finds herself compelled to abandon her young or to adjust her pace to theirs.* Finally, unless one assumes the singular and fortuitous concatenations of circumstances of which I shall speak in the sequel and which could very well never have occurred, it is for all intents and purposes clear that he who first made himself clothes or a Dwelling, thereby provided himself with things that are not very necessary, since he had done without them until then, and since it is not evident why he could not have tolerated as a grown man a mode of life he had tolerated from childhood.

[13] Alone, idle, and always near danger, Savage man must like to sleep and be a light sleeper like the animals which, since they think little, sleep, so to speak, all the time they do not think. Self-preservation being almost his only care, his most developed faculties must be those that primarily serve in attack and defense, either in order to overcome his prey or to guard against becoming another animal's prey: By contrast, the organs that are perfected only by softness and sensuality must remain in a state of coarseness which precludes his being in any way delicate; and since his senses differ in this respect, his touch and taste will be extremely crude; his sight, hearing and smell most subtle: Such is the animal state in general, and according to Travelers' reports, it also is the state of *[141]* most Savage Peoples. It is therefore not surprising that the Hottentots of the Cape of Good Hope can sight Ships with the naked eye as far out on the high seas as the Dutch can with Telescopes, nor that the Savages of America track the Spaniards by smell just as well as the best Dogs might have done, nor that all those Barbarous Nations tolerate their nakedness without discomfort, whet their taste with hot Peppers, and drink European Liquors like water.

[14] Until now I have considered only Physical Man; let us now try to view him from the Metaphysical and Moral side.

* There may be a few exceptions to this. For example that of the animal from the province of Nicaragua which resembles a Fox, has feet like a man's hands and, according to Corréal, has a pouch under its belly into which the mother puts her young when she has to flee. This is probably the same animal which in Mexico is called *Tlaquatzin,* and to the female of which Laët attributes a similar pouch serving the same purpose.

[15] I see in any animal nothing but an ingenious machine to which nature has given senses in order to wind itself up and, to a point, protect itself against everything that tends to destroy or to disturb it. I perceive precisely the same thing in the human machine, with this difference that Nature alone does everything in the operations of the Beast, whereas man contributes to his operations in his capacity as a free agent. The one chooses or rejects by instinct, the other by an act of freedom; as a result the Beast cannot deviate from the Rule prescribed to it even when it would be to its advantage to do so, while man often deviates from it to his detriment. Thus a Pigeon would starve to death next to a Bowl filled with the choicest meats, and a Cat atop heaps of fruit or of grain, although each could very well have found nourishment in the food it disdains if it had occurred to it to try some; thus dissolute men abandon themselves to excesses which bring them fever and death; because the Mind depraves the senses, and the will continues to speak when Nature is silent.

[16] Every animal has ideas, since it has senses; up to a point it even combines its ideas, and in this respect man differs from the Beast only as more does from less: Some Philosophers have even suggested that there is a greater difference between one given man and another than there is between a given man and a given beast; it is, then, not so much the understanding that constitutes the specific difference between man and the other animals, as it is his property of being a free agent. Nature commands every animal, and the Beast obeys. Man *[142]* experiences the same impression, but recognizes himself free to acquiesce or to resist; and it is mainly in the consciousness of this freedom that the spirituality of his soul exhibits itself: for Physics in a way explains the mechanism of the senses and the formation of ideas; but in the power of willing, or rather of choosing, and in the sentiment of this power are found purely spiritual acts about which nothing is explained by the Laws of Mechanics.

[17] But even if the difficulties surrounding all these questions left some room for disagreement about this difference between man and animal, there is another very specific property that

distinguishes between them and about which there can be no argument, namely the faculty of perfecting oneself; a faculty which, with the aid of circumstances, successively develops all the others, and resides in us in the species as well as in the individual, whereas an animal is at the end of several months what it will be for the rest of its life and its species is after a thousand years what it was in the first year of those thousand. Why is man alone liable to become an imbecile? Is it not that he thus returns to his primitive state and that, whereas the Beast, which has acquired nothing and also has nothing to lose, always keeps its instinct, man, losing through old age or other accidents all that his *perfectibility* had made him acquire, thus relapses lower than the Beast itself? It would be sad for us to be forced to agree that this distinctive and almost unlimited faculty is the source of all of man's miseries; that it is the faculty which, by dint of time, draws him out of that original condition in which he would spend calm and innocent days; that it is the faculty which, over the centuries, causes his enlightenment and his errors, his vices and his virtues to arise, and eventually makes him his own and Nature's tyrant (IX). It would be frightful to be obliged to praise as a beneficent being him who first suggested to the inhabitant of the Banks of the Orinoco the use of the Slats he ties to his Children's temples, and which insure at least a measure of their imbecility and of their original happiness.

[18] Savage Man, left by Nature to bare instinct alone, or rather, compensated for any lack of instinct by faculties capable of making up for it at first, and *[143]* of afterwards raising him far above nature, will then begin with purely animal functions: (X) to perceive and to sense will be his first state, which he will have in common with all animals. To will and not to will, to desire and to fear, will be the first and almost the only operations of his soul until new circumstances cause new developments in it.

[19] Regardless of what the Moralists may say about it, human understanding owes much to the Passions which, as is commonly admitted, also owe much to it: It is by their activity that our reason perfects itself; we seek to know only because we desire to enjoy, and it is not possible to conceive of why someone

without desires or fears would take the trouble of reasoning. The Passions, in turn, owe their origin to our needs, and their progress to our knowledge; for one can desire or fear things only in terms of one's ideas about them, or by the simple impulsion of Nature; and Savage man, deprived of every sort of enlightenment, experiences only the Passions of the latter kind; his desires do not exceed his Physical needs (XI); the only goods he knows in the Universe are food, a female, and rest; the only evils he fears are pain, and hunger; I say pain, and not death; for an animal will never know what it is to die, and the knowledge of death and of its terrors was one of man's first acquisitions on moving away from the animal condition.

[20] If I had to do so, I could easily buttress this sentiment with facts, and show that in all Nations of the world progress of the Mind proportioned itself exactly to the needs which Peoples received from Nature or to which circumstances subjected them, and consequently to the passions which inclined them to satisfy those needs. I would show how in Egypt the arts arose and spread with the flooding of the Nile; I would follow their progress among the Greeks, where they were seen to spring up, grow, and rise to the Heavens amid the Sands and Rocks of Attica, without being able to take root on the fertile Banks of the Eurotas; I would point out that in general the Peoples of the North *[144]* are more industrious than those of the south because they can less afford not to be so, as if Nature wanted in this way to equalize things, by endowing Minds with the fertility it denies the Soil.

[21] But without invoking the uncertain testimonies of History, who fails to see that everything seems to remove from Savage man the temptation as well as the means to cease being savage? His imagination depicts nothing to him; his heart asks nothing of him. His modest needs are so ready to hand, and he is so far from the degree of knowledge necessary to desire to acquire greater knowledge, that he can have neither foresight nor curiosity. The spectacle of Nature becomes so familiar that he grows indifferent to it. Forever the same order, forever the same revolutions; he lacks the wit to wonder at the greatest marvels; and it is not to him that one would turn for the Philosophy man

needs in order to be able for once to observe what he has seen every day. His soul, which nothing stirs, yields itself wholly to the sentiment of its present existence, with no idea of the future, however near it may be, and his projects, as narrow as his views, hardly extend to the close of day. Such is still nowadays the extent of the Carib's foresight: he sells his Cotton bed in the morning and comes weeping to buy it back in the evening, having failed to foresee that he would need it for the coming night.

[22] The more one meditates on this subject, the greater does the distance between pure sensations and the simplest knowledge grow in our eyes; and it is inconceivable how a man could, by his own strength alone, without the help of communication and without the goad of necessity, have crossed such a wide divide. How many centuries perhaps elapsed before men were in a position to see any other fire than that of Heaven? How many different chance occurrences must they have needed before they learned the most common uses of this element? How many times must they have let it go out before they mastered the art of reproducing it? And how many times did each one of these secrets perhaps die together with its discoverer? What shall we say about agriculture, an art requiring so much labor and foresight: dependent on many other arts which can quite obviously be pursued *[145]* only in a society that has at least begun, and which we use not so much to draw forth from the Earth foods it would readily yield without agriculture, as to force it to satisfy predilections that are more to our taste? But let us suppose that men had multiplied so much that natural produce no longer sufficed to feed them; a supposition which, incidentally, would point to one great advantage for the human Species in this way of life. Let us suppose that without forges and Workshops, the tools for Farming had dropped from Heaven into the Savages' hands; that these men had overcome the mortal hatred they all have of sustained work; that they had learned to foresee their needs sufficiently far ahead, that they had guessed how to cultivate the Earth, sow seed, and plant Trees; that they had found the art of grinding Wheat and of fermenting grapes; all of them things which the Gods had to be made to teach

them for want of being able to conceive how they could have learned them on their own; what man would, after all this, be so senseless as to torment himself with cultivating a Field that will be despoiled by the first passer-by, man or beast, who fancies this harvest; and how will everyone resolve to spend his life doing hard work when the more he needs its rewards, the more certain he is not to reap them? In a word, how can this situation possibly dispose men to cultivate the Earth as long as it has not been divided among them, that is to say as long as the state of Nature is not abolished?

[23] Even if we should wish to suppose a Savage man as skillful in the art of thinking as our Philosophers make him out to be; even if, following their example, we should make of him a Philosopher as well, who discovers alone the most sublime truths, who by chains of the most abstract reasoning establishes for himself maxims of justice and reason derived from the love of order in general or from the known will of his Creator; in a word even if we should suppose him to have a mind as intelligent and as enlightened as it must be—and, indeed, is found to be—heavy and stupid, what use would the Species derive from all this Metaphysics which could not be communicated, and would perish with the individual who *[146]* had invented it? What progress could Mankind make, scattered in the Woods among the Animals? And how much could men perfect and enlighten one another who, having neither a fixed Dwelling nor any need of one another, might meet no more than twice in their life, without knowing and speaking with one another?

[24] If one considers how many ideas we owe to the use of speech; How much Grammar exercises and facilitates the operations of the Mind; if one thinks about the inconceivable efforts and the infinite time the first invention of Languages must have cost; if one adds these reflections to those that preceded, then one can judge how many thousands of Centuries would have been required for the successive development in the human Mind of the Operations of which it was capable.

[25] Let me be allowed briefly to consider the perplexities regarding the origin of Languages. I could leave it at here

quoting or restating the Abbé de Condillac's investigations of this matter, all of which fully confirm my sentiment, and which perhaps suggested its first idea to me. But since the manner in which that Philosopher resolves the difficulties he himself raises regarding the origin of instituted signs shows that he assumed what I question, namely some sort of society already established among the inventors of language, I believe that I ought to supplement the reference to his reflections with reflections of my own, in order to exhibit these same difficulties in the light best suited to my subject. The first difficulty that arises is to imagine how languages could have become necessary; for, Men having no relationships with one another and no need of any, one cannot conceive the necessity or the possibility of this invention if it was not indispensable. I would be ready to say, as many others do, that Languages arose in the domestic dealings between Fathers, Mothers and Children: but not only would this fail to meet the objections, it would be to commit the fallacy of those who, in reasoning about the state of Nature carry over into it ideas taken from Society, always see the family assembled in one and the same dwelling and its members maintaining among themselves as intimate and as permanent a union as they do among us, where so many common interests *[147]* unite them; whereas in this primitive state, without Houses or Huts or property of any kind, everyone bedded down at random and often for only a single night; males and females united fortuitously, according to chance encounters, opportunity, and desire, without speech being an especially necessary interpreter of what they had to tell one another; they parted just as readily (XII). The mother at first nursed her Children because of her own need; then, habit having made them dear to her, she nourished them because of theirs; as soon as they had the strength to forage on their own, they left even the Mother; and since almost the only way to find one another again was not to lose sight of one another in the first place, they soon were at the point of not even recognizing each other. Note, further, that since the Child has all of its needs to explain, and hence has more things to say to the Mother than the Mother has to the Child, it is the child that must contribute most to the invention, and that the language it uses must largely be of its own making; which multiplies Languages by as many as there are individuals who speak them; their roving and vagabond life further contributes to this multiplication of languages, since it allows no idiom enough time to become stable; for to say that the Mother dictates to the Child the words it will have to use in order to ask her for one thing or another shows how Languages already formed are taught, but it does not teach how they are formed.

[26] Let us suppose this first difficulty overcome: Let us for a moment cross the immense distance that must have separated the pure state of Nature from the need for Languages; and, by assuming them to be necessary (XIII), let us inquire how they might have begun to get established. New difficulty, even worse than the preceding one; for if Men needed speech in order to learn how to think, they needed even more to know how to think in order to find the art of speech; and even if it were understood how the sounds of the voice came to be taken for the conventional interpreters of our ideas, it would still leave open the question of what could have been the interpreters of that convention for ideas which have no sensible object and which could therefore not be pointed to by gesture or by voice; so that it is scarcely possible to frame *[148]* tenable conjectures about the origin of this Art of communicating one's thoughts and of establishing exchanges between Minds: a sublime Art which is already so far from its Origin but which the Philosopher sees as still so immensely far removed from perfection that no one is bold enough to assert categorically it will ever be reached, even if the revolutions which time necessarily brings about were suspended in its favor, even if Prejudices were to retire from Academies or fall silent before Them, and They could attend to this thorny topic for Centuries together without interruption.

[27] Man's first language, the most universal, the most energetic and the only language he needed before it was necessary to persuade assembled men, is the cry of Nature. Since that cry was wrested from him only by a sort of instinct on urgent occasions, to implore for help in great dangers or relief in violent ills, it was not of much use in the ordinary course of life, where more moderate sentiments prevail. When men's

ideas began to expand and to multiply, and closer communication was established among them, they sought more numerous signs and a more extensive language: They multiplied the inflections of the voice and added gestures which are by their Nature more expressive, and less dependent for their meaning on prior agreement. Thus they expressed visible and moving objects by means of gestures, and objects that strike the ear by imitative sounds: but because gesture indicates almost only present or easily described objects and visible actions; because it is not universally serviceable since darkness or an interfering body render it useless, and because it requires attention rather than exciting it; it finally occurred to men to substitute for it the articulations of the voice which, although they do not stand in the same relation to some ideas, are better suited to represent them all, inasmuch as they are instituted signs; a substitution which can only have been made by common consent, which men whose crude vocal apparatus had as yet had no practice must have found it rather difficult to implement, and which is even more difficult to conceive of in itself, since this unanimous agreement must have been motivated, and since speech *[149]* seems to have been very necessary in order to establish the use of speech.

[28] It would seem that the first words men used had in their Mind a much wider reference than do words used in already formed Languages, and that since they were ignorant of the Division of Discourse into its constituent parts, they at first assigned to each word the meaning of an entire proposition. When they began to distinguish between subject and predicate, and verb and noun, which was no mean feat of genius, substantives were at first just so many proper names, the present infinitive was the only tense of verbs, and as for adjectives, the very notion must have developed only with great difficulty, because every adjective is an abstract word and abstractions are difficult and not particularly natural Operations.

[29] Every object was at first given a particular name without regard to kinds and Species, which these first Institutors were not in a position to distinguish; and all particulars presented themselves to their mind in isolation, just as they are in the

picture of Nature. If one Oak was called A, another Oak was called B; for the first idea one derives from two objects is that they are not the same, and it often takes a good deal of time to notice what they have in common: so that the more limited knowledge was, the more extensive the Dictionary grew. The clutter of all this Nomenclature was not easily cleared; for, in order to subsume the beings under common and generic designations, their properties and differences had to be known; observations and definitions were needed, that is to say much more Natural History and Metaphysics than the men of that time could have had.

[30] Besides, general ideas can enter the Mind only with the help of words, and the understanding grasps them only by means of propositions. That is one of the reasons why animals could not frame such ideas, nor ever acquire the perfectibility that depends on them. When a Monkey unhesitatingly goes from one nut to another, *[150]* are we to think that he has the general idea of that sort of fruit and compares its archetype with these two particulars? Surely not; but the sight of one of these nuts recalls to his memory the sensations he received from the other, and his eyes, modified in a certain way, announce to his taste how it is about to be modified. Every general idea is purely intellectual; if the imagination is at all involved, the idea immediately becomes particular. Try to outline the image of a tree in general to yourself, you will never succeed, in spite of yourself it will have to be seen as small or large, bare or leafy, light or dark, and if you could see in it only what there is in every tree, the image would no longer resemble a tree. Purely abstract beings are either seen in this same way, or conceived of only by means of discourse. Only the definition of a Triangle gives you its genuine idea: As soon as you [frame the] figure [of] one in your mind, it is some one given Triangle and not another, and you cannot help making its lines perceptible or its surface colored. Hence one has to state propositions, hence one has to speak in order to have general ideas: for as soon as the imagination stops, the mind can proceed only by means of discourse. If, then, the first Inventors could give names only to the ideas they already had, it follows that the first substantives could never

have been anything but proper names.

[31] But when, by means which I cannot conceive, our new Grammarians began to expand their ideas and to generalize their words, the Inventors' ignorance must have restricted this method to within very narrow bounds; and as they had at first gone too far in multiplying the names of particulars because they did not know kinds and species, they subsequently made too few species and kinds because they had not considered the Beings in all their differences. To carry the divisions sufficiently far would have required more experience and enlightenment than they could have had, and more research and work than they were willing to devote to it. If even nowadays new species are daily discovered which had so far escaped all our observations, think how many must have eluded men who judged things only by their first impression! As for primary Classes and the most *[151]* general notions, it would be superfluous to add that they, too, must have escaped them: How, for instance, would they have imagined or understood the words matter, mind, substance, mode, figure, motion, since our Philosophers, who have been using them for such a long time, have considerable difficulty understanding them themselves, and since, the ideas attached to these words being purely Metaphysical, they found no model of them in Nature?

[32] I pause after these first steps and beg my Judges to suspend their Reading here, to consider, in the light of the invention of Physical nouns alone, that is to say in the light of the most easily found part of Language, how far it still has to go in order to express all of men's thoughts, to assume a stable form, to admit of being spoken in public, and to influence Society: I beg them to reflect on how much time and knowledge it took to find numbers (XIV), abstract words, Aorists, and all the tenses of Verbs, particles, Syntax, to connect Propositions, arguments, and to develop the entire Logic of Discourse. As for myself, frightened by the increasing difficulties, and convinced of the almost demonstrated impossibility that Languages could have arisen and been established by purely human means, I leave to anyone who wishes to undertake it, the discussion of this difficult Problem: which was the more necessary, an already

united Society for the institution of Languages, or already invented Languages for the establishment of Society?

[33] Whatever may be the case regarding these origins, it is at least clear from how little care Nature has taken to bring Men together through mutual needs and to facilitate their use of speech, how little it prepared their Sociability, and how little of its own it has contributed to all that men have done to establish the bonds of Sociability. Indeed, it is impossible to imagine why, in that primitive state, a man would need another man any more than a monkey or a Wolf would need his kind, or, assuming that need, to imagine what motive could induce the other to attend to it, or even, if he did, how they might agree on terms. I know that we are repeatedly told that nothing would have been as miserable as man in that state; and if it is true, as I believe [152] I have proven, that he could only after many Centuries have had the desire and the opportunity to leave it, then that would be an Indictment of Nature, not of him whom nature had so constituted; but if I understand this term *miserable* correctly, it is a word either entirely devoid of sense, or which merely signifies a painful privation and suffering of Body or soul: Now, I should very much like to have it explained to me what kind of misery there can be for a free being whose heart is at peace and body in health. I ask, which of the two, Civil life or natural life, is more liable to become intolerable to those who enjoy it? We see around us almost only People who complain of their existence, even some who deprive themselves of it as far as they are able, and the combination of divine and human Laws hardly suffices to put a halt to this disorder: I ask whether anyone has ever heard tell that it so much as occurred to a Savage who is free to complain of life and to kill himself? One ought, then, to judge with less pride on which side genuine misery lies. Nothing, on the contrary, would have been as miserable as Savage man dazzled by enlightenment, tormented by Passions, and reasoning about a state different from his own. It was by a very wise Providence that the faculties he had in potentiality were to develop only with the opportunities to exercise them, so that they might not be superfluous and a burden to him before their time, nor belated and useless in time

of need. In bare instinct he had all he needed to live in the
state of Nature, in cultivated reason he has only what he needs
to live in society.

[34] It would at first seem that men in that state, having
neither moral relations of any sort between them, nor known
duties, could be neither good nor wicked, and had neither vices
nor virtues, unless these words are taken in a physical sense and
the qualities that can harm an individual's self-preservation are
called vices, and those that can contribute to it, virtues; in
which case he who least resists the simple impulsions of Nature
would have to be called the most virtuous: But without straying
from the ordinary sense, we should suspend the judgment we
might pass on such a situation, and be wary of our Prejudices
until it has been established, Scale in hand, whether there are
more virtues than vices among [153] civilized men, or whether
their virtues are more advantageous than their vices are detri-
mental, or whether the progress of their knowledge is sufficient
compensation for the harms they do one another in proportion
as they learn of the good they should do, or whether their
situation would not, on the whole, be happier if they had
neither harm to fear nor good to hope for from anyone, than
they are by having subjected themselves to universal dependence
and obligated themselves to receive everything from those who
do not obligate themselves to give them anything.

[35] Above all, let us not conclude with Hobbes that because
he has no idea of goodness, man is naturally wicked, that he is
vicious because he does not know virtue, that he always refuses
to those of his kind services which he does not believe he owes
them, or that by virtue of the right which he with reason assigns
himself to the things he needs, he insanely imagines himself to
be the sole owner of the entire Universe. Hobbes very clearly
saw the defect of all modern definitions of Natural right: but
the conclusions he draws from his own definition show that he
understands it in a sense that is no less false. By reasoning on
the basis of the principles he established, this Author should
have said that, since the state of Nature is the state in which the
care for our own preservation is least prejudicial to the self-
preservation of others, it follows that this state was the most

conducive to Peace and the best suited to Mankind. He says precisely the contrary because he improperly included in Savage man's care for his preservation the need to satisfy a multitude of passions that are the product of Society and have made Laws necessary. A wicked man is, he says, a sturdy Child; it remains to be seen whether Savage Man is a sturdy Child. Even if it were granted him that it is, what would he conclude? That if this man were as dependent on others when he is sturdy as he is dependent on them when weak, he would not stop at any kind of excess, that he would strike his Mother if she were slow to give him the breast, that he would strangle one of his young brothers if he inconvenienced him, that he would bite another brother's leg if he hurt or bothered him; but being sturdy and being dependent are two contradictory assumptions in the state of Nature; Man is weak when he is dependent, and he is emancipated before he is sturdy. *[154]* Hobbes did not see that the same cause that prevents the Savages from using their reason, as our Jurists claim they do, at the same time prevents them from abusing their faculties, as he himself claims they do; so that one might say that Savages are not wicked precisely because they do not know what it is to be good; for it is neither the growth of enlightenment nor the curb of the Law, but the calm of the passions and the ignorance of vice that keep them from evil-doing; *so much more does the ignorance of vice profit these than the knowledge of virtue profits those.* There is, besides, another Principle which Hobbes did not notice and which, having been given to man in order under certain circumstances to soften the ferociousness of his vanity or of the desire for self-preservation prior to the birth of vanity (XV), tempers his ardor for well-being with an innate repugnance to see his kind suffer. I do not believe I need fear any contradiction in granting to man the only Natural virtue which the most extreme Detractor of human virtues was forced to acknowledge. I speak of Pity, a disposition suited to beings as weak and as subject to so many ills as we are; a virtue all the more universal and useful to man as it precedes the exercise of all reflection in him, and so Natural that the Beasts themselves sometimes show evident signs of it. To say nothing of the tenderness Mothers feel for

their young and of the dangers they brave in order to protect
them, one daily sees the repugnance of Horses to trample a
living Body underfoot; an animal never goes past a dead animal
of its own Species without some restlessness: Some even give
them a kind of burial; and the mournful lowing of Cattle
entering a Slaughter-House conveys their impression of the
horrible sight that strikes them. It is a pleasure to see the author
of the *Fable of the Bees* forced to recognize man as a compas-
sionate and sensitive Being and, in the example he gives of it,
abandon his cold and subtle style to offer us the pathetic picture
of a man locked up, who outside sees a ferocious Beast tearing
a Child from his Mother's breast, breaking his weak limbs with
its murderous fangs, and tearing the Child's throbbing entrails
with its claws. What dreadful *[155]* agitation this witness to an
event in which he takes no personal interest whatsoever must
experience. What anguish he must suffer at this sight, for not
being able to give any help to the fainted Mother or the dying
Child.

[36] Such is the pure movement of Nature prior to all reflection: such is the force of natural pity which the most depraved
morals still have difficulty destroying, since in our theaters one
daily sees being moved and weeping at the miseries of some
unfortunate person, people who, if they were in the Tyrant's
place, would only increase their enemy's torments; like blood-
thirsty Sulla, so sensitive to ills which he had not caused, or
that Alexander of Pherae who dared not attend the performance
of a single tragedy for fear that he might be seen to moan with
Andromache and Priam, but who listened without emotion to
the cries of so many citizens daily being murdered on his orders.

> *When nature gave man tears,*
> *She proclaimed that he was tender-hearted.*

[37] Mandeville sensed clearly that for all their morality, men
would never have been anything but monsters if Nature had not
given them pity in support of reason: but he did not see that
from this single attribute flow all the social virtues he wants to
deny men. Indeed, what are generosity, Clemency, Humanity, if
not Pity applied to the weak, the guilty, or the species in
general? Even Benevolence and friendship, properly understood,

are the products of a steady pity focused on a particular object; for what else is it to wish that someone not suffer, than to wish that he be happy? Even if it were true that commiseration is nothing but a sentiment that puts us in the place of him who suffers, a sentiment that is obscure and lively in Savage man, developed but weak in Civil man, what difference could this idea make to the truth of what I say, except to give it additional force? Indeed commiseration will be all the more energetic in proportion as the Onlooking animal identifies more intimately with the suffering animal: Now this identification must, clearly, have been infinitely closer in the state of Nature than in the state *[156]* of reasoning. It is reason that engenders vanity, and reflection that reinforces it; It is what turns man back upon himself; it is what separates him from everything that troubles and afflicts him: It is Philosophy that isolates him; it is by means of Philosophy that he secretly says at the sight of a suffering man, perish if you wish, I am safe. Only dangers that threaten the entire society still disturb the Philosopher's tranquil slumber, and rouse him from his bed. One of his kind can with impunity be murdered beneath his window; he only has to put his hands over his ears and to argue with himself a little in order to prevent Nature, which rebels within him, from letting him identify with the man being assassinated. Savage man has not this admirable talent; and for want of wisdom and of reason he is always seen to yield impetuously to the first sentiment of Humanity. In Riots, in Street-brawls, the Populace gathers, the prudent man withdraws; it is the rabble, it is the Marketwomen who separate the combatants and keep honest folk from murdering each other.

[38] It is therefore quite certain that pity is a natural sentiment which, by moderating in every individual the activity of self-love, contributes to the mutual preservation of the entire species. It is pity which carries us without reflection to the assistance of those we see suffer; it is pity which, in the state of Nature, takes the place of Laws, morals, and virtue, with the advantage that no one is tempted to disobey its gentle voice; it is pity which will keep any sturdy Savage from robbing a weak child or an infirm old man of his hard-won subsistence if he hopes he can

find his own elsewhere: It is pity which instead of the sublime maxim of reasoned justice *Do unto others as you would have them do unto you* inspires all Men with this other maxim of natural goodness, much less perfect but perhaps more useful than the first: *Do your good with the least possible harm to others*. It is, in a word, in this Natural sentiment rather than in subtle arguments that one has to seek the cause of the repugnance to evil-doing which every human being would feel even independently of the maxims of education. Although Socrates and Minds of his stamp may be capable of acquiring virtue through reason, Mankind would long ago *[157]* have ceased to be if its preservation had depended solely on the reasonings of those who make it up.

[39] With such sluggish passions and such a salutary curb, fierce rather than wicked, and more intent on protecting themselves from the harm they might suffer than tempted to do any to others, men were not prone to very dangerous quarrels: since they had no dealings of any kind with one another; since they therefore knew neither vanity, nor consideration, nor esteem, nor contempt; since they had not the slightest notion of thine and mine, or any genuine idea of justice; since they looked on any violence they might suffer as an easily repaired harm rather than as a punishable injury, and since they did not even dream of vengeance except perhaps mechanically and on the spot like the dog that bites the stone thrown at him; their disputes would seldom have led to bloodshed if they had had no more urgent object than Food: but I see one that is more dangerous, which it remains for me to discuss.

[40] Among the passions that stir man's heart, there is one that is ardent, impetuous, and makes one sex necessary to the other, a terrible passion that braves all dangers, overcomes all obstacles, and in its frenzy seems liable to destroy Mankind when it is destined to preserve it. What must become of men possessed by this unbridled and brutal rage, lacking modesty, lacking restraint, and daily feuding over their loves at the cost of their blood?

[41] It has to be granted, first of all, that the more violent the passions, the more necessary are Laws with which to contain

them: but quite aside from the fact that the disorders and the crimes they daily cause among us sufficiently prove the inadequacy of the Laws in this respect, it would still be worth inquiring whether these disorders did not arise together with the Laws themselves; for then, even if they could repress them, it is surely the very least to expect of them that they put a stop to an evil which would not exist without them.

[42] Let us begin by drawing a distinction between the moral and the Physical in the sentiment of love. The Physical is the general desire which moves one sex to unite with the other; the moral is what gives this desire its distinctive character and focuses it exclusively on a single object, *[158]* or at least gives it a greater measure of energy for this preferred object. Now it is easy to see that the moral aspect of love is a factitious sentiment; born of social practice, and extolled with much skill and care by women in order to establish their rule and to make dominant the sex that should obey. This sentiment, since it is based on certain notions of merit or of beauty which a Savage is not in a position to possess, and on comparisons he is not in a position to make, must be almost nonexistent for him: For as his mind could not frame abstract ideas of regularity and of proportion, so his heart cannot feel the sentiments of admiration and of love that arise, without our even noticing it, from applying these ideas; he heeds only the temperament he received from Nature, and not a taste which he could not have acquired, and any woman suits him.

[43] Limited to the Physical aspect of love alone, and fortunate enough not to know preferences that exacerbate its sentiment and increase its difficulties, men must feel the ardors of temperament less frequently and less vividly, and hence have fewer and less cruel quarrels among themselves. The imagination, which wreaks such havoc among us, does not speak to Savage hearts; everyone peacefully awaits the impulsion of Nature, yields to it without choice with more pleasure than frenzy, and the need once satisfied, all desire is extinguished.

[44] It is therefore indisputable that love itself, like all the other passions, acquired only in society the impetuous ardor that so often causes it to be fatal among men, and it is all the

more ridiculous to portray Savages as constantly murdering one another in order to satisfy their brutality, as that opinion goes directly counter to experience, and as the Caribs, which of all existing Peoples have so far departed least from the state of Nature, are in fact also the most peaceful in their loves and the least given to jealousy, even though they live in a scorching Climate, which always seems to stir these passions to greater activity. *[159]*

[45] Regarding inferences that might, in a number of animal species, be drawn from the fights of Males that bloody our poultry yards at all seasons or cause our forests to resound with their cries in Springtime as they feud over a female, the first thing is to exclude from consideration all species in which Nature has clearly established different relations in the relative strength of the Sexes than among us: Thus Cock-fights do not provide a basis for inferences about the human species. In species where the Proportion is better observed, the cause for such fights can only be either the scarcity of females in comparison with the number of Males, or the periods of exclusion during which the female consistently rejects the male's approaches, which is equivalent to the first cause; for if each female tolerates the male only two months out of the year, then it is in this respect tantamount to having the number of females reduced by five-sixths: Now, neither of these alternatives applies to the human species, where the number of females generally exceeds that of males, and where, even among Savages, females have never been known to have periods of heat and of rejection, as do those of other species. Moreover, among several of these animals, where the entire species ruts at the same time, there comes one terrible moment of common ardor, tumult, disorder, and fighting: a moment which does not occur in the human species, where love is never cyclical. It therefore does not follow from the fights of some animals for the possession of females, that the same thing would happen to man in the state of Nature; and even if it did follow, since such dissensions do not destroy the other species, it seems at least reasonable that they would not be any more fatal to ours, and it is quite evident that they would still wreak less havoc in the state of nature than

they do in Society, especially in Countries where Morals still count for something and the jealousy of Lovers and the vengeance of Husbands daily cause Duels, Murders and worse; where the duty of eternal fidelity only makes for adulteries, and where even the Laws of continence and of honor inevitably increase debauchery and multiply abortions.

[46] Let us conclude that, wandering in the forests without industry, *[160]* without speech, without settled abode, without war, and without ties, without any need of others of his kind and without any desire to harm them, perhaps even without ever recognizing any one of them individually, subject to few passions and self-sufficient, Savage man had only the sentiments and the enlightenment suited to this state, that he sensed only his true needs, looked only at what he believed it to be in his interest to see, and that his intelligence made no more progress than his vanity. If he by chance made some discovery, he was all the less in a position to communicate it as he did not recognize even his Children. The art perished with the inventor; there was neither education nor progress, generations multiplied uselessly; and as each one of them always started at the same point, Centuries went by in all the crudeness of the first ages, the species had already grown old, and man remained ever a child.

[47] If I have dwelt at such length on the assumption of this primitive condition, it is because, having ancient errors and inveterate prejudices to destroy, I believed I had to dig to the root and to show in the depiction of the genuine state of Nature how far inequality, even natural inequality, is from having as much reality and influence in that state as our Writers claim.

[48] Indeed it is easy to see that among the differences that distinguish men, several are taken to be natural although they are exclusively the result of habit and of the different kinds of life men adopt in Society. Thus a sturdy or a delicate temperament, together with the strength or the weakness that derive from it, are often due more to a tough or an effeminate upbringing than to the bodies' primitive constitution. The same is true of strengths of Mind, and education not only introduces differences between Minds that are cultivated and those that are

not, but it also increases the differences that obtain between cultivated Minds in proportion to their culture; for if a Giant and a Dwarf travel the same road, every step they take will give the Giant an added advantage. Now if one compares the prodigious variety of educations and ways of life that prevails in the different orders of the civil state with the simplicity and the uniformity of animal and savage life, where all eat the same foods, live in the same *[161]* fashion, and do exactly the same things, it will be evident how much smaller the difference between man and man must be in the state of Nature than in the state of society, and how much natural inequality in the human species must increase as a result of instituted inequality.

[49] But even if Nature displayed as much partiality in the distribution of its gifts as is claimed, what advantage would the more favored enjoy at the expense of the others in a state of things that allowed for almost no relations of any sort between them? Where there is no love, of what use is beauty? Of what use is wit to people who do not speak, and cunning to those who have no dealings with one another? I constantly hear it repeated that the stronger will oppress the weak; but explain to me what the word "oppression" here means. Some will dominate by violence, the others will groan, subjected to all of their whims: that is precisely what I see among us, but I do not see how the same could be said about Savage men, whom it would even be rather difficult to get to understand what subjection and domination are. A man might seize the fruits another has picked, the game he killed, the lair he used for shelter; but how will he ever succeed in getting himself obeyed by him, and what would be the chains of dependence among men who possess nothing? If I am chased from a tree, I need only go to another; if I am tormented in one place, who will keep me from going somewhere else? Is there a man so superior to me in strength, and who, in addition, is so depraved, so lazy and so ferocious as to force me to provide for his subsistence while he remains idle? He will have to make up his mind not to let me out of his sight for a single moment and to keep me very carefully tied up while he sleeps, for fear that I might escape or kill him: that is to say that he is obliged to incur willingly a great deal more

trouble than he seeks to avoid and than he causes me. After all this, what if his vigilance relaxes for a moment? What if an unexpected noise makes him turn his head? I take twenty steps into the forest, my chains are broken, and he never sees me again in his life.

[50] Without needlessly drawing out these details, everyone must *[162]* see that since ties of servitude are formed solely by men's mutual dependence and the reciprocal needs that unite them, it is impossible to subjugate a man without first having placed him in the position of being unable to do without another; a situation which, since it does not obtain in the state of Nature, leaves everyone in it free of the yoke, and renders vain the Law of the stronger.

[51] Having proved that Inequality is scarcely perceptible in the state of Nature and that its influence there is almost nil, it remains for me to show its origin and its progress through the successive developments of the human Mind. Having shown that *perfectibility,* the social virtues and the other faculties which Natural man had received in potentiality could never develop by themselves, that in order to do so, they needed the fortuitous concatenation of several foreign causes which might never have arisen and without which he would eternally have remained in his primitive condition; it remains for me to consider and bring together the various contingencies that can have perfected human reason while deteriorating the species, make a being wicked by making it sociable, and from so remote a beginning finally bring man and the world to the point where we now find them.

[52] I admit that since the events I have to describe could have occurred in several ways, I can choose between them only on the basis of conjectures; but not only do such conjectures become reasons when they are the most probable that can be derived from the nature of things and the only means available to discover the truth, it also does not follow that the consequences I want to deduce from mine will therefore be conjectural since, on the principles I have just established, no other system could be framed that would not give me the same results and from which I could not draw the same conclusions.

[53] This will exempt me from expanding my reflections about how the lapse of time makes up for the slight likelihood of events; about the astonishing power of very slight causes when they act without cease; about the impossibility of on the one hand rejecting certain hypotheses without, on the other, being in a position to attach to them the certainty of facts; about how, when two facts given as real are to be connected by a sequence of intermediate facts that are unknown or believed *[163]* to be so, it is up to history, if available, to provide the facts that connect them; in the absence of history, it is up to Philosophy to ascertain similar facts that might connect them; finally about this, that with respect to outcomes, similarity reduces facts to a much smaller number of different classes than people imagine. It is enough for me to submit these issues for consideration to my Judges: it is enough for me to have seen to it that vulgar Readers need not consider them.

[164]

PART II

[1] The first man who, having enclosed a piece of ground, to whom it occurred to say *this is mine* and found people sufficiently simple to believe him, was the true founder of civil society. How many crimes, wars, murders, how many miseries and horrors Mankind would have been spared by him who, pulling up the stakes or filling in the ditch, had cried out to his kind: Beware of listening to this impostor; you are lost if you forget that the fruits are everyone's and the Earth no one's: But in all likelihood things had by then reached a point where they could not continue as they were; for this idea of property, depending as it does on many prior ideas which could only arise successively, did not take shape all at once in man's mind: Much progress had to have been made, industry and enlightenment acquired, transmitted, and increased from one age to the next, before this last stage of the state of Nature was reached. Let us therefore take up the thread earlier, and try to fit this slow succession of events and of knowledge together from a single point of view, and in their most natural order.

[2] Man's first sentiment was that of his existence, his first care that of its preservation. The Earth's products provided him with all the assistance he needed, instinct moved him to use them. Hunger and other appetites caused him by turns to experience different ways of existing, one of which prompted him to perpetuate his species; and this blind inclination, devoid of any sentiment of the heart, produced only a purely animal act. The need satisfied, the two sexes no longer recognized one another, and even the child no longer meant anything to the Mother as soon as it could do without her.

[3] Such was the condition of nascent man; such was the life of an animal at first restricted to pure sensations, *[165]* and scarcely profiting from the gifts Nature offered him, let alone dreaming of wresting anything from it; but difficulties soon presented themselves; it became necessary to learn to overcome

them: the height of Trees which prevented him from reaching their fruits, competition from the animals trying to eat these fruits, the ferociousness of the animals that threatened his very life, everything obliged him to attend to bodily exercise; he had to become agile, run fast, fight vigorously. The natural weapons, branches and stones, were soon at hand. He learned to overcome the obstacles of Nature, fight other animals when necessary, contend even with men for his subsistence, or make up for what had to be yielded to the stronger.

[4] In proportion as Mankind spread, difficulties multiplied together with men. Differences of terrain, Climate, seasons, could have forced them to introduce differences into their ways of life. Barren years, long and harsh winters, scorching all-consuming Summers, required renewed industry on their part. On seashores and Riverbanks they invented line and hook; and became fishermen and Fish-eaters. In forests they made bows and arrows and became Hunters and Warriors; in cold Countries they covered themselves with the skins of the beasts they had killed; lightning, a Volcano, or some happy accident acquainted them with fire, a new resource against the rigors of winter: They learned to conserve this element, then to reproduce it, and finally to prepare the meats they had previously devoured raw.

[5] This repeated interaction of the various beings with himself as well as with one another must naturally have engendered in man's mind perceptions of certain relationships. The relations which we express by the words great, small, strong, weak, fast, slow, fearful, bold, and other such ideas, compared as need required and almost without thinking about it, finally produced in him some sort of reflection, or rather a mechanical prudence that suggested to him the precautions most necessary for his safety.

[6] The new enlightenment that resulted from this development increased his superiority over the other animals by acquainting him with it. He learned to set [166] traps for them, he tricked them in a thousand ways, and although a number of them might surpass him in strength at fighting or in speed at running, in time he became the master of those that could be of service to him and the scourge of those that could harm him.

That is how his first look at himself aroused the first movement of pride in him; that is how, while he was as yet scarcely able to discriminate ranks, and considered himself in the first rank as a species, he was from afar preparing to claim first rank as an individual.

[7] Although others of his kind were not for him what they are for us, and he had scarcely more dealings with them than with the other animals, they were not neglected in his observations. The conformities which time may have led him to perceive between them, his female and himself, led him to judge regarding those he did not perceive, and seeing that they all behaved as he would have done in similar circumstances, he concluded that their way of thinking and of feeling fully corresponded to his own, and this important truth, once it was firmly settled in his mind, made him follow, by a premonition as sure as Dialectics and more rapid, the best rules of conduct to observe with them for his advantage and safety.

[8] Taught by experience that love of well-being is the sole spring of human actions, he was in a position to distinguish between the rare occasions when common interest should make him count on the help of his kind, and the even rarer occasions when competition should make him suspicious of them. In the first case he united with them in a herd, or at most in some kind of free association that obligated no one and lasted only as long as the transitory need that had formed it. In the second case, everyone sought to seize his own advantage, either by open force if he believed that he could do so; or by skill and cunning if he felt he was the weaker.

[9] That is how men might imperceptibly have acquired some crude idea of mutual engagements and of the advantage of fulfilling them, but only as far as present and perceptible interest could require; for foresight was nothing to them and, far from being concerned with a distant future, they did not even give a thought to the next day. If a Deer was to be caught, everyone [167] clearly sensed that this required him faithfully to keep his post; but if a hare happened to pass within reach of one of them, he will undoubtedly have chased after it without a scruple and, having caught his own prey, have cared very little about

having caused his Companions to miss theirs.

[10] It is easy to understand that such dealings did not require a language much more refined than that of Crows or of Monkeys, which troop together in approximately the same way. Some inarticulate cries, many gestures, and a few imitative noises must, for a long time, have made up the universal Language, [and] the addition to it, in every Region, of a few articulated and conventional sounds—the institution of which is, as I have already said, none too easy to explain—made for particular languages, crude, imperfect and approximately like those which various Savage Nations still have today. I cover multitudes of Centuries in a flash, forced by time running out, the abundance of things I have to say, and the almost imperceptible progress of the beginnings; for the more slowly events succeeded one another, the more quickly can they be described.

[11] This initial progress finally enabled man to make more rapid progress. The more the mind became enlightened, the more industry was perfected. Soon ceasing to fall asleep underneath the first tree or to withdraw into Caves, they found they could use hard, sharp stones as hatchets to cut wood, dig up earth, and make huts of branches which it later occurred to them to daub with clay and mud. This was the period of a first revolution which brought about the establishment and the differentiation of families, and introduced a sort of property; from which perhaps a good many quarrels and Fights already arose. However, since the stronger were probably the first to make themselves dwellings they felt they could defend, it seems plausible that the weak found it simpler and safer to imitate them than to try to dislodge them: and as for those who already had Huts, a man must rarely have tried to appropriate his neighbor's, not so much because it did not belong to him as because it was of no use to him, and he could not get hold of it without risking a very lively fight with the family that occupied it. *[168]*

[12] The first developments of the heart were the effect of a new situation that brought husbands and Wives, Fathers and Children together in a common dwelling; the habit of living together gave rise to the sweetest sentiments known to man,

conjugal love and Paternal love. Each family became a small Society, all the better united as mutual attachment and freedom were its only bonds; and that is when the first difference was established in the ways of life of the two Sexes, which until then had had but one. Women became more sedentary and grew accustomed to looking after the Hut and Children, while the man went in quest of the common subsistence. As a result of their slightly softer life, both Sexes also began to lose something of their ferociousness and vigor; but while each separately grew less fit to fight wild beasts, in exchange it became easier to assemble in order to resist them in common.

[13] In this new state, with a simple and solitary life, very limited needs, and the implements they had invented to provide for them, men enjoyed a great deal of leisure which they used to acquire several sorts of conveniences unknown to their Fathers; and that was the first yoke which, without thinking of it, they imposed on themselves, and the first source of evils they prepared for their Descendants; for not only did they, in this way, continue to weaken body and mind, but since these conveniences, by becoming habitual, had almost entirely ceased to be enjoyable, and at the same time had degenerated into true needs, it became much more cruel to be deprived of them than to possess them was sweet, and men were unhappy to lose them without being happy to possess them.

[14] One here gets a somewhat better view of how the use of speech is imperceptibly established or perfected in the bosom of each family, and can further conjecture how various particular causes could enlarge language and accelerate its progress by making it more necessary. Great floods or earthquakes surrounded inhabited Areas with waters or precipices; Revolutions of the Globe broke off portions of the Continent and carved them into Islands. It seems likely that a common Idiom was formed earlier among men brought into closer proximity with one another in this fashion, and forced *[169]* to live together, than among those who roamed freely through the forests of the Mainland. Thus it is very possible that Islanders, after their first attempts at Navigation, introduced the use of speech among us; and it is at least very likely that Society and languages arose in Islands and were

perfected there before they were known on the Continent.

[15] Everything begins to change in appearance. Men, who until now had roamed in the Woods, having become more settled, gradually come together, unite in various troops, and finally in every region form a particular Nation united in morals and character, not by Rules or Laws, but by the same kind of life and of foods, and the influence of a shared Climate. Permanent proximity cannot fail in the end to give rise to some bond between different families. Young people of the opposite sex live in adjoining Huts, the transient dealings demanded by Nature soon lead to others that are no less sweet and, as a result of mutual visits, are more permanent. They grow accustomed to attend to different objects and to make comparisons; imperceptibly they acquire ideas of merit and of beauty which produce sentiments of preference. The more they see one another, the less they can do without seeing one another still more. A tender and sweet sentiment steals into the soul, and at the least obstacle becomes an impetuous frenzy; jealousy awakens together with love; Discord triumphs, and the gentlest of all passions receives sacrifices of human blood.

[16] As ideas and sentiments succeed one another, as the mind and the heart grow active, Mankind continues to grow tame, relations expand, and bonds tighten. It became customary to gather in front of the Huts or around a large Tree: song and dance, true children of love and leisure, became the amusement or rather the occupation of idle men and women gathered together. Everyone began to look at everyone else and to wish to be looked at himself, and public esteem acquired a value. The one who sang or danced best; the handsomest, the strongest, the most skillful, or the most eloquent came to be the most highly regarded, and this was the first step at once toward inequality and vice: *[170]* from these first preferences arose vanity and contempt on the one hand, shame and envy on the other; and the fermentation caused by these new leavens eventually produced compounds fatal to happiness and innocence.

[17] As soon as men had begun to appreciate one another and the idea of regard had taken shape in their mind, everyone claimed a right to it, and one no longer could with impunity

fail to show it toward anyone. From this arose the first duties of
civility even among Savages, and from it any intentional wrong
became an affront because, together with the harm resulting
from the injury, the offended party saw in it contempt for his
person, often more unbearable than the harm itself. Thus everyone punishing the contempt shown him in a manner proportionate to the stock he set by himself, vengeance became
terrible, and men bloodthirsty and cruel. This is precisely the
stage reached by most of the Savage Peoples known to us; and
it is for want of drawing adequate distinctions between ideas
and noticing how far these Peoples already were from the first
state of Nature, that many hastily concluded that man is naturally
cruel and that he needs political order in order to be made
gentle, whereas nothing is as gentle as he in his primitive state
when, placed by Nature at equal distance from the stupidity of
the brutes and the fatal enlightenment of civil man, and restricted
by instinct and by reason alike to protecting himself against the
harm that threatens him, he is restrained by Natural pity from
doing anyone harm without being moved by anything to do
anyone harm, even after harm has been done to him. For
according to the axiom of the wise Locke, *"Where there is no
property, there can be no injury."*

[18] But it must be noted that beginning Society and the
already established relations among men, required in them
qualities different from those they derived from their primitive
constitution; that, since morality was beginning to enter into
human Actions and since, before there were Laws, everyone was
sole judge and avenger of the offenses he had received, the
goodness suited to the pure state of Nature was no longer the
goodness suited to nascent Society; that punishments had to
become more severe in proportion as the opportunities to offend
became more frequent, and that the terror of vengeance had
[171] to take the place of the Laws' restraint. Thus, although
men now had less endurance, and natural pity had already
undergone some modification, this period in the development
of human faculties, occupying a just mean between the indolence
of the primitive state and the petulant activity of our vanity,
must have been the happiest and the longest-lasting epoch. The

more one reflects on it, the more one finds that this state was the least subject to revolutions, the best for man (XVI), and that he must have left it only by some fatal accident which, for the sake of the common utility, should never have occurred. The example of the Savages, almost all of whom have been found at this point, seems to confirm that Mankind was made always to remain in it, that this state is the genuine youth of the World, and that all subsequent progress has been so many steps in appearance toward the perfection of the individual, and in effect toward the decrepitude of the species.

[19] As long as men were content with their rustic huts, as long as they confined themselves to sewing their clothes of skins with thorns or fish bones, adorning themselves with feathers and shells, painting their bodies different colors, perfecting or embellishing their bows and arrows, carving a few fishing Canoes or a few crude Musical instruments with sharp stones; in a word, so long as they applied themselves only to tasks a single individual could perform, and to arts that did not require the collaboration of several hands, they lived free, healthy, good, and happy as far as they could by their Nature be, and continued to enjoy the gentleness of independent dealings with one another: but the moment one man needed the help of another; as soon as it was found to be useful for one to have provisions for two, equality disappeared, property appeared, work became necessary, and the vast forests changed into smiling Fields that had to be watered with the sweat of men, and where slavery and misery were soon seen to sprout and grow together with the harvests.

[20] Metallurgy and agriculture were the two arts the invention of which brought about this great revolution. For the Poet it is gold and silver; but for the Philosopher it is iron and wheat that civilized men, and ruined Mankind. Indeed, both were *[172]* unknown to the Savages of America who have therefore always remained such; even other Peoples seem to have remained Barbarians as long as they engaged in one of these Arts without the other; and perhaps one of the main reasons why Europe had political order, if not earlier then at least more continuously and better than the other parts of the world, is that it is both the most abundant in iron and the most fertile in wheat.

[21] It is very difficult to conjecture how men came to know and to use iron: for it is not plausible that they on their own imagined extracting the ore from the mine and doing what is required to prepare it for smelting, before they knew what the outcome would be. On the other hand, it is even less plausible to attribute this discovery to some accidental fire, as mines are formed only in arid places bare of trees and plants, so that it might seem that Nature had taken precautions to withhold this fatal secret from us. The only remaining alternative, then, is that some extraordinary event, such as a Volcano throwing up molten metal, will have given its Witnesses the idea of imitating this operation of Nature; even then, they must also be assumed to have had a good deal of courage and foresight to undertake such strenuous labor and to anticipate so far in advance the advantages they might derive from it; which really only accords with minds already more skilled than these must have been.

[22] As for agriculture, its principle was known long before its practice was established, and it is scarcely possible that men constantly engaged in drawing their subsistence from trees and plants, would not fairly soon have the idea of how Nature proceeds in the generation of Plants; but their industry probably turned in that direction only rather late, either because trees which, together with hunting and fishing, provided their food, did not require their care, or for want of knowing the use of wheat, or for want of implements to cultivate it, or for want of anticipating future need, or, finally, for want of means to prevent others from appropriating the fruit of their labor. Once they had become more industrious, they probably began by cultivating a few vegetables or roots with sharp stones or pointed sticks *[173]* around their Huts, long before they knew how to thresh and grind wheat and had the implements necessary for large-scale cultivation, to say nothing of the fact that in order to devote oneself to this occupation and sow fields, one has to be resigned to lose something at first for the sake of gaining a great deal subsequently; a precaution that is very alien to the turn of mind of Savage man who, as I have said, has trouble anticipating in the morning what his needs will be in the evening.

[23] The invention of the other arts was therefore necessary

to force Mankind to attend to the art of agriculture. As soon as men were needed to melt and forge iron, others were needed to feed them. The more the number of workers increased, the fewer hands were engaged in providing for the common subsistence, without there being fewer mouths to consume it; and as some had to have foods in exchange for their iron, the others finally discovered the secret of using iron to increase foods. Thus arose on the one hand plowing and agriculture, and on the other the art of working metals and multiplying their uses.

[24] From the cultivation of land, its division necessarily followed; and from property, once recognized, the first rules of justice necessarily followed: for in order to render to each his own, it has to be possible for each to have something; moreover, as men began to extend their views to the future and all saw that they had some goods to lose, there was no one who did not have to fear reprisals against himself for wrongs he might do to another. This origin is all the more natural as it is impossible to conceive the idea of nascent property in any other way than in terms of manual labor: for it is not clear what more than his labor man can put into things he has not made, in order to appropriate them. It is labor alone which, by giving the Cultivator the right to the product of the land he has tilled, therefore also gives him a right to the land, at least until the harvest, and so from one year to the next, which, as it makes for continuous possession, is easily transformed into property. When the Ancients, says Grotius, gave Ceres the title legislatrix and a festival celebrated in her honor the name Thesmophoria, they thereby indicated that the division *[174]* of land produced a new kind of right. Namely the right of property different from that which follows from natural Law.

[25] Things could have remained equal in this state if talents had been equal and if, for example, the use of iron and the consumption of foods had always been exactly balanced; but this proportion, which nothing maintained, was soon upset; the stronger did more work; the more skillful used his to better advantage; the more ingenious found ways to shorten the work; the Ploughman had greater need of iron, or the smith greater need of wheat, and by working equally, the one earned much

while the other had trouble staying alive. That is how natural inequality insensibly unfolds together with the inequality of associations, and how the differences among men, developed by their different circumstances, become more perceptible, more permanent in their effects, and begin to exercise a corresponding influence on the fate of individuals.

[26] Things having reached this point, it is easy to imagine the rest. I shall not pause to describe the successive invention of the other arts, the progress of languages, the testing and exercising of talents, the inequality of fortunes, the use or abuse of Wealth, nor all the details that attend them and which everyone can easily add. I shall limit myself to a brief glance at Mankind placed in this new order of things.

[27] Here, then, are all our faculties developed, memory and imagination brought into play, vanity interested, reason become active, and the mind almost at the limit of the perfection of which it is capable. Here are all natural qualities set in action, each man's rank and fate set, not only in terms of the quantity of goods and the power to benefit or harm, but also in terms of mind, beauty, strength or skill, in terms of merit or talents, and, since these are the only qualities that could attract regard, one soon had to have them or to affect them; for one's own advantage one had to seem other than one in fact was. To be and to appear became two entirely different things, and from this distinction arose ostentatious display, deceitful cunning, and all the vices that follow in their train. Looked at in another way, man, who had previously been free and independent, is now so to speak subjugated by a *[175]* multitude of new needs to the whole of Nature, and especially to those of his kind, whose slave he in a sense becomes even by becoming their master; rich, he needs their services; poor, he needs their help, and moderate means do not enable him to do without them. He therefore constantly has to try to interest them in his fate and to make them find their own profit, in deed or in appearance, in working for his: which makes him knavish and artful with some, imperious and harsh with the rest, and places him under the necessity of abusing all those he needs if he cannot get them to fear him and does not find it in his interest to serve them usefully.

Finally, consuming ambition, the ardent desire to raise one's
relative fortune less out of genuine need than in order to place
oneself above others, instills in all men a black inclination to
harm one another, a secret jealousy which is all the more
dangerous as it often assumes the mask of benevolence in order
to strike its blow in greater safety: in a word, competition and
rivalry on the one hand, conflict of interests on the other, and
always the hidden desire to profit at another's expense; all these
evils are the first effect of property, and the inseparable train of
nascent inequality.

[28] Before its representative signs were invented, wealth
could scarcely consist in anything but lands and livestock, the
only real goods men can possess. Now, once inheritances had
increased in number and size to the point where they covered
all the land and all adjoined one another, men could no longer
aggrandize themselves except at one another's expense, and the
supernumeraries whom weakness or indolence had kept from
acquiring an inheritance of their own, grown poor without
having lost anything because they alone had not changed while
everything was changing around them, were obliged to receive
or to seize their subsistence from the hands of the rich; and
from this began to arise, according to the different characters of
the poor and the rich, domination and servitude, or violence
and plunder. The rich, for their part, had scarcely become
acquainted with the pleasure of dominating than they disdained
all other pleasures, and using their old Slaves to subject new
ones, they thought only of subjugating and enslaving their
neighbors; like those ravenous wolves which once they have
tasted human flesh, [176] scorn all other food and from then on
want only to devour men.

[29] Thus, as the most powerful or the most miserable claimed,
on the basis of their strength or of their needs, a kind of right
to another's goods, equivalent, according to them, to the right
of property, the breakdown of equality was followed by the
most frightful disorder: thus the usurpations of the rich, the
Banditry of the Poor, the unbridled passions of all, stifling
natural pity and the still-weak voice of justice, made men greedy,
ambitious, and wicked. A perpetual conflict arose between the

right of the stronger and the right of the first occupant, which
ended only in fights and murders (XVII). Nascent Society gave
way to the most horrible state of war: Mankind, debased and
devastated, no longer able to turn back or to renounce its
wretched acquisitions, and working only to its shame by the
abuse of the faculties that do it honor, brought itself to the
brink of ruin.

> *Shocked by the novelty of the evil,*
> *at once rich and miserable,*
> *He seeks to escape his wealth, and*
> *hates what he had just prayed for.*

[30] It is not possible that men should not at last have reflected
on such a miserable situation and the calamities besetting them.
The rich, above all, must soon have sensed how disadvantageous
to them was a perpetual war of which they alone bore the full
cost, and in which everyone risked his life while only some also
risked goods. Besides, regardless of the color they might lend
to their usurpations, they realized well enough that they were
only based on a precarious and abusive right, and that since
they had been acquired solely by force, force could deprive
them of them without their having any reason for complaint.
Even those whom industriousness alone had enriched could
scarcely base their property on better titles. No matter if they
said: It is I who built this wall; I earned this plot by my labor.
Who set its boundaries for you, they could be answered; and by
virtue of what do you lay claim to being paid at our expense
for labor we did not impose on you? Do you not know that a
great many of your brothers perish or suffer from need for what
you have in excess, and that you required the express and
unanimous *[177]* consent of Mankind to appropriate for yourself
anything from the common subsistence above and beyond your
own? Lacking valid reasons to justify and sufficient strength to
defend himself; easily crushing an individual, but himself crushed
by troops of bandits; alone against all, and unable, because of
their mutual jealousies, to unite with his equals against enemies
united by the common hope of plunder, the rich, under the

pressure of necessity, at last conceived the most well-considered project ever to enter man's mind; to use even his attackers' forces in his favor, to make his adversaries his defenders, to instill in them other maxims and to give them different institutions, as favorable to himself as natural Right was contrary to him.

[31] To this end, after exhibiting to his neighbors the horror of a situation which armed all of them against one another, made their possessions as burdensome to them as their needs, and in which no one found safety in either poverty or wealth, he easily invented specious reasons to bring them over to his purpose: "Let us unite," he told them, "to protect the weak from oppression, restrain the ambitious, and secure for everyone the possession of what belongs to him: Let us institute regulations of Justice and of peace to which all are obliged to conform, which favor no one, and which in a way make up for the vagaries of fortune by subjecting the powerful and the weak alike to mutual duties. In a word, instead of turning our forces against ourselves, let us gather them into a supreme power that might govern us according to wise Laws, protect and defend all the members of the association, repulse common enemies, and keep us in eternal concord."

[32] Much less than the equivalent of this Discourse was needed to sway crude, easily seduced men who, in any event, had too much business to sort out among themselves to be able to do without arbiters, and too much greed and ambition to be able to do for long without Masters. All ran toward their chains in the belief that they were securing their freedom; for while they had enough reason to sense the advantages of a political establishment, *[178]* they had not enough experience to foresee its dangers; those most capable of anticipating the abuses were precisely those who counted on profiting from them, and even the wise saw that they had to make up their mind to sacrifice one part of their freedom to preserve the other, as a wounded man has his arm cut off to save the rest of his Body.

[33] Such was, or must have been, the origin of Society and of Laws, which gave the weak new fetters and the rich new forces (XVIII), irreversibly destroyed natural freedom, forever

fixed the Law of property and inequality, transformed a skillful usurpation into an irrevocable right, and for the profit of a few ambitious men henceforth subjugated the whole of Mankind to labor, servitude and misery. It is easy to see how the establishment of a single Society made the establishment of all the others indispensable, and how, in order to stand up to united forces, it became necessary to unite in turn. Societies, multiplying and expanding rapidly, soon covered the entire face of the earth, and it was no longer possible to find a single corner anywhere in the universe where one might get free of the yoke and keep one's head out of the way of the often ill-guided sword everyone perpetually saw hanging over it. Civil right having thus become the common rule of the Citizens, the Law of Nature no longer obtained except between different Societies where, under the name of Right of nations, it was tempered by a few tacit conventions in order to make commerce possible and to replace natural commiseration which, losing in the relations between one Society and another almost all the force it had in the relations between one man and another, no longer dwells but in a few great Cosmopolitan Souls who cross the imaginary barriers that separate Peoples and, following the example of the sovereign being that created them, embrace the whole of Mankind in their benevolence.

[34] The Bodies Politic thus remaining in the state of Nature among themselves, soon experienced the inconveniences that had forced individuals to leave it, and this state became even more fatal among these great Bodies than it had previously been among the individuals who made them up. From it arose the National Wars, Battles, murders, reprisals which [179] make Nature tremble and shock reason, and all those horrible prejudices which rank the honor of spilling human blood among the virtues. The most honest men learned to count it as one of their duties to slay their kind; in time men were seen to massacre one another by the thousands without knowing why; and more murders were committed in a single day's fighting, and more horrors at the capture of a single town than had been committed in the state of Nature for centuries together over the entire face of the earth. Such are the first discernible effects of the division

of Mankind into different Societies. Let us return to their institution.

[35] I know that some have attributed other origins to Political Societies, such as the conquests by the more powerful, or the union of the weak; and the choice between these causes does not make a difference to what I want to establish: however, the cause of their origin which I have just expounded seems to me the most natural for the following reasons: 1. That, in the first case, the Right of conquest, since it is not a Right, could not have served as the foundation for any other Right, for the Conqueror and the conquered Peoples always remain in a state of War with one another unless the Nation, restored to full freedom, voluntarily chooses its Victor as its Chief. Until that time, regardless of what may have been the terms of capitulation, as they were based on nothing but violence and are consequently null by that very fact, there can, on this hypothesis, be neither genuine Society, nor Body Politic, nor any Law other than that of the stronger. 2. That, in the second case, the words *strong* and *weak* are equivocal; that during the interval that separates the establishment of the Right of property or of the first occupant and that of political Governments, the meaning of these terms is better conveyed by the terms *poor* and *rich,* because in fact, prior to the Laws, a man had no other means of subjugating his equals than by attacking their goods or making some of his own goods over to them. 3. That the Poor, having nothing to lose but their freedom, it would have been a great folly for them to deprive themselves voluntarily of the only good they had left, without gaining anything in exchange; that the rich, on the contrary, being so to speak sensitive in every part of their Goods, it was much easier to hurt them, and that they consequently *[180]* had to take more precautions to protect themselves from it; and that, finally, it is reasonable to believe that a thing was invented by those to whom it is useful rather than by those whom it harms.

[36] Nascent Government had no constant and regular form. For want of Philosophy and of experience, only present inconveniences were noticed, and men gave thought to remedying the others only as they became manifest. Despite all the labors

of the wisest Lawgivers, the Political state always remained imperfect because it was almost the product of chance and, having begun badly, time revealed its defects and suggested remedies but could never repair the vices of the Constitution; it was constantly being patched; whereas the thing to do would have been to begin by purging the threshing floor and setting aside all the old materials, as Lycurgus did in Sparta, in order afterwards to erect a good Building. Initially Society consisted of but a few general conventions which all individuals pledged to observe, and of which the Community made itself the guarantor toward each one of them. Experience had to show how weak such a constitution was, and how easily violators could escape conviction or punishment for wrongs of which the Public alone was to be both witness and judge; the Law had to be eluded in a thousand ways, inconveniences and disorders had to keep multiplying, before it at last occurred to them to entrust the dangerous custody of the public authority to individuals, and to commit the task of enforcing the People's deliberations to Magistrates: for to say that the Chiefs were chosen before the confederation was established, and that the Ministers of the Laws existed before the Laws themselves, is an assumption that does not allow of serious refutation.

[37] It would be no more reasonable to believe that Peoples initially threw themselves unconditionally and irrevocably into the arms of an absolute Master, and that the first means of providing for the common safety that proud and untamed men imagined was to rush headlong into slavery. Indeed, why did they give themselves superiors if not to defend them against oppression, and to protect their goods, their freedoms and their lives, which are, so to speak, the constituent *[181]* elements of their being? Now, since in the relations between man and man the worst that can happen to one is to find himself at the other's discretion, would it not have been counter to good sense to begin by surrendering into the hands of a Chief the only things they needed his help in order to preserve? What equivalent could he have offered them for the concessions of so fine a Right; and if he had dared to exact it on the pretext of defending them, would he not straightway have received the answer of the

Fable: What more will the enemy do to us? It is therefore incontrovertible, and it is the fundamental maxim of all Political Right, that Peoples gave themselves Chiefs to defend their freedom, and not to enslave them. *If we have a Prince,* said Pliny to Trajan, *it is so that he may preserve us from having a Master.*

[38] Politicians propound the same sophisms about the love of freedom that Philosophers propounded about the state of Nature; on the basis of the things they see, they judge of very different things which they have not seen, and they attribute to men a natural inclination to servitude because of the patience with which the men they have before their eyes bear their servitude, not realizing that it is as true of freedom as it is of innocence and virtue, that one appreciates their worth only as long as one enjoys them oneself, and loses the taste for them as soon as they are lost. I know the delights of your Country, said Brasidas to a Satrap who was comparing the life of Sparta with that of Persepolis, but you cannot know the pleasures of mine.

[39] As an untamed Steed bristles its mane, stamps the ground with its hoof, and struggles impetuously at the very sight of the bit, while a trained horse patiently suffers whip and spur, so barbarous man will not bend his head to the yoke which civilized man bears without a murmur, and he prefers the most tempestuous freedom to a tranquil subjection. Man's natural dispositions for or against servitude must therefore not be judged by the degradation of enslaved Peoples but by the prodigious feats of all free Peoples to protect themselves against oppression. I know that the former do nothing but incessantly boast of the peace and quiet they enjoy in their chains, and that *they call the most miserable servitude peace:* but when I see the others sacrifice pleasures, rest, wealth, *[182]* power, and life itself for the sake of preserving this one good which those who have lost it hold in such contempt; when I see Animals born free and abhorring captivity smash their heads against the bars of their prison; when I see multitudes of completely naked Savages scorn European voluptuousness and brave hunger, fire, the sword, and death in order to preserve nothing but their independence, I feel that it is not for Slaves to reason about freedom.

[40] As for Paternal authority, from which some have derived absolute Government and all Society, without invoking Locke's or Sidney's proofs to the contrary, it suffices to note that nothing in the world is farther from the ferocious spirit of Despotism than the gentleness of this authority which looks more to the advantage of the one who obeys than to the utility of the one who commands; that by the Law of Nature the Father is the Child's master only as long as it needs his help, that beyond that point they become equal, and that then the son, perfectly independent of the Father, owes him only respect and not obedience; for gratitude is indeed a duty that ought to be performed, but it is not a right that can be exacted. Instead of saying that civil Society is derived from Paternal power, it should, on the contrary, be said that this power derives its principal force from civil Society: an individual was recognized as the Father of many only once they remained assembled around him; the Father's goods, of which he is truly the Master, are the bonds that keep his children dependent on him, and he may give them no more of a share of his estate than is proportional to how well they have deserved of him by continual deference to his wishes. Now subjects, far from being in a position to expect a similar favor from their Despot—since they belong to him as his own, they and everything they possess, or at least since that is what he claims—are reduced to receiving as a favor whatever portion of their goods he leaves them; he dispenses justice when he despoils them; he dispenses grace when he lets them live.

[41] If one continued thus to examine the facts in terms of Right, one would find no more solidity than truth in the voluntary establishment of Tyranny, and it would be difficult to show the validity of a contract which obligated *[183]* only one of the parties, in which one side granted everything and the other nothing, and which could only prove prejudicial to the one who commits himself. This odious System is very far from being even today that of Wise and good Monarchs, and especially of the Kings of France, as may be seen in various places in their Edicts, and in particular in the following passage of a famous Text published in 1667 in the

name and by the orders of Louis XIV. *Let it therefore not be said that the Sovereign is not subject to the Laws of his State, since the contrary proposition is a truth of the Right of Nations, which flattery has sometimes challenged, but which good Princes have always defended as a tutelary divinity of their States. How much more legitimate it is to say with the Wise Plato that the perfect felicity of a Kingdom is that a Prince be obeyed by his Subjects, that the Prince obey the Law, and that the Law be right and always directed to the public good.* I shall not pause to inquire whether, since freedom is man's noblest faculty, one is not debasing one's Nature, placing oneself at the level of Beasts enslaved by instinct, offending even the Author of one's being, if one unreservedly renounces the most precious of all his gifts and submits to committing all the crimes he forbids us in order to please a ferocious and insane Master, nor whether that sublime workman ought to be more irritated at seeing his finest work destroyed than at seeing it dishonored. I shall ignore, if one wishes, the authority of Barbeyrac who, following Locke, explicitly declares that no one may sell his freedom to the point of submitting to an arbitrary power that treats him according to its fancy: *For,* he adds, *that would be to sell one's very life, of which one is not master.* I shall only ask by what Right those who were not afraid to debase themselves to this point could subject their posterity to the same ignominy, and on its behalf renounce goods which it does not owe to their liberality and without which life itself is a burden to all who are worthy of it?

[42] Pufendorf says that just as one transfers one's goods to another by conventions and Contracts, so too can one divest oneself of one's freedom in favor of someone else. That seems to me to be a very bad argument; for, first of all, the goods I alienate become something altogether foreign to me, and abuse of them is a matter of indifference *[184]* to me; but it is important to me that my freedom not be abused, and I cannot risk becoming the instrument of a crime without incurring the guilt of the evil I shall be forced to commit. Moreover, since the Right of property is only by convention and human institution, every man can dispose of what he possesses as he pleases: but the same does not hold for the essential Gifts of Nature, such as

life and freedom, which everyone is permitted to enjoy and of
which it is at least doubtful that one has the Right to divest
oneself; in depriving oneself of the one, one debases one's
being; in depriving oneself of the other one annihilates it as
much as in one lies; and as no temporal good can compensate
for either, it would be an offense against both Nature and reason
to renounce them at any price whatsoever. But even if one
could alienate one's freedom as one can one's goods, it would
be very different with respect to Children, who enjoy the
Father's goods only by transmittal of his right, whereas freedom,
since it is a gift they have from Nature in their capacity as
human beings, their Parents had no Right to divest them of it;
so that just as violence had to be done to Nature in order to
establish Slavery, Nature had to be altered in order to perpetuate
that Right. And the Jurists who have gravely pronounced that
the child of a Slave would be born a Slave, have in other words
decided that a human being would not be born a human being.

[43] It therefore seems to me certain not only that Governments did not begin with Arbitrary Power, which is but their
corruption, their ultimate stage, and which at last returns them
to the sole Law of the stronger for which they at first were the
remedy, but also that even if this is how they did begin, Arbitrary
Power, being by its Nature illegitimate, cannot have served as
the foundation for the Rights of Society nor, consequently, for
instituted inequality.

[44] Without at present entering into the inquiries that still
remain to be pursued regarding the Nature of the fundamental
Pact of all Government, I here limit myself in accordance with
the common opinion to considering the establishment of the
Body Politic as a true Contract between the People and the
Chiefs it chooses for itself; a Contract by which both Parties
obligate themselves to observe the Laws stipulated in it and
which form the bonds of their union. The People having, in
regard to Social relations, united all their *[185]* wills, into one
single will, all the articles on which this will pronounces itself
become so many fundamental Laws that obligate all the members
of the State without exception, and one of which regulates the
selection and the power of the Magistrates charged with attending

to the execution of the other Laws. This power extends to everything that can preserve the Constitution but not as far as to change it. To it are joined honors that render the Laws and their Ministers respectable and, for the Ministers personally, prerogatives compensating them for the strenuous labors which good administration requires. The Magistrate, for his part, obligates himself to use the power entrusted to him only in conformity with the intention of the Constituents, to maintain everyone in the peaceful enjoyment of what belongs to him, and on all occasions to prefer the public utility to his self-interest.

[45] Before experience had shown or knowledge of the human heart had led [men] to anticipate the inevitable abuses of such a constitution, it must have appeared all the better, as those who were charged with attending to its preservation themselves had the greatest interest in its being preserved; for, the Magistracy and its Rights being established only by the fundamental Laws, as soon as these are destroyed, the Magistrates would cease to be legitimate, the People would no longer be bound to obey them, and since it would have been the Law and not the Magistrate that constituted the essence of the State, everyone would by Right revert to his Natural freedom.

[46] If one but paused to reflect on it attentively, this would be confirmed by new reasons, and it would be evident from the Nature of the Contract that it could not be irrevocable: for if there were no superior power capable of guaranteeing the Contracting parties' fidelity or of forcing them to fulfill their reciprocal engagements, the Parties would remain sole judges in their own case, and each would always have the Right to renounce the Contract as soon as he found either that the other had violated its terms, or that the terms ceased to suit himself. It is on this principle that the Right to abdicate can, it seems, be based. Now, considering, as we are doing, only human institution, if the Magistrate, who has all the power in his hand and who appropriates to himself all the advantages of the Contract, nevertheless had the right to renounce his autho/186/rity, then there is all the more reason that the People, who pay for all of the Chiefs' faults, should have the Right to

renounce Dependence. But the frightful dissensions, the infinite disorders which this dangerous power would necessarily entail, show more than anything else does, how much human Government needed a more solid base than reason alone, and how necessary for the public repose it was that the divine will intervene to give to Sovereign authority a sacred and inviolable character which might deprive the subjects of the fatal Right to dispose of it. If Religion had performed only this good for men, it would be enough for them all to have to cherish and adopt it, even with its abuses, since it still spares more blood than fanaticism causes to flow: but let us follow the thread of our hypothesis.

[47] The different forms of Governments owe their origin to the greater or lesser differences between individuals at the time of Institution. Was one man preeminent in power, wealth, or prestige? He alone was elected Magistrate, and the State became Monarchic; if several, nearly equal among themselves, surpassed all the others, they were elected together, and there was an Aristocracy; those between whose fortune or talents there was less disparity and who had distanced themselves least from the state of Nature, retained the supreme Administration in common, and formed a Democracy. Time confirmed which of these forms was the most advantageous to men. Some remained exclusively subject to Laws, others were soon obeying Masters. Citizens wanted only to keep their freedom, subjects thought only of depriving their neighbors of theirs, because they found it insufferable that others enjoy a good which they no longer enjoyed themselves. In a word, on one side were wealth and Conquests, and on the other happiness and virtue.

[48] In these different Governments all Magistracies were at first Elective; and when Wealth did not prevail, preference was accorded to merit, which confers a Natural Ascendancy, and to age, which confers experience in business and equanimity in deliberations. The Hebrews' elders, the Spartan Gerontes, the Roman Senate, and the very Etymology of our word *Seigneur,* show how [187] respected Old Age formerly was. The more Elections settled on men of advanced age, the more frequent they became, and the more their cumbersomeness made itself

felt; intrigues arose, factions were formed, the parties became embittered, civil Wars flared up; at last the blood of Citizens was sacrificed to the alleged happiness of the State, and men were on the verge of relapsing into the Anarchy of former times. The ambition of the Foremost men took advantage of these circumstances to perpetuate their offices within their families: The People, already accustomed to dependence, repose, and the comforts of life, and already past the state where they could break their chains, consented to let their servitude increase in order to secure their tranquility, and that is how Chiefs, having become hereditary, grew accustomed to look upon their Magistracy as a family estate and upon themselves as the proprietors of the State of which they at first were only the Officers, to call their Fellow-Citizens their Slaves, to number them like Cattle among the things that belonged to them, and to call themselves equals of the Gods and Kings of Kings.

[49] If we follow the progress of inequality through these different revolutions, we will find that the establishment of the Law and Right of property was its first term; the institution of Magistracy, the second; the conversion of legitimate into arbitrary power the third and last; so that the state of wealth and poverty was authorized by the first Epoch; that of powerful and weak by the second, and that of Master and Slave by the third, which is the last degree of inequality and the stage to which all the others finally lead, until new revolutions either dissolve the Government entirely or bring it closer to legitimate institution.

[50] In order to understand the necessity of this progress one has to consider not so much the motives for the establishment of the Body Politic, as the form it assumes in execution, and the inconveniences it brings about: for the same vices that make social institutions necessary, make their abuse inevitable; and since, with the sole exception of Sparta where the Law primarily attended to the Children's education, and where Lycurgus established morals that almost made the addition of *[188]* Laws unnecessary, Laws, in general less strong than the passions, contain men without changing them; it would be easy to prove that any Government which, without being corrupted or altered, always functioned in accordance with the end of its institution,

would have been instituted unnecessarily, and a Country where no one eluded the Laws and abused the Magistracy, would need neither Magistrates nor Laws.

[51] Political distinctions necessarily introduce civil distinctions. Growing inequality between the People and its Chiefs soon makes itself felt among private individuals, and gets modified there in a thousand ways according to passions, talents, and circumstances. The Magistrate cannot usurp illegitimate power without establishing clients to whom he is forced to yield some part of it. Besides, Citizens let themselves be oppressed only so far as they are carried away by blind ambition and, looking beneath more than they look above themselves, come to hold Domination dearer than independence, and consent to bear chains so that they might impose chains on others in turn. It is very difficult to reduce to obedience someone who does not seek to command, and the cleverest Politician would never succeed in subjugating men whose only wish was to be Free; but inequality readily spreads among ambitious and pusillanimous souls, always ready to risk their fortune, and almost equally ready to dominate or serve according to whether it proves favorable or adverse to them. Thus there must have come a time when the eyes of the People were so dazzled that their leaders only had to say to the least of men, be Great, you and your entire race, and he at once appeared great to everyone as well as in his own eyes, and his Descendants were exalted still further in proportion to their distance from him; the more remote and uncertain the cause, the greater the effect; the more idlers could be counted in a family, the more illustrious it became.

[52] If this were the place to go into details, I could easily explain how, even without the Government's intervention, inequality of credit and authority becomes inevitable among Private Individuals (XIX) as soon as, united in one Society, they are forced to [189] compare themselves one with the other, and to take the differences they find into account in the constant use they have to make of one another. These differences are of several kinds; but in general, since wealth, nobility or rank, Power and personal merit are the principal distinctions by which people measure themselves in Society, I would prove that the

harmony or conflict of these various forces is the surest sign of
a well or a badly constituted State: I would show that of these
four sorts of inequality, as personal qualities are the origin of
all the others, wealth is the last to which they are finally
reduced, because, being the most immediately useful to well-
being and the easiest to transmit, it can readily be used to buy
all the rest. This observation makes it possible to judge rather
accurately of the extent to which any People has moved from
its original institution, and how far it has gone toward the
ultimate stage of corruption. I would indicate how much this
universal desire for reputation, honors, and preferment which
consumes us all, stimulates talents and strengths and sets them
off against one another, how much it excites and multiplies the
passions and, in making all men competitors, rivals, or rather
enemies, how many reverses, how many successes, how many
catastrophies of every kind it causes daily by leading so many
Contenders to enter the same lists: I would show that it is to
this ardor to have ourselves talked about, to this frenzy to
distinguish ourselves which almost always keeps us outside
ourselves, that we owe what is best and what is worst among
men, our virtues and our vices, our Sciences and our errors, our
Conquerors and our Philosophers, that is to say a multitude of
bad things for a small number of good ones. Finally, I would
prove that if one sees a handful of powerful and rich men at
the pinnacle of greatness and fortune while the mass crawls in
obscurity and misery, it is because the former value the things
they enjoy only to the extent that the others are deprived of
them, and they would cease to be happy if, without any change
in their own state, the People ceased to be miserable.

[53] But these details would alone provide material for a
considerable work in which the advantages and inconveniences
of any Government relative to the Rights of the state of Nature
would be weighed, and in which would be revealed all *[190]*
the different guises that inequality has assumed to this day and
may in future Centuries assume, according to the Nature of
these Governments and to the revolutions time will necessarily
bring about in them. One would see the multitude oppressed
from within as a consequence of the very precautions it had

taken against threats from without; one would see oppression constantly grow without the oppressed ever being able to know where it might end, or what legitimate means they might still have to stop it. One would see the Rights of Citizens and National freedoms die out little by little, and the protestations of the weak treated as seditious rumblings. One would see politics restrict the honor of defending the common cause to a mercenary portion of the People: One would see as a result taxes become necessary, the discouraged Cultivator leave his field even in Peacetime, and abandon his plow to gird on the sword. One would see arise the fatal and bizarre rules regarding the point of honor: One would see the defenders of the Fatherland sooner or later become its Enemies, forever holding the dagger over their fellow-citizens, and a time would come when they would be heard to say to their Country's oppressor

If you order me to plunge the sword into my brother's breast,
Or my father's throat, or even my pregnant wife's womb,
I shall do so, though my right arm be unwilling.

[54] From the extreme inequality of Conditions and fortunes, from the diversity of passions and talents, from the useless arts, the pernicious arts, the frivolous Sciences, would arise masses of prejudices equally contrary to reason, happiness and virtue; one would see Chiefs foment everything that can weaken assembled men by disuniting them; everything that can give Society an air of apparent concord while sowing seeds of real division; everything that can inspire mistrust and mutual hatred in the different orders by setting their Rights and interests at odds, and so strengthen the Power that contains them all.

[55] It is from the lap of this disorder and these revolutions that Despotism, gradually raising its hideous head *[191]* and devouring everything good and wholesome it may have seen anywhere in the State, would finally succeed in trampling Laws and People underfoot, and establishing itself on the ruins of the Republic. The times preceding this last change would be times of troubles and calamities: but in the end everything would be swallowed up by the Monster; and Peoples would no longer

have Chiefs or Laws, but only Tyrants. From that moment on there would also no longer be any question of morals and virtue; for wherever Despotism rules, *where honesty offers no hope,* it suffers no other master; as soon as it speaks, there is no consulting probity or duty, and the blindest obedience is the only virtue left to Slaves.

[56] Here is the last stage of inequality, and the ultimate point which closes the Circle and meets the point from which we set out: Here all private individuals again become equal because they are nothing and, the Subjects no longer having any other Law than the Master's will, nor the Master any other rule than his passions, notions of the good and the principles of justice again vanish. Here everything reverts to the sole Law of the stronger and consequently to a new State of Nature, different from that with which we began in that the first was the state of Nature in its purity, whereas this last is the fruit of an excess of corruption. There is, in any event, so little difference between the two states, and the Contract of Government is so utterly dissolved by Despotism, that the Despot is Master only as long as he is the stronger, and that as soon as he can be expelled he has no grounds to protest against violence. The uprising that finally strangles or dethrones a Sultan is as legal an action as those by which, the day before, he disposed of his Subjects' lives and goods. Force alone maintains him, force alone over-throws him; thus everything happens in accordance with the Natural order; and whatever may be the outcome of these brief and frequent revolutions, no one can complain of another's injustice, but only of his own imprudence or misfortune.

[57] By thus discovering and retracing the forgotten and lost roads that must have led man from the Natural state to the Civil state; by restoring, in addition to the intermediary *[192]* stages I have just indicated, those which the pressure of time caused me to omit or the imagination failed to suggest to me, any attentive Reader cannot fail but be struck by the immense distance that separates these two states. It is in this slow succession of things that he will find the solution to an infinite number of problems of ethics and of Politics which Philosophers are unable to solve. He will sense that, since the Mankind of one age is not the

Mankind of another age, the reason why Diogenes did not find a man is that he was searching among his contemporaries for a man of a period that was no more: Cato, he will say, perished with Rome and freedom, because he was out of place in his century, and the greatest of men only amazed the world he would have governed five hundred years earlier. In a word, he will explain how the human soul and passions, by imperceptible alterations change in Nature, so to speak; why the objects of our needs and of our pleasures change in the long run; why, as original man gradually vanishes, Society no longer offers to the eyes of the wise man anything but an assemblage of artificial men and factitious passions which are the product of all these new relationships and without true foundation in Nature. Observation fully confirms what reflection teaches us on this subject: Savage man and civilized man differ so much in their inmost heart and inclinations that what constitutes the supreme happiness of the one would reduce the other to despair. The first breathes nothing but repose and freedom, he wants only to live and to remain idle, and even the Stoic's ataraxia does not approximate his profound indifference to everything else. By contrast, the Citizen, always active, sweats, scurries, constantly agonizes in search of still more strenuous occupations: he works to the death, even rushes toward it in order to be in a position to live, or renounces life in order to acquire immortality. He courts the great whom he hates, and the rich whom he despises; he spares nothing to attain the honor of serving them; he vaingloriously boasts of his baseness and of their protection and, proud of his slavery, he speaks contemptuously of those who have not the honor of sharing it. What a Sight for a Carib the difficult and envied labors of a European Statesman must be! How many cruel deaths would not *[193]* this indolent Savage prefer to the horror of such a life, which is often not even sweetened by the pleasure of doing well? But in order to see the purpose of so many cares, the words *power* and *reputation* would have to have some meaning in his mind; he would have to learn that there is a sort of men who count how they are looked upon by the rest of the universe for something, who can be happy and satisfied with themselves on the testimony of

others rather than on their own. That, indeed, is the genuine
cause of all these differences: the Savage lives in himself;
sociable man, always outside himself, is capable of living only
in the opinion of others and, so to speak, derives the sentiment
of his own existence solely from their judgment. It is not part
of my subject to show how such a disposition engenders so
much indifference to good and evil together with such fine
discourses on morality; how everything being reduced to appearances, everything becomes factitious and play-acting: honor,
friendship, virtue, and often even vices in which one at length
discovers the secret of glorying; how, in a word, forever asking
of others what we are, without ever daring to ask it of ourselves,
in the midst of so much Philosophy, humanity, politeness, and
Sublime maxims, we have nothing more than a deceiving and
frivolous exterior, honor without virtue, reason without wisdom,
and pleasure without happiness. It is enough for me to have
proved that such is not man's original state, and that the spirit
of Society alone, together with the inequality society engenders,
change and alter all our natural inclinations in this way.

[58] I have tried to give an account of the origin and the
progress of inequality, the establishment and the abuse of
political Societies, in so far as these things can be deduced from
the Nature of man by the light of reason alone, and independently
of the sacred Dogmas that endow Sovereign authority with the
Sanction of Divine Right. It follows from this account that
inequality, being almost nonexistent in the state of Nature, owes
its force and growth to the development of our faculties and
the progress of the human Mind, and that it finally becomes
stable and legitimate by the establishment of property and Laws.
It follows, further, that moral inequality, authorized by positive
right alone, is contrary to Natural Right whenever it is not *[194]*
directly proportional to Physical inequality; a distinction which
sufficiently determines what one ought to think in this respect
of the sort of inequality that prevails among all civilized Peoples;
since it is manifestly against the Law of Nature, however defined,
that a child command an old man, an imbecile lead a wise man,
and a handful of people abound in superfluities while the
starving multitude lacks in necessities.

[195]

ROUSSEAU'S NOTES

EPISTLE DEDICATORY, page 120

I Herodotus relates that after the murder of the false Smerdis, when the seven liberators of Persia gathered to deliberate about the form of Government they would give the State, Otanes's opinion strongly favored a republic; an opinion all the more extraordinary in the mouth of a Satrap in that, in addition to any claim he might have had to the Empire, the great fear more than death any sort of Government that forces them to respect men. Otanes, as might be expected, was not heeded, and seeing that they were going to proceed to the election of a Monarch he, who wanted neither to obey nor to command, freely yielded to the other Contenders his right to the crown, asking in return only that he himself and his posterity be free and independent; which was granted him. Even if Herodotus had not told us the restriction placed upon this Privilege, it would necessarily have to be assumed; otherwise Otanes, not recognizing any sort of Law and not accountable to anyone, would have been all-powerful in the State, and more powerful than the King himself. But it was scarcely likely that a man capable in a case like this of being satisfied with such a prerogative, was capable of abusing it. Indeed, there is no evidence that this right ever caused the least trouble in the Kingdom, due either to the wise Otanes, or to any one of his descendants.

PREFACE, page 129

II [1] With the very first step I take, I confidently lean on one of those authorities that are respectable to Philosophers because they are due to a solid and sublime reason which philosophers alone are capable of discovering and appreciating.

[2] "However much it may be in our interest to know ourselves, I wonder whether we do not know better everything that is not ourselves. Provided by Nature with organs destined exclusively for our preservation, we use them only to receive foreign impressions, we seek only to spread outward, and to exist outside ourselves; too busy *[196]* multiplying the functions of our senses and extending the external scope of our being, we rarely use that internal sense which reduces us to our true dimensions, and sets off from us everything that does not belong to it.

Yet this is the sense we must use if we wish to know ourselves; it is the only one by which we can judge ourselves; but how is this sense to be made active and given its full scope? How is our Soul, within which it resides, to be freed of all of our Mind's illusions? We have lost the habit of using it, it has remained without exercise amidst the riot of our bodily sensations, it has been dried up in the fire of our passions; the heart, the Mind, the senses, everything has worked against it." *Hist[oire] Nat[urelle]* IV:151, *de la Nat[ure] de l'homme.*

DISCOURSE, page 141

III [1] The changes which a long practice of walking on two feet may have produced in man's structure, the similarities that can still be observed between his arms and the Forelegs of Quadrupeds, and the inference drawn from the way they walk, may have given rise to some doubts about which way of walking must have been most natural to us. All children begin by walking on all fours and need our example and lessons to learn to stand upright. There are even Savage Nations, such as the Hottentots, which greatly neglect their Children and let them walk on their hands for so long that they afterwards have considerable trouble getting them to straighten up; the children of the Caribs of the Antilles do the same. There are various instances of Quadruped men, and I could cite among others that of the Child found in 1344 near Hesse where he had been raised by Wolves, and who subsequently said at the Court of Prince Henry that if it had been up to himself alone, he would have preferred to return among them rather than to live among men. He had become so accustomed to walk like those animals, that wood Splints had to be tied on him which forced him to hold himself upright and keep his balance on his two feet. The same was true of the Child found in 1694 in the forests of Lithuania, and who lived among Bears. He gave, says M. de Condillac, no sign of reason, walked on his hands and feet, had no language, and made sounds which in no way resembled those of a human being. The little Savage of Hanover who several years ago was brought to the Court of England had all the trouble in the world getting adjusted to walking on two feet, and in 1719 two more Savages were found in the Pyrenees, who roamed the mountains in the manner of quadrupeds. As for the possible objection that this means to deprive ourselves of the use of the hands, to which we owe so many advantages; besides the fact that *[197]* the example of the monkeys shows that the hand can very well be used in both ways, it would only prove that man can assign to his limbs a more convenient destination than Nature's, and not that Nature destined man to walk otherwise than it teaches him to do.

[2] But there are, it seems to me, much better reasons for holding that man is a biped. First of all, even if it were shown that he could originally have been structured differently than he visibly is, and nevertheless eventually become what he is, that would not be reason enough to conclude that that is how it did happen: For besides showing that these changes are possible, it would also have to be shown that they are at least likely, before accepting them. Moreover, while it does seem that man's arms could have served him for Legs in case of need, that is the only observation that lends this system support, as against a great many others that are contrary to it. The principal ones are: that if man had walked on all fours, then the manner in which his head is attached to his body, instead of directing his gaze horizontally as is that of all other animals and as is his own when he walks upright, would have kept his eyes fixed on the earth, a situation that is scarcely favorable to the preservation of the individual; that the tail he lacks and for which he has no use in walking on two feet, is useful to quadrupeds, and that none of them is without it; that the woman's breast, while very well placed for a biped holding her child in her arms, is so poorly placed for a quadruped that none has it so placed; that the hindquarters being inordinately high in relation to the forelegs, which is why we drag ourselves around on our knees when we walk on all fours, the whole would have made for an Animal that is ill-proportioned and walks uncomfortably; that if he had set his foot down flat as he does his hand, he would have had one less articulation in his hind leg than other animals have, namely that which joins the Canon bone to the Tibia; and that if he set down only the tip of the foot, as he would probably have been constrained to do, the tarsus, even disregarding the many bones that make it up, would seem to be too big to take the place of the canon, and its Articulations with the Metatarsus and the Tibia too close together to give the human leg in this position the same flexibility as the legs of quadrupeds. The example of Children, taken as it is from an age when natural strengths are not yet developed nor the limbs firm, proves nothing at all, and I would as soon say that dogs are not destined to walk because for several weeks after their birth they only crawl. Moreover, particular facts are of little force against the universal practice of all men, of even those from Nations which, since they had no communication with the others, could not have imitated them in anything. A Child abandoned in some forest before it could walk, and raised by some beast, will have followed

its Nurse's example by learning to walk as she does; it could have acquired through habit a dexterity it did not get from Nature; and *[198]* just as people lacking an arm succeed, by dint of practice, to do with their feet everything we do with our hands, so will it finally have succeeded in using its hands as feet.

DISCOURSE, page 142

IV [1] Should there be among my Readers so poor a Physicist as to raise objections regarding this assumption of the natural fertility of the earth, I will answer him with the following passage.

[2] "Since plants draw much more substance for their nourishment from air and water than they do from the earth, it happens that when they decay they restore more to the earth than they had drawn from it; besides, a forest regulates rainwater by preventing evaporation. Thus, in a woods left untouched for a long time, the layer of earth which supports vegetation would increase considerably; but since Animals restore less to the earth than they take from it, and men consume enormous quantities of wood and plants for fire and other uses, it follows that in an inhabited country the layer of topsoil must invariably decrease and eventually become like the ground of Arabia Petraea and so many other Provinces of the Orient which, indeed, is the oldest inhabited Clime, and where [now] only Salt and Sand are found; for the fixed Salt of Plants and of Animals remains, while all their other parts are volatilized." M. de Buffon, *Hist[oire] nat[urelle]*.

[3] To this may be added the factual proof of the great number of trees and of plants of all kinds that filled almost all the desert Islands discovered in recent centuries, and of what history tells us about the huge forests that had to be cut down everywhere on earth as it was populated or civilized. I shall make the following three additional remarks on this subject. The first is that, if there is a kind of vegetation that could compensate for the depletion of vegetable matter which, according to M. de Buffon's reasoning, is due to animals, then it is mainly woods, the crowns and leaves of which collect and absorb more water and moisture than do other plants. The second is that the destruction of topsoil, that is to say the loss of the substance suited to vegetation, must accelerate in proportion as the earth is more cultivated and as its more industrious inhabitants consume its various productions in greater quantities. My third and most important remark is that the fruits of Trees provide animals with a more abundant supply of food than can other [forms of] vegetation, an experiment I have myself

performed by comparing the production of two pieces of ground equal in size and quality, the one covered with chestnut trees, and the other sown with wheat.

DISCOURSE, page 142

V Among Quadrupeds the two most universal distinguishing features of the carnivorous species are drawn from the shape of the Teeth and from the conformation of the Intestines. The Animals that live only off vegetation all have blunt teeth, *[199]* like the Horse, the Ox, the Sheep, the Hare; but the Carnivores have them pointed, like the Cat, the Dog, the Wolf, the Fox. As for Intestines, Frugivorous Animals have some, such as the Colon, which are not found among carnivorous Animals. It therefore seems that Man, whose Teeth and Intestines are like those of the Frugivorous Animals, should naturally be placed in that Class, and this opinion is confirmed not only by anatomical observations: but the records of Antiquity also lend it considerable support. "Dicaearchus," says St. Jerome, "relates in his Books on Greek Antiquities that during the reign of Saturn, when the Earth was still fertile by itself, no man ate Flesh, but all lived off the Fruits and the Vegetables that grew naturally" (Bk. II, *Adv[versus] Jovian[um]*). This opinion may further be bolstered by the accounts of several modern Travelers; François Corréal, among others, reports that most of the inhabitants of the Lucayes whom the Spaniards transported to the Islands of Cuba, Santo Domingo, and elsewhere, died for having eaten flesh. It is evident from this that I forgo many advantages of which I could avail myself. For since prey is almost the only object about which Carnivores fight, and Frugivores live in constant peace with one another, it is clear that if the human species were of the latter kind, it could have subsisted much more easily in the state of Nature, and would have had much less need and many fewer occasions to leave it.

DISCOURSE, page 143

VI [1] All knowledge requiring reflection, all Knowledge acquired only from chains of ideas and perfected only successively, seems to be altogether beyond the reach of Savage man for want of communication with his kind, that is to say for want of the instrument used in such communication, and of the needs that make it necessary. His knowledge and efforts are restricted to jumping, running, fighting, throwing a stone, climbing a tree. But while these are the only things he knows, he, in return, knows them much better than do we who have not the same need of them as has he; and since these activities depend exclusively on the use of the Body and cannot be communicated or improved from one individual to the next, the first man could have been just as skilled at them as his most remote descendants.

[2] The reports of travelers are full of examples of the strength and vigor of men from the barbarous and Savage Nations; they praise their skill and facility scarcely less; and since it takes only eyes to observe these things, nothing prevents our crediting what eyewitnesses warrant in these matters. I draw some examples at random from the first books that come to hand. *[200]*

[3] "The Hottentots," says Kolben, "are better at fishing than the Europeans of the Cape. They are equally skilled with net, hook and spear, in bays as in rivers. They are no less skillful at catching fish by hand. They are incomparably adept at swimming. Their way of swimming is somewhat surprising and altogether peculiar to them. They swim with their body upright and their hands stretched out of the water, so that they appear to be walking on land. In the most turbulent sea and when the waves are so many mountains, they as it were dance on the crest of the waves, rising and falling like a piece of cork."

[4] "The Hottentots," the same Author further says, "are surprisingly skilled hunters, and how lightfootedly they run passes the imagination." He is surprised at their not putting their skill to bad use more frequently, although they do sometimes do so, as may be judged from the example he gives of it. "A Dutch sailor disembarking at the Cape," he says, "asked a Hottentot to follow him into Town with a roll of tobacco weighing about twenty pounds. When they both were at some distance from the Crew, the Hottentot asked the Sailor whether he could run. Run, the Dutchman answers, yes, quite well. Let us see, replies the African, and escaping with the tobacco, he disappeared almost instantly. The Sailor, dumbfounded by such marvelous speed, gave no thought to pursuing him, and never again saw either his tobacco or his porter.

[5] "They are so quick of eye and so sure of hand that Europeans simply cannot match them. At a hundred paces they will hit a target the size of a half-penny with a stone, and what is more astonishing, instead of fixing their eyes on the target as do we, they engage in constant movements and contortions. Their stone is as if carried by an invisible hand."

[6] Father du Tertre says about the Savages of the Antilles approximately the same things that have just been read about the Hottentots of

the Cape of Good Hope. He mainly praises the accuracy of their shooting with their arrows birds on the wing and swimming fish, which they then retrieve by diving. The Savages of North America are no less famous for their strength and their skill: and here is an example by which to judge of the strength and skill of the Indians of South America.

[7] In the year 1746, an Indian from Buenos Aires, having been sentenced to the Galleys in Cadiz, proposed to the Governor to buy back his freedom by risking his life at a public festival. He promised to tackle the fiercest Bull singlehanded and armed with only a rope, bring him low, grapple him with his rope by any part of the body he would be told to, saddle him, bridle him, ride him, fight thus mounted two more of the fiercest Bulls brought from the Torillo, and put them all [201] to death one after the other the moment he was ordered to do so, all without anyone's help; which was granted him. The Indian kept his word and succeeded in everything he had promised; for the way in which he went about it, and the full details of the fight, one can consult the first Volume in 12° of the *Observations sur l'histoire naturelle* by M. Gautier, p. 262, whence this fact is taken.

DISCOURSE, page 144

VII "The life-span of Horses," says M. de Buffon, "like that of all other animal species, is proportional to the duration of their growth. Man, who takes fourteen years to grow, may live six or seven times as long, that is to say ninety or a hundred years: The Horse, whose growth is completed in four years, may live six or seven times as long, that is to say twenty-five or thirty years. Possible counterexamples to this rule are so rare that they should not even be regarded as exceptions from which to draw conclusions; and since draught horses reach their full size in less time than do riding horses, they also live less long and are old by the time they have reached the age of fifteen."

DISCOURSE, page 144

VIII I believe I see between carnivorous and frugivorous animals another still more general difference than the one I mentioned in Note V, since it applies to birds as well. This difference consists in the number of young, which never exceeds two to a litter in species that live exclusively off vegetation, and generally exceeds that number for carnivorous animals. It is easy to know Nature's destination in this regard by the number of teats, which is only two for every female of the first species, like the Mare, the Cow, the Goat, the Doe, the Ewe, etc., and is always six or eight for the other females, like the Bitch, the Cat, the she-Wolf, the Tigress, etc. The Hen, the Goose, the Duck, all of which are carnivorous Birds, as well as the Eagle, the Sparrow-hawk, the Barn-owl, also lay and hatch a great many eggs, something that never happens in the case of the Pigeon, the Dove, or the Birds that eat absolutely nothing but grain, and generally lay and hatch no more than two eggs at a time. The reason that may account for this difference is that the animals living only off grasses and plants, since they spend almost all day foraging and are forced to spend much time feeding themselves, could not properly nurse many young, whereas the carnivores, since they take their meal almost in an instant, can more easily and more frequently return both to their young and to their hunt, and repair the expense of such a large quantity of Milk. All this calls for many individual observations and reflections; but this is not the place for them, and I am satisfied to have shown the most general System of Nature in this part, a System which *[202]* provides a new reason for taking man out of the Class of carnivorous animals and placing him among the frugivorous species.

DISCOURSE, page 149

IX [1] A famous Author, calculating the goods and evils of human life and comparing the two sums, found the last greatly exceeded the first and that, all things considered, life was a rather poor gift for man. I am not at all surprised by his conclusion; he drew all his arguments from the constitution of Civil man: if he had gone back to Natural man, it is likely that he would have reached very different results, that he would have noticed that man suffers almost no evils but those he has given himself, and that Nature would have been justified. It is not without difficulty that we have succeeded in making ourselves so unhappy. When, on the one hand, one considers men's tremendous labors, so many Sciences fathomed, so many arts invented, so many forces employed; abysses filled, mountains razed, rocks sundered, rivers made navigable, lands cleared, lakes dug, swamps drained, huge buildings erected on land, the sea covered with Vessels and Sailors; and when, on the other hand, one inquires with a little meditation into the true advantages that have resulted from all this for the happiness of the human species; one cannot but be struck by the astonishing disproportion there is between these things, and deplore man's blindness which, in order to feed his insane pride and I know not what vain self-admiration, causes him eagerly to run after all the miseries of which he is susceptible, and which beneficent Nature had taken care to keep from him.

[2] Men are wicked; a sad and constant experience makes proof unnecessary; yet man is naturally good, I believe I have proved that; what, then, can have depraved him to this point, if not the changes that occurred in his constitution, the progress he has made, and the knowledge he has acquired? Let human Society be ever so much admired, it remains none the less true that it necessarily moves men to hate one another in proportion as their interests cross, to render one another apparent services and in effect to do one another every imaginable harm. What is one to think of dealings in which every private person's reason dictates to him maxims directly contrary to those the public reason preaches to the body of Society, and in which everyone profits from the others' misfortunes? There is perhaps not a single well-to-do person whom greedy heirs and often his own children do not secretly wish dead; not a Vessel at Sea whose loss would not be good news to some Merchant; not a single commercial house which a dishonest debtor would not like to see burn together with all the papers in it; not a single People that does not rejoice at the disasters of its neighbors. That is how we find our advantage in what harms our kind, and how one man's loss almost always makes for another's prosperity *[203]*: but what is more dangerous still is that public calamities are waited and hoped for by a host of private individuals. Some wish for illnesses, others for death, others for war, others for famine; I have seen horrible men weep in sorrow at the prospects of a good harvest, and the great and deadly London fire which cost so many unfortunates their lives or their belongings, perhaps made more than ten thousand people's fortune. I know that Montaigne blames the Athenian Demades for having had a Workman punished who, by selling coffins very dear, profited greatly from the death of Citizens: But the reason Montaigne adduces, that everyone would have to be punished, clearly confirms my own. Let us therefore look through our frivolous displays of beneficence to what goes on in the recesses of men's hearts, and reflect on what must be the state of things in which all men are forced both to caress and to destroy one another, and in which they are born enemies by duty and knaves by interest. If, in return, I am told that Society is so constituted that every man gains by serving the rest; I shall reply that that would all be very well if he did not gain even more by harming them. There is no profit, however legitimate, that is not exceeded by the profit to be made illegitimately, and the wrong done a neighbor is always more lucrative than any services. It

therefore only remains a matter of finding ways to ensure one's impunity, and that is the end to which the powerful put all their strength and the weak all their cunning.

[3] Savage man, once he has supped, is at peace with all of Nature and a friend to all of his kind. Must he sometimes contend for his meal? He never comes to blows without first having compared the difficulty of prevailing with that of finding his sustenance elsewhere; and since pride has no share in the fight, it ends with a few fisticuffs; the victor eats, the vanquished goes off to seek his fortune, and everything is once again at peace: but with man in Society it is all a very different business; first necessities have to be provided for, and then superfluities; next come delicacies, and then immense wealth, and then subjects, and then Slaves; he has not a moment's respite; what is most singular is that the less natural and urgent the needs, the more the passions increase and, worse still, so does the power to satisfy them; so that after long periods of prosperity, after having swallowed up a good many treasures and ruined a good many men, my Hero will end up by cutting every throat until he is the sole master of the Universe. Such, in brief, is the moral picture if not of human life, at least of the secret aspirations of the heart of every Civilized man.

[4] Compare without prejudices the state of Civil man with that of Savage man, and determine if you can, how many new gates in addition to his wickedness, his needs, and his miseries, the first has opened to pain and to death. If you consider the mental suffering that consumes us, the violent passions that exhaust and waste us, the excessive labors *[204]* which overburden the poor, the even more dangerous softness to which the rich abandon themselves, and which cause the first to die of their needs and the others of their excesses. If you think of the horrendous combinations of foods, their noxious seasonings, the spoiled provisions, the adulterated drugs, the villainies of those who sell them, the mistakes of those who administer them, the poisonous Utensils in which they are prepared; if you take note of the epidemics bred by the bad air wherever multitudes of men are gathered together, of those occasioned by the delicacy of our way of living, the to and fro between indoors and out, the use of clothes put on or taken off with too few precautions, and all the cares which our excessive sensuality has turned into necessary habits and which it then costs us our life or our health to neglect or to be deprived of altogether; if you take into account the fires and the earthquakes that consume or topple entire Cities, killing their inhabitants by the thousands; in a word, if you bring together the dangers which all of these causes continually gather over our heads,

you will sense how dearly Nature makes us pay for the contempt we have shown for its lessons.

[5] I shall not here repeat about war what I have said about it elsewhere; but I do wish informed people were, for once, willing and ready to tell the public in detail about the horrors committed in armies by the Contractors of food and Hospital supplies; their none-too-secret maneuvers, by which the most brilliant armies fade into less than nothing, would be seen to cause the death of more Soldiers than are mowed down by the enemy's sword. Another and no less shocking calculation is to reckon the number of men yearly swallowed up by the sea as a result of hunger, or scurvy, or Pirates, or fire, or shipwrecks. It is obvious that established property and hence Society must also be held accountable for the murders, poisonings, highway robberies, and even for the punishments of these crimes, punishments that are necessary to prevent greater evils but which, by making the murder of one man cost the lives of two or more, do nevertheless really double the loss to the human species. How many shameful ways there are to prevent the birth of human beings and to cheat Nature: Either by those brutal and depraved tastes that insult her most charming work, tastes which neither Savages nor animals have ever known, and which in civilized countries have arisen only from a corrupt imagination; or by those secret abortions, worthy fruits of debauchery and of a vicious honor, or by the exposure or murder of large numbers of children, the victims of their parents' poverty or their Mothers' barbarous shame; or, finally, by the mutilation of the unfortunates who have a portion of their existence and their entire posterity sacrificed to vain songs or, worse still, to the brutal jealousy of a few men: A mutilation which, in this last case, doubly outrages Nature, *[205]* in the treatment inflicted on those who suffer it, and in the use to which they are destined.

[6] But are there not a thousand even more frequent and more dangerous cases, when paternal rights openly offend humanity? How many talents are buried and inclinations forced by the unwise constraint of Fathers! How many who would have distinguished themselves if they had occupied a suitable position, die miserable and dishonored in some other position for which they had no taste! How many happy but unequal marriages have been broken or upset, and how many chaste wives dishonored by an order of [social] conditions that is always in contradiction with the order of nature! How many other bizarre unions formed by interest and disowned by love and reason! How many even honest and virtuous husbands and wives torture one another because

they were poorly matched! How many young and unhappy victims of their Parents' greed plunge into vice or spend their sad days in tears, and groan in indissoluble bonds which the heart rejects and gold alone forged! Sometimes the fortunate are those whose courage and very virtue tear them from life before some barbarous violence forces them to spend it in crime or in despair. Forgive me for it, Father and Mother forever deserving of sorrow: I embitter your suffering reluctantly; but may it serve as an eternal and terrible example to anyone who dares, in the very name of nature, to violate the most sacred of its rights!

[7] If I have spoken only of the badly formed unions that are the product of our political condition, are the unions over which love and sympathy presided thought to be free of inconveniences? What if I undertook to show the human species assaulted at its very source and even in the most sacred of all ties, ties regarding which one no longer dares to heed Nature until after one has consulted fortune, and with respect to which civil disorder so jumbles virtues and vices that continence becomes a criminal precaution and the refusal to give life to another human being an act of humanity? But without tearing the veil that covers so many horrors, let us leave it at pointing out the evil for which others must provide the remedies.

[8] Add to all this the many unhealthy trades that shorten life or destroy the temperament; such as work in mines, the various treatments of metals and minerals, especially Lead, Copper, Mercury, Cobalt, Arsenic, Realgar; those other perilous trades that daily cost many workers' lives, some of them Roofers, others Carpenters, others Masons, others working in quarries; combine all of these considerations, I say, and it will be evident that the reasons for the decrease in the species that has been noted by more than one Philosopher, may be found in the establishment and the perfection of Societies.

[9] Luxury, impossible to prevent among men greedy for their own comfort and other men's regard, soon completes [206] the evil which Societies had begun, and on the pretext of providing a livelihood for the poor who should never have been made so in the first place, it impoverished everyone else, and sooner or later depopulates the State.

[10] Luxury is a remedy much worse than the evil it pretends to cure; or rather, it is itself the worst of all evils in any State whatever, large or small, and which, in order to feed the hosts of Lackeys and of miserable people it has created, oppresses and ruins both the farmer and the Citizen; like those scorching south winds which, blanketing grass and foliage with all-devouring insects, deprive useful animals of

their sustenance, and carry famine and death wherever they make themselves felt.

[11] From Society and the luxury which it engenders arise the liberal and the mechanical Arts, Commerce, Letters; and all those useless things that cause industry to flourish, and enrich and ruin States. The reason for this decline is very simple. It is easy to see that agriculture must, by its nature, be the least lucrative of all the arts; for since the use of its product is the most indispensable to all men, its price must be proportioned to the poorest men's faculty [to pay]. From that same principle the following rule may be derived, that in general the Arts are lucrative in inverse proportion to their usefulness, and that the most needed arts must in the end become the most neglected. Which shows what one ought to think regarding the true advantages of industry and the real effect that results from its progress.

[12] Such are the perceptible causes of all the miseries into which opulence in the end plunges the most admired Nations. As industry and the arts spread and flourish, the scorned farmer, weighed down by taxes needed to support Luxury, and condemned to spend his life between labor and hunger, abandons his fields to go look in the Cities for the bread which he should be bringing there. The more the stupid eyes of the People are struck with admiration by capital cities; the more one should bemoan to see the Countryside abandoned, the fields lie fallow, and the highways overrun by unfortunate Citizens turned beggars or thieves and destined someday to end their misery on the wheel or a dunghill. That is how the State, while it on one side grows rich, grows weak and is depopulated on the other, and how the most powerful Monarchies, after much labor to grow opulent and empty, end up by being the prey of the poor Nations that succumb to the fatal temptation to invade them, and grow rich and weak in their turn, until they are themselves invaded and destroyed by others.

[13] Let someone deign to explain to us for once what could have produced those swarms of Barbarians who for so many centuries swept over Europe, Asia, and Africa? Was it to the quality of their Arts, the Wisdom of their Laws, the excellence of their polity, that they owed this enormous population? Let our learned men kindly tell us why, instead of multiplying to such an extent, these ferocious and brutal men, lacking enlightenment, lacking restraints, lacking education, were not forever killing off each other over their pastures or [207] their hunting grounds? Let them explain to us how these miserable people could have been so bold as to look straight in the face of such clever people as we ourselves were, with such fine military discipline, such

fine Codes, and such wise Laws? Finally, why is it that, ever since
Society was perfected in the countries of the North, and they there
went to such trouble to teach men their mutual duties and the art of
living together agreeably and peacefully, nothing like the great numbers
of men which it used to produce is any longer seen to come from
there. I rather fear that it might finally occur to someone to answer me
that all these great things, to wit the Arts, the Sciences, and the Laws
were most Wisely invented by men as a Salutary plague to prevent the
excessive increase of the species, for fear that this world, which is
destined for us, might in the end become too small for its inhabitants.

[14] What, then? Must Societies be destroyed, thine and mine anni-
hilated, and men return to live in forests with Bears? A conclusion in
the style of my adversaries, which I would rather anticipate than leave
them the shame of drawing it. O you, to whom the celestial voice has
not made itself heard, and who recognize no other destination for your
species than to end this short life in peace; you who are able to leave
behind in the Cities your fatal acquisitions, your restless minds, your
corrupted hearts, and your unbridled desires; resume your ancient and
first innocence since it is in your power to do so; go into the woods to
lose sight and memory of your contemporaries' crimes, and do not fear
that you are debasing your species when you renounce its enlightenment
in order to renounce its vices. As for men like myself, whose passions
have forever destroyed their original simplicity, who can no longer
subsist on grass and acorns, nor do without Laws or Chiefs; Those who
were honored in their first Father with supernatural lessons; those who
will see in the intention of giving from the beginning a morality to
human actions which they would not have acquired for a long time,
the reason for a precept indifferent in itself and inexplicable in any
other System: Those, in a word, who are convinced that the divine
voice called all Mankind to the enlightenment and the happiness of the
celestial Intelligences; they will, all of them, try, by practicing the
virtues which they obligate themselves to perform as they learn to
know them, to deserve the eternal prize they must expect for it; they
will respect the sacred bonds of the Societies of which they are
members; they will love their kind and serve them with all their power;
they will scrupulously obey the Laws and the men who are their
Authors and their Ministers; they will honor above all the good and
wise Princes who will know how to forestall, cure, and palliate the
host of abuses and of evils that are forever ready to overwhelm us;
They will animate the zeal of those worthy Chiefs by showing them,
without fear or flattery, the grandeur of their task and the sternness of

their duty; But they will be none the less contemptuous of a constitution which can be maintained only with the help of so many respectable people more often wished *[208]* for than available, and from which, in spite of all their cares, there always arise more real calamities than apparent advantages.

DISCOURSE, page 149

X [1] Of the men we know, either on our own, or from Historians, or from travelers; some are black, others white, others red; some wear their hair long, others have nothing but curly wool; some are almost entirely covered with hair, others have not even any on their Face; there have been, and perhaps there still are, Nations of men of gigantic size; and, leaving aside the fable about Pygmies which may well be no more than an exaggeration, the Laplanders and especially the Greenlanders are known to be well below the average size for man; it is even claimed that there are entire Peoples with tails like quadrupeds; and, without placing blind faith in the accounts of Herodotus and of Ctesias, one can at least draw the following very plausible conclusion from them, that, if good observations had been possible in those ancient times when different people differed in their ways of life more than they do today, then much more striking varieties in the shape and bearing of the body would also have been noted among them. All these facts, of which it is easy to provide incontrovertible proofs, can surprise only those who are in the habit of looking exclusively at the objects around them, and are ignorant of the powerful effects of differences in Climates, air, foods, ways of life, habits in general and, above all, of the astonishing force of uniform causes acting continuously on long successions of generations. Nowadays, when commerce, Travels and conquests bring different Peoples closer together, and their ways of life grow constantly more alike as a result of frequent communication, certain national differences are found to have diminished and, for example, everyone can see that present-day Frenchmen are no longer the tall, fair-skinned and blond-haired bodies described by Latin Historians, although time, together with the admixture of Franks and Normans, who are themselves fair and blond, should have made up for whatever the contact with the Romans may have taken away from the influence of the Climate on the population's natural constitution and complexion. All these observations about the varieties which a thousand causes may produce, and indeed have produced in the human Species, lead me to wonder whether various animals similar to men, which travelers have without much observation taken for Beasts, either because of some differences they noticed in their outward conformation, or merely because these Animals did not speak, might not indeed be genuine Savage men whose race, dispersed in the woods in ancient times, had had no occasion to develop any of its virtual faculties, had not acquired any degree of perfection, and was still in the primitive state of Nature. Let us give an example of what I mean. *[209]*

[2] ."In the Kingdom of the Congo," says the translator of the Hist[oire] des Voyages, "are found many of those big Animals called *Orang-outangs* in the East Indies, which occupy something like a middle position between the human species and the Baboons. Battel relates that in the forests of Mayomba, in the Kingdom of Loango, two kinds of Monsters are found, the larger of which are called *Pongos,* and the others *Enjokos.* The first bear an exact resemblance to man; but they are much heavier and quite tall. Together with a human face, they have very deep-set eyes. Their hands, cheeks, ears are hairless, except for their rather long eyebrows. Although the rest of their body is rather hairy, this body hair does not grow especially dense, and it is of a dunnish color. Finally, the only feature that distinguishes them from men is their leg, which is without a calf. They walk upright, with the hand holding one another by the hair of the Neck; they live in the woods; They sleep in Trees where they build themselves a kind of roof that protects them from rain. Their food is fruit or Wild nuts. They never eat flesh. The Negroes who travel through the forests are in the habit of lighting fires at night. They notice that in the morning, when they have left, the Pongos take their place around the fire, and do not leave it until it has died out: for although they are very dextrous, they have not sense enough to keep the fire going by adding wood to it.

[3] "Sometimes they walk in troops and kill Negroes making their way through the forests. They even attack elephants that come to graze in the places where they live, and make it so uncomfortable for them by striking them with their fists or with sticks that they force them to run away roaring. Pongos are never taken alive; because they are so sturdy that ten men would not be enough to stop them: But the Negroes do take many of their Young after having killed the Mother to whose Body the little one clings fast: when one of these Animals dies, the others cover its body with a Heap of branches or boughs. Purchas adds that in the conversations he had had with Battel, he learned from him that a Pongo had kidnapped a little Negro from him, who spent a whole month in the Society of these Animals; For they do no harm whatever to the human beings they surprise, at least not when these do

not look at them, as the little Negro had observed. Battel has not described the second species of monster.

[4] "Dapper confirms that the Kingdom of the Congo is full of the animals called Orang-outangs, that is to say inhabitants of the woods, in the Indies, and Quojas-Morros by the Africans. This Beast is, he says, so similar to man that it has entered the mind of some travelers that it might have been the offspring of a woman and a monkey: a chimera dismissed even by the Negroes. One of these animals was brought from the Congo to Holland and presented to Prince Frederick-Henry of Orange. *[210]* It was as tall as a three-Year old Child and of moderate girth, but square and well-proportioned, quite agile and quite lively; its legs fleshy and sturdy, the front of its body bare, but the back covered with black hair. At first sight its face resembled that of a man, but its nose was flat and snubbed; its ears, too, were those of the human Species; its breast, for it was a female, was plump, its navel deep-set, its shoulders nicely articulated, its hands divided into fingers and thumbs, its calves and heels thick and fleshy. It often walked upright on its legs, it could lift and carry rather heavy loads. When it wanted to drink it took the cover of the pot with one hand and held the bottom with the other. Afterwards it gracefully wiped its lips. It lay down to sleep, its head on a Pillow, covering itself so skillfully that it might have been mistaken for a human being in bed. The Negroes tell strange tales about this animal. They maintain not only that it takes women and girls by force, but that it dares to attack armed men; In a word, it is quite likely that it is the Satyr of the Ancients. Perhaps Merolla is only referring to these Animals when he relates that Negroes sometimes capture Savage men and women in their hunts."

[5] These species of Anthropomorphic animals are again mentioned in the third volume of the same Histoire des Voyages under the names *Beggos* and *Mandrills;* but restricting ourselves to the preceding accounts, one finds in the description of these supposed monsters striking conformities with the human species, and smaller differences than might be pointed to between one human being and another. It is not clear from these passages what the Authors' reasons are for refusing to call the Animals in question Savage men, but it is easy to conjecture that it is because of their stupidity, and also because they did not speak; weak reasons for those who know that, although the organ of speech is natural to man, speech itself is nevertheless not natural to him, and who recognize the extent to which his perfectibility may have raised Civil man above his original state. The small number of lines comprising these descriptions permits us to judge how poorly these

Animals have been observed, and with what prejudices they were seen. For example, they are characterized as monsters, and yet it is conceded that they reproduce. In one place Battel says that the Pongos kill the Negroes traveling through the forest, in another place Purchas adds that they do them no harm even when they surprise them; at least not when the Negroes do not insist on looking at them. The Pongos gather around the fires lit by the Negroes once these have left, and they in turn leave once the fire has died out; that is the fact; here, now, is the observer's commentary: *For although they are very dextrous, they have not sense enough to keep the fire going by adding wood to it.* I should like to guess how Battel, or Purchas, his *[211]* compiler, could have known that the Pongos' departure was an effect of their stupidity rather than of their will. In a Climate such as that of Loango, fire is not something Animals particularly need, and if Negroes light them, they do so less against the cold than to frighten ferocious beasts; it is therefore perfectly plain that after having for a while been cheered by the flames or having thoroughly warmed up, the Pongos grow bored with always staying in one place, and go off to forage, which requires more time than if they ate flesh. Besides, the majority of animals, not excepting man, are known to be naturally lazy, and they shun every kind of care that is not absolutely necessary. Finally, it seems very strange that the Pongos, whose dexterity and strength is extolled, the Pongos who know how to bury their dead and how to make themselves roofs out of branches, should not know how to push embers into a fire. I remember having seen a monkey perform the same operation which it is claimed the Pongos cannot perform; it is true that, as my ideas were not at the time turned in that direction, I myself committed the mistake for which I reproach our travelers, and I neglected to examine whether it had indeed been the monkey's intention to keep the fire going, or whether it had simply been, as I believe, to imitate the action of a human being. Be that as it may; it is well demonstrated that the Monkey is not a variety of man; not only because it is deprived of the faculty of speaking, but especially because it is certain that this species lacks the faculty of perfecting itself which is the specific characteristic of the human species. Experiments [about] which seem not to have been conducted sufficiently carefully with the Pongos and the Orang-outang to allow the same conclusion to be drawn regarding them. However, if the Orang-outang or others did belong to the human species, there is one way in which the crudest observers could satisfy themselves on the question even with a demonstration; but not only would a single generation not suffice for this experiment, it must also be regarded as impracticable because what is but an assumption would have to have been demonstrated as true before the test to confirm the fact could be tried in innocence.

[6] Precipitous judgments that are not the fruit of an enlightened reason are liable to run to extremes. Our travelers do not hesitate to make beasts by the name of *Pongos, Mandrills, Orang-outangs* of the same beings which the Ancients made into Divinities by the name of *Satyrs, Fauns,* and *Sylvans.* Perhaps after more accurate investigations it will be found that they are neither beasts nor gods, but men. In the meantime it seems to me quite as reasonable to rely in this matter on Merolla, a learned Cleric, an eyewitness, and a man who, for all his naïveté, was intelligent, as on the Merchant Battel, on Dapper, on Purchas, and the other Compilers. *[212]*

[7] What would have been the judgment of such Observers about the Child found in 1694 of whom I spoke above, who gave no sign of reason, walked on his hands and feet, had no language, and formed sounds in no way resembling those of a man. It took him a long time, continues the same Philosopher who provides me with this fact, before he could utter a few words, and then he did so in a barbarous manner. As soon as he could speak, he was questioned about his first state, but he no more remembered it than we remember what happened to us in the Cradle. If, unfortunately for him, this child had fallen into our travelers' hands, there can be no doubt that after taking note of his silence and stupidity, they would have decided to send him back into the woods or to lock him up in a Menagerie; after which they would have spoken about him learnedly in fine reports as a most curious Beast that rather resembled a man.

[8] Although the inhabitants of Europe have for the past three or four hundred years overrun the other parts of the world, and are constantly publishing new collections of travels and reports, I am convinced that the only men we know are the Europeans; what is more, the ridiculous prejudices that have not died out even among Men of Letters, would make it appear that under the pompous name "the study of man," everyone studies scarcely anything other than the men of his country. Regardless of how much individuals may come and go, it would seem that Philosophy does not travel, and indeed one People's Philosophy is but little suited for another. It is clear why that should be so, at least with respect to faraway places: there are scarcely more than four sorts of men who make extended journeys: Sailors, Merchants, Soldiers and Missionaries. Now it is scarcely to be expected that the first three Classes would provide good Observers, and as for those in

the fourth, even if they are not subject to prejudices of station as are all the others, one has to believe that since they are absorbed by the sublime vocation that calls them, they would not readily engage in inquiries that appear to be matters of pure curiosity and would distract them from the labors to which they destine themselves. Besides, to preach the Gospel usefully requires only zeal, and God grants the rest; but to study men requires talents which God does not commit himself to grant to anyone, and which are not always the lot of Saints. One cannot open a travel book without coming upon descriptions of characters and morals; yet one is utterly astounded to find that these people who have described so many things, have said only what everybody already knew, that all they were able to perceive at the other end of the world is what they could perfectly well have noticed without leaving their street, and that the telling traits that differentiate Nations and strike eyes made to see, have almost always escaped theirs. Hence that fine adage of ethics so much harped on by the ruck of Philosophasters, that men are everywhere the same, that, since they everywhere have the same passions and the same vices, it is quite useless to seek to characterize *[213]* different Peoples; which is about as well argued as it would be to say that it is impossible to distinguish between Peter and James because both have a nose, a mouth, and eyes.

[9] Shall we never see reborn the happy times when Peoples did not pretend to Philosophize, but the Platos, the Thales, and the Pythagorases, seized with an ardent desire to know, undertook the greatest journeys merely in order to learn, and went far off to shake the yoke of National prejudices, to get to know men by their conformities and their differences, and to acquire that universal knowledge that is not exclusively of one Century or of one country but of all times and of all places, and thus is, so to speak, the common science of the wise?

[10] One admires the largess of a few men who, animated by curiosity, have at great expense made or sponsored voyages to the Orient with Learned men and Painters, there to make drawings of ruins and to decipher or copy Inscriptions; but I find it difficult to conceive how, in a Century that prides itself on remarkable knowledge, there are not two like-minded men, rich, one in money and the other in genius, both loving glory and aspiring to immortality, one of whom would sacrifice twenty thousand crowns of his fortune and the other ten years of his life for the sake of a notable voyage around the world; during which to study, not forever stones and plants, but, for once, men and morals, and who, after so many centuries spent in measuring

and examining the house, finally decided that they want to know its inhabitants.

[11] The Academicians who have traveled through the Northern parts of Europe and the Southern parts of America were more intent on visiting them as Geometers than as Philosophers. Yet, since they were both at once, the regions seen and described by such men as La Condamine and Maupertuis cannot be regarded as altogether unknown. The Jeweller Chardin, who traveled like Plato, has left nothing more to be said about Persia; China seems to have been well observed by the Jesuits; Kempfer gives a tolerable idea of the little he saw in Japan. Except for these accounts, we do not know the Peoples of the East Indies, who are exclusively visited by Europeans more interested in filling their purses than their heads. All of Africa and its numerous inhabitants, as remarkable in character as they are in color, still remain to be studied; the whole earth is covered with Nations of which we know only the names, and yet we pretend to judge mankind! Let us suppose a Montesquieu, a Buffon, a Diderot, a Duclos, a d'Alembert, a Condillac, or men of that stamp, traveling with a view to instruct their compatriots, observing and describing as they know how to do, Turkey, Egypt, Barbary, the Empire of Morocco, Guinea, the lands of the Bantus, the interior and the East coasts of Africa, the Malabars, Mongolia, the banks of the Ganges, the Kingdoms of Siam, Pegu and Ava, China, Tartary, and above all Japan: then, in the other *[214]* Hemisphere, Mexico, Peru, Chile, the Lands [around the Straits] of Magellan, without forgetting the Patagonians, true or false, Tucumán, Paraguay if possible, Brazil, finally the Caribbean, Florida, and all the Wild regions, this being the most important voyage of all and the one that should be undertaken with the greatest care; let us suppose that on their return from these memorable travels, these new Hercules set down at leisure the natural, Moral, and Political History of what they had seen, then we would ourselves see a new world issue from their pen, and would thus learn to know our own: I say that when such Observers assert about a given Animal that it is a man and about another that it is a beast, they will have to be believed; but it would be most simple-minded to rely in this matter on coarse travelers about whom one might sometimes be tempted to ask the same question they pretend to answer about other animals.

DISCOURSE, page 150

XI That seems most evident to me, and I cannot conceive where our Philosophers would have arise all the passions they attribute to Natural man. With the single exception of the Physically necessary, which

Nature itself requires, all our other needs are needs only by habit, prior to which they were not needs, or by our desires, and one does not desire what one is not in a position to know. Whence it follows that, since Savage man desires only the things he knows, and knows only the things the possession of which is in his power or easy to achieve, nothing must be so calm as his soul and nothing so limited as his mind.

DISCOURSE, page 153

XII [1] I find in Locke's Civil Government an objection that seems to me too specious to permit me to ignore it. "The end of society between Male and Female," says this philosopher, "being not barely procreation, but the continuation of the species; this society ought to last, even after procreation, so long as is necessary to the nourishment and support of the young ones, who are to be sustained by those that got them, till they are able to shift and provide for themselves. This rule, which the infinite wisdom of the creator hath set to the works of his hands, we find the creatures inferior to man steadily and precisely obey. In those animals which feed on grass, the Society between male and female lasts no longer than the very act of copulation; because the teat of the Dam being sufficient to nourish the young, till they be able to feed on grass, the male only begets, but concerns not himself for the female or young, to whose sustenance he can contribute nothing. But in beasts of prey the Society lasts longer: because the Dam not being able well to subsist herself, and nourish her offspring by her own prey alone, *[215]* a more laborious, as well as more dangerous way of feeding than by feeding on grass, the assistance of the male is necessary to the maintenance of their common family, if one may use the term, which cannot subsist till they are able to prey for themselves, but by the care of Male and Female. The same is to be observed in all birds, except some Domestic ones, where plenty of food excuses the cock from feeding the young brood; it is to be observed that while the young in their nest need food, the male and the female take some there, till the young are able to use their wing, and provide for themselves.

[2] "And herein I think lies the chief, if not the only reason why the male and female in Mankind are obliged to a longer Society than other creatures. The reason is that the Woman is capable of conceiving and is commonly with child again, and brings forth too a new birth long before the former is out of a dependency for support on his parents' help, and able to shift for himself, and has all the assistance due to him from his parents. Whereby the Father, who is obliged to take care for those he hath begot, and to do so for a long time, is also under an

obligation to continue in conjugal Society with the same woman from whom he had them, and to remain in that Society much longer than other creatures, whose young being able to subsist of themselves, before the time of procreation returns again, the bond between the male and the female dissolves of itself, and they are fully at liberty, till the season which customarily summons animals to join together, obliges them again to choose new mates. Wherein one cannot but admire the wisdom of the creator who having given to man foresight, and an ability to lay up for the future, as well as to supply the present necessity, wanted and arranged it so that Society of man should be much more lasting, than of male and female amongst the other creatures; that so their industry might be encouraged, and their interest better united, to make provision, and lay up goods for their common issue, as nothing is more prejudicial to Children than uncertain and vague mixture, or easy and frequent dissolutions of conjugal Society."

[3] The same love of truth that led me to present this objection in all sincerity, moves me to accompany it with a few remarks in order, if not to refute it, at least to elucidate it.

[4] 1. In the first place, I shall note that moral proofs are without great force in matters of Physics, and that they serve rather to provide reasons for existing facts than to ascertain the real existence of these facts. Yet that is the kind of proof Mr. Locke uses in the passage I have just cited; for although it may be *[216]* advantageous to the human species that the union between man and woman be permanent, it does not follow that it was so established by Nature; otherwise it would have to be said that Nature also instituted Civil Society, the Arts, Commerce, and everything that is claimed to be useful to men.

[5] 2. I do not know where Mr. Locke found that the Society of Male and Female lasts longer among animals of prey than among those that live off grass, and that [among them] the one helps the other to feed the young: For it does not appear that the Dog, the Cat, the Bear, or the Wolf recognize their female better than the Horse, the Ram, the Bull, the Stag, or all other Quadrupeds recognize theirs. It would seem, on the contrary, that if the female did need the male's assistance to preserve her young, this would be so above all in the species that live exclusively off grass, because the Mother needs much time to graze, and during that whole stretch she is forced to neglect her brood, whereas a female Bear's or Wolf's prey is devoured in an instant, and she has more time to suckle her young without suffering any hunger. This reasoning is confirmed by an observation about the relative number of teats and of young which distinguishes the carnivorous from the

frugivorous species, and about which I spoke in Note VIII. If that
observation is correct and general, then a woman's having only two
teats and rarely giving birth to more than one child at a time is one
more strong reason for doubting that the human species is naturally
Carnivorous, so that it would seem that in order to draw Locke's
conclusion, his argument would have to be turned completely upside
down. This same distinction is no more solid when applied to birds.
For who can believe that the union of Male and Female is more lasting
among vultures and Ravens than among Turtle-doves? We have two
species of domestic birds, the Duck and the Pigeon, that provide us
with examples directly contrary to this Author's System. The Pigeon,
which lives exclusively off grain, remains united with its female, and
they feed their young in common. The Duck, whose omnivorousness is
well known, recognizes neither its female nor its young, and does not
in any way help with their subsistence; and among Chickens, a species
scarcely less carnivorous, there is no evidence that the Cock worries
about the brood at all. If in other species of birds the Male does share
with the Female the care of feeding the young, it is because Birds,
since they cannot fly at first and the Mother cannot suckle them, are
much less able to do without the Father's assistance than Quadrupeds,
where the Mother's teat suffices, at least for a time.

[6] 3. A good deal of uncertainty surrounds the principal fact which
serves as the basis for Mr. Locke's entire argument: For in order to
know whether, as he claims, in the pure state of Nature the woman is
commonly with child again and brings forth too a new birth long
before the former is able to shift for himself, would require experiments
which Locke has surely not performed, and which no *[217]* one is in a
position to perform. The continual cohabitation of Husband and Wife
provides such direct occasion to expose oneself to a new pregnancy
that it is rather difficult to believe that fortuitous encounters or the
impulsion of temperament alone would have produced as frequent
effects in the pure state of Nature as in that of conjugal Society; a delay
which might perhaps contribute to the children's becoming more
robust and might, besides, be compensated for by [having] the faculty
to conceive prolonged to a more advanced age in women who abused
it less in their youth. Regarding Children, there are a good many reasons
to believe that their strength and their organs develop later among us
than they did in the primitive state of which I speak. The original
weakness they owe to their Parents' constitution, the care taken to
swaddle and cramp all their limbs, the softness in which they are
reared, perhaps the use of another milk than their Mother's, everything

thwarts and delays in them the first progress of Nature. Their being obliged to mind a thousand things to which their attention is constantly being drawn while their bodily strength is not given any exercise, may further considerably hamper their growth; it is therefore likely that if, instead of first overloading and tiring their minds in a thousand ways, their Bodies were allowed to move as actively and constantly as Nature seems to expect them to do, they could walk, act, and fend for themselves much earlier.

[7] 4. Finally, Mr. Locke at most proves that man might well have a motive for remaining attached to the woman when she has a Child; but he does not at all prove that he must have been attached to her before its birth and during the nine months of pregnancy. If a given woman is of no interest to a man throughout those nine months, if she even becomes unknown to him, why will he help her after the birth? Why will he help her rear a Child he does not even know is his, and whose birth he neither willed nor foresaw? Mr. Locke obviously presupposes what is in question: For it is not a matter of knowing why a man remains attached to a woman after the birth, but why he gets attached to her after the conception. Once the appetite is satisfied, the man no longer needs this woman, nor the woman this man. He has not the least worry nor, perhaps, the least idea of the consequences of his action. One goes off in this direction, the other in that, and there is no likelihood that at the end of nine months they will remember ever having known each other: For the kind of memory by which one individual manifests preference for another individual for the act of procreation requires, as I prove in the text, more progress or corruption of the human understanding than it can be assumed to have in the state of animality that is here at issue. Another woman can, therefore, satisfy a man's new desires as conveniently as can the woman he had previously known, and another man can similarly satisfy [218] the woman, assuming she is prompted by the same appetite during the state of pregnancy, which may reasonably be doubted. But if, in the state of Nature, the woman no longer experiences the passion of love after the child has been conceived, then the obstacle to her Society with the man becomes much greater still, since she then no longer needs either the man who impregnated her or any other. There is, therefore, no reason for the man to seek out the same woman, nor for the woman to seek out the same man. Locke's argument therefore collapses, and all of that Philosopher's Dialectic has not protected him against the error Hobbes and others committed. They had to explain a fact of the state of Nature, that is to say of a state where men lived isolated, and where one

particular man had no motive whatsoever to remain near some other particular man, nor perhaps, which is far worse, did men have any motive to remain near one another; and it did not occur to them to transport themselves beyond the Centuries of Society, that is to say beyond those times when men always have a reason to remain close to one another, and when a particular man often has a reason to remain by the side of a particular man or a particular woman.

DISCOURSE, page 154

XIII I do not propose to embark on the philosophical reflections that might be made regarding the advantages and the drawbacks of this institution of languages; I am not one to be granted leave to attack vulgar errors, and lettered people respect their prejudices too much to bear my supposed paradoxes patiently. Let us therefore let speak the Persons in whom it is not deemed a Crime to dare sometimes to take the side of reason against the opinion of the multitude. "Nor would the happiness of mankind be in any way diminished if, after the evil and the confusion of so many languages has been banished, [all] mortals eagerly practiced [this] one art, and everything were allowed to be expressed in signs, movements, and gestures. But as things now stand, the condition of the animals, which are commonly held to be dumb, appears in this respect to be much better than ours, for they can make their feelings and thoughts known without interpreter faster and perhaps more felicitously than any men can do, especially when they are speaking a foreign language" (Is[aac] Vossius, de Poëmat[um] Cant[u] et Viribus Rythmi, p. 66).

DISCOURSE, page 157

XIV Plato, showing how necessary ideas of discrete quantity and its relations are in the least of arts, rightly mocks the Authors of his time who claimed that Palamedes had invented numbers at the siege of Troy, as if, says that Philosopher, Agamemnon could until then have been ignorant of how many legs he had. Indeed, one senses how impossible it is for society and the arts to have reached the level they already were at by the time of the siege of Troy, without men's having the use of numbers and of reckoning: but the fact that a knowledge of numbers is necessary before other knowledge can be acquired, does not make it any easier to imagine how numbers were invented; once their names are known, it is easy to explain their meaning, and to evoke the ideas which these names *[219]* represent; but in order to invent them, and before conceiving of these very ideas, one had, so to speak, to have become adept at philosophical meditation, to have practiced considering the beings exclusively in their essence, and independently of all other perception, an abstraction that is very arduous, very metaphysical, not very natural, and yet without which these ideas could never have been transposed from one species or kind to another, nor numbers have become universal. A savage could separately consider his right leg and his left leg, or view them together in terms of the indivisible idea of a pair, without ever thinking that he had two of them; for the representative idea that depicts an object to us is one thing, and the numerical idea that specifies it, is another. Still less could he reckon up to five, and although by fitting his hands one to the other he could have noticed that the fingers matched exactly, he was far from dreaming of their numerical equality; he no more knew the number of his fingers than of his hairs; and if, after having made him understand what numbers are, someone had told him that he had as many toes as fingers, he might perhaps have been very surprised, on comparing them, to find it true.

DISCOURSE, page 160

XV [1] *Amour propre* [vanity] and *Amour de soi-même* [self-love], two very different passions in their nature and their effects, must not be confused. Self-love is a natural sentiment which inclines every animal to attend to its self-preservation and which, guided in man by reason and modified by pity, produces humanity and virtue. Vanity is only a relative sentiment, factitious, and born in society, which inclines every individual to set greater store by himself than by anyone else, inspires men with all the evils they do one another, and is the genuine source of honor.

[2] This being clearly understood, I say that in our primitive state, in the genuine state of nature, Vanity does not exist; For, since every individual human being views himself as the only Spectator to observe him, as the only being in the universe to take any interest in him, as the only judge of his own merit, it is not possible that a sentiment which originates in comparisons he is not capable of making, could spring up in his soul: for the same reason, this man could have neither hatred nor desire for vengeance, passions that can arise only from the opinion of having received some offense; and since it is contempt or the intent to harm, and not the harm itself, that constitutes the offense, men who are unable to appreciate one another or to compare themselves

with one another, can do each other much violence when there is some advantage in it for them, without ever offending one another. In a word, every man viewing his kind scarcely differently from the way he would view Animals of another species, can rob the weaker of his prey or yield his own to the stronger without considering these acts of pillage as anything but *[220]* natural occurrences, without the slightest stirring of arrogance or resentment, and with no other passion than the pain or pleasure at success or failure.

DISCOURSE, page 177

XVI [1] It is a most remarkable thing that for all the years the Europeans have been tormenting themselves to bring the Savages of the various parts of the world over to their way of life, they should not yet have been able to win over a single one of them, not even with the assistance of Christianity; for our missionaries sometimes make Christians of them, but never Civilized men. Nothing can overcome their invincible repugnance against adopting our morals and living in our way. If these poor Savages are as unhappy as they are said to be, by what inconceivable depravation of judgment do they consistently refuse either to adopt political society in imitation of us, or to learn to live happy among us; whereas, one reads in a thousand places that Frenchmen and other Europeans have voluntarily taken refuge among these Nations, spent their entire lives there, without any longer being able to leave such a strange way of life, and one even sees sensible Missionaries regret with emotion the calm and innocent days they spent among those much despised peoples? If it be answered that they are not sufficiently enlightened to judge soundly of their state and of ours, I will reply that the assessment of happiness is less the business of reason than of sentiment. Besides, that answer can be turned against us with even greater force; for the distance is greater between our ideas and the frame of mind required to appreciate the Savages' taste for their way of life, than between the Savages' ideas and ideas that might enable them to conceive of our way of life. Indeed, after a few observations they can readily see that all our labors are directed at only two objects: namely, the comforts of life for oneself, and consideration from others. But how are we to imagine the sort of pleasure a Savage takes in spending his life alone in the depths of the forests, or fishing, or blowing into a poor flute without ever managing to draw a single note from it and without troubling to learn to do so?

[2] On a number of occasions, Savages have been brought to Paris,

London, and other cities; people have scurried to spread out before them our luxury, our wealth, and all of our most useful and most interesting arts; all this never excited in them anything other than a stupid admiration, without the slightest stirring of covetousness. I remember, among others, the Story of a chief of some North Americans who was brought to the Court of England about thirty years ago. A thousand things were placed before his eyes in order to give him some present he might like, but nothing was found that he seemed to care for. Our weapons seemed to him heavy and clumsy, our shoes hurt his feet, he found our clothes cumbersome, he rejected everything; finally it was noticed that, having picked up a wool blanket, he seemed to take pleasure in wrapping it around his shoulders; *[221]* you will at least allow, someone straightway said to him, the usefulness of this furnishing? Yes, he answered, it seems to me almost as good as an animal skin. He would not even have said that, if he had worn both in the rain.

[3] I will perhaps be told that it is habit which, by attaching everyone to his way of life, prevents Savages from feeling what is good in ours: And on that basis it must, to say the least, appear very extraordinary that habit should prove stronger in preserving the Savages' taste for their misery than the Europeans' enjoyment of their felicity. But to meet this last objection with an answer that admits of not a single word in reply—without invoking all the young Savages whom vain efforts have been made to Civilize; without speaking of the Greenlanders or of the inhabitants of Iceland whom attempts have been made to raise and rear in Denmark, and all of whom sorrow and despair caused to perish, either of yearning, or in the sea across which they had tried to swim back to their country—I shall limit myself to citing a single well-attested example which I submit to the scrutiny of admirers of the European Political order.

[4] "All the efforts of the Dutch Missionaries of the Cape of Good Hope never Succeeded in converting a single Hottentot. Van der Stel, Governor of the Cape, having taken one of them in infancy, had him brought up in the principles of the Christian Religion and in the observance of European customs. He was richly dressed, taught several languages, and his progress fully corresponded to the care taken with his education. The Governor, expecting much from his mind, sent him to India with a Commissioner-General who employed him usefully in the Company's business. After the Commissioner's death, he returned to the Cape. A few days after his return, during a visit to some Hottentot relatives of his, he decided to divest himself of his European garb and

dress in a Sheepskin. He returned to the Fort in this new apparel carrying a package with his former clothes, and presenting them to the Governor, he addressed this discourse to him.* *Be so good, Sir, as to note that I forever renounce these trappings. I also renounce the Christian Religion for the rest of my life; my resolution is to live and die in the Religion, the ways, and the customs of my Ancestors. The one favor I ask of you is to leave me the Necklace and the Cutlass I am wearing. I shall keep them for love of you.* Straightway, without awaiting Van der Stel's answer, he ran off, and was never again seen at the Cape" (*Histoire des Voyages,* vol. 5, p. 175).

DISCOURSE, page 182

XVII It might be objected that in such a disorder men, instead of stubbornly slaughtering one another, would have dispersed if there had been no limits on their *[222]* dispersion. But, in the first place, these limits would at least have been those of the world, and if one thinks of the excessively large population that results from the state of Nature, one has to conclude that, in that state, the earth would soon have been covered with men who would thus have been forced to stay together. Besides, they would have dispersed if the evil had been swift, and the change had taken place from one day to the next; but they were born under the yoke; by the time they felt its weight, they were in the habit of bearing it, and were content to wait for the opportunity to shake it. Finally, as they were already accustomed to a thousand comforts that forced them to stay together, dispersion was no longer as easy as in the first times when, no one needing anyone but himself, everyone made his decision without waiting for anyone else's consent.

DISCOURSE, page 183

XVIII Marshal de V*** related that in one of his Campaigns, when the excessive frauds of a Food Contractor had made the army suffer and grumble, he roundly took the man to task and threatened to have him hanged. *The threat does not bother me,* the scoundrel brashly replied, *and I am pleased to tell you that a man who commands a hundred thousand crowns does not get hanged.* I do not know how it happened, the Marshal naïvely added, but he was indeed not hanged, although he deserved it a hundred times.

* See the frontispiece [p. 116].

DISCOURSE, page 194

XIX Distributive justice would be at odds with the rigorous equality
of the state of Nature, even if it were practicable in civil society; and
as all the members of the State owe it services proportionate to their
talents and strengths, the Citizens ought, in their turn, to be differentiated
and favored in proportion to their services. It is in this sense that a
passage in Isocrates has to be understood, in which he praises the first
Athenians for having correctly discerned the more advantageous of the
two sorts of equality, one of which consists in allotting the same
advantages to all Citizens indifferently, and the other in distributing
them according to each one's merit. These skillful politicians, adds the
orator, by banishing the unjust equality which draws no distinction
between wicked and good men, inviolably adhered to the equality
which rewards and punishes each according to his merit. But, in the
first place, never has a society existed, regardless of the degree of
corruption they may have reached, where no distinction was drawn
between wicked and good men; and in matters of morals, where the
Law cannot prescribe a sufficiently precise standard to serve as a rule
for the Magistrate, it very wisely forbids him to pass judgment on
persons, and restricts him to judgments on Actions, in order not to
leave the Citizens' fate or rank to the Magistrate's discretion. Only
morals as pure as the Ancient Romans' can bear Censors, and such
tribunals would soon have overturned everything among us: It is up to
public esteem *[223]* to draw the distinction between wicked and good
men; the Magistrate is judge of rigorous right only; but the people is
the genuine judge of morals; a judge of integrity and even enlightenment
on this point, sometimes deceived, but never corrupted. The ranks of
the Citizens ought, therefore, to be regulated not according to their
personal merit, which would be to leave to the Magistrate the means
of applying the Law in an almost arbitrary fashion, but according to the
real services they render to the State, which admit of more exact
assessment.

LETTER
by J. J. ROUSSEAU
to M. PHILOPOLIS

[1] You wish me to reply, Sir, since you ask me questions. Besides, the work at issue is dedicated to my Fellow-Citizens; in defending it I justify the honor they did me in accepting it. I leave aside the good and the bad things said about me in your Letter, because they more or less make up for one another, they interest me little and the public less, and none of it has any bearing on the quest for truth. I therefore begin with the argument you regard as crucial to the question I tried to solve.

[2] The state of society, you tell me, results immediately from man's faculties, and hence from his nature. To wish man not to become sociable would, therefore, be to wish that he not be a man, and to criticize society is to attack God's work. Allow me, Sir, in turn to submit a difficulty to you, before solving yours. I would spare you this detour if I knew a better way of reaching the goal.

[3] Let us assume that someday scientists discovered both the secret of hastening old age and the art of getting men to use this unusual discovery. It might not prove as difficult to persuade them to do so as may at first appear. For reason, that great conveyor of all our foolishness, would not fail us with this one. The Philosophers, above all, and all sensible men, in order to shake the yoke of the passions and enjoy that *[231]* prized repose of soul, would hasten to attain the age of Nestor, and willingly give up the desires that can be satisfied in order to escape those that have to be stifled. Only a few dolts, though blushing for their weakness, would foolishly wish to remain young and happy instead of growing old for the sake of being wise.

[4] Let us assume that it thereupon occurred to a singular, bizarre spirit, in a word to a man of paradoxes, to reproach the others for the absurdity of their maxims, to prove to them that in their quest for tranquility they are rushing to their death, that for all their reasonableness they only talk nonsense, and

that if they have to be old someday, they should at least try to be so as late as possible.

[5] There is no need to ask whether our sophists, afraid to see their Mystification exposed, would not rush to interrupt this troublesome speaker: "Wise seniors," they would say to their followers, "thank Heaven for the graces it bestows on you, and forever rejoice at having heeded its will so well. True, you are decrepit, listless, rheumy; that is man's inexorable fate; but your mind is sound; all your limbs are paralyzed, but you speak like oracles, and if your aches daily increase, your Philosophy increases with them. Be sorry for the impetuous youths whose brute health deprives them of the advantages associated with your weakness. Happy infirmities, that gather around you so many skilled Pharmacists who are supplied with more drugs than you have complaints, so many learned physicians who are thoroughly familiar with your pulse, who know the Greek names for all your rheumatisms, so many eager sympathizers and loyal heirs who lead you pleasantly to your last hour. How much help you would have foregone if you had not known how to inflict on yourselves the ills that made them necessary."

[6] Can we not easily imagine them then apostrophizing our heedless alarm-sounder, and addressing him approximately as follows:

[7] "Rash haranguer, stop these impious discourses. Dare you thus blame the will of him [232] who made mankind? Is not old age a state that follows from man's constitution? Is it not natural for man to grow old? What, then, are you doing with your seditious discourses, if not attacking a Law of nature and hence the will of its Creator? Since man grows old, God wants him to grow old. Are facts anything other than the expression of his will? Recognize that man young, is not the man God wanted to make, and that in order to obey his orders promptly one must hasten to grow old."

[8] Assuming all this, I ask you, Sir, whether the man of paradoxes should remain silent or reply and, if he should reply, kindly to let me know what he should say, and I will then try to meet your objection.

[9] Since you mean to attack me in terms of my own system,

please do not forget that in my view society is natural to mankind as decrepitude is to the individual, and that Peoples need arts, Laws and Governments, as old men need crutches. The only difference is that old age is a state that follows from the nature of mankind not, as you maintain, immediately, but only, as I have proved, with the help of external circumstances which might have been or not been, or might at least have occurred sooner or later, and hence might have hastened or retarded the progress. [As] a number of these circumstances even depend on men's will, I was compelled to assume, for the sake of strict symmetry, that the individual has the power to hasten his old age just as the species has the power to delay its old age. Since the state of society thus has an ultimate limit which men have it in their power to reach either sooner or later, it is not useless to show them the danger of going so fast, and the miseries of a condition which they take to be the perfection of the species.

[10] To the list of the ills which beset men, and which I hold to be their own work, you rejoin, Leibniz and yourself, that all is good, and that providence is thus justified. I was far from believing that it needed the help of the Leibnizian, or, indeed, of any other Philosophy for its justification. Do you yourself seriously think that any System *[233]* of Philosophy whatsoever could be more blameless than the Universe, and that a Philosopher's arguments exonerate providence more convincingly than do God's works? Besides, to deny the existence of evil is a most convenient way of excusing the author of that evil; the stoics formerly made themselves a laughingstock for less.

[11] According to Leibniz and to Pope, whatever is, is good. If there are societies, it is because the general good requires that there be societies; if there are none, the general good requires that there be none, and if someone persuaded men to return to live in the forests, it would be good that they return to live there. One must not bring to bear on the nature of things an idea of good or evil drawn solely from the relations between them, for things may be good relative to the whole although evil in themselves. What contributes to the general good may be a particular evil which it is permissible to get rid of if

possible. For if this evil, when tolerated, is useful to the whole, the opposite good which one attempts to substitute for it will, once it takes effect, be no less useful to it. If all is good as it is, then, by parity of reason, if someone tries to alter the state of things, it is good that he try to alter it; and whether it be good or bad that he succeed can be learned only from the outcome, and not from reason. None of this prevents a particular evil from being a real evil for the person who suffers it. It was good for the whole that we be civilized since that is what we are, but it would certainly have been better for us if we were not so. Leibniz could never have derived anything from his system to refute that proposition; and it is evident that optimism rightly understood neither supports nor subverts my position.

[12] I therefore need answer neither Leibniz nor Pope, but only yourself, who, without drawing any distinction between universal evil, which they deny, and particular evil, which they do not deny, claim that simply because a thing exists it is not permissible to wish that it exist differently. But, Sir, if all is good as it is, then all was good as it was before there were Governments and Laws, hence it was at least superfluous to establish them, and in that case Jean-Jacques would, with [the help of] your system, have had an easy time of it against Philopolis. If all is good as it is in the [234] way in which you understand it, what is the point of correcting our vices, curing our ills, removing our errors? Of what use are our pulpits, our Courts, our Academies? Why call the Doctor when you have a fever? How do you know whether the good of the greatest whole, which you do not know, does not require you to be delirious, and whether the health of the inhabitants of Saturn or of Sirius would not suffer because yours was restored? Let everything go as it may, so that everything always go well. If everything is as best it can be, then you must blame any action whatsoever. For since any action, as soon as it occurs, necessarily brings about some change in the state things are in, one cannot touch anything without doing wrong, and the most absolute quietism is the only virtue left to man. Finally, if all is good as it is, then it is good that there be Laplanders, Eskimos, Algonquins, Chickasaws, Caribs, who do without our political order, Hotten-

tots who have no use for it, and a Genevan who approves of them. Leibniz himself would grant that.

[13] Man, you say, is such as the place he was to occupy in the universe required. But men differ so much according to times and places that with this kind of logic, inferences from the particular to the Universal are liable to lead to rather contradictory and inconclusive conclusions. A single error in Geography is enough to overturn the whole of this supposed doctrine which deduces what ought to be from what is seen [to be]. An Indian will say that it is the way of Beavers to hole up in dens, man ought to sleep in the open, in a Hammock stretched between trees. No, no, the Tartar will say, man is made to sleep in a Wagon. Poor people, our Philopolises will exclaim with an air of pity, don't you see that man is made to build cities! When it comes to thinking about human nature, the true Philosopher is neither an Indian nor a Tartar, neither from Geneva nor from Paris, but is a man.

[14] That the monkey is a Beast, I believe it, and I have stated my reason for believing it; you are good enough to inform me that the Orang-outang also is one, but I must admit that given the facts I cited, that seemed to me a difficult fact to prove. You philosophize too well to settle such questions as lightly as do our travelers *[235]* who are sometimes ready without much ado to rank their own kind among the beasts. You would, therefore, certainly place the public in your debt, and instruct even naturalists, if you told us by what means you settled that question.

[15] In my Epistle Dedicatory I congratulated my Fatherland for having one of the best governments that can be: In the body of the Discourse I showed that there could be very few good Governments: I do not see the contradiction you find in this. But how do you know, Sir, that if my health permitted I would go and live in the woods rather than among my Fellow-Citizens for whom you know my affection? So far was I from saying anything of the sort in my work, that you must, rather, have found in it very powerful reasons for not choosing that kind of life. I am much too sensible in my own person of how difficult it is for me not to live with men as corrupt as myself, and even

the wise man, if there is one, will not nowadays seek happiness in a desert. If one can, one ought to settle in one's Fatherland, in order to love and to serve it. Happy he who, failing that opportunity, can at least live in friendship in the common Fatherland of Mankind, in that vast sanctuary open to all men, where austere wisdom and exuberant youth are equally at ease; where humanity, hospitality, gentleness and all the charms of an easy society reign; where the Poor man still finds Friends, virtue examples that energize it, and reason guides that enlighten it. One can profitably watch the spectacle of life on that great Stage of fortune, vice and, sometimes, virtues; but one should end one's life in peace in one's own country.

[16] It seems to me, Sir, that you censure me most severely for a remark that appears to me to be perfectly correct but which, regardless of whether it is correct or not, has not in my text the meaning you are pleased to attribute to it by the addition of a single Letter. *If nature intended us to be saints,* you have me say, *I almost dare assert that the state of reflection is a state against Nature, and that a man who reflects is a depraved Animal.* I confess to you that if I had confounded health and saintliness in this fashion, and if the proposition were true, I would think myself very likely to become a great saint *[236]* in the next world or at least always to be in good health in this one.

[17] I conclude, Sir, by answering your last three questions. I shall not avail myself of the time you allow me to think about them; I had taken care to do so beforehand.

[18] *Would a man or any other sentient Being that had never known pain, experience pity and be moved at the sight of a child being murdered?* I answer that he would not.

[19] *Why does the Populace, to which M. Rousseau attributes such a large dose of pity, so avidly glut itself with the spectacle of a wretch dying on the wheel?* For the same reason that you go to the Theater to weep and to see Seide murder his Father, or Thyestes drink his son's blood. Pity is such a delicious sentiment that it is not surprising one seeks to experience it. Besides, everyone is secretly curious to learn the movements of Nature as that fearful moment which none can escape draws

near. Add to that the pleasure of, for two months, being the neighborhood orator and movingly describing to one's neighbors the fine death of the man most recently broken on the wheel.

[20] *Is the affection which female animals display for their young directed toward these young or toward the mother?* First toward the mother because of her need, thereafter toward the young out of habit. I had said so in the Discourse. *If perchance it were toward her, the well-being of the young would be all the more securely guaranteed.* I should think so too. However, this maxim must be construed narrowly rather than broadly, for as soon as the Chicks have hatched, the Hen seems to have no need of them, and yet she yields to none in maternal solicitude.

[21] These, Sir, are my answers. Note, moreover, that in this discussion, as in that about the first discourse, I am always the monster who maintains that man is naturally good, and my adversaries are always the honest folk who, for the sake of public edification, try to prove that nature made only scoundrels.

[22] I am, as much as one can be of someone one does not know,

Sir, etc.

REPLY
to CHARLES-GEORGES LE ROY

[1] I do not Know about that resemblance, nor do I know why, if there were no fruit, man would not eat grass or shoots, and use his hands or claws to dig for roots as even any number of our [civilized] men have frequently done in desert places where they have lived off roots for very long periods of time. In addition, people are forever telling me about long winters, without being prepared to take into account that more than half the earth hardly has any winter at all, the trees do not lose their foliage, and there is fruit all year long. The arguments against me are always drawn from a Paris, or a London, or some other small corner of the world, whereas I try to draw mine from the world itself.

[2] The difficulty carnivores have in finding their prey wherever men have cleared and cultivated the land, might not arise if the whole earth had been left fallow; certain it is, that you can place a cat or a wolf in a position where it would take it no more than twenty minutes out of every twenty-four hours to get its food; whereas on any assumption you care to make, a horse or an ox will always need to spend several hours grazing so that, by and large, they will always be at a disadvantage. Besides, regardless of what observation may establish about particular facts, the proof that all is well regulated is drawn from a general and incontrovertible fact, namely that all species survive: but I do understand that we, and especially I, can often err in the choice and application of the rules.

ESSAY
ON THE ORIGIN OF LANGUAGES
in which Something is said about Melody and Musical Imitation

CHAPTER ONE

OF THE VARIOUS MEANS OF COMMUNICATING
OUR THOUGHTS

[1] Speech differentiates man from the other animals; language differentiates one nation from another; where a man is from is known only once he has spoken. Usage and need cause everyone to learn the language of his country; but what causes this [particular] language to be the language of his country and not of another? In order to tell, one has to go back to some cause that depends on locality and antedates even morals: since speech is the first social institution, it owes its form to natural causes alone.

[2] As soon as one man was recognized by another as a sentient, thinking Being, similar to himself, the desire or the need to communicate to him his sentiments and thoughts made him seek the means to do so. Such means can only be drawn from the senses, the only instruments by which one man can act upon another. Hence the institution of sensible signs to express thought. The inventors of language did not go through this [chain of] reasoning, but instinct suggested to them its conclusion. We have but two general means of acting on someone else's senses, namely movement and the voice. Movement acts immediately through touch, or mediately through gesture. Since the first reaches no farther than arm's length, it cannot communicate at a distance; but the other extends as far as does the field of vision. That leaves only sight and hearing as passive organs of language among men dispersed.

[3] Although the language of gesture and that of the voice are equally natural, the first is easier and less dependent on conventions. For more objects strike our eyes than our ears, and shapes exhibit greater variety than do sounds. They are also more expressive and say more in less time. Love, it is said, was the inventor of drawing. Love might also have invented speech,

though less happily. Dissatisfied with speech, love disdains it:
it has livelier ways of expressing itself. How many things the
girl who took such pleasure in tracing her Lover's shadow was
telling him! What sounds could she have used to convey this
movement of the twig?

[4] Our gestures signify nothing but our natural restlessness;
they are not the ones about which I wish to speak. Only
Europeans gesticulate while speaking; one would think that the
power of their speech resided entirely in their arms; to which
they further add the power of their lungs, and all to scarcely
any avail. After a Frenchman has huffed and puffed and gone
through all kinds of bodily contortions to deliver himself of
long speeches, a Turk takes his pipe from his mouth for a
moment, quietly says two words, and crushes him with a single
pithy saying.

[5] Ever since we have learned to gesticulate we have forgotten
the art of pantomime, for the same reason that, with all of our
fancy grammars, we no longer understand the symbols of the
Egyptians. What the ancients said most forcefully they expressed
not in words, but in signs; they did not say it, they showed it.

[6] Consult ancient history; you will find it filled with such
ways of addressing arguments to the eyes, and they never fail to
produce a more certain effect than all the discourses that might
have been put in their place. An object, presented before
anything is said, stimulates the imagination, arouses curiosity,
holds the mind in suspense and anticipation of what will be
said. I have noticed that Italians and people from Provence,
with whom gesture usually precedes speech, in this way manage
to get themselves listened to more attentively and even with
greater pleasure. But the most vigorous speech is that in which
the Sign has said everything before a single word is spoken.
Tarquin, Thrasybulus lopping off the heads of the poppies,
Alexander putting his ring to his favorite's mouth, Diogenes
walking in front of Zeno, did they not speak more effectively
than with words? What circumlocutions would have expressed
the same ideas equally well? Darius, waging war in Scythia,
receives from the King of the Scythians a frog, a bird, a mouse,
and five arrows. The Herald transmits his gift in silence and

departs. This terrible harangue was understood, and Darius had no more urgent desire than to get back to his country as best he could. Substitute a letter for these signs: the more it threatens the less it frightens; it is mere bluster, and Darius would simply have laughed at it.

[7] When the Levite of Ephraim wanted to avenge the death of his wife he did not write to the Tribes of Israel; he divided her body into twelve pieces which he sent to them. At this ghastly sight they rushed to arms, crying with one voice: *No, never has anything like this happened in Israel, from the day when our fathers left Egypt until this day!* And the Tribe of Benjamin was exterminated.* Nowadays it would have been turned into lawsuits, debates, perhaps even jokes; it would have dragged on, and the most ghastly crime would finally have remained unpunished. King Saul, returning from the fields, in like fashion dismembered his plow oxen and used a similar sign to rouse Israel to assist the city of Jabesh. The Jews' Prophets and the Greeks' Lawgivers who frequently presented visible objects to the people, spoke to them better with these objects than they would have done with long discourses, and the way in which, according to Athenaeus, the orator Hyperides got the courtesan Phryne acquitted without urging a single word in her defense, is yet another instance of a mute eloquence that has at all times proven effective.

[8] Thus one speaks much better to the eyes than to the ears: no one fails to feel the truth of Horace's judgment in this regard. The most eloquent discourses are even seen to be those with the most images embedded in them, and sounds are never more vigorous than when they produce the effect of colors.

[9] But when it is a question of moving the heart and enflaming the passions, things stand entirely differently. The successive impression made by discourse, striking with cumulative impact, arouses a very different emotion in you from that produced by the presence of the object itself, which you take in completely at one glance. Imagine a situation where you know perfectly well that someone is in pain; you are not likely

* Only six hundred of its men, without any women or children, were left.

to be easily moved to tears at the sight of the afflicted person; but give him the time to tell you everything he feels and you will soon burst into tears. Only thus do the scenes of tragedy produce their effect.* Pantomime alone, unaccompanied by discourse, will leave you almost unmoved; discourse unaccompanied by gesture will wring tears from you. The passions have their gestures but also their accents; and these accents, which cause us to shudder, these accents to which one cannot close one's ear and which by way of it penetrate to the very depths of the heart, in spite of ourselves convey to it the [e]motions that wring them [from us], and cause us to feel what we hear. Let us conclude that visible signs make for more accurate imitation, but that interest is aroused more effectively by sounds.

[10] This leads me to think that if we had never had any but physical needs, we might very well never have spoken and [yet] have understood one another perfectly by means of the language of gesture alone. We might have established societies differing but little from those now in existence, societies which might even have attained their end more successfully; we might have instituted laws, chosen chiefs, invented arts, established commerce and, in a word, done almost as many things as we have been doing with the help of speech. The epistolary language of Salaams** relays the secrets of oriental gallantry from one end to the other of the best-guarded Harems without fear of jealous [masters]. The mutes of the Grand Vizier understand one another, and they understand everything they are told by means of signs quite as well as it can be stated in discourse. Mr. Pereyre and those who, like himself, teach mutes not only to speak but to know what they are saying are, after all, compelled first to teach them another, equally complicated language, by means of which to enable them to understand spoken language.

---

* I have said elsewhere why feigned miseries affect us more than real ones do. There are people who sob at tragedies but never in their lives took pity on a single unhappy person. The invention of the theater is marvelously suited to flatter our vanity with all the virtues we lack.

** Salaams are any number of the most common objects, such as an orange, a ribbon, a piece of coal, etc., the sending of which conveys a meaning known to all lovers in the country where this language has currency.

244   ESSAY ON THE ORIGIN OF LANGUAGES

[11] Chardin says that in India traders take one another by the hand and, by varying their grip in ways no one can see, transact all their business in public and yet secretly, without having exchanged a single word. Imagine them blind, deaf, and mute, they would understand one another no less well; which shows that, in order to form a language, a single one of the two senses by which we are active would suffice.

[12] It would also seem from these observations, that the invention of the art of communicating our ideas is a function not so much of the organs we use in such communication as of a faculty peculiar to man which causes him to use his organs for this purpose and which, if he lacked them, would cause him to use others to the same end. Let man be as crudely structured as you please; no doubt he will acquire fewer ideas; but provided only that there is some means of communication between himself and his kind by which one man can act and the other feel, they will succeed in eventually communicating to one another all the ideas they have.

[13] Animals have a structure more than adequate for this kind of communication, yet none of them has ever put it to this use. Here, it seems to me, is a most distinctive difference. I do not doubt that animals that work and live together, such as Beavers, ants, bees, have some natural language as a means of communicating with one another. There is even reason to believe that the language of Beavers and that of ants are gestural and speak only to the eyes. Be that as it may; precisely because these various languages are natural, they are not acquired; the animals that speak them have them at birth; they all have them, and everywhere they have the same one; they do not change languages, nor do they make any progress whatsoever in them. Conventional language belongs to man alone. That is why man makes progress in good as well as in evil, and why animals do not. This single distinction seems to be far-reaching. They say that it can be explained by a difference in organs. I should be curious to see that explanation.

CHAPTER TWO

THAT THE FIRST INVENTION OF SPEECH IS NOT DUE
TO THE NEEDS BUT TO THE PASSIONS

[1] It would seem, then, that the needs dictated the first gestures, and the passions wrung the first utterings [*voix*]. Once the clues which the facts provide are followed up in the light of these distinctions, it may prove necessary to think about the origin of languages altogether differently from the way in which it has been thought about until now. The genius of the oriental languages, the oldest ones known to us, completely contradicts the didactic development they are imagined to have followed. These languages are in no way methodical or reasoned; they are lively and figurative. The speech of the first men is represented to us as [if they had been] Geometers' languages, whereas we can see that they were Poets' languages.

[2] It had to be so. Man did not begin by reasoning but by feeling. It is claimed that men invented speech in order to express their needs; that seems to me an untenable opinion. The natural effect of the first needs was to separate men, not to unite them. It had to be so for the species to spread and the earth to be promptly populated, otherwise mankind would have crowded into one corner of the earth, while the rest remained desert.

[3] From this alone it clearly follows that the origin of languages is not due to men's first needs; it would be absurd for the cause of their separation to give rise to the means to unite them. Where, then, may this origin be found? In the moral needs, the passions. All the passions unite men, while the necessity to seek their subsistence forces them to flee one another. Not hunger, nor thirst, but love, hatred, pity, anger wrung their first utterings [*voix*] from them. Fruit does not shrink from our grasp, one can eat it without speaking; one stalks in silence the prey one means to devour; but in order to

move a young heart, to repulse an unjust aggressor, nature
dictates accents, cries, plaints: here [then] are the oldest invented
words, and here is why the first languages were songlike and
passionate before they were simple and methodical. None of
this is true without qualification; but I shall come back to it in
the sequel.

CHAPTER THREE

THAT THE FIRST LANGUAGE MUST HAVE BEEN FIGURATIVE

[1] Just as the first motives that moved man to speak were
passions, his first expressions were Tropes. Figurative language
arose first, proper [or literal] meaning was found last. Things
were called by their true name only once they were seen in
their true form. At first men spoke only poetry; only much later
did it occur to anyone to reason.

[2] Now, I sense the reader stopping me here, and asking
how an expression can be figurative before it has a proper [or
literal] meaning, since the figure consists solely in the transposing
of meaning. I grant that; but in order to understand me, it is
necessary to substitute the idea which the passion presents to
us for the word which we are transposing; for words are
transposed only because ideas also are; otherwise figurative
language would signify nothing. Let me therefore reply with an
example.

[3] A savage, upon meeting others, will at first have been
frightened. His fright will have made him see these men as
larger and stronger than himself; he will have called them
Giants. After much experience he will have recognized that,
since these supposed Giants are neither bigger nor stronger than
he, their stature did not fit the idea he had initially attached to
the word Giant. He will therefore invent another name common
both to them and to himself, for example the name *man,* and he
will restrict the name *Giant* to the false object that had struck
him during his illusion. That is how the figurative word arises

before the proper [or literal] word does, when passion holds our eyes spellbound and the first idea which it presents to us is not that of the truth. What I have said regarding words and names applies equally to turns of phrase. Since the illusory image presented by passion showed itself first, the language answering to it was invented first; subsequently it became metaphorical, when the enlightened mind recognized its original error and came to use expressions of that first language only when moved by the same passions as had produced it.

CHAPTER FOUR

OF THE DISTINCTIVE CHARACTERISTICS OF THE FIRST LANGUAGE AND OF THE CHANGES IT MUST HAVE UNDERGONE

[1] Simple sounds issue naturally from the throat, and the mouth is naturally more or less open; but the modifications of tongue and palate, by which we articulate, require attention and practice; we do not make them without intending to make them; all children must learn them, and some do not do so easily. In all languages the liveliest exclamations are inarticulate; cries, moans are nothing but utterings [*voix*]; mutes, that is to say deaf persons, utter only inarticulate sounds. Father Lamy cannot even imagine how men could ever have invented any other sounds, had God not expressly taught them to speak. Articulations are few in number; sounds are numberless, and the accents placed on them can similarly be multiplied; all musical notes are so many accents; it is true that our speech has only three or four; but the chinese have many more; on the other hand, they have fewer consonants. To this source of combinations add that of meter or quantity, and you will have a greater variety not only of words, but of syllables, than the richest language needs.

[2] I do not doubt that if the first language still existed, it would have preserved certain primitive characteristics, indepen-

dently of vocabulary and syntax, which would distinguish it from all other languages. Not only must all of the phrases of this language be in images, sentiments, figures of speech; but in its mechanical aspect it would have to answer to its primary aim and convey to the ear as well as to the understanding the almost inescapable impressions of passion seeking to communicate itself. Since our natural utterings [*voix*] are inarticulate, words would have few articulations; a few interspersed consonants would eliminate the hiatus between vowels, and so suffice to make them smooth and easy to pronounce. On the other hand, its sounds would be extremely varied, and variety of accent would make the same utterings [*voix*] greater in number; quantity and rhythm would make possible still further combinations; so that, since utterings [*voix*], sounds, accent, and quantity, which are by nature, would leave little to be done by articulations, which are by convention, men would sing rather than speak; most root words would be sounds imitating either the accent of the passions or the effect of sensible objects: onomatopoeia would constantly make its presence felt.

[3] This language would have many synonyms to describe the same being in its different relations;* it would have few adverbs and abstract words to express these relations. It would have many augmentatives, diminutives, compound words, expletives, to endow periods with cadence and sentences with fullness; it would have many irregularities and anomalies; it would neglect grammatical analogy in favor of the euphony, variety, harmony and beauty of sounds. Instead of arguments it would have pithy sayings; it would persuade without convincing, and depict without demonstrating; in some respects it would resemble Chinese, in others Greek, in still others Arabic. Develop these ideas in all their ramifications, and you will find that Plato's *Cratylus* is not as ridiculous as it appears to be.

---

* Arabic is said to have more than a thousand different words for *camel,* more than a hundred for *sword,* etc.

CHAPTER FIVE

OF WRITING

[1] Anyone who studies the history and progress of languages will see that as utterings [*voix*] grow increasingly monotone, consonants increase in number, and that as accents disappear and quantities are equalized, they are replaced by grammatical combinations and new articulations; but these changes take place only gradually. In proportion as needs increase, as [men's] dealings [with one another] grow more involved, as enlightenment spreads, the character of language changes; it becomes more precise and less passionate; it substitutes ideas for sentiments; it no longer speaks to the heart but to the reason. As a result accent dies out and articulation becomes more pervasive; language becomes more exact and clear, but more sluggish, subdued, and cold. This progress seems entirely natural to me.

[2] Another way to compare languages and to ascertain how ancient they are is drawn from writing, the age being in inverse proportion to the perfection of this art. The cruder the writing, the more ancient the language. The original method of writing is not to depict sounds but the objects themselves, either directly as did the Mexicans, or by allegorical figures as the Egyptians did in ancient times. This state corresponds to passionate language, and it already presupposes some social life as well as needs engendered by the passions.

[3] The second way is to represent words and propositions by conventional characters; which is possible only once the language is fully formed and an entire people is united by shared Laws; for it already involves a twofold convention. Such is the writing of the Chinese; this [way of writing] is truly to depict sounds and to speak to the eyes.

[4] The third is to break up the speaking voice into a number of elementary parts such as vowels and consonants, by means of which all imaginable words and syllables could be formed. This way of writing, which is the one we use, must have been

imagined by people engaged in commerce who, since they traveled in a number of countries and had to speak a number of languages, were compelled to invent characters that could be common to all of them. To do this is not exactly to depict speech, but to analyze it.

[5] These three ways of writing correspond fairly accurately to the three different states in terms of which it is possible to consider men assembled into nations. The depiction of objects suits savage peoples; signs of words and propositions, barbarian peoples; and the alphabet, civilized peoples.

[6] This last-mentioned invention ought not, therefore, to be regarded as a proof of the great antiquity of the people who invented it. On the contrary, the alphabet is likely to have been discovered by a people intent on communicating with other peoples speaking other languages, peoples contemporary with it and possibly more ancient. The same cannot be said of the two other methods. However, I grant that if we keep to history and the known facts, alphabetical writing appears to go as far back as any other. But it is not surprising that we lack records of times when people did not write.

[7] It is scarcely likely that those to whom it first occurred to analyze speech into elementary signs would initially have made very precise divisions. Later, when they perceived the inadequacy of their analysis, some increased the number of letters in their alphabet, as did the Greeks. Others were satisfied to vary the meaning or the sound of letters by placing or combining them differently. That is how the inscriptions on the ruins of Tchelminar which Chardin has transcribed for us appear to have been written. They exhibit only two shapes or characters* which, however, differ in size and face in different directions. Yet, to judge by the perfection of the arts which the beauty of the characters indicates,** and by the admirable monuments on

* "People are surprised," says Chardin, "that two shapes can make up so many letters; as for myself, I do not find it so very astonishing, since the letters of our alphabet, which are 23 in number, are nevertheless made up of only two lines, the straight and the curved; which is to say that with a *C* and an *I* we form all the letters that make up our words."

** "This character is very beautiful in appearance, with nothing unclear or

which these inscriptions are found, this unknown and almost awesomely ancient language must have been well developed at the time. I do not know why there is so little discussion of these astonishing ruins. When I read their description in Chardin, I feel transported to another world. All of this strikes me as intensely thought-provoking.

[8] The art of writing does not in any way depend on that of speaking. It depends on needs of a different nature, which develop sooner or later depending on circumstances that are altogether independent of how long a people has been in existence, and might never have arisen in very ancient Nations. It is not known for how many centuries the art of hieroglyphs was perhaps the Egyptians' only writing; and the fact that a civilized people may find such writing adequate is proven by the example of the Mexicans, whose writing was even less convenient.

[9] When the Coptic alphabet is compared with the Syriac or with the Phoenician alphabet, it is readily evident that one derives from the other, and it would not be surprising if the latter were the original, nor if the more recent people had instructed the more ancient in this respect. It is also clear that the Greek Alphabet derives from the Phoenician; indeed, it is evident that it must derive from it. Regardless of whether

---

barbarous about it. . . . It would seem that the letters were gilded; for several, especially capitals, still show some gold, and it is surely admirable and astounding that this gilding should have withstood exposure to the elements for all these centuries. . . . It is not, however, at all surprising that not a single one of the world's scholars has ever made any sense of this writing, for it in no way resembles any writing that has come down to us; whereas all the systems of writing now known, except the Chinese, exhibit many affinities with one another and appear to derive from the same source. What is most astonishing about all this is that the Parsees, who are the descendants of the ancient Persians and who preserve and perpetuate their religion, not only are no more familiar with these characters than we are, but that their own characters no more resemble them than ours do. . . . From which it follows that either it is a cabalistic character—which is unlikely, since it is used routinely and naturally everywhere throughout the building, and there is none other by the same chisel—or that it is of an antiquity so great that we hardly dare state it." Indeed Chardin would lead one to infer, judging from this passage, that this character had already been forgotten at the time of Cyrus and of the Magi, and was as unknown then as it is today.

Cadmus or someone else brought it over from Phoenicia, it seems certain, in any case, that the Greeks did not set out in quest of it, but that the Phoenicians brought it over themselves: for they were the first and almost the only one of the Asian or African Peoples to engage in trade with Europe,* and they came to the Greeks long before the Greeks visited them; which in no way proves that the Greek People is less ancient than the Phoenician.

[10] At first the Greeks not only took over the Phoenicians' characters, but even the direction of their lines from right to left. Later it occurred to them to write in furrows, that is to say by returning alternately from left to right and from right to left.** Finally they wrote as we do now, beginning every line anew from left to right. This progress[ion] is altogether natural: writing in furrows is unquestionably the easiest to read. I am even surprised that it was not adopted along with printing; but since writing this way by hand is difficult, it must have fallen into disuse when manuscripts became more numerous.

[11] But even though the greek alphabet derives from the Phoenician alphabet, it by no means follows that the Greek language derives from the Phoenician language. The first proposition does not at all entail the second, and it would appear that the Greek language was already very ancient, at a time when the art of writing was still recent and even imperfectly developed among the Greeks. Up to the time of the siege of Troy they had only sixteen letters, if that many. It is said that Palamedes added four and Simonides the remaining four. All this is rather farfetched. On the other hand, latin, a more modern language, had a complete alphabet almost from its beginning, though the first Romans hardly made use of it, since they began to write down their history so late, and lustra were only marked off with nail[-head]s.

[12] Besides, there is no absolutely fixed number of letters or of elements of speech; some have more, some fewer, depending on the language and on the various modifications accorded to

---

* I hold the Carthaginians to be Phoenicians since they were a colony of Tyre.
** See Pausanias, *Arcad*[*ia*]. That is also how the Latins wrote in the beginning; hence, according to Marius Victorinus, the word *versus*.

vowels [*voix*] and consonants. Those who recognize only
five vowels are seriously mistaken: the Greeks had seven written
vowels, the first Romans six;* the Gentlemen of Port Royal
recognize ten, M. Duclos seventeen; and I have no doubt that
many more would be found, had the ear been habituated to be
more sensitive to the various modifications which it is capable
of [discriminating], and the mouth better trained [to produce]
the various modifications which it is capable of [producing].
Depending on the refinement of the organ[s of speech and
hearing], a greater or smaller number of these modifications will
be discovered between the acute *a* and the grave *o,* between
the open *i* and the open *e,* etc. Anyone can experience this by
moving from one vowel to the next in a continuous, modulated
voice; for to the extent that habit has made one more or less
sensitive to them, one can single out a greater or lesser number
of these nuances and mark each with its own distinctive character,
and this habituation depends on the kinds of vocalizations [*voix*]
common in the language to which the organ [of speech or
hearing] imperceptibly conforms. Much the same can be said
about articulated letters, or consonants. But that is not how most
nations went about it. They took over one another's alphabets,
and represented very different utterings [*voix*] and articulations
by the same characters. That is why, unless one is very well
trained, one invariably sounds ridiculous reading in a language
other than one's own, no matter how faithful its spelling is [to
the way it sounds].

[13] Writing, which might be expected to fix [or to stabilize]
language, is precisely what alters it; it changes not its words but
its genius; it substitutes precision for expressiveness. One conveys
one's sentiments in speaking, and one's ideas in writing. In
writing one is compelled to use every word in conformity with
common usage; but a speaker alters meanings by his tone of
voice, determining them as he wishes; since he is less constrained
to be clear, he stresses forcefulness more; and a language that
is written cannot possibly retain for long the liveliness of one
that is only spoken. What gets written down are words [*voix*],

---

* "Greek records seven vowels, Romulus six, later usage five, once the *y* was
rejected as Greek." Mart[ianus] Capel[la]. I. iii.

not sounds; yet in an accented language it is the sounds, the accents, the inflections of every sort, that constitute the greatest part of the vigor of the language, and it is because of them that in a given sentence an otherwise common expression proves to be the only proper one. The means employed to compensate for this [feature of spoken language] enlarge [and] stretch written language, and as they pass from books into discourse, they enervate speech itself.* When we say everything as it would get written, all we do is to read as we speak.

CHAPTER SIX

WHETHER IT IS LIKELY THAT HOMER KNEW HOW TO WRITE

[1] Regardless of what we may be told about the invention of the Greek alphabet, I believe it to be much more recent than it is said to be, and I base this opinion mainly on the character of the language. It has often occurred to me to doubt not only that Homer knew how to write, but even that in his time anyone wrote. I am very sorry that this doubt is so categorically contradicted by the Story of Bellerophon in the *Iliad;* since I, no less than Father Hardouin, have the misfortune to be rather stubborn about my paradoxes, if I were less ignorant I would be sorely tempted to extend my doubts to that Story itself, and to tax it with having been uncritically interpolated by the compilers of Homer. Not only are there few traces of this art to be found in the rest of the *Iliad;* but I dare say that the entire

* The best such means, and one that would be free from this defect, would be punctuation, had it not been left in such an imperfect state. Why, for example, have we not a vocative mark? The question mark, which we do have, was much less necessary; in our language at least, one can see from the construction alone whether or not a question is being asked. *Are you coming* and *you are coming* are not the same. But how is one to distinguish in writing a man who is being mentioned from one being addressed? Here is a real equivocation, one which the vocative mark would have removed. The same equivocation occurs in irony, when accent fails to convey it.

Odyssey is but a tissue of stupidities and inanities which one or two letters would have reduced to thin air, whereas the Poem becomes reasonable and even rather well plotted on the assumption that its Heroes knew nothing of writing. If the *Iliad* had been written it would have been sung much less often, Rhapsodes would have been less in demand, and their number would have increased less. No other poet has been sung so much with the possible exception of Tasso in Venice; and he only by Gondoliers, who are not great readers. The variety of dialects used by Homer is further strong presumptive evidence. Writing assimilates and blends the dialects which speech differentiates, and everything imperceptibly tends to conform to a common model. In proportion as a nation reads and studies, its dialects fade, and finally they survive only in vernacular form among the people, which reads little and writes not at all.

[2] Now since these two Poems are later than the siege of Troy, it is hardly likely that the Greeks who conducted that siege were acquainted with writing, while the Poet who sang of it was not. For a long time these Poems were written only in men's memories; they were compiled in written form rather late and with considerable difficulty. It was when Greece began to abound in books and written poetry that the whole charm of Homer's poetry came to be felt by comparison. The other Poets wrote, Homer alone had sung, and these divine songs ceased to be listened to with delight only after Europe was blanketed with barbarians who took it upon themselves to judge what they were incapable of feeling.

CHAPTER SEVEN

OF MODERN PROSODY

[1] We have no idea of a sonorous and harmonious language that speaks as much by means of sounds as by means of utterances [or words, *voix*]. It is an error to believe that written accents can replace vocal accents: written accents are invented

only once vocal accent is lost.* What is more, we believe that we have accents in our language, although we have none whatsoever. Our supposed accents are nothing but vowels or signs of quantity; they do not indicate any variation in sound. The proof is that all of these accents are produced either by unequal duration or by altered positions of the lips, the tongue, or the palate, all of which make for variety of utterings [*voix*]; none by changes in the glottis, which make for variety of sounds. Thus when our circumflex does not indicate a simple uttering [*voix*], it indicates either a long vowel or nothing at all. Let us now see what it was for the Greeks.

* Some scholars claim, counter to the common opinion and to the evidence of all ancient manuscripts, that the Greeks knew and used the written signs called "accents," and they base their opinion on two texts, both of which I will transcribe in order to permit the Reader to assess their true meaning.

Here is the first, taken from Cicero's treatise *On the Orator,* Book III, Section 44: "After this painstaking labor [of ordering words], there remains rhythm and harmony of phrasing which, I fear, Catulus, may appear puerile to you. Indeed, according to the ancient masters, prose exhibited something analogous to verse, namely a kind of number; they wanted the phrases in speeches punctuated by pauses for breath and not because of shortness of breath, nor did they want them indicated by copyists' marks, but by phrasing. Isocrates is said to have been the first who, as his disciple Naucrates put it, in order to flatter the ear, established the rule of subjecting prose, which until then had been without rule, to a rhythm. Indeed, the musicians, who were formerly also poets, in order to please, invented these two ways, verse and song, so that the rhythm of the words and the harmony of the sounds might prevent a surfeit of the ear. They thought that they should transfer these two innovations, I mean the art of regulating the voice, and that of indicating the end of phrases by some rhythmical pattern, from poetry into eloquence to the full extent that discourse, a serious matter, might permit it."

Here is the second, drawn from Isidore's *Origins,* Book I, Chapter 20: "In addition, there are signs found in the most celebrated writers, and the ancients introduced them into verse and prose in order to punctuate their writings. The sign is a specific mark, placed in the manner of a letter in order in each case to indicate the phrase pattern. The number of signs introduced in verse is 26, and their names are given below."

To me this indicates that the good copyists of Cicero's time separated words and that they used signs equivalent to our punctuation. It also indicates to me the invention of number [*i.e.,* meter] and of prose declamation attributed to Isocrates. But I see nothing at all here of written signs or accents, and even if I did, it would justify only a single conclusion which I do not deny and which is in perfect conformity with my principles, namely that when the Romans began to study Greek, the Copyists, in order to help them with its pronunciation, invented signs for accents, aspiration, and prosody; but it would not at all follow that these signs were used by the Greeks, who had no need of them.

[2] "Dionysus of Halicarnassus says that on the acute accent
the tone was raised, and on the grave it was lowered by a
fifth; the prosodic accent was thus also a musical accent,
especially the circumflex, where the voice, after having risen
by a fifth, dropped by another fifth on the same syllable."* This
passage and its context clearly indicate that M. Duclos does not
recognize a musical accent in our language, but only the
prosodic and the vocal accents. In addition to these there is an
orthographic accent which in no way affects the voice, or the
sound, or the quantity, but which sometimes indicates an
omitted letter, as does the circumflex, while at other times it
specifies the meaning of an otherwise equivocal monosyllable,
such as the so-called grave accent that distinguishes the adverb
of place *où* [where] from the disjunctive particle *ou* [or], and *à*
[to] used as an article from the same *a* [has] used as a verb. The
accent differentiates between these monosyllables for the eye
alone, nothing differentiates between their pronunciation."** Thus
the definition of the accent generally accepted by the French
does not fit a single one of the accents in their language.

[3] I fully expect that some of their grammarians, having been
taught that accents mark a raising or a lowering of the voice,
will here again tax me with paradoxes and, for want of paying
sufficiently close attention to experience, they will think that
they are using different movements of the glottis to produce the
very accents which they produce exclusively by opening the
mouth or placing the tongue in different ways. Now, here is
what I suggest they do in order to verify what actually takes
place, and to prove my point incontrovertibly.

[4] Attune your voice perfectly to some musical instrument
and on this unison note pronounce, one after the other, all the
most variously accented French words you can think of; since
only the grammatical and not the rhetorical accent is at issue
here, these different words need not even make any sustained

* M. Duclos, *Rem[arques] sur la gram[maire] génér[ale] et raisonnée,* p. 30.
** It might seem that this is the accent by which the Italians distinguish
between, for example, the verbal form *è* [is] and the conjunction *e* [and]; but
the first is perceptible to the ear as a stronger and more emphatic sound, which
makes the accent with which it is written a vocal accent; Buonmattei should
not have failed to make this observation.

sense. Make a note of whether, as you speak in this fashion, you do not indicate all the accents as distinctly and as clearly at this one level of sound as you would if you spoke unhampered, varying the tone of your voice. Now assuming this to be the case, and indisputably it is, I say that, since all your accents are expressed at the same pitch, they do not indicate different sounds. I cannot imagine what might be said in rebuttal to this.

[5] Any language in which the same words can be set to several melodies, has no settled musical accent. If the accent were fixed, so would the melody be; as soon as the tune is a matter of choice, accent counts for naught.

[6] All modern European languages are more or less in the same situation; I do not even exclude Italian. Italian is no more a musical language than is French. The difference is simply that one lends itself to music and the other does not.

[7] All this tends to confirm the following principle, that by a natural progress all lettered languages must change character and lose vigor as they gain in clarity; that, in proportion to the effort to perfect grammar and logic, this progress is accelerated, and that in order to cause a language to grow rapidly frigid and monotonous one need only establish academies among the people who speak it.

[8] Derivative languages are recognized by the discrepancy between spelling and pronunciation. The older and the purer languages are, the less arbitrary is their pronunciation, and hence the less complicated are the characters that indicate pronunciation. "All of the ancients' prosodic signs," says M. Duclos, "even assuming that they were used with great consistency, still were not as important as usage." I would go further, and say that they replaced it. The ancient Hebrews had neither punctuation nor accents, they did not even have vowels. When other Nations began to try to speak Hebrew and the Jews spoke other languages, their own lost its accent; [punctuation] signs and [vowel] points became necessary to set it in order, and this restored the meaning of words far more than it did the pronunciation of the language. The Jews of today, speaking Hebrew, would no longer be understood by their ancestors.

[9] In order to know English, one has to learn it twice; the

first time to read it, and the second to speak it. If a foreigner glances at the book from which an Englishman is reading aloud, he will perceive no connection at all between what he sees and what he hears. Why is that? Because England was conquered by a succession of peoples and, while the words continued to be written as before, their pronunciation has often changed. There is a considerable difference between the signs that establish the meaning of what is written and the signs that govern pronunciation. It would be easy to construct a language made up exclusively of the consonants, which would be very clear in its written form, but could not be spoken. Algebra is, in some respects, just such a language. When the spelling of a language is clearer than its pronunciation, it indicates that this language is written more than it is spoken: such may have been the learned language of the Egyptians; such are for us the dead languages. In the case of languages burdened with useless consonants, writing even seems to have preceded speech; and it is difficult to resist the suspicion that this is what happened with Polish. If it did, then Polish must be the most frigid of all languages.

CHAPTER EIGHT

GENERAL AND LOCAL DIFFERENCES
IN THE ORIGIN OF LANGUAGES

[1] Everything I have said so far applies to primitive languages in general and to such progress as results from their age, but it explains neither their origin nor their differences. The principal cause for the differences between them is local, a consequence of the climates in which they are born and of the manner in which they are formed, [and] it is to this cause that one has to go back in order to understand the general and characteristic difference that is found to obtain between the languages of the south and those of the north. The great failing of Europeans is always to philosophize about the origin of things in the light of

what happens right around them: they never fail to show us the first men living in a barren, harsh land, dying of cold and hunger, anxious to secure shelter and clothing; everywhere they see only the snow and ice of Europe, without taking into account that, like all other species, mankind was born in the warm regions, and that in two-thirds of the globe winter is hardly known. When one proposes to study men, one has to look close by; but in order to study man one has to learn to cast one's glance afar; one has to begin by observing the differences in order to discover the properties.

[2] Mankind, born in the warm countries, spreads to the cold ones; there it increases, and eventually flows back into the warm countries. To this action and reaction are due the earth's revolutions and the ceaseless agitation of its inhabitants. Let us try to follow the very order of nature in our inquiries. I am entering upon a long digression about a topic so hackneyed as to have become trivial, but to which one nevertheless always has to return, however unwillingly, in order to discover the origin of human institutions.

CHAPTER NINE

THE FORMATION OF SOUTHERN LANGUAGES

[1] In the first times* men, scattered over the face of the earth, had no society other than that of the family, no laws other than those of nature, no language other than gesture and a few inarticulate sounds.** They were not bound by any idea of common brotherhood and, since they had no arbiter other than

---

* I call first the times of men's dispersion, regardless of the age one chooses to assign to mankind at that period.
** Genuine languages have not a domestic origin; only a more comprehensive and lasting convention can establish them. The savages of America almost never speak except when away from home; in his hut everyone remains silent and speaks to his family by means of signs; and such signs are infrequent because a savage is less restless, less impatient than a European, has fewer needs, and takes care to attend to them himself.

force, they believed themselves to be one another's enemies. Their weakness and ignorance gave them that opinion. Since they knew nothing, they feared everything; they attacked in self-defense. A man abandoned alone on the face of the earth at the mercy of mankind, had to be a ferocious animal. He was ready to inflict on others all the harm he feared from them. Fear and weakness are the sources of cruelty.

[2] Social attachments develop in us only with our knowledge. Pity, although natural to man's heart, would remain forever inactive without imagination to set it in motion. How do we let ourselves be moved to pity? By transporting ourselves outside ourselves; by identifying with the suffering being. We suffer only to the extent that we judge him to suffer; it is not in ourselves but in him that we suffer. Think how much acquired knowledge this transport presupposes! How could I imagine evils of which I have no idea? How could I suffer when I see another suffer, if I do not even know that he suffers, if I do not know what he and I have in common? Someone who has never reflected cannot be clement, or just, or pitying; any more than he can be wicked and vindictive. He who imagines nothing feels only himself; in the midst of mankind he is alone.

[3] Reflection is born of the comparison of ideas, and it is their variety that leads us to compare them. Whoever sees only a single object has no occasion to make comparisons. Whoever sees only a small number, and always the same ones from childhood on, still does not compare them, because the habit of seeing them deprives him of the attention required to examine them; but as a new object strikes us, we want to know it, and we look for relations between it and the objects we do know; that is how we learn to observe what we see before us, and how what is foreign to us leads us to examine what touches us.

[4] Apply these ideas to the first men, and you will see the reason for their barbarism. Since they had never seen anything other than what was around them, they did not know even that; they did not know themselves. They had the idea of a Father, a son, a brother, but not of a man. Their hut held all those who were like themselves; a stranger, an animal, a monster were all

the same to them: outside of themselves and their family, the whole universe was naught to them.

[5] Hence the apparent contradictions one sees in the fathers of nations: so much naturalness and so much inhumanity, such ferocious ways [*moeurs*] and such tender hearts, so much love for their family and aversion toward their species. All their sentiments, focused on those close to them, were therefore the more vigorous. Everything they knew, they held dear. Hostile to the rest of the world, which they neither saw nor knew, they hated only what they could not know.

[6] These times of barbarism were the golden age, not because men were united but because they were separated. Everyone, it is said, considered himself to be master of everything; that may be so; but no one knew or desired more than was ready to hand; his needs, far from drawing him closer to those like himself, drew him away from them. Men may have attacked one another upon meeting, but they rarely met. Everywhere the state of war prevailed, yet the whole earth was at peace.

[7] The first men were hunters or shepherds, and not tillers of the soil; the first goods were herds, not fields. Before ownership of the earth was divided, no one thought of cultivating it. Agriculture is an art that requires tools; to sow in order to reap is a measure requiring foresight. Man in society seeks to expand; isolated man contracts. Beyond where his eye can see or his arm reach there no longer is either right or property for him. Once the Cyclops has rolled the stone in front of the entrance to his cave, his herds and he are safe. But who would protect the harvest of a man whom the laws do not protect?

[8] I will be told that Cain was a tiller of the ground and that Noah planted a vineyard. Why not? They were alone; what did they have to fear? Besides, that does nothing to counter my point; I have stated above how I conceive of the first times. When Cain became a fugitive, he was, after all, compelled to give up agriculture; the wandering life of Noah's descendants must have made them forget it also. The earth had to be populated before it could be cultivated; the two cannot readily be done together. During the first dispersion of mankind, until the family was stabilized and man had a fixed dwelling, there

was no more agriculture. Peoples that do not settle cannot possibly cultivate the soil. Such formerly were the Nomads, such were the Arabs living in their tents, the Scythians in their wagons, such are still the wandering Tartars and the savages of America in our time.

[9] As a rule, of all of the peoples whose origin we know, the first barbarians are found to be voracious and carnivorous rather than agricultural and granivorous. The Greeks [refer by] name [to] the person who first taught them to till the soil, and they would seem not to have learned this art until comparatively late. But when they add that until the time of Triptolemus they lived solely off acorns, they make an implausible claim and one which their own history belies; for they had been eating meat prior to Triptolemus, since he forbade them to eat it. Besides, it would seem that they did not take this prohibition very seriously.

[10] At Homer's feasts an ox is slaughtered to regale one's guests, as one might nowadays slaughter a suckling pig. On reading that Abraham served a calf to three people, that Eumaeus had two kids roasted for Ulysses's dinner, and that Rebecca did the same for her husband's, one may gather what tremendous devourers of meat men were in those times. To get a notion of the meals of the ancients one need only consider the meals of present-day savages; I almost said those of Englishmen.

[11] The first cake that was eaten was the communion of mankind. When men began to settle, they cleared a bit of land around their hut; it was a garden rather than a field. The little grain they gathered was ground between two stones, made into a few cakes baked in ashes, or over embers, or on a hot stone, and eaten only at feasts. This ancient practice, consecrated among the Jews by Passover, is preserved to this day in Persia and in the [East] Indies. There they eat only unleavened breads, and these breads, made up of thin sheets, are baked and eaten at every meal. Only when more bread came to be needed did it occur to people to leaven it, for small quantities do not readily lend themselves to leavening.

[12] I know that large-scale agriculture already prevailed at the time of the patriarchs. It must have been introduced into

Palestine quite early, since Egypt is so close. The book of Job, perhaps the oldest of all extant books, refers to cultivation of the fields; it lists five hundred pairs of oxen as part of Job's wealth. The reference to pairs indicates that these oxen were yoked for work; it is explicitly stated that these oxen were ploughing when the Sabeans carried them off, and one can readily gather what an expanse of land five hundred teams of oxen must have ploughed.

[13] All this is true; but let us not confuse different times. What we call the age of the patriarchs is very remote from the first age. Scripture lists ten generations between them in those centuries when men lived to a very advanced age. What did they do during those ten generations? We know nothing about it. Since they lived scattered and almost without society, they scarcely spoke: how could they have written and, given the regularity of their solitary life, what events would they have transmitted to us?

[14] Adam spoke; Noah spoke; granted. Adam had been taught by God himself. When they separated, the children of Noah gave up agriculture, and the common language perished together with the first society. This would have happened even if there had never been a tower of babel. Isolated individuals living on desert islands have been known to forget their own language. After several generations away from their country men rarely preserve their original language, even when they work together and live in society with one another.

[15] Scattered throughout this vast desert of a world, men relapsed into the dull barbarism they would have been in if they had been born of the earth. By following [the thread of] these entirely natural ideas the authority of Scripture can easily be reconciled with ancient records, and there is no need to treat as fables traditions that are as old as are the peoples that have handed them down to us.

[16] In that brutish state, they had to live. The more active, the more robust, those who were always on the move, could only live off fruit and the hunt: so they became hunters, violent, bloodthirsty and, in time, they became warriors, conquerors, usurpers. History has stained its records with the crimes of these

first Kings; war and conquests are nothing but manhunts. Once they had conquered, it only remained for them to devour men. That is what their successors learned to do.

[17] The greater number, less active and more peaceable, stopped as soon as they could, gathered cattle, tamed them, taught them to heed man's voice, learned to tend them and increase their number so as to have them for food; and that is how pastoral life began.

[18] Human industry expands with the needs that give it rise. Of the three ways of life available to man, hunting, herding, and agriculture, the first develops strength, skill, speed of body, courage and cunning of soul; it hardens man and makes him ferocious. The land of the hunters does not long remain that of the hunt.* Game has to be pursued over great distances; hence horsemanship. Game that flees has to be caught; hence light weapons—the sling, the arrow, the javelin. The pastoral art, father of repose and of the indolent passions, is the most self-sufficient art; it almost effortlessly provides man with food and clothing; it even provides him with his dwelling. The tents of the first shepherds were made of animal skins; so were the roofs of the ark and the tabernacle of Moses. As for agriculture, it arises later and involves all the arts; it introduces property, government, laws, and gradually wretchedness and crimes, which for our species are inseparable from the knowledge of good and evil. Hence the Greeks did not view Triptolemus merely as the inventor of a useful art, but as a founder and a wise man to whom they owed their first regulations and their first laws. Moses, on the other hand, appears to have disapproved of agriculture in attributing its invention to a wicked man and making God reject his offerings. The first tiller of the ground would seem to have proclaimed by his character the bad effects of his art. The author of Genesis had seen farther than had Herodotus.

* The practice of hunting is not at all favorable to population [growth]. This was noted at the time that the Islands of Santo Domingo and Tortuga were inhabited by buccaneers, and it is confirmed by the state of northern America. None of the fathers of large nations were hunters by [e]state; all of them were farmers or shepherds. Hunting must, then, in their case, be viewed less as a primary means of subsistence than as a supplement to the pastoral state.

[19] The preceding division corresponds to the three states of man considered in relation to society. The savage is a hunter, the barbarian a herdsman, civil man a tiller of the ground.

[20] So that regardless of whether one inquires into the origin of the arts or studies the earliest morals [or ways of life, *moeurs*], everything is seen to be related in its principle to the means by which men provide for their subsistence; and of these, the means that unite men are a function of climate and of the nature of the soil. Hence the diversity of languages and their contrasting characteristics must also be explained by the same causes.

[21] Mild climates, lush and fertile lands were the first to be populated and the last where nations were formed, because there men could more easily do without one another, and the needs that cause society to be born made themselves felt later.

[22] Assume perpetual spring on earth; assume water, cattle, pastures everywhere; assume men issuing from the hands of nature and dispersed throughout all this: I cannot imagine how they would ever have renounced their primitive liberty and left the isolated and pastoral existence that so well suits their natural indolence,* in order to impose on themselves without any necessity the slavery, the labors, and the miseries that are inseparable from the state of society.

[23] He who willed man to be sociable inclined the globe's axis at an angle to the axis of the universe by a touch of the finger. With this slight motion I see the face of the earth change and the vocation of mankind settled; I hear, far off, the joyous cries of a heedless multitude; I see Palaces and Cities raised; I see the birth of the arts, laws, commerce; I see peoples forming, expanding, dissolving, succeeding one another like the waves of the sea; I see men clustered in a few points of their habitation

---

* The extent to which man is naturally lazy, is simply inconceivable. It would seem that he lives solely in order to sleep, to vegetate, to remain motionless; he can scarcely decide to go through the motions required to keep from dying of hunger. Nothing sustains the savages' love of their state as much as this delicious indolence. The passions that cause man to be restless, provident, active, are born only in society. To do nothing is man's primary and strongest passion after that of self-preservation. Upon looking at it more closely, it would be found that, even among us, people work only in order to get to rest, that it is still laziness that makes us industrious.

in order there to devour one another, and turn the remainder of the world into a frightful desert, a worthy monument to social union and the usefulness of the arts.

[24] The earth nourishes men; but after the first needs have dispersed them, other needs unite them, and it is only then that they speak and cause others to speak about them. I must be allowed time to explain my meaning, so that I am not found to be in contradiction with myself.

[25] When one inquires into where the fathers of mankind were born, whence the first colonies came, the first emigrations originated, you will not name the happy climes of Asia Minor or of Sicily or Africa, or even Egypt; you will name the sands of Chaldea, the rocks of Phoenicia. You will find that it is so at all times. Regardless of how many Chinese live in China, Tartars also go to live there; the Scythians inundated Europe and Asia; the mountains of Switzerland are currently pouring into our fertile regions a continuous stream of colonists that gives no indication whatsoever of drying up.

[26] It is said to be natural for the inhabitants of a barren land to leave it for a better. Very well; but why does this better land make room for others, instead of swarming with its own inhabitants? To leave a barren land, one has to be there in the first place; why then are so many men born there rather than elsewhere? Harsh lands might be expected to be populated only with the excess from fertile lands, and yet we see the opposite to be the case. Most Latin peoples called themselves aboriginal,* whereas Magna Graecia, which is more fertile, was populated exclusively by foreigners. All Greek peoples acknowledged that they originally grew out of various colonies, except the one whose soil was the worst, namely the Attic people, who called themselves Autochthonous or self-born. Finally, without piercing the night of time, modern centuries provide one conclusive piece of evidence: indeed, where on the earth is the climate drearier than in what has been called the factory of mankind?

[27] Human associations are in large measure the work of

* The terms *Autochthons* and *Aborigines* merely mean that the first inhabitants of the land were savage, without societies, without laws, without traditions, and that they populated it before they spoke.

accidents of nature: local floods, overflowing seas, volcanic eruptions, major earthquakes, fires started by lightning and destroying forests, everything that must have frightened and dispersed the savage inhabitants of a land, must afterwards have brought them together to restore in common their common losses. The traditions about natural disasters which were so common in ancient times show what instruments providence used to force humans to come together. Ever since societies have been established, these great accidents have ceased and become increasingly rare; it would seem that this too has to be so; the same calamities that brought together men who were scattered, would disperse those who are united.

[28] The revolutions of the seasons are another more general and more permanent cause, one that must have produced the same effect in the climates that are subject to it. Forced to make provisions for winter, people have to help one another and are thus compelled to establish some kind of convention amongst themselves. When expeditions become impossible and they can no longer get about because of the extreme cold, boredom unites them as much as [did] need: the Lapps, buried in their ice, the Eskimos, the most savage of all peoples, come together in their caverns in winter, and in summer they act as if they had never known one another. Increase their development and their enlightenment by one degree, and they will be united forever.

[29] Neither man's stomach nor his intestines are made to digest raw meat, and he generally cannot stand its taste. With the possible single exception of the Eskimos whom I just mentioned, even savages grill their meats. Fire, in addition to being necessary for cooking meats, also delights the eye, and its warmth is pleasing to the body. The sight of the flame, which causes animals to flee, attracts men.* Around a common hearth

---

* Fire gives much pleasure to animals as well as to man, once they have become accustomed to its sight and felt its gentle warmth. Often it would even prove no less useful to them than to us, if only to warm their young. Yet no one has ever heard of any animal, wild or domestic, which, even by imitating us, has acquired the skills required to make fire. And these are the reasoning beings that are said to form an evanescent prehuman society, although their intelligence could not rise to the level of drawing sparks from a stone and catching them [on tinder], or at least of keeping some abandoned fire going! Upon my word, the philosophers quite openly mock us. Their writings clearly show that they indeed take us for beasts.

people gather, feast, dance; the sweet bonds of familiarity imperceptibly draw man to his kind, and on this rustic hearth burns the sacred fire that introduces the first sentiments of humanity into men's hearts.

[30] In warm lands, unevenly scattered springs and rivers are further meeting places, all the more necessary inasmuch as men can do without water even less than they can do without fire. Barbarians who live off their herds are especially in need of common watering places, and we learn from the history of the most remote ages that that is indeed where their treaties as well as their quarrels began.* Easy access to water can delay the emergence of society among those who live where it is plentiful. In arid places, on the other hand, people had to cooperate in sinking wells and digging ditches to provide water for their cattle. Associations of men are found there almost from time immemorial, for the land had either to remain desert or to be made inhabitable by man's labor. But our tendency to refer everything to our own practices calls for a few reflections on this subject.

[31] The first state of the earth differed greatly from its present state, when it is seen embellished or disfigured by men's hand. The chaos which the Poets feigned among the elements did prevail among its productions. In those remote times when revolutions were frequent, when numberless accidents altered the nature of the soil and the features of the terrain, everything grew in a jumble, trees, vegetables, shrubs, grasses: no species had time to seize for its own the terrain that best suited it, and to choke out the others there; they would separate slowly, gradually, and then a sudden upheaval would jumble everything.

[32] The relation between man's needs and the productions of the earth is such that, as long as it is populated, everything subsists; but before men united had, by their common labors, introduced a balance among its productions, they could all subsist only if nature alone attended to the equilibrium which the hand of man preserves today; nature maintained or restored this equilibrium by revolutions, just as men maintain or restore it by their inconstancy. Men were not yet at war with one

* See the instance of the one as well as of the other between Abraham and Abimelech in connection with the well of the Oath, in chapter 21 of *Genesis*.

another, but the elements seemed to be; men did not burn cities, dig mines, fell trees; but nature sparked volcanoes, aroused earthquakes, the fire of heaven devoured forests. A bolt of lightning, a flood, a volcanic eruption did then in a few hours what a hundred thousand human arms now do in a century. I see no other way in which the system could have subsisted and the equilibrium maintained itself. In the two realms of organic beings, the larger species would in the long run have absorbed the smaller:* the entire earth would soon have been covered with nothing but trees and ferocious beasts; eventually everything would have perished.

[33] The water cycle which nourishes the earth would, little by little, have broken down. Mountains get worn down and smaller, rivers silt up, the sea rises and spreads, everything imperceptibly tends toward the same level; men's hand slows this drift and delays this progress; without them it would proceed faster, and the earth might perhaps already be under water. Springs are poorly distributed and, prior to human labor, they flowed less evenly, fertilized the earth less [adequately], made its inhabitants' supply of drinking water more difficult. Rivers were often inaccessible, and their banks steep or marshy: since human art did not retain them in their beds, they often overflowed, flooded one bank or the other, changed directions and course, divided into various branches; sometimes they would dry up, sometimes quicksands blocked access to them; it was as if they did not exist, and men died of thirst surrounded by water.

[34] How many arid lands there are that are inhabitable only thanks to men's draining or chaneling of rivers. Almost the

---

* It is claimed that by a kind of natural action and reaction, the various species of the animal kingdom would of themselves remain in a perpetual balancing [or seesaw] which would be tantamount to their being in equilibrium. Once the devouring species has increased too much at the expense of the devoured species, the first, so the argument goes, finding no more food, will have to decrease and allow the other time to replenish its numbers; until it again provides ample food for the first and once more decreases while the devouring species is replenished anew. But such an oscillation seems quite implausible to me: for according to this system there has to be a period during which the preyed-upon species increases and the predator species decreases; which seems to me to be altogether contrary to reason.

whole of Persia subsists only by means of this artifice; China abounds in People because of its many canals; without their canals, the Low Countries would be flooded by rivers, as they would be flooded by the sea without their dikes; Egypt, the most fertile country on earth, is inhabitable only as a result of human labor. On the great plains where there are no rivers and where the grade is not sufficiently steep, there is no alternative to wells. So that the reason why the first peoples mentioned in history did not live in lush lands or easily accessible shores is not that these happy climes were deserted, but that their numerous inhabitants could do without one another and therefore lived isolated in their families with no outside communication for a longer time. But in arid regions, where water could only be had from wells, people had no alternative but to get together to dig them, or at least to agree about their use. Such must have been the origin of societies and of languages in warm lands.

[35] Here the first ties between families were established; here the first meetings between the sexes took place. Young girls came to fetch water for the household, young men came to water their herds. Here eyes accustomed from childhood to [see] always the same objects began to see sweeter ones. The heart was moved by them and, swayed by an unfamiliar attraction, it grew less savage and felt the pleasure of not being alone. Imperceptibly water came to be more needed, the cattle were thirsty more often; one arrived in haste, and left with reluctance. In this happy age when nothing recorded the hours, nothing required them to be counted; the only measure of time was enjoyment and boredom. Beneath old oaks, conquerors of years, spirited young people gradually forgot their ferociousness; little by little they tamed one another; in striving to make themselves understood, they learned to make themselves intelligible. Here the first festivals took place; feet skipped with joy, an eager gesture no longer proved adequate, the voice accompanied it with passionate accents, pleasure and desire merged into one and made themselves felt together. Here, finally, was the true cradle of peoples, and from the pure crystal of the fountains sprang the first fires of love.

[36] What! were men born of the earth before that time? Did

generation succeed upon generation without union between the sexes and without any mutual understanding? No, there were families, but there were no Nations; there were domestic languages, but there were no popular languages; there were marriages, but there was no love. Each family was self-sufficient and propagated itself from its own stock alone: children of the same parents grew up together and gradually found ways to make themselves intelligible to one another; the distinction between the sexes appeared with age, natural inclinations sufficed to unite them, instinct served in lieu of passion, habit in lieu of predilection, people became man and wife without having ceased to be brother and sister.* None of this was sufficiently lively to untie tongues, none of it such as to draw forth the accents of the ardent passions sufficiently frequently to establish them as institutions; and the same may be said of the occasional, not very pressing needs that may have led some men to collaborate on common labors; one started the basin of the fountain, another later finished it, often without their having had the slightest need of any agreements, and sometimes without even having seen one another. In a word, in mild climates, in fertile regions, it took all the liveliness of the agreeable passions to start men speaking. The first languages, daughters of pleasure rather than of need, long remained under the aegis of their father; their seductive accent faded only with the sentiments that had given them birth, when new needs introduced among men, forced everyone to think only of himself and to withdraw his heart within himself.

---

* The first men had to marry their sisters. In view of the simplicity of the first morals, this practice continued without prejudice as long as families remained isolated and even after the most ancient peoples had come together; but the law that abolished it is no less sacred for being by human institution. Those who view it solely in terms of the bond it established between families fail to see its most important aspect. In view of the intimacy between the sexes that inevitably attends upon domestic life, the moment such a sacred law ceased to speak to the heart and to awe the senses, men would cease to be upright, and the most frightful morals would soon cause the destruction of mankind.

CHAPTER TEN

THE FORMATION OF THE LANGUAGES OF THE NORTH

[1] Eventually all men become alike, but the order of their progress differs. In southern climates, where nature is prodigal, needs are born of the passions; in cold countries, where nature is miserly, the passions are born of the needs, and the languages, sad daughters of necessity, reflect their harsh origin.

[2] Although man can become accustomed to inclement weather, to cold, discomfort, even to hunger, there is a point beyond which nature succumbs. Whatever is weak perishes, the victim of these cruel ordeals; whatever remains is strengthened, and there is no middle ground between vigor and death. That is why northern peoples are so sturdy; they did not, initially, grow sturdy because of the climate; rather, only those who were sturdy survived in that climate; and it is not surprising that the children preserve their fathers' good constitution.

[3] It is immediately evident that men who are more sturdy must have a less delicate vocal apparatus, their voices must be rougher and stronger. Besides, what a difference there is between the touching inflections that issue from movements of the soul, and the cries wrested by physical needs: In those dreadful climates where everything is dead nine months out of the year, where the sun warms the air for a few weeks only in order to let the inhabitants know the benefits of which they are deprived and to prolong their misery, in those regions where the earth yields whatever it yields only after much labor and where the source of life seems to reside more in the arms than in the heart, men, constantly involved in providing for their subsistence, hardly thought about gentler bonds, everything was confined to physical impulsion, opportunity dictated choice, ease dictated preference. Idleness, which feeds the passions, yielded to labor, which represses them. Before they could think about living happily, men had to think about living. Mutual need united them far more effectively than sentiment would have done,

society was formed solely through industry, the ever-present danger of perishing did not permit of a language restricted to gesture, and their first word was not *love me* [*aimez-moi*] but *help me* [*aidez-moi*].

[4] The two expressions, although quite similar, are pro-nounced in a very different tone [of voice]. Not feeling, but understanding had to be conveyed; so that it was a matter not of energy but of clarity. In the place of accent, which was not forthcoming from the heart, they used strong, [easily] perceived articulations, and if the form of the language to some extent made any natural impression, that impression contributed still further to its harshness.

[5] Indeed, men of the North are not without passions, but theirs are passions of another kind. In warm climates the passions are voluptuous, related to love and softness. Nature does so much for those who live there, that there is almost nothing left for them to do. As long as an Asian has women and rest, he is content. But in the North, where people consume a great deal and the soil is barren, men, subject to so many needs, are easily irritated; everything that happens around them worries them: since they have a hard time subsisting, the poorer they are, the more they cling to the little they have; to get close to them is to threaten their lives. That is what accounts for their irascible temperament, so quick to lash out furiously at everything that offends them. Their most natural utterings [*voix*] therefore are those of anger and threats, and they are invariably accom-panied by strong articulations which make them harsh and noisy.

CHAPTER ELEVEN

REFLECTIONS ON THESE DIFFERENCES

[1] Such, in my opinion, are the most general physical causes of the characteristic difference between primitive languages. Southern languages must have been lively, resonant, accentuated,

eloquent, and often obscure because of their vigor; northern languages must have been muted, crude, articulated, shrill, monotone and clear, more because of their words than because of good construction. Modern languages, though they have been intermingled and recast hundreds of times, still retain something of these differences: French, English, German are the private languages of men who help one another, who argue with one another in a deliberate manner, or of excited men who get angry; but the ministers of the Gods proclaiming the sacred mysteries, wise men giving laws to their people, leaders swaying the masses must speak Arabic or Persian.* Our languages are better written than spoken, and it is more pleasant to read us than it is to listen to us. In contrast, oriental languages lose their life and warmth when they are written down: only half the meaning is conveyed by the words, all its vigor is in the accents. To form an opinion about the genius of the Orientals from their books is like painting a man's portrait from his corpse.

[2] In order to assess men's actions properly, one has to consider them in all their relations, and that is something we are simply not taught to do. When we put ourselves in the place of others, we always put ourselves in their place as circumstances have modified us, not as they must have modified them, and when we think that we are judging them in the light of reason, we are merely comparing their prejudices with ours. Because he can read a little Arabic, a man smiles as he peruses the Koran; if he had heard Mohammed himself proclaim it in that eloquent rhythmic language, in that rich and persuasive voice which seduced the ear before it did the heart, constantly infusing his succinct sayings with the accent of enthusiasm, he would have prostrated himself and cried: *Great Prophet, Messenger of God, Lead us to glory, to martyrdom; we want to conquer or to die for you.* Fanaticism always appears ludicrous to us, because it has no voice to command a hearing among us. Even our fanatics are not true fanatics; they are merely knaves or fools.

---

* Turkish is a northern language.

Instead of inflections for men inspired, our languages provide only cries for men possessed by the Devil.

CHAPTER TWELVE

THE ORIGIN OF MUSIC

[1] Together with the first utterings [*voix*], the first articulations or the first sounds were formed, depending on the kind of passion that dictated either of them. Anger wrests [from us] threatening cries which the tongue and the palate articulate; but the voice of tenderness is gentler: it is modulated by the glottis and becomes a sound. Its accents, however, are more or less frequent, its inflections more or less acute depending on the sentiment that accompanies it. Thus cadence and sounds are born together with syllables: passion rouses all of the [vocal] organs to speech and adorns the voice with their full brilliance; thus verse, song, speech have a common origin. Around the fountains which I have mentioned, the first speeches were the first songs: the periodic and measured recurrences of rhythm, the melodious inflections of accents, caused poetry and music to be born together with language; or rather, all this was nothing other than language itself in those happy climates and those happy ages when the only pressing needs that required another's collaboration were needs born of the heart.

[2] The first stories, the first declamations, the first laws were in verse; poetry was discovered before prose; it had to be so, since the passions spoke before reason did. The same was true of music: at first there was no music other than melody, nor any other melody than the varied sound of speech; accents made up the song, quantities made up measure, and people spoke as much by sonorities and rhythm as by articulations and sounds. Speech and song were formerly one, says Strabo; and, he adds, this shows poetry to be the source of eloquence.* He should

* *Geogr[aphy]*, B[oo]k I.

have said that both sprang from the same source and were
initially the same thing. In view of the way in which the earliest
societies united, was it surprising that the first stories were set
in verse and that the first laws were sung? Is it surprising that
the first Grammarians subordinated their art to music and were
at one and the same time teachers of both?*

[3] A language that has only articulations and utterings [*voix*]
is therefore in possession of only half its resources: true, it
conveys ideas; but to convey sentiments and images it still needs
rhythm and sounds [or sonorities], that is to say a melody; that
is what the Greek language had, and ours lacks.

[4] We are always astounded by the prodigious effects of
eloquence, poetry, and music among the Greeks. We can make
no sense of them, because we no longer experience anything
like them, and all we can bring ourselves to do, in view of the
strong evidence regarding them, is to pretend that we believe
them as a concession to our scholars.** Burette, having transcribed
some pieces of Greek music as best he could into our musical
notation, was so naïve as to have these pieces performed at the
Academy of Belles Lettres, and the Academicians were so for-
bearing as to listen to them. I rather admire such an experiment
in a country whose music all other nations find indecipherable.
Give any foreign Musician you please a solo from a French opera

* "Archytas and Aristoxenus, indeed, thought grammar comprehended under
music, and that the same persons taught both subjects. . . . But so did Eupolis,
in whose work Prodamus teaches both music and letters. And Maricas, that is to
say Hyperbolus, acknowledges that the musicians teach him nothing but letters."
Quintilian, B[oo]k I, ch[apter] 10.
** Some allowance must probably always be made for Greek exaggeration,
but to make such allowances to a point where all differences vanish is really
too great a concession to modern prejudice. "It was," says the Abbé Terrasson,
"when the music of the Greeks at the time of Amphion or of Orpheus was at
the level at which we now find it in the towns farthest removed from the
capital, that it interrupted the flow of rivers, attracted oaks, and caused rocks to
move. Nowadays, when it has reached a very high level of perfection, it is much
beloved, its beauties are even understood, but it leaves everything in place. The
same was true of the verses of Homer, a poet born in times which, in comparison
with the times that followed, still preserved something of the childhood of the
human spirit. Men were enthralled by his verses, whereas nowadays they merely
enjoy and appreciate the verses of good poets." There is no denying that the
Abbé Terrasson was occasionally philosophic, but he certainly gives no proof of
it in this passage.

to perform, and I defy you to recognize any part of it. Yet these very Frenchmen took it upon themselves to pass judgment on the melody of one of Pindar's Odes set to Music two thousand years ago!

[5] I have read that American Indians, seeing the amazing effects of firearms, used to pick musket balls up off the ground, and, after hurling them with a loud outcry, were utterly surprised to find that they had not killed anyone. Our orators, our musicians, our scholars are like those Indians. The wonder is not that we no longer achieve with our music what the Greeks achieved with theirs; the wonder would, rather, be that the same effects could be produced with such very different instruments.

CHAPTER THIRTEEN

OF MELODY

[1] Man is modified by his senses, unquestionably; but because we fail to distinguish between modifications, we confuse their causes; we attribute both too much and too little power to sensations; we do not realize that often they affect us not only as sensations but as signs or images, and that their moral effects also have moral causes. Just as the sentiments which painting arouses in us are not due to colors, the power which music exercises over our souls is not the product of sounds. Beautiful colors, nicely modulated, give the eye pleasure, but that pleasure is purely sensory. It is the drawing, the imitation that endows these colors with life and soul, it is the passions which they express that succeed in arousing our own, the objects which they represent that succeed in affecting us. Interest and sentiment do not depend on colors; the lines of a touching painting touch us in an etching as well: remove them from the Painting, and the colors will cease to have any effect.

[2] Melody does in music exactly what drawing does in painting; it indicates the lines and shapes, of which the chords

and sounds are but the colors; but, it will be said, melody is no more than a succession of sounds; undoubtedly; but by the same token drawing is also nothing more than an arrangement of colors. An orator uses ink to set down his writings: does that mean that ink is a most eloquent liquid?

[3] Suppose a country where they had no idea of drawing, but where many people who spent their lives combining, mixing, grading colors, believed that they excelled in painting; those people would argue about our painting exactly as we argue about the music of the Greeks. If they were told about the emotion which beautiful paintings arouse in us and the charm of being moved by a pathetic scene, their scholars would immediately delve into the matter, comparing their colors with ours, seeing whether our green is more delicate or our red more brilliant; they would inquire what combinations of colors have the power to cause weeping and what others to arouse anger. The Burettes of that country would patch together a few rag-tag scraps of our paintings; whereupon people would ask themselves with some astonishment what is so wonderful about that coloration.

[4] But if, in a neighboring nation, someone began tracing a line, a sketch, some as yet unfinished figure, it would all be regarded as so much scribbling, as willful and baroque painting, and for the sake of preserving [good] taste they would restrict themselves to that simple beauty which really expresses nothing but which causes beautiful modulations, large slabs of strong color, extended transitions between hues, to vibrate without a single line.

[5] Finally they might perhaps by dint of progress get to the experiment with the prism. Straightway some famous artist would be sure to erect a fancy system on the basis of it. Gentlemen, he would say to them, if we are to philosophize properly we must go back to the physical causes. Here you have the resolution of light, the primary colors, their relationships, their proportions, the true principles of the pleasure you derive from painting. All this mysterious talk about drawing, representation, shape is pure imposture on the part of French painters who think that with their imitations they can arouse I know not

what movements in the soul, when it is well known that there are only sensations. You hear wonderful reports about their painting, but look at my hues.

[6] French painters, he would continue, may have noticed the rainbow, nature may have endowed them with some taste for nuance and some instinct for coloration. I, however, have shown you the great, the true principles of the art. What am I saying, of the art? Of all the arts, Gentlemen, of all the Sciences. The analysis of colors, the measurement of prismatic refractions provide you with the only precise relations to be found in nature, with the rule for all relations. Now, everything in the universe is only relations. One therefore knows everything once one knows how to paint, one knows everything once one knows how to match colors.

[7] What would we say about a painter so lacking in sense and taste that he would reason in this way, stupidly limiting the pleasure painting gives us to the physical aspects of his art? What would we say about a musician who, filled with similar prejudices, believed that harmony alone is the source of the great effects of music? We would send the former off to paint the woodwork, and condemn the other to compose French operas.

[8] As painting, then, is not the art of combining colors in ways pleasing to the eye, music is not the art of combining sounds in ways pleasing to the ear. If there were no more than that to them, they would both be natural sciences, not fine arts. Imitation alone raises them to that rank. What makes painting one of the imitative arts? Drawing. What makes music another? Melody.

CHAPTER FOURTEEN

OF HARMONY

[1] The beauty of sounds is by nature; their effect is entirely physical; it is due to the interaction of the different particles of air set in motion by the sounding body and by all of its

constituent parts, [continuing] perhaps to infinity: all of these taken together, produce a pleasant sensation: everyone in the universe will take pleasure in listening to beautiful sounds; but unless this pleasure is enlivened by familiar melodic inflections it will not be [totally] delightful, it will not become utter pleasure [*volupté*]. The songs which, to us, are the most beautiful will only moderately affect an ear completely unaccustomed to them; it is a language for which one has to have the Dictionary.

[2] Regarding harmony properly so called, the situation is even less auspicious. Since all of its beauties are by convention, it does not in any way appeal to ears untutored in it; to experience and to appreciate it requires long-standing familiarity with it. Rude ears perceive our consonances as mere noise. It is not surprising that when the natural proportions are altered, natural pleasure disappears.

[3] A sound carries with it all of its accompanying overtones, so related [to it] in terms of intensity and intervals as to produce its most perfect harmony. Add to it the third or fifth or some other consonant interval, and what you have done is not to augment it but to double it; you retain the relation of interval while changing that of intensity: by emphasizing one consonant interval and not the others, you upset the proportion. By trying to do better than nature, you do worse. Your ear and your taste are spoiled by a misunderstanding of art. By nature there is no other harmony than unison.

[4] M. Rameau contends that comparatively simple trebles naturally suggest their basses, and that a person with a true but untrained ear will naturally sing this bass. That is a musician's prejudice, contradicted by all experience. A person who has never heard either bass or harmony will not only fail to find them on his own, he will even dislike them if he should hear them, and he will very much prefer simple unison.

[5] Even after a thousand years spent reckoning the relations of sounds and the laws of harmony, how can that art ever be turned into an art of imitation? What would be the principle of this supposed imitation, of what is harmony the sign, and what have chords in common with our passions?

[6] Ask the same question about melody, and the answer is

immediately evident, it is in the reader's mind all along. By imitating the inflections of the voice, melody expresses plaints, cries of suffering or of joy, threats, moans; all the vocal signs of the passions fall within its province. It imitates the accents of [various] languages as well as the idiomatic expressions commonly associated in each one of them with given movements of the soul; it not only imitates, it speaks; and its language, though inarticulate, is lively, ardent, passionate, and a hundred times more vigorous than speech itself. This is where musical imitation acquires its power, and song its hold on sensitive hearts. In some [musical] systems, harmony can contribute to these [effects] by linking the succession of sounds in accordance with a few laws of modulation, by making intonations more accurate and providing the ear with reliable evidence of this accuracy, by reconciling barely perceptible inflections and fixing them to consonant, connected intervals. But by placing constraints on melody at the same time, harmony deprives it of energy and expressiveness, it eliminates the passionate accent in favor of intervals, it restricts to only two modes songs that should have as many modes as there are tones of voice, and it eradicates and destroys a great many sounds or intervals that do not fit into its system; in a word, it separates song and speech to such an extent that these two languages contend, thwart one another, deprive one another of any truth, and cannot be united in the treatment of a passionate subject without appearing absurd. That is why the people always find it ridiculous to have strong, serious passions expressed in song; for they know that in our languages these passions have no musical inflections at all, and that men of the north no more die singing than do Swans.

[7] By itself, harmony is not even adequate to express what would seem to fall entirely within its province. Thunder, murmuring waters, winds, storms are but poorly rendered by simple chords. Do what you may, mere noise says nothing to the mind; objects have to speak in order to make themselves heard; in every imitation, some sort of discourse must always complement the voice of nature. A musician who tries to render noise with noise errs; he knows neither the weaknesses nor the strengths of his art; he judges of it without taste or insight; teach him that

he must render noise with song, that if he wished to make frogs croak, he would have to make them sing; for it is not enough for him merely to imitate, he must do so in a way that both moves and pleases; without that, his dreary imitation is nothing and, by failing to arouse anyone's interest, it fails to make any impression.

CHAPTER FIFTEEN

THAT OUR LIVELIEST SENSATIONS OFTEN ACT BY WAY OF MORAL IMPRESSIONS

[1] As long as sounds continue to be considered exclusively in terms of the excitation they trigger in our nerves, the true principles of music and of its power over men's hearts will remain elusive. In a melody, sounds act on us not only as sounds but as signs of our affections, of our sentiments; that is how they arouse in us the [e]motions which they express and the image of which we recognize in them. Something of this moral effect can be discerned even in animals. One Dog's barking attracts another. When my cat hears me imitate a miaowing, he is immediately alert, restless, tense. As soon as he notices that it is I, imitating the sounds of a cat, he relaxes and sits back. What accounts for this difference in impressions, since there is none in the excitation of the nerve fibers and the cat itself was initially deceived?

[2] If the major impact our sensations have upon us is not due to moral causes, then why are we so sensitive to impressions which are meaningless to barbarians? Why does music that most moves us seem but an empty noise to the ear of a Carib? Are his nerves of a different nature from ours, why are they not excited in the same way, or why do the same excitations affect some people so strongly and others hardly at all?

[3] As proof of the physical power of sounds, people refer to the cure of Tarantula bites. The example proves the opposite. It is not the case that absolute sounds or the same tunes are the

indicated cure for everyone who has been stung by that insect; rather, each one of them requires tunes with a melody he knows and lyrics he can understand. An Italian requires Italian tunes, a Turk would require Turkish tunes. One is affected only by accents that are familiar; the nerves respond to them only insofar as the mind inclines them to it; one has to understand the language in which one is being addressed if one is to be moved by what one is told. Bernier's Cantatas are said to have cured a French musician of the fever; they would have given one to a musician of any other nation.

[4] The same differences can be observed in relation to all the other senses, down to the crudest of them. Let a man, with his hand resting and his glance focusing on one and the same object, alternately believe that it is and that it is not alive; although what strikes his senses is the same, what a difference in the impression! The roundness, whiteness, firmness, gentle warmth, springy resistance, rhythmic swelling are pleasant but dull to the touch, once he no longer believes that underneath them he can feel the throbbing and beating of a heart full of life.

[5] I know only one sense the reactions of which are without any moral component: taste. That is why a sweet tooth is the dominant vice only of people who feel nothing.

[6] Whoever wishes to philosophize about the power of sensations must therefore begin by distinguishing between exclusively sensory impressions and the intellectual and moral impressions which we receive by way of the senses but of which the senses are merely the occasional causes; let him avoid the error of attributing to sensible objects a power which they either lack or derive from the affections of the soul which they represent to us. Colors and sounds can do much as representations and signs, and little as simple objects of sensation. Sequences of sounds or of chords may perhaps give me a moment's pleasure; but in order to delight and to move me, these sequences must provide something that is neither sound nor chord, and will succeed in moving me in spite of myself. Even songs that are merely pleasant but say nothing, become boring; for it is not so much the ear that conveys pleasure to the heart as the

heart that conveys it to the ear. I believe that if these ideas had been explored more adequately, much foolish speculation about ancient music could have been avoided. But in this century, when every effort is made to materialize all the operations of the soul and to deprive human sentiments of all morality, I should be greatly surprised if the new philosophy did not prove as fatal to good taste as it does to virtue.

CHAPTER SIXTEEN

FALSE ANALOGY BETWEEN COLORS AND SOUNDS

[1] Physical observations have occasioned every kind of absurdity in discussions of the fine arts. The analysis of sound has revealed the same relations as has the analysis of light. Straightway the analogy was seized upon, without regard for experience or reason. The systematizing spirit has jumbled everything and, since it proved impossible to paint for the ears, it was decided to sing to the eyes. I have seen the famous clavichord on which music was supposedly produced with colors; what a gross misunderstanding of how nature operates it was, not to see that the effect of colors is due to their permanence and that of sounds to their succession.

[2] The full wealth of coloration is spread out all at once over the face of the earth. Everything is seen at first glance; but the more one looks, the more one is enchanted. One need only go on admiring and contemplating forever.

[3] The same is not true of sound; nature does not analyze it and separate out its harmonics; on the contrary, it hides them under the appearance of unison; or if, sometimes, it does separate them in the modulated song of man or in the warbling of certain birds, it does so successively and one after the other; it inspires songs, not chords, it dictates melody, not harmony. Colors are the ornament of inanimate beings; all matter is colored; but sounds proclaim movement; the voice proclaims a being endowed with sense; only animate bodies sing. It is not

the mechanical flutist that plays the flute, but the engineer who measured the flow of air and made the fingers move.

[4] Thus every sense has its own proper realm. The realm of music is time, that of painting is space. To multiply the number of sounds heard all at once, or to present colors one after the other, is to alter their economy, it is to substitute the eye for the ear, and the ear for the eye.

[5] You say: just as every color is determined by the angle of refraction of the ray that causes it, so is every sound determined by the number of vibrations of the sounding body in a given span of time. Now, since the relations between these angles and these numbers are the same, the analogy is obvious. Granted; but it is an analogy of reason, not of sensation, and [besides], it is not to the point. In the first place, the angle of refraction is both perceptible and measurable, whereas the number of vibrations is neither. Sounding bodies being subject to the influence of the air constantly change their size and the sounds they give forth. Colors last, sounds vanish, and one can never be certain that the sounds that arise next are the same as those that have just died away. Moreover, every color is absolute, independent, whereas every sound is for us only relative, and distinct only by contrast. By itself a sound has no absolute character by which it might be recognized; it is low or high, loud or soft in relation to another sound; in itself it is none of these. Nor is a given sound by nature anything within the harmonic system: it is neither tonic, nor dominant, nor harmonic, nor fundamental; for all of these properties are only relationships, and since the entire system can vary from low to high, every sound changes its rank and position in the system as the system changes in degree. But the properties of colors are not at all functions of relationships. Yellow is yellow, independently of red and of blue; it is everywhere perceptible and recognizable, and as soon as its angle of refraction has been determined we can be sure of obtaining the same yellow every time.

[6] Colors are not in the colored bodies but in the light; an object must be illuminated in order to be visible. Sounds also need a moving agent, and in order for them to exist the sounding body has to be set in motion. Sight here enjoys a further

advantage: for the constant emanation [of light] from the stars is the natural agency by which sight is acted upon, whereas nature by itself engenders few sounds and, short of believing in the harmony of the heavenly spheres, living beings are needed to produce it.

[7] Painting is thus seen to be closer to nature, while music is more closely related to human art. Music is also felt to [involve our] interest more than does painting, precisely because it brings man closer to man and always gives us some idea about our own kind. Painting is often dead and inanimate; it can transport you to the middle of a desert; but as soon as vocal signs strike your ear, they herald a being like yourself; they are, so to speak, the organs of the soul, and if they also depict solitude, they tell you that you are not alone in it. Birds whistle, man alone sings; and it is not possible to hear a song or a symphony without immediately telling oneself: another being endowed with sense is present.

[8] One of the great advantages the musician enjoys is that he can paint things that cannot be heard, whereas the Painter cannot represent things that cannot be seen; and the greatest wonder of an art that acts solely through movement is that it can fashion it even into an image of repose. Sleep, the quiet of night, solitude, and silence itself have a place in the spectacles of music. It is known that noise can produce the effect of silence and silence the effect of noise, as when one falls asleep while being read to in an even and monotonous voice and wakes up the moment the reading stops. But the effect of music on us is more profound, in that it excites in us through one of the senses, affects similar to those that can be aroused through another; and since that relation is perceptible only if the impression is strong, painting, which lacks the requisite strength, cannot imitate music as music imitates it. Though the whole of nature be asleep, he who contemplates it is not asleep; and the musician's art consists in substituting for the imperceptible image of the object, that of the [e]motions which that object's presence excites in the beholder's heart. It will not only churn up the sea, fan the flames of a conflagration, cause rivers to run, rain to fall, and streams to swell, but will also depict the

desolation of dreadful deserts, dusk the walls of a subterranean dungeon, appease the storm, clear and still the air and, from the orchestra, spread renewed freshness through the woodlands. It will not represent these things directly, but it will excite in the soul the very same sentiments which one experiences upon seeing them.

CHAPTER SEVENTEEN

A MUSICIANS' ERROR THAT IS HARMFUL TO THEIR ART

Note how everything constantly brings us back to the moral effects about which I have spoken, and how far the musicians who account for the impact of sounds solely in terms of the action of air and the excitation of [nerve] fibers are from understanding wherein the power of this art consists. The more closely they assimilate it to purely physical impressions, the farther away they remove it from its origin, and the more they also deprive it of its primitive energy. By abandoning the accents of speech and adhering exclusively to the rules of harmony, music becomes noisier to the ear and less pleasing to the heart. It has already ceased to speak; soon it will no longer sing, and once that happens it will no longer, for all its chords and harmony, have any effect on us.

CHAPTER EIGHTEEN

THAT THE MUSICAL SYSTEM OF THE GREEKS HAS NO RELATION WHATSOEVER TO OURS

[1] How did these changes come about? By a natural change in the character of languages. It is well known that our harmony is a gothic invention. People who claim to discover the system of the Greeks in ours talk foolishness. The system of the Greeks was absolutely not harmonic in our sense of the term, except

for what was required to tune instruments according to perfect consonances. All peoples with stringed instruments have to tune them by consonances, whereas those without them exhibit inflections in their songs which we call false because they do not fit into our system and we have no notations for them. This has been observed in the songs of American savages, and it should also have been observed in the various intervals of Greek music if it had been studied with less partiality for our own music.

[2] The Greeks divided their Scale into tetrachords as we divide our keyboard into octaves; and the same divisions recurred regularly in each of their tetrachords as they do in each of our octaves; a similarity which would not have been preserved in the unity of the harmonic mode, and would not even have been suspected. But since one proceeds by smaller intervals when speaking than when singing, it was natural for them to view the repetition of tetrachords in their oral melody, as we do the repetition of octaves in our harmonic melody.

[3] The only consonances they acknowledged are the consonances they call perfect; they excluded thirds and sixths from this class. Why did they do so? Because they did not know, or at least in practice excluded the minor interval of the whole tone, and their consonances were not tempered in any degree; as a consequence all their major thirds were too great and their minor thirds too small by a comma, and so their major and minor sixths were reciprocally altered in the same way. Now, try to imagine what notions of harmony and what harmonic modes are possible once thirds and sixths are excluded from the class of consonances! If, with a true sense for harmony, they had perceived the consonances which they did allow, then these consonances would at least have been implicit in their songs, and the unsounded consonance of the root sequences would have lent its name to the diatonic sequences it implied. Far from having fewer consonances than we, they would have had more; and, for example, since they understood the bass *do sol,* they would have called the second *do re* a consonance.

[4] But, someone might object, why diatonic sequences? Because of an instinct that inclines us to choose the most convenient

inflections in an accented and singing language: because the voice took a middle course between the extreme glottal modifications that are required in order constantly to sound the large intervals of consonances on the one hand, and the difficulty of controlling intonation in the very complicated relationships of smaller intervals on the other, it naturally hit on intervals smaller than consonances and simpler than commas: which is not to say that smaller intervals did not also serve a function in the more pathetic forms.

CHAPTER NINETEEN

HOW MUSIC DEGENERATED

[1] As language became perfected, melody imperceptibly lost some of its former vigor by imposing new rules on itself, and the calculation of intervals replaced delicacy of inflection. That, for example, is how the enharmonic genus gradually fell into disuse. Once theater had assumed a fixed form, all singing in it was restricted to prescribed modes; and as the rules for imitation were multiplied, the language of imitation grew weaker.

[2] The study of philosophy and the progress of reasoning, having perfected grammar, deprived language of the lively and passionate tone that had originally made it so songlike. Composers, who at first had been in the pay of Poets and worked only under their direction and as it were at their dictation, became independent of them at the time of Melanippides and Philoxenus. It is about this license that Music complains so bitterly in a comedy by Pherecrates, a passage of which has been preserved for us by Plutarch. Thus as melody began to be less closely tied to speech, it imperceptibly assumed a separate existence, and music became increasingly independent of words. That was also the period when the wonders gradually ceased which it had wrought when it was but the accent and the harmony of poetry, and when it endowed poetry with a power over the passions which speech has since exercised only over

the reason. Indeed, once Greece abounded in Sophists and Philosophers it no longer had famous poets or musicians. In cultivating the art of convincing [men], the art of moving [them] was lost. Even Plato, jealous of Homer and Euripides, decried the one and was incapable of imitating the other.

[3] Soon servitude added its influence to that of philosophy. Greece in chains lost the fire that warms only free souls, and she never recovered for the praise of her tyrants the tone in which she had sung her Heroes. The influx of Romans further diluted what harmony and accent the language had kept. Latin is a duller and a less musical tongue and, on adopting music, harmed it. The way people sang in the capital came little by little to affect the singing in the provinces; the theaters of Rome had a harmful effect on those of Athens; by the time Nero was carrying off prizes, Greece had ceased to deserve them; and the same melody shared by two languages suited each of them less well.

[4] Finally the catastrophe occurred which destroyed the progress of the human spirit, without eliminating the vices that were its product: Europe, overrun by barbarians and subjugated by ignorant men, at one and the same time lost her sciences, her arts, and the universal instrument of both, a harmonious and perfected language. These crude men whom the North had fathered, gradually accustomed all ears to the coarseness of their speech; their harsh voices, devoid of accents, were noisy without being sonorous. The Emperor Julian compared the speech of the Gauls to the croaking of frogs. Since all of their articulations were as grating as their voices were nasal and dull, they could impart brilliance to their singing only by stressing vowel sounds in order to cover up the profusion and the harshness of their consonants.

[5] This noisy singing, combined with the inflexibility of [their vocal] organ[s], compelled these newcomers as well as the subject peoples who imitated them, to make all sounds more sustained in order to make them intelligible. Labored articulation and stressed sounds contributed equally to rob melody of all sense of measure and rhythm. Since the hardest thing to pronounce was always the transition from one sound to the next,

the best they could do was to pause at each sound as long as possible, increase its volume, and let it burst forth as vehemently as possible. Soon song was nothing but a dreary and slow succession of drawled and shouted sounds, devoid alike of sweetness, measure, and grace; and although some scholars have pointed out that in latin singing the distinction between long and short syllables had to be observed, we are at least certain that verse was sung like prose, and that not feet, nor rhythm, nor any kind of measured song were of any further concern.

[6] Since song was thus deprived of all melody and consisted solely in the volume and duration of sounds, it must eventually have suggested ways in which it might be made still more resonant with the aid of consonances. Several voices, constantly drawing out in unison endlessly long sounds, chanced upon a few chords which made the noise seem pleasant to them by accentuating it: and that is how the use of descant and of counterpoint began.

[7] For I know not how many centuries, musicians kept going in circles about vain questions which they debated because they did not know the principle of an effect which they knew [perfectly well]. Even the most tireless reader could not stand eight to ten long chapters of verbiage in Jean de Muris for the sake of finding out whether it is the fifth or the fourth which should be the lower interval in an octave divided into two consonances; and four hundred years later, equally dreary lists of all the basses that must carry a sixth instead of a fifth are still to be found in Bontempi. In the meantime, however, harmony imperceptibly took the direction prescribed to it by analysis, until finally the invention of the minor mode and of dissonances introduced into it the arbitrariness in which it abounds, and which only prejudice prevents us from perceiving.*

* By reducing the whole of harmony to the very simple principle of the resonance of strings in their aliquot [or constituent] parts, M. Rameau bases the minor mode and the dissonance on his supposed findings that a vibrating sonorous string induces vibrations in longer strings at the lower twelfth and the lower major seventeenth. According to him these strings vibrate and quiver over their entire length, but do not resonate. That strikes me as very odd physics; it is rather as if one were to say that the sun is shining but it is impossible to see anything.

[8] Once melody was forgotten and the attention of musicians had focused entirely on harmony, everything gradually turned toward this new object; form, mode, scale, everything acquired a new complexion: harmonic successions came to determine the sequence of parts. Once this sequence had usurped the name of melody, it indeed became impossible to fail to recognize its mother's features in this new melody; and as our musical system thus gradually became purely harmonic, it is not surprising that spoken accent should have suffered as a result, and that for us music should have lost all of its vigor.

[9] That is how singing gradually became an art entirely separate from speech, from which it originates; how the harmonic aspects of sounds caused the inflections of the voice to be forgotten; and how music, restricted to the exclusively physical effect of combinations of vibrations, finally came to be deprived of the moral effects it used to produce when it was doubly the voice of nature.

CHAPTER TWENTY

THE RELATION OF LANGUAGES TO GOVERNMENTS

[1] This progress[ion] is neither accidental nor arbitrary; it is due to the vicissitudes of things. Languages are naturally formed according to men's needs; they change and become transformed as these same needs change. In ancient times, when persuasion

---

Since these longer strings produce only the sound of the highest note because they are divided, vibrate, and resonate in unison with it, they blend their sound with its sounds, and thus seem not to emit any sound of their own. The error consists in believing that they were seen to have vibrated over their entire length, and in not having observed the nodes carefully. We know from experience, and M. Tartini has confirmed it, that two strings which form any given harmonic interval can make their fundamental heard in the bass even without a third string: but a single string has no other fundamental than its own; it produces no resonance or vibration in its multiples, but only in its unison and its aliquot [or constituent] parts. Since sound has no other cause than the vibration of the sounding body, and since the effect always follows the unimpeded action of the cause, it is nonsense to separate vibrations from resonance.

served in lieu of public force, eloquence was necessary. Of what use would it be today, when public force replaces persuasion? It requires neither art nor figures of speech to say *such is my pleasure.* What discourses then remain to be addressed to the people assembled? Sermons. And why should those who deliver them care whether they persuade the people, since the people do not award privileges? Popular languages have become as thoroughly useless as has eloquence. Societies have assumed their final forms: nothing can be changed in them anymore except by arms and cash, and since there is nothing left to say to the people but *give money,* it is said with posters on street corners or with soldiers in private homes; for this there is no need to assemble anyone; on the contrary, subjects must be kept scattered; that is the first maxim of modern politics.

[2] Some languages are conducive to liberty; namely, the sonorous, rhythmic, harmonious languages in which speech can be made out from far away. Ours are made for the buzz in the Sultan's Council Chamber. Our preachers agonize, work themselves into a sweat in the Churches, and still no one has any idea of what they have said. After they have worn themselves out shouting for an hour, they leave the pulpit half-dead. Surely it was not worth the effort.

[3] Among the ancients it was easy to be heard by the people in a public square; one could speak in one for an entire day without strain. Generals delivered formal speeches to their Troops; they could make themselves heard without wearing themselves out. Modern historians who included formal speeches in their histories have made themselves a laughingstock. Imagine someone delivering a formal speech in French to the people of Paris in the Place Vendôme. If he shouts at the top of his voice, people will hear that he is shouting, but they will not make out a single word. Herodotus read his history to the people of Greece assembled out of doors, and he met with universal applause. Nowadays, an academician who reads a paper at a public session can hardly be heard at the back of the hall. The reason there are fewer mountebanks in the marketplaces of France than of Italy is not that in France people listen to them less, but only that they cannot hear them as well. M. d'Alembert

believes that a French recitative could be delivered in the Italian manner; it would have to be spoken directly into the ear, or it would simply not be heard. Now, I maintain that any language in which it is not possible to make oneself understood by the people assembled is a servile language; it is impossible for a people to remain free and speak that language.

[4] I conclude these reflections which, though superficial, may give rise to more profound ones, with the passage that suggested them to me.

[5] *To describe and to give examples of the extent to which character, the morals, and the interests of a people influence its Language would provide matter for a rather philosophical inquiry.**

---

* *Remarques sur la gram[maire] génér[ale] et raison[née]*, by M. Duclos, p. 11.

EDITOR'S NOTES

The present standard edition of Rousseau's works is Jean-Jacques Rousseau, *Oeuvres complètes,* B. Gagnebin and M. Raymond, eds. (Paris: Pléiade, 1959–   ), of which four volumes have so far appeared; it includes all the works translated in this volume, except the *Essay on the Origin of Languages;* the bracketed italic numbers throughout the translations refer to the pagination of the original in the Pléiade edition; all references to that edition in the following notes are abbreviated *OC,* followed by a Roman numeral indicating the volume, and an Arabic numeral indicating the page(s).

The present standard edition of Rousseau's correspondence is Jean Jacques Rousseau, *Correspondance complète,* collected, edited, and annotated by R. A. Leigh (Geneva: Institut et Musée Voltaire; Oxford: The Voltaire Foundation at the Taylor Institution, 1965–   ). Forty-three volumes of this remarkable work have so far appeared; all references to it throughout the present volume are abbreviated *CC,* followed by a Roman numeral indicating the volume, and an Arabic numeral indicating the page(s).

FIRST DISCOURSE, pages 1–27

The Dijon *Académie des sciences et belles lettres* announced the topic of its 1750 prize essay competition—"Has the restoration of the Sciences and Arts contributed to the purification of morals?"—in the October 1749 *Mercure de France.* Entries had to be submitted by April 1, 1750, and they were to take up no more than half an hour's reading time. The Academy reached its decision in July, and announced it in August. It is worth noting that in that announcement, it expressly stated that Rousseau's essay won first place because he had answered its question in the negative. The only other entry to have done so as well, took second place. The Academy also took note of the strongly republican tone of Rousseau's *Discourse,* and expressly stated that it was awarding it the prize in spite of it.

Rousseau on several occasions in later life recalled his excitement on first reading the announcement of the Academy's topic. He had gone to visit his friend Diderot, who had just been released from the Vincennes dungeon but was still confined to the castle grounds for having—anonymously—published his *Pensées Philosophiques* (1746) and his *Letter about the Blind* (1749). He had a copy of the latest issue of the *Mercure de France* in his pocket, and as he was walking along he began to leaf through it. When he came upon the announcement of the Academy question he was so overwhelmed by the rush of thoughts it aroused in him, that he had to sit down by the side of the road to try and sort them out. Almost a quarter of a century later, in the second of four important autobiographical letters to Malesherbes, he wrote: "Everything I have been able to retain of the great truths which during a quarter of an hour illumined me beneath that tree, has been feebly scattered throughout my three principal writings, this first discourse, the one on inequality, and the treatise on education [*Emile*], which three works are inseparable and together form a single whole" (12 January 1762; *OC* I: 1136; see also *Confessions* VIII, *OC* I: 350–352, 356, and *Rousseau Juge de Jean Jacques* II, *OC* I: 828f).

The major recent editions of the *First Discourse* are:

George R. Havens, *Jean Jacques Rousseau: Discours sur les sciences et les arts, édition critique avec une introduction et un commentaire* (New York: Modern Language Association of America, 1946).

François Bouchardy's critical edition in the Pléiade *Oeuvres complètes* III: 1–30, 1137–1156.

Michel Launay's critical edition in the Intégrale *Oeuvres complètes,* 3 vols. (Editions du Seuil, 1967, 1971), II: 52–68.

Claude Pichois and René Pintard, *Jean-Jacques entre Socrate et Caton* (Paris: Corti, 1972) contains interesting and previously unpublished fragments and drafts of the *First Discourse* and of related texts; they have been included in the appendix to the more recent printings of the third volume of the Pléiade edition of the *Oeuvres complètes.*

L. Delaruelle, "Les sources principales de J.-J. Rousseau dans le Premier Discours à l'académie de Dijon," *Revue d'histoire littéraire de la France* (1912), 19: 245–271, remains helpful.

The Dijon Academy and the circumstances surrounding the 1750 competition are described in Marcel Bouchard, *L'Académie de Dijon et le premier Discours de Rousseau* (Paris, 1950).

I have also consulted the annotated translations by Roger D. and Judith R. Masters, *Jean-Jacques Rousseau, the First and Second Discourses* (New York: St. Martin's Press, 1964); Kurt Weigand, *Jean-Jacques Rousseau, Schriften zur Kulturkritik: Die zwei Diskurse von 1750 u. 1755; eingeleitet, übersetzt und herausgegeben,* 2nd ed. (Hamburg: Meiner, 1971); Henning Ritter, ed., *J. J. Rousseau: Schriften,* 2 vols. (Munich: Hanser, 1978); Dietrich Leube *et al., Jean-Jacques*

Rousseau, Sozialphilosophische und Politische Schriften (Munich: Winkler, 1981), annotations by Eckhart Koch.

Discourse   Rousseau called five of his works "Discourses": The present writing, that on *Inequality*, the *Political Economy*, a *Discourse on the Virtue Most Necessary for Heroes*, and a *Discourse on Riches.* The so-called *First* and *Second Discourses*, as well as that on heroic virtue, were occasioned by Academy competitions. They may therefore have called for oratorical flourishes, and at least the appearance of being suited to public delivery. They may therefore also appear to be more popular than formal "Treatises," which is what he calls both the *Social Contract* (in the prefatory Note to that work) and *Emile* (in the letter to Malesherbes cited in the second paragraph of these notes). But the *Discourse on Political Economy*, commissioned and written as an article for the *Encyclopedia*, suffices to show that he looked upon the "discourse" as a flexible form. Machiavelli called his major work *Discourses*; Hobbes refers to the *Leviathan* as "my Discourse of Civil and Ecclesiastical Government" (in the last paragraph of that work); Locke calls his *Treatises of Government* a "Discourse" in the very first line of his preface to them; Algernon Sidney wrote *Discourses Concerning Government*; the list could be extended almost at will, and it would certainly not have to be restricted to popular or political works alone.

A Citizen of Geneva   Rousseau, however, stresses the political character of the work from the first: the author has a political identity, but has no personal name. Strictly speaking, he could not claim Genevan citizenship at this time. He had forfeited it by converting to Catholicism just before he turned sixteen, in 1728. He reconverted to Protestantism and was restored to Genevan citizenship on August 1, 1754. He was later to say that he put *Citizen of Geneva* only on the title page of books which he thought would do his native city honor (*La Nouvelle Héloïse*, 2nd preface, *OC* II: 27).

Here I am the barbarian   *Barbarus hic ego sum quia non intelligor illis*, from Ovid, *Tristia* V: X, line 37. Rousseau slightly altered a verse Ovid wrote while exiled among the Sarmatians, a tribe closely related to the Scythians. Just as the sophisticated poet from Imperial Rome felt that the Sarmatians took him for a barbarian, so Rousseau expected sophisticated *ancien régime* France to mistake his defense of austere republican virtue for a defense of barbarism. In the event he did not prove wrong. He had cited the same line from Ovid at the end of an

early letter to de Conzié (17 January 1742, *CC* I: 139, no. 43), and
that same year he had also used it as the epigraph to a collection of
youthful writings, *La Muse allobroge* (*The Boorish Muse*) (Leigh, *CC*
I: 143, n.dd; Ch. Guyot in *OC* II: 1123n); he again chose it as an
epigraph for the important late apologetic text, *Dialogues, Rousseau
Juge de Jean-Jacques, OC* I: 657). Samuel Pufendorf, whose *Droit de
la nature et des gens* (*Right of Nature and of Nations*) Rousseau
knew well, quotes the same verse of Ovid's in the context of his
discussion of the origin of language (*Droit,* Bk. IV: ch. 1, §vi,
note a).

Barillot & Son, Geneva   It would seem that although the first edition
of the *Discourse* appeared with a Genevan publisher's name on the
title page, it was brought out by Pissot in Paris, in January 1751 (Leigh,
CC II: 135f).

For an edition of the *Discourse* that was also to include the replies
to objections translated in the present volume, Rousseau wrote the
following prefatory note:

> What is fame? Here is the unfortunate work to which I owe mine.
> Certainly this piece which earned me a prize and made me a name, is
> mediocre at best, and, I dare say, it is one of the slightest in this entire
> collection. What an abyss of miseries the author would have been spared
> if this first writing had been received only as it deserved to be! But it
> seemed fated that an initially unjust acclaim should gradually bring down
> on me strictures that are even more so.

The dissatisfaction which he here voices with the *Discourse* refers
exclusively to its rhetorical and literary features. He never retracted
the views he developed in it.

The "at first unjust," that is to say undeserved, "acclaim" which he
mentions was quite extraordinary. He describes it briefly in *Confessions*
VIII, *OC* I: 363f. The subsequent, even more unjust, "strictures"
culminated in 1762 with the Paris Parliament's condemning the *Emile*
and ordering Rousseau's arrest, and in Geneva's condemning and
publicly burning both the *Emile* and the *Social Contract,* and also
ordering their author's arrest. Other expulsions followed, and Rousseau
had to flee from one refuge to another for many years.

[2] The League   Organized in 1576 by the Duc de Guise in order to
rally Catholic resistance to Huguenot advances in France and overthrow
King Henry III.

[3] notes ... additions easy to recognize   They have, on the contrary, proven quite difficult to identify. Most probably one of the notes he added is his discreet reference to Diderot's *Pensées Philosophiques,* which had been publicly condemned shortly after its publication in 1746. Most probably one of the additions is the passage in which he speaks of "the sentiment of that original freedom for which they [men] seemed born" (I: 3; *cf.* Bouchardy's note in the Pléiade edition, p. 1240, and Launay, *Jean-Jacques Rousseau écrivain politique* [Grenoble: A.C.E.R., 1971], pp. 141–145; Pichois and Pintard, *op. cit.,* pp. 40, 75). But regardless of what may have been the specific changes he made in his final text, Rousseau is here clearly saying that they sharpened his criticism of the Enlightenment and the *ancien régime.*

We are deceived . . . *Decipimus specie recti,* from Horace, *On the Art of Poetry,* line 25, where Horace says that it is the poets who are thus deceived.

[4] Has the restoration . . . to be examined The Academy's question, Has the restoration of the arts and sciences helped to purify morals?, appears to call for either a yes or a no answer. Rousseau begins by restating that question, and suggesting a third alternative: the arts and sciences have neither purified morals, nor have they failed to do so; rather, they have positively corrupted them. With that reformulation, he completely alters the terms of the discussion.

[5] learned Associations . . . the truly Learned *Savant* (n., adj.), "learned," is etymologically related to *science,* "knowledge," as "artist" is to "art"; it may range in meaning from "scholar(ly)" to "scientist" or "scientific"; similarly, *science,* as in the title of this *Discourse,* is not restricted in meaning to "science" in the narrow sense of the term, or to "natural science," but means "knowledge" or "learning" in any of its senses; as, for example, in Bacon's *Advancement of Learning,* a work of which the present *Discourse* is an almost point-by-point criticism. "Arts," in the title as well as throughout this *Discourse,* must also be understood in the broad and now somewhat old-fashioned sense which includes skills and crafts as well as the fine arts.

[8] the Throne of Constantine Constantinople, the modern Istanbul, was conquered by the Turks in 1453.

[9] that original freedom for which they seemed born *Cf.* "Man is born free, everywhere he is in chains." *Social Contract* I: 1.

[9]* Ichthyophagi Literally "fish-eaters"; the episode is also mentioned by Montesquieu, *Spirit of Laws* XXI: 8.

[11] **virtue ... the strength and vigor of the soul** Michel de
Montaigne (1533–1592), whose *Essays* are a constant source and
guide for the early Rousseau, uses the expression, though not as a
definition of virtue, in "Of the Younger Cato," *Essays* I: 37 (*Oeuvres
complètes,* A. Thibaudet and M. Rat, eds. [Paris: Pléiade edition, 1962,
p. 225], cited hereafter as *OC;* and in *The Complete Essays,* translated
by Donald Frame, Stanford University Press, 1958); Rousseau uses the
expression again in this *Discourse* [49]. He develops the view that
strength of soul defines heroic virtue, and that the younger Cato is the
embodiment of that form of virtue, in his 1751 *Discourse on this
Question: "What is the Virtue most Necessary for Heroes?"* (*OC* II:
1272f).

[14] **Pyrrhonism** The skepticism or zeteticism founded by Pyrrho of
Elis (*c.* 365–*c.* 275 B.C.) that seeks suspension of judgment or *epoche*
and imperturbability or *ataraxia* (Diogenes Laertius, *Lives and Opinions
of Philosophers* IX: 61–108, see 107); "Pyrrhonism" is therefore
commonly regarded as undermining the bases of loyalty and social life.

[14]* **I like, says Montaigne** In "On the Art of Conversing," *Essays*
III: 8 (*OC* 901; Frame tr., 702); the exception is most probably
Diderot.

[17] **Consider Egypt ... Sesostris** Legendary Egyptian ruler in the
13th century B.C. (see Herodotus, *Histories* II: 102–110). **conquered
by Cambyses** Second king of Persia, he conquered Egypt in 525 B.C.
by the Greeks Alexander the Great conquered it in 332 B.C.; **the
Romans** conquered it under Augustus, in 30 B.C.; **the Arabs** did so
under Calif Omar I, in 638 A.D.; **the Turks** did so in 1517.

[18] **Consider Greece ... twice vanquished Asia** In the Trojan
War, and at Salamis in 480 B.C. **the Macedonian's yoke** Philip of
Macedon's (382–336 B.C.) defeat of the allied armies of Athens and
Thebes at the battle of Chaeronea in 338 B.C. marked the end of Greek
independence. **Demosthenes** The greatest of Athenian orators (385–
322 B.C.), he tried to alert his compatriots to the Macedonian danger
before Chaeronea, and to rouse them against Macedonian rule after it.

[19] **Rome ... Ennius** Regarded by the Romans as their first poet
(239–189 B.C.). **Terence** The Roman comic poet (*c.* 185–159 B.C.).
Romulus, who founded Rome in 735 B.C. was, according to tradition,
a **shepherd. Ovid** (43 B.C.–18 A.D.) Rousseau here refers to him as
the author of *The Art of Love,* although he had drawn on another poem

of his for the epigraph of this *Discourse*. **Catullus** (84–54 B.C.), writer of erotic poems. **Martial** (40–104 A.D.), writer of epigrammatic satires of social life. **Arbiter of good taste** Petronius, author of the *Satyricon,* and a companion of the Emperor Nero (14–68 A.D.), who put him in charge of the Imperial pleasures in 66 A.D. (*cf.* Tacitus, *Annals* XVI: 18f). Nero is again excoriated in the speech which Rousseau has Pyrrhus deliver, this *Discourse* [32].

[21] China ... the yoke of the ... Tartar Genghis Khan invaded China in the first quarter of the 13th century.

[22] Persians ... a Philosophical Romance Xenophon (430–354 B.C.), *Education of Cyrus;* Rousseau's remark suggests that he regards Xenophon's account as truer than the factually true accounts of antiquarians; he called his own *Emile* a romance (Bk. V, *OC* IV: 777; tr. 416). **the Scythians** The warlike and proverbially savage nomad people who in classical antiquity lived in what are now southwestern Russia and the Balkans. As the epigraph to this *Discourse* indicates, Rousseau knew perfectly well that opinions about the Scythians were, to say the least, divided: Montaigne speaks well of them in several essays, from which Rousseau draws in the present *Discourse, e.g.,* "Of Pedantry," *Essays* I: 25 (*OC* 143, tr. 106); "Of Cannibals," *Essays* I: 31 (*OC* 206f, tr. 154f). In the *Second Discourse* (p. 160 above), he quotes a passage in which Justin praises them. But he also knew Herodotus's account (*Histories* IV: 1–143), and the tradition according to which, as Pufendorf put it, the Scythians ate human flesh and killed their own children on the pretext of religion (*Droit* II: 3, §viii); see also, Shakespeare, *King Lear* I. i. 116–118. Gibbon summarizes what was known of the Scythians at the time in *Decline and Fall* (ch. 26). **the Germans ... whose simplicity ... a pen weary** Tacitus (*c.* 55–120 A.D.), whose description of the spirit in which he wrote about the Germans Rousseau here quotes literally (*Germania* XIX: 20). **that rustic nation** Presumably the Swiss.

[22]* happy Nations ... Montaigne unhesitatingly prefers "Of Cannibals," *Essays* I: 31 (in particular *OC* 204, 213, tr. 153, 159). Rousseau exaggerates Montaigne's preference for the cannibals' polity to Plato's *Laws.* What Montaigne says is that he regrets knowledge of the American Indians' way of life was not available "at a time when there were men better able to judge of it than we are; I regret that Lycurgus and Plato did not have it, for it seems to me that what experience shows us about those nations exceeds not only all the pictures with which poetry has embellished the golden age and all of its inventions in fancying a happy human condition, but also the conception and the very desire of philosophy."

[23]* **the Athenians' ... upright Tribunal** The Areopagus. **the Romans think of medicine** Plutarch, *Life of Marcus Cato, the Censor,* xii; Montaigne, "Of the Resemblance of Children to Fathers," *Essays (OC* 745, tr. 581). **the Spaniards ... forbid their lawyers** Montaigne, "Of Experience," *Essays* III: 13 *(OC* 1043, tr. 816).

[24] **a Tyrant was ... assembling** Peisistratos (605–527 B.C.) is traditionally said to have caused Homer's *Iliad* and *Odyssey* to be collected and organized into the form in which they have been handed down, and to have made them the basis of Athenian public education; Cicero, *Of the Orator* III: 34; see also Diderot's *Encyclopedia* article "Bibliothèque" ("Library").

[27] **"I have," he says ...** Rousseau is here paraphrasing Plato's *Apology of Socrates,* 21c–22b in the translation of it which Diderot had made during his confinement at Vincennes. See *Oeuvres complètes,* Diekmann, Proust, Varloot eds. (Paris: Hermann, 1978), vol. IV, pp. 251–253. Rousseau merely follows Diderot's translation in speaking of "artists" where Socrates speaks of "artisans."

[31] **the elder Cato** Marcus Porcius Cato (234–149 B.C.), surnamed the Censor, was a consul, general, diplomat, traditional model of stern Roman republican virtue and consistent opponent of Greek learning and sophistication, who in his private capacity practiced agriculture and wrote an early treatise on the subject. **Epicurus** (*c.* 342–270 B.C.) taught materialism and hedonism. **Zeno** (336–264 B.C.) founded the Stoic sect. **Arcesilaus** (*c.* 315–240 B.C.) was the founder of Academic Skepticism. They are roughly contemporaries, and together represent the dominant post–Socratic-and-Aristotelian philosophical alternatives in antiquity (see also *Observations* [39]*, p. 41*). *Ever since ...* Seneca (*c.* 3 B.C.–65 A.D.), *Letters to Lucillus* 95 (13), cited by Montaigne in "Of Pedantry," *Essays* I: 25 *(OC* 140, tr. 103), from which Rousseau quotes at length later in this *Discourse* [51]*.

[32] **Fabricius** Roman general, consul and censor (d. *c.* 250 B.C.), traditionally surnamed "The Just," noted for his incorruptibility and his dignified bearing in the face of adversity (see especially Vergil, *Aeneid* V: 843f; Seneca, *On Providence* 3; Plutarch, *Life of Pyrrhus* XVIII: 20f). In Cicero's judgment, both Fabricius and Marcus Porcius

Cato possessed only a popular virtue, not virtue proper (*On Duties* III: iv, 16). **prey of a flute-player** Again the Emperor Nero. **Cineas** Ambassador of Pyrrhus, he is reported by Plutarch to have spoken of the Roman Senate in these terms (*Life of Pyrrhus* XIX, near the end).

Rousseau penciled this famous prosopopeia of Fabricius during the rush of inspiration he experienced on the road to Vincennes on first reading the Dijon Academy's question.

[33] **Louis XII ... Henry IV** Kings of France. The first, surnamed "Father of the People," ruled 1498–1515. The second, surnamed "The Great," ruled 1589–1610; in 1598, he issued the Edict of Nantes, guaranteeing the religious and political rights of Protestants.

[36] **an ancient tradition** In his "Letter to Grimm" [17], Rousseau tells how he was led to wonder about the ancient Egyptians' view of the sciences by a passage in Plato (see pp. 57f). The reference is to the *Phaedrus* (274c–275b), where Socrates has an Egyptian king reject the god Theuth's gift of the arts, and especially of writing, on the grounds that it would do more harm than good.

[36]* **the Prometheus fable** The version of this fable which Rousseau here cites is drawn from Plutarch's essay "How to Profit from One's Enemies," 2. It is an essay which he rereads and rethinks to the very end of his life: See *Rêveries* IV, *OC* I: 1024; *The Reveries of the Solitary Walker,* translated by Charles E. Butterworth (New York: Harper & Row, 1982), p. 43.

All ancient sources—Hesiod's *Works and Days* (42–105), *Theogony* (561–616), Aeschylus's *Prometheus Bound,* Plato's *Statesman* (274 c–d)—agree in showing Prometheus's gift accompanied by suffering for men. Plutarch has his Prometheus go on to say that fire can also profit those who learn how to use it. That is also the conclusion suggested by the title of his essay. That conclusion is entirely consistent with Rousseau's argument in the remainder of the *Discourse*.

Plutarch has Prometheus himself warn against the dangers of fire; the frontispiece assigns that task to Rousseau: "Prometheus's torch is the torch of the Sciences made to quicken great geniuses; . . . the Satyr who, seeing fire for the first time, runs toward it and wants to embrace it, represents the vulgar who, seduced by the brilliance of Letters, indiscreetly give themselves over to study; . . . the Prometheus who cries out and warns them of the danger is the Citizen of Geneva" ("About a New Refutation," [11], pp. 94f above).

Rousseau gave much thought to the illustrations for his works. He found this frontispiece, drawn by Pierre, very bad, whereas he found that for the *Second Discourse* very good (letter of 26 December 1757; *CC* IV: 408, no. 595).

[37] the well to which truth has withdrawn In his "Letter to Grimm" [28] (p. 60 above), Rousseau rightly points out that the expression is as old as philosophy itself. It is commonly attributed to Democritus (fl. 420 B.C.) (Fragment 117); Montaigne cites it, gives its source, and rejects it in "On the Art of Discussion," *Essays* III: 8 (*OC* 906, tr. 708), an essay from which Rousseau had quoted above.

[38]* the Peripatetics Or Aristotelians. René **Descartes** (1596–1650) had propounded his theory of extended substance and vortices in order to provide a rigorously mathematical and mechanical physics; *cf. Le Monde* (Adam-Tannery ed. XI: 43–47), *Principles of Philosophy* (II: 33–35; III: 45–53; IV: 2). Descartes's theory was overthrown by Newton.

[39] in what ratios bodies attract one another Newton's law of universal gravitation: bodies attract one another in direct proportion to their mass and in inverse proportion to the square of their distance. **the proportions . . . swept** Kepler's second law: the vector radius from the sun to a planet sweeps out equal areas in equal times. **man sees everything in God** The doctrine propounded by Nicolas Malebranche (1638–1715) in *Recherche de la vérité (Search after Truth)*. **two clocks** An image used by Gottfried Wilhelm von Leibniz (1646–1716) to illustrate his doctrine of the preestablished harmony (*e.g., Second Eclaircissement du Nouveau Système;* and Bayle, *Dictionnaire,* "Rorarius," note h, near the end). **what stars may be inhabited** Probably refers to Bernard Le Bovier de Fontenelle's (1657–1757) work of scientific popularization, *Entretiens sur la pluralité des mondes (Conversations about the Multiplicity of Worlds)*. **insects reproduce** A subject studied during the decades preceding the writing of this *Discourse* by R.-A. Ferchaud de Réaumur (1683–1757), as well as by Charles Bonnet (1720–1793), both of whom Rousseau knew; Bonnet later wrote a refutation of Rousseau's *Second Discourse* under the pseudonym Philopolis (see pp. 231–237 above).

[41] sumptuary laws That is to say, laws to tax and curb luxury; Rousseau returns to the issue in his "Letter to Raynal" [7] p. 29 above, and in the "Observations" [51]f, p. 44 above. He deals with it at some length in the *Discourse on Political Economy* (*OC* III: 252; translation by Charles Sherover [New York: Harper & Row, 1984], p. 151). In the

Considerations on . . . Poland, he again stresses that sumptuary laws cannot possibly extirpate luxury (*OC* III: 965; W. Kendall tr. [Indianapolis: Library of Liberal Arts, 1972], 18). **this paradox** That the pursuit of personal wealth and the promotion of luxury contribute to the common weal; or, as Mandeville put it in the subtitle to his *Fable of the Bees,* "Private Vices, Publick Benefits." This at the time rather novel doctrine of some English economists had recently been brought to the attention of the French public by J.-F. Melon, and it had been cleverly popularized by Voltaire in two notorious poems, "Le Mondain" (1736), and "Défense du Mondain, ou l'apologie du luxe" (1737). Although Rousseau does not here name these poems and their author, they are very clearly the targets of this criticism: he apostrophizes Voltaire by name three paragraphs later. **The ancient political Thinkers** The same thought is stated in almost the same words by Charles-Louis de Secondat, baron de Montesquieu (1689–1755), *Of the Spirit of the Laws* (1748) III: 3. **One will tell you** "Sir Petty assumed, in his calculations, that a man in England is worth what he would be sold for in Algiers. That must be true only of England. There are countries where a man is worth nothing; and others where he is worth less than nothing" (Montesquieu, *Of the Spirit of the Laws* XXIII: 17, and *cf.* III: 13). The reference is to Sir William Petty, author of *Essay on Political Arithmetick* (1680); Algiers is where Moorish pirates sold Christian prisoners into slavery. **Sybarite . . . Lacedaemonians** The inhabitants of the Greek city of Sybaris were so notorious for their love of luxury that their name has remained a synonym for dissolutencss. Sybaris was destroyed by the Crotoniats in 515 B.C. The Sybarites claimed that the Crotoniats had Spartan help. The Crotoniats denied it. Herodotus, after reporting these conflicting claims, invites the reader to decide between them (*Histories* V, 44f). Rousseau clearly believes the Crotoniats' version of the events.

[42] **The Monarchy of Cyrus** Alexander the Great conquered Persia in 334 B.C.; **the Scythians** resisted the Persians under Darius (512 B.C.) and later the Macedonians under Alexander. **Two famed Republics** Rome and Carthage—which Montesquieu compares (in *Causes de la grandeur des Romains* IV) in the same terms as those in which Rousseau here compares them—Rome defeating Carthage in the Punic wars, 265–242 B.C., 218–201 B.C., 146 B.C. **The Roman Empire** fell to the barbarian invasions of the Goths, the Vandals, and the Huns. **The Franks** conquered the Gauls, and **the Saxons** invaded Britain in the 5th and 6th centuries. **poor Mountaineers** The Swiss defeated the Hapsburgs of Austria in 1315 and 1386 and Charles the Bold, Duke of

Burgundy, in 1476. **Charles the Fifth's heir** Philip II of Spain (1527–1598) was, as an early English translator of the *Discourse* remarks, defeated by "[t]he *Hollanders* whose chief Employment was the *Herring-ʾishery*"; they successfully rebelled against Spanish rule in 1568, and a decade later established their independence (*A Discourse . . . By a Citizen of Geneva,* R. Wynne, A.M., tr., London, 1752, p. 32n).

[44] **famed Arouet** More famed, of course, in his public guise and by his pen name, Voltaire (1694–1778).

[44]* **reflections [by] Plato** In the *Republic* V: 451c–464b; Rousseau frequently returned to this question; for example, in *Discourse on Inequality,* Epistle Dedicatory [20] and Part I [42] with the editorial note; Book V of *Emile;* and throughout the *Nouvelle Héloïse.*

[45] **Carle** Vanloo (1705–1765) and Jean-Baptiste-Marie **Pierre** (1713–1789) were renowned painters. **Praxiteles** and **Phidias,** the greatest sculptors of classical Greece. Jean-Baptiste **Pigal[le]** (1714–1785) was a fashionable sculptor.

[47] **the Goths ravaged Greece** Under Alaric I, in the early 5th century. **Charles the Eighth** King of France (1483–1498) who conquered Tuscany and Naples in 1495. Both episodes are taken almost literally from Montaigne's "Of Pedantry," *Essays* I: 25 (*OC* 143, tr. 106); but in Montaigne the remark about the effects of studies on martial polities served as an introduction to the illustrative episodes, whereas in Rousseau it serves as their conclusion. Montaigne had earlier been speaking of Sparta, and it is to Sparta that he refers when speaking of "this martial polity." Rousseau failed to make the verbal change required by his paraphrase of Montaigne's paragraph, and hence his reference to "this" martial polity remains without an antecedent. The whole of Montaigne's essay is particularly relevant to the argument of the subsequent three paragraphs.

[49] **Cannae . . . Trasimene** Hannibal's greatest victories against Rome, in 216 and 217 B.C., respectively. **crossed the Rubicon** In 49 B.C., thereby in effect bringing the Republic to an end.

[50] **more strength and vigor than . . . bravery** "So sensible were the Romans of the imperfection of valor without skill and practice, that, in their language, the name of an army was borrowed from the word which signified exercise (*exercitus ab exercitando*)." Gibbon, *Decline and Fall,* ch. 1; see also Cicero, *On Duties* I: 61–92. On **strength and vigor** *Cf.* this *Discourse* [11], p. 5 above.

[51] **said a Wise man** Montaigne, in "Of Pedantry," *Essays* I: 25 (*OC* 137, tr. 101); the whole of Rousseau's long note immediately following is also drawn from that essay (*OC* 141f, tr. 104f).

[51]* **Pens Philosoph** Diderot, *Pensées Philosophiques* VIII: "Of some people it ought to be said not that they fear God, but that they are afraid of him." Even this discreet reference was quite daring, since his friend's book had been publicly condemned in 1746; *cf.* the "Preface" [3], p. 2 above, and the editorial note.

[51]** **the greatest of their Kings** Agesilaus (early 9th century B.C.), see Plutarch, *Sayings of the Spartans,* 67. **Plato** In *Alcibiades* I: 121d–122a; however, see also Plato, *Laws* III: 694a–698a. **Astyages, in Xenophon** This frequently cited episode is found in *Education of Cyrus* I:iii, 17; Montaigne's paraphrase, which Rousseau is here citing, comes much closer to equating the just with the legal than does Cyrus's teacher in Xenophon's account. τύπτω "I hit." *genere demonstrativo* The school term for the rhetorical form which Aristotle calls epideictic; *cf.* Aristotle, *Rhetoric* I: 3, with Quintillian, *Institutes* II: xx, 23.

[55] **great Monarch** Louis XIV (reigned 1643–1715) established numerous academies.

[56] **his august successor** Louis XV, who reigned 1715–1774. **imitated by all the Kings** Among them by Stanislas, deposed king of Poland, to whose "Observations" about this *Discourse* Rousseau replied at length (pp. 31–52 above).

[57] **there are no bodies** George Berkeley (1685–1753). **no substance other than matter, and no God other than the world.** Since Rousseau is attributing both of these tenets to one doctrine, and since the equation between God and the world most clearly points to Baruch Spinoza (1632–1677), it would seem that he is here suggesting that Spinoza was a materialist, a bold but defensible interpretation, *cf.* *Ethics* I: 15 (scholium), and letter no. 56 with Bayle, *Dictionnaire, s.v.* Spinoza, note N, II. **neither virtues nor vices** Evidently the philosophers' "internal doctrine" (see the editorial note on "Observations" [39]*, p. 313 below), in the form given to that doctrine by Diderot and practiced by his epigone Melchior Grimm; *cf.* Diderot's letter to Landois of 26 June 1756 and Grimm's *Correspondance littéraire* for 1 July and 15 July 1756, with *Rousseau Juge de Jean-Jacques,* Dialogue II (*OC* I: 841f), Dialogue I (*OC* I: 695); *cf. Confessions* IX (*OC* I: 468), *Rêveries* III (*OC* I: 1022, tr. 38). **men**

are wolves Thomas Hobbes (1588–1679), near the beginning of the Epistle Dedicatory to his *De Cive* or *On the Citizen* (1651), remarks that "both sayings are very true: 'that man to man is a kind of God; and that man to man is an arrant wolf.'" *De Cive*, H. Warrander, ed. (Oxford: Clarendon Press, 1983), p. 24; hereafter cited as *On the Citizen;* cf. Plautus, *Asinaria,* II, iv, 88.

[58] Leucippus Founded the atomist school (mid-5th century B.C.). **Diagoras** Disciple of the atomists, he was surnamed "the Atheist," and in 411 B.C. Athens prosecuted him for impiety. **the dangerous reveries of Hobbes** In the Epistle Dedicatory to his 1649 French translation of Hobbes's *On the Citizen* which Rousseau used, Sorbière had expressed his preference for "the reveries of Hobbes, Gassendi, and Descartes," to the more serious thoughts of some other philosophers. Rousseau's own last writing was called *Reveries.*

[58]* Sultan Achmed [III] Ruled from 1703 to 1730, and established a printing press in 1727. The anecdote about **Calif Omar,** who ruled 634–641, is recounted in Diderot's *Encyclopedia* article, "Bibliothèque" ("Library"). **Gregory the Great** Pope from 590 to 604 who was reputed to have had all pagan books in the Palatine library destroyed, and in the *Pensées Philosophiques* to which Rousseau had earlier referred—this *Discourse* [51]—Diderot speaks of Gregory's "barbarous zeal" against letters, adding "[i]f it had been up to that Pontiff alone, we would be in the condition of the Mohamedans, who are reduced to reading nothing but their Koran" (no. XLIV). As for Gregorian chant, see *Essay on . . . Languages,* pp. 291f above.

[59] Verulam Francis Bacon (1561–1626) was created Baron Verulam in 1618. **Descartes** See also this *Discourse* [38]*, and on **Newton** see [39]; on Bacon, Descartes, and Newton, see also Jean Le Rond d'Alembert's (1717–1783) *Preliminary Discourse to the Encyclopedia* (pt. II, near the beginning), an important manifesto of the Enlightenment which appeared within a year of this *Discourse* of Rousseau's. **feel the strength to go forth alone** Descartes describes himself as doing so in his *Discourse on Method* II (Gilson ed.), 16:24–30. **The Prince of Eloquence** M. Tullius Cicero (106–43 B.C.), orator, statesman, philosopher, was consul in 63 B.C. **perhaps the greatest of Philosophers** Bacon was Lord Chancellor in 1618.

[61] speak well . . . act well The Athenians and the Spartans; cf. Plutarch, *Marcus Cato* XXII: 4, cited by Montaigne, again in "Of Pedantry," *Essays* I: 25 (*OC* 142, tr. 105).

LETTER TO RAYNAL, pages 28–30

Guillaume-Thomas-François Raynal (1713–1796) is now primarily remembered as the author of the *Philosophical and Political History of the Europeans' Institutions and Commerce in the Two Indies* (1770), a work noted for its anticlerical and politically audacious views. He had been a Jesuit, but had left the Order in the late 1740s. In 1750 he became the editor of the *Mercure de France*. By this time he and Rousseau knew one another. In the June 1751 issue of the *Mercure* he published some brief and quite friendly "Observations on the *Discourse* that was crowned at Dijon" in the guise of a summary of comments by a number of unnamed critics. The same issue also carried the present "Letter" of Rousseau's, replying to these "Observations."

The "Letter" to Raynal has most recently been edited by Bouchardy, *Oeuvres complètes* (Pléiade ed.) III: 31–33; and by Launay, *Oeuvres complètes* (Intégrale ed.) II: 70–71, who also reproduces Raynal's "Observations" (p. 69); as does Ludwig Tente, *Die Polemik um den ersten Discours in Frankreich und Deutschland,* Dissertation (Kiel: Christian-Albrechts-Universität zu Kiel, 1974), pp. 126f.

The italicized passages in the "Letter" are Rousseau's citations from the text he is discussing.

[2] I myself said that it is worse than ignorance   *First Discourse* [8], p. 4 above.

[7] They add that   Mistakenly italicized in the Pléiade edition.

[8] spare me the trouble of transcribing   Both ask what the practical consequences of Rousseau's argument are for states as well as for individuals.

[13] the opponent . . . I am threatened with   Raynal had said that there were rumors of a forthcoming rebuttal of the *Discourse* by an Academician from "one of the better cities"; he was presumably alerting Rousseau to Stanislas's "Reply."

OBSERVATIONS, pages 31–52

The September 1751 issue of the *Mercure de France* carried an anonymous "Reply" to the First *Discourse,* and Rousseau's "Observations" about it appeared in October 1751. Rousseau knew that his anonymous critic was Stanislas Leszinski (1677–1766), formerly Stanislas I, twice deposed king of Poland and the father-in-law of Louis XV of France, and he several times alludes to his critic's high station. In the *Confessions* he recalls this exchange with King Stanislas. "I seized the opportunity to show the public how a private person might defend the cause of truth even against a sovereign. It is difficult to take a tone at once more proud and more respectful than the tone I took to answer him" (Bk. VIII; *OC* I: 366).

The *Observations* have most recently been edited by Bouchardy, *Oeuvres complètes* (Pléiade ed.) III: 35–57; by Launay, *Oeuvres complètes* (Intégrale ed.) II: 76–86, who also reprints Stanislas's "Reply" to the *Discourse, op. cit.,* pp. 72–76; as does Ludwig Tente, *Die Polemik um den ersten Discours, op. cit.,* pp. 158–169.

The italicized passages are, again, Rousseau's direct quotations from the text he is discussing.

[11] **too little common measure** Between a King praising a commoner, and a commoner praising a King.

[11]* **Pliny** The Younger (61–*c.* 113) wrote a *Panegyric* of the Emperor Trajan from which Rousseau quotes on p. 187 above.

[12]** *The Love of Letters Inspires ... Virtue* See also Rousseau's remarks on this topic in his "Letter ... about a New Refutation" [5], pp. 91f above.

[17] **Egyptians' vessels** *Exodus* 3:22, 12:35.

[22] **impious ... Alfonse X** King of Spain (1252–1284) and a keen student of astronomy, he is reported to have said that if God had asked him, he would have given him advice on how to improve the Creation. See, for example, Bayle, *Dictionary,* "Castille," note H.

[26] **one modern people** The Swiss, *Discourse* [22]. **drawing abhorrent comparisons** Between ancient or alien nations and contemporary European societies.

[27] **I am here asked** *I.e.,* in King Stanislas's "Reply."

[27]* **Preface to the Encyclopedia** Usually referred to as the *Preliminary Discourse,* this manifesto of the Enlightenment was written in 1751 by Jean Le Rond d'Alembert. Part II ends with a brief discussion of the argument of the *First Discourse.*

[36] **Josephus and Philo** Flavius Josephus, Jewish historian (37–*c.*

95) wrote the *Jewish Antiquities* and the *Jewish War*. Philo, called
Judaeus (20 B.C.–45 A.D.), a philosopher, sought to synthesize Platonic
and Biblical thought. **the Sadducees . . . the Pharisees** Religious
parties or, as Josephus, who himself was a Pharisee, said (*Jewish War*
II: 18, ii–xiv), philosophical sects among the Jews; the Pharisees
affirmed, and the Sadducees denied, that in addition to the written law,
Moses had received a divine oral law at Sinai; accordingly, the Pharisees
affirmed and the Sadducees denied the immortality of the soul. Jesus
taxed the first with hypocrisy, and the second with irreligion (*Mark*
12:18–27; cf. *Luke* 20:27–39, *Matthew* 22:23).

[36]* *Bourgeois Gentilhomme* Molière's play was first performed in
1670.

[39] **Saint Justin Martyr** Christian apologist, martyred in Rome
around 165.

[39]* **Lucian** The Greek satirical writer (125–190) is best known for
his *Dialogues of the Dead*. **Tertullian** Powerful and influential Christian
apologist (*c.* 155–*c.* 220). **The Epicureans . . . the Academics . . .
the Stoics** Views about religion held by the major philosophical schools
are reported and discussed most fully in Cicero's dialogue *On the
Nature of the Gods,* to which Rousseau alludes in the last paragraph of this long note. **Cyrenaics, as reported by Diogenes Laertius**
A school of hedonism founded by Aristippus of Cyrene, a sometime
companion of Socrates (Plato, *Phaedo* 59c); Rousseau here quotes
from the account of Aristippus in Diogenes Laertius's (3rd century A.D.)
Lives and Opinions of the Eminent Philosophers (II: 98f): *Sustulit
amicitiam quod ea nequè insipientibus neque sapientibus adsit . . .
Probabile dicebat prudentem virum non seipsum pro patria periculis
exponere, neque enim pro insipientium commodis amittendam esse
prudentiam. Furto quoque et adulterio et sacrilegio cum tempestivum
erit daturum operam sapientem. Nihil quippe horum turpe naturâ
esse. Sed auferatur de hisce vulgaris opinio, quae è stultorum
imperitorumque plebeculâ conflata est . . . sapientem publicè absque
ullo pudore ac suspicione scortis congressurum.* **Pythagoras** (fl.
540–510 B.C.). The doctrine primarily associated with his name is that
"the principles of numbers are the elements of all the beings" (Aristotle,
Metaphysics I: 5, 986a 1 and context). His school drew a distinction
between the *acousmatics,* or those of his followers who had heard
only summaries of his teaching, and the *mathematicians,* or those who
had learned the fully elaborated teaching. Diderot refers to this doctrine

of double truth in his Encyclopedia article "Pythagorisme." **The internal doctrine ... the Chinese ... Atheists or Philosophers** Jean Baptiste Barbeyrac, in the preface to his French edition of Pufendorf's *Right of Nature and of Nations,* which Rousseau knew well, writes about a Chinese philosopher "whose sentiments prevail to this day": "His disciples have an *external doctrine* which they preach to the people in order, they say, to hold it to its duties, and which consists in teaching that there is a real difference between good and evil, the just and the unjust, and that there is another life where one will be rewarded or punished for what one has done in this life. But the *internal doctrine,* which is only for the initiates, reduces itself to a kind of *Spinozism* which wipes out religion and morals" (p. LXXV). So, too, Locke: "the Jesuits themselves, the great encomiasts of the Chinese, do all to a man agree, and will convince us that the sect of the literati, or learned, keeping to the old religion of China, and the ruling party there, are all of them atheists." *An Essay Concerning Human Understanding* I: 4, §viii; see also Bayle, *Dictionary,* "Spinoza," note B; and the editorial note about the "internal doctrine" to *First Discourse* [57], p. 308 above.

[39]** **Clement of Alexandria** (*c.* 150–*c.* 215) was author of, among others, an *Hortatory Address to the Greeks* aimed at converting them.

[43] **subject the word of God to the rules of Grammar** Gregory the Great; the remark is reported by Bayle, *Dictionary,* "Gregory," note M, as well as by Diderot, *Pensées Philosophiques* (1746), no. XLIV; on Pope Gregory, see also *First Discourse* [58]*.

[48] *not in the manner of Aristotle* Non Aristotelico more, sed Piscatorio.

[51] *for every Aristippus ...* The founder of the Cyrenaic school of philosophy; see [39]*, above.

[53] **hypocrisy an homage vice pays to virtue** François de La Rochefoucauld (1613–1680), *Maxims* (1678 ed.), no. 218. **beautiful souls** or *belles âmes,* are, as the context indicates, passionate and forthright, and even their faults may be innocent, in contrast to petty, calculating hypocrites, who are suspect even when they do what is right. The heroine and the hero of the *Nouvelle Héloïse* are "beautiful souls" (I: x; I: xiii; IV: xii; *OC* II: 52, 62, 459); Julie's husband, M. de Wolmar, on the other hand, is a "noble soul" (II: vi; *OC* II: 209). Rousseau used the expression "beautiful souls" as the caption for the

seventh illustration in the novel, an engraving which depicts the heroine and her husband welcoming her former lover to their home (*OC* II: 766f). He calls special attention to the caption, and hence to the expression and to what he means by it, in the second preface to the novel (*OC* II: 13); the term and the notion become important in Romanticism, especially in German Romanticism. **Louis-Dominique Bourguignon,** *alias* **Cartouche** Notorious chief of a band of brigands (1693–1721). **Cromwell** Rousseau taxes Oliver Cromwell (1599–1658) with being a hypocrite for seeking worldly power in the name of religion (also *Of the Social Contract* IV: 8).

[55]* are found together ... all the other things These two lines are unaccountably omitted in the Pléiade and the Intégrale editions.

[62]* the Philosopher I ... mentioned D'Alembert, in the *Preliminary Discourse* to the *Encyclopedia*, mentioned at [27]*.

[65] a great Prince King Stanislas, to whom these "Observations" are addressed, had founded the Royal Academy of Sciences and Letters of Nancy in the very year of this exchange, 1751.

LETTER TO GRIMM, pages 53-64

As Rousseau points out in his first sentence, Gautier's refutation appeared in the October 1751 issue of the *Mercure*. Canon Joseph Gautier (d. 1776) is fully identified by the titles he lists at the head of his "Refutation," and by which Rousseau therefore addresses him in this rejoinder. Gautier owed his various positions to the patronage of King Stanislas, who had also only recently established the Academy of Nancy.

Rousseau is known to have been working on this rejoinder to Gautier at the same time as he was working on his "Observations" on King Stanislas's criticism of his *Discourse,* and it seems reasonable to think of the two rejoinders together. In the "Observations" he had tried to persuade King Stanislas, as he had earlier tried to persuade the Dijon Academy, to adopt a position at odds with their inclination and their self-interest narrowly construed. Gautier, on the other hand, begins, as Rousseau correctly points out, with some rather fawning references to his royal patron, and he ends with an open appeal to his fellow Academicians' narrow self-interest. This leads Rousseau to draw a sharp contrast, both at the beginning and at the end of the present "Letter," between himself, the citizen of a free city and the spokesman for its best interests, and Gautier, the member of learned professions and of an Academy under royal patronage and the spokesman for their interests. The "Letter" is thus made to illustrate one of the major themes of the *Discourse* which initially occasioned this exchange.

The ostensible addressee of the "Letter," Baron Friedrich-Melchior Grimm (1723–1807) belonged to Diderot's circle. At the time of this writing, he and Rousseau were good friends. Grimm took over the editorship of the *Correspondance littéraire* from Raynal in 1753, and he became an influential figure on the Paris literary and cultural scene. Later he and Rousseau broke, and Rousseau asked his publisher to omit Grimm's name from the title of this letter. The relations with Grimm form a major strand in the story Rousseau tells in the *Confessions*.

This "Letter to Grimm," dated November 1, 1751, appeared in pamphlet form. It has most recently been edited by Bouchardy, *Oeuvres complètes* (Pléiade ed.) III: 59–70; and by Launay, *Oeuvres complètes* (Intégrale ed.) II: 100–106, who also reprints Gautier's "Refutation," *op. cit.*, pp. 93–99; as does Tente, *Die Polemik, op. cit.*, pp. 184–202.

The italicized passages throughout Rousseau's text are, again, direct quotations from the text he is discussing.

[3] the Prosopopeia of Louis the Great   In defense of the arts and sciences which Gautier wrote in imitation and refutation of Rousseau's prosopopeia of Fabricius, *Discourse* [32].

[6] our soldiers are not Réaumurs and Fontenelles   Gautier had mentioned Réaumur and Maupertuis; René-Antoine Ferchault de Réaumur (1683–1757), renowned scientist; Bernard le Bovier de Fontenelle (1657–1757), for almost half a century the permanent Secretary of the Academy of Sciences, widely influential popularizer of the new science, and vigorous partisan of the moderns; Pierre Louis Moreau de Maupertuis (1698–1759), distinguished mathematician and natural philosopher, became president of the Berlin Academy of Sciences.

[7] Herodotus, Strabo ... Tacitus   In contradiction to Rousseau's praise of the Scythians, the early Germans, and the early Persians, Gautier refers to the reports of the Scythians' harsh ways in Herodotus (*c.* 480–*c.* 425 B.C.), *Histories* IV: 1–143, and in Strabo (63 B.C.–25 A.D.), *Geography* VII: 300–303; to the unfavorable description of the early Germans by the Roman geographer Pomponius-Mela (1st century A.D.); and to the revulsion at the Persians' harems and their Magis' tolerance of incest expressed by Charles Rollin (1661–1741) in his widely read and translated *Histoire ancienne,* Bk. IV, ch. 4, art. iv. Rousseau, on the other hand, had referred to Xenophon (430–352 B.C.), at *Discourse* [22] and [50]*, and to Tacitus (*c.* 55–120 A.D.) at *Discourse* [22].

[15] **"We readily inquire . . . *what blockheads!"***   Montaigne, *Essays* I: 25, "On Pedantry" (*OC* 135, tr. 100); Rousseau reversed the order of Montaigne's text, which begins "Call out . . ."

[17] **a passage in Plato**   *Phaedrus* 274c–275c, *cf. Discourse* II [36]; **Ozymandias** Legendary king of Egypt, presumably Ramses II, who ruled from about 1300 to 1232 B.C. In his *Refutation,* Gautier refers to Diodorus of Sicily's (1st century B.C.) report (*Hist.* I: 1, 49) that Ozymandias had built the first public library, and had inscribed on its portal "Remedies for the Soul's Ills"; the episode is also recounted in Diderot's *Encyclopedia* article "Bibliothèque."

[21] **Carneades**   Gautier refers to the famous episode when the Greek philosopher Carneades (214–129 B.C.), founder of the Third or New Academy, in Rome on an embassy, publicly argued in support of natural right one day, and just as vigorously argued against it the next day; to the elder Cato's indignation at this display, and to his sharp condemnation of Greek philosophy; and to the fact that in his old age that same Cato studied Greek in order to read Plato's dialogue on the immortality of the soul, the *Phaedo,* in the original.

[25] **the Stoics . . . in my camp**   In the passage just quoted by Rousseau, Gautier had spoken of *"stoic sternness."*

[28] ***truth . . . to the bottom of a well***   *Discourse* [37] and editorial note.

[29] **I notice that M. Gautier**   Rousseau omitted this paragraph in some editions of this text.

[33] ***The victories of the Athenians over . . . even the Lacedaemonians***   Reading *même* as Gautier had written, rather than *mêmes* as both the Pléiade and the Intégrale editions do. **what I said about the defeat of Xerxes . . . outcome of the Peloponnesian War** Xerxes, king of Persia (485–465 B.C.), whose attempted invasion of Greece was finally repulsed at Salamis in 480 B.C. In the *Discourse,* Rousseau had said that by this time the Persians had become corrupted, whereas the Athenians were corrupted by the arts and sciences in the course of the subsequent century; and within seventy-five years, in 405 B.C., the

Peloponnesian War ended with the defeat of Athens by Sparta. *funds intended for the war are used* Reading *destinés* and *employés,* as Gautier had written and the sense demands, instead of erroneously repeating *destinés* as both the Pléiade and the Intégrale editions do.

[38] the Utrecht Gazette . . . account of M. Gautier's Work This indeed most laudatory page about Gautier's *Reply* is reproduced in Tente, *op. cit.,* pp. 204f. As Rousseau points out in his "Last Reply" [74]* (p. 89 above), Gautier wrote an answer to the present "Letter."

LAST REPLY, pages 65–89

This "Reply" was occasioned by a lengthy *Discourse on the Benefits of the Sciences and Arts, by M. Bordes,* initially read before the Academy of Lyon in June 1751, printed in the December issue of the *Mercure,* and published in pamphlet form in the spring of the following year. Charles Bordes (1711–1781) and Rousseau had been friends some ten years earlier, when Rousseau lived in Lyon. At the time, Rousseau addressed two verse Epistles to Bordes (*OC* II: 1130–1133), and he recalls that period at the beginning of Book VII of the *Confessions.* In the next Book, he refers briefly to the present exchange with Bordes and to Bordes's later animus toward him (*OC* I: 280–281, 366).

The "Last Reply" has most recently been edited by Bouchardy, *Oeuvres complètes* (Pléiade ed.) III: 71–96; and by Launay, *Oeuvres complètes* (Intégrale ed.) II: 141–153, who also reprints Bordes's *Discourse, op. cit.,* pp. 134–141; as does Tente in *Die Polemik, op. cit.,* pp. 303–323.

Italicized passages throughout the "Last Reply" are, again, Rousseau's citations from the text he is discussing.

Let us not appear to remain silent Ne, dum tacemus, non verecundiae sed diffidentiae causâ tacere videamur, St. Cyprian (c. 210–258), *Against Demetrianus.*

[4]* the famous Philosopher Plutarch, in his essay "Of Envy and Hatred," which is also the source of the anecdote in the next paragraph of Rousseau's note.

[5] It cost Socrates** Meletus brought charges against him in the name of the poets, Anytus in the name of the artisans and the politicians, and Lycon in the name of the orators (Plato, *Apology of Socrates,* 23e– 24a). Just as in his paraphrase of the *Apology* in the *First Discourse*

[27]–[29], Rousseau had made no mention of Socrates's criticism of the political men, so here he omits to mention that charges were brought against him in their name. **when I asserted that Socrates would not have had to drink the hemlock** *Discourse* [33].

[12]* memorable examples of continence Plutarch, in his essay "On Curiosity" (par. XIII), tells how **Cyrus** of Persia (*c.* 585–529 B.C.) and **Alexander** the Great (356–323 B.C.) both chose not to behold women of great beauty lest they be distracted by their charms. Elsewhere he concludes an account of the conduct of the Elder—not the Younger—**Scipio** (*c.* 236–184 B.C.) on conquering the Spanish city of New Carthage. "But one thing above all the rest, chiefly increased his praise, and won him great love and good-will, as a mirror and example of all virtue. There was a young lady taken prisoner, that in beauty excelled all the women in Carthage: whom he carefully caused to be kept, and preserved from violence and dishonour. And afterwards, when he knew that she was married unto Lucceius, Prince of the Celtibarians, he sent for her husband that was a very young man, and delivered her unto him, untouched or dishonoured. Lucceius not forgetting his noble courtesy unto her, did let all his subjects understand the great bounty, modesty, and excellency of all kinds of virtues that were in this Roman general: and shortly after he returned again to the Roman's camp with a great number of horsemen" (*Lives,* Scipio African, North tr.). An ancient shield in the French Royal Collection at the Louvre known as "Scipio's Shield" had, according to tradition, been given to Scipio on that occasion (Delaruelle, "Les sources . . . ," *op. cit.,* p. 248, n. 3). **Falises was conquered . . . Pyrrhus driven out** Pyrrhus defeated the Romans in two successive campaigns (280 and 279 B.C.), inflicting—but also sustaining—great losses. The Romans were ready to continue to do battle regardless of the cost to them. Pyrrhus could not do so, and therefore had to abandon his Italian campaign; hence the expression "Pyrrhic victory." **the Poet Dryden** John Dryden (1631–1700).

[16] abandoned to *the faculties of instinct* alone The expression is Bordes's, in a passage which Rousseau quotes in this "Reply" [40].

[35] Caryatids Classical columns in the form of draped female figures.

[38] Did not Ochus shine . . . Atlas . . . Zoroaster . . . Zamolxis Religious innovators, although Ochus or Artaxerxes III, king of Persia (358–338 B.C.), seems out of place in this list. **Philosophy . . . among the Barbarians** *Cf.* Plato, *Republic* VI: 499c. *Miltiades* led the victorious Athenians against the Persians in the battle of Marathon, in 490 B.C. *Themistocles* (*c.* 523–459 B.C.) fortified Piraeus, the port of Athens, and persuaded Athens to build up its navy; he later led the victorious Greeks against the Persians in the battle of Salamis, in 480 B.C. *Aristides,* surnamed the Just, fought at Marathon and at Salamis, and led the Athenians in the final decisive battle against the Persians at Plataea in 479 B.C. Two years later he achieved leadership of the Maritime Confederacy in Athens; the laws which he drew up for that confederacy were regarded as exemplary. **Socrates'**s dates are 469–399 B.C.; **Plato**'s are 429–347 B.C.

[40] **Cicero's eloquence . . . his civic-spiritedness** Cicero was consul in 63 B.C., when Catiline's conspiracy was discovered. He exposed and prosecuted the conspirators, and his speeches on the occasion are models of civic oratory.

[42] **the foresight of that boor Themistocles** See Herodotus, VII: 144; Thucydides, *Peloponnesian Wars* I: 14; Plutarch's *Life,* 4. **who did not know how to play the flute** According to Cicero, it was the lyre he did not know how to play: *Tusculan Disputations* I, ii, 4.

[46] **Thermopylae** The mountain pass held by Spartan King Leonidas against the vastly superior invading Persian forces. When he learned that he had been betrayed, he dismissed all allies and, with only three hundred of his countrymen, fought the advancing enemy to the death in 480 B.C. (Herodotus VII: 202–226).

[46]* **Pericles** (495–429 B.C.), political leader of Athens during what is often called the city's Golden Age. Rousseau's doubts about his political leadership echo those raised by Plato and, less directly, by Thucydides. **Alcibiades** (450–404 B.C.), the brilliant and flamboyant public figure, had advised the Athenians to launch the ruinous Sicilian expedition. Thucydides, in his account of the episode, leaves open the possibility, as Rousseau does here, that Alcibiades might have brought that expedition to a successful conclusion (*Peloponnesian Wars* VI: xv).

[47] **the Ephors** The five overseers elected annually in Sparta, and who exercised very great authority in all of the city's affairs.

[49]* **It is not Rousseau . . . it is Montaigne** In "Of the Younger Cato," *Essays* I: 37 (*OC* 226, Frame tr. 170).

[49]** **Curius, refusing the presents** Curius Dentatus defeated the

Samnites in his first consulship, in 290 B.C., and Pyrrhus in his second consulship in 275 B.C.

[49] **Tiberius** (42 B.C.–37 A.D.), emperor of Rome (14–37 A.D.) known for his suspicious and cruel nature. **Catherine de Medici** (1519–1589), cruel Regent of France, largely responsible for the Saint Bartholomew Massacre of Protestants (1572).

[51] *Cato* ... **the model of the purest virtue**   Marcus Porcius Cato (95–46 B.C.) surnamed Utican, great-grandson of Cato the Censor, on whom he modeled himself. He was an adherent of the Stoic sect. He had consistently opposed Caesar's ambitions, and when Caesar's armies prevailed, Cato chose to take his life rather than survive the Republic. He quickly became a legendary hero of Republicanism. See Seneca, *Letters to Lucillus* XCV: 59–71; his *On Providence,* from which Rousseau quotes in the next paragraph; and especially Plutarch's *Life* of Cato. Rousseau calls Cato "the greatest of men" in the *Second Discourse* II [57], and in the *Letter to d'Alembert* (Fuchs ed., Droz, 1948, p. 38, A. Bloom translation [Free Press, 1960], p. 29); in the *Discourse on Political Economy* [30] (*OC* III: 255), and in the *Discourse on the Virtue Most Necessary to a Hero,* he compares and contrasts Cato with Socrates (*OC* II: 1268).

[52] *Behold a spectacle* ...   *Ecce spectaculum dignum ad quod respiciat, intentus operi suo, Deus. Ecce par Deo dignum, vir fortis cùm malâ fortunâ compositus. Non video, inquam, quid habeat in terris Jupiter pulchrius, si convertere animum velit, quàm ut spectet Catonem, jàm partibus non semel fractis, nihilominus inter ruinas publicas erectum* (Seneca, *On Providence* [3]).

[53] *a Brutus*   Lucius Junius Brutus, leader of the revolt that rid Rome of the Tarquins (510 B.C.) and established the Republic; his sons Titus and Tiberius having conspired to restore the Tarquins, Brutus condemned them to death. *Decius* Mus, Publius, Roman consul in 340 B.C., dedicated himself to the gods of the underworld for the sake of victory by the Roman armies. *Lucretia,* wife of Lucius Collatinus, committed suicide after being raped by Sextus Tarquinius. The ensuing outrage led to the overthrow of the Tarquins in the insurrection led by Lucius Junius Brutus (Plutarch, *The Life of Publius Valerius Publicola,* in the beginning). In 1754 Rousseau began a play, "The Death of Lucretia." L. *Virginius* slew his daughter to save her from being enslaved by the tyrannical Decemvir Appius Claudius; the public outrage against the Decemvirs expressed itself in an uprising which restored the Republic

(449 B.C.); on the Decemvirs, see also *On the Social Contract* III: 28. *Scaevola* or "the left-handed," the name given to C. Mucius. When the Etruscan King Porsena marched against Rome to restore the Tarquins to the throne (507 B.C.), C. Mucius tried to kill him. Caught in the attempt and threatened with torture, he plunged his right hand into a bed of live coals to show his indifference to pain. Early in his *Confessions* Rousseau recalls how, when he was a child, he got so carried away while telling the story of Scaevola, that he walked over to a brazier, ready to reenact the scene he was recounting (*OC* I: 9).

[57] **Philip's stratagems**   Philip (382–336 B.C.), king of Macedonia, gradually conquered the Greek cities on the Macedonian coast and eventually defeated an alliance led by Athens at the Battle of Chaeroneia in 338 B.C., thereby putting an end to the independence of Greece.

[57]* **Titus**   Titus Flavius Sabinus Vespasianus, emperor of Rome (79–81). **"As a private person ...** *Privatus atque etiam sub patre principe, ne odio quidem, nedum vituperatione publicâ caruit. At illi ea fama pro bono cessit, conversaque est in maximas laudes* (Suetonius, *Lives of the Caesars,* Bk. VIII: 1, vii).

[61] **Cortés**   Hernando Cortés led the Spanish conquest of Mexico 1519–1521. **Guatimozin** The Aztec chief defeated by Cortés and executed by his orders; the story of his proud bearing was widely known, *e.g.,* Voltaire, *Essai sur les moeurs,* ch. 143 (near the end); *Encyclopedia,* "Mexico"; Raynal, *Philosophical and Political History,* Bk. VI, ch. 9.

[64] *It would appear,* **we are told**   The last three words are erroneously attributed to Rousseau instead of to Bordes by the editors of the Pléiade as well as of the Intégrale edition. Rousseau is here quoting a sentence in which Bordes is quoting a sentence from *Discourse* [57].

[65] **Hebert**   A jeweler who supplied the Court at the time of this writing. **Lafrenaye** A painter. **Dulac** Unidentified. **Martin** The name of two renowned cabinetmakers (Bouchardy, *OC* III: 1278).

[66] **"A good mind needs little learning"**   *Paucis est opus litteris ad mentem bonam* (Seneca, *Moral Letters,* 106, near the end).

[67] *We are told to mourn the education of the Persians*   See *Discourse* [22] and [51]*, and references. **"Be he Trojan or Rutulian"** *Tros Rotulusve fuat* (Vergil, *Aeneid* X: 108).

[69] *can delude only informed minds.* **I don't know how to reply**

Rousseau pretends not to realize that *informed* is a misprint for *uninformed* in Bordes's text.

[71] **Melon** Jean-François Melon (1680–1738), author of an *Essai politique sur le commerce* (2nd enlarged edition, 1734), and of an "Apology of Luxury." In addition to his defense of luxury, that is to say of a public policy favoring the pursuit of material well-being and affluence unhampered by moral restraints or sumptuary laws, Melon strongly defended slavery on economic grounds.

[74]* **I am told that M. Gautier** *Cf.* "Letter to Grimm" [38], pp. 62f.

LETTER ABOUT A NEW REFUTATION, pages 90–95

The *Refutation* that occasioned this "Letter" appeared in late 1751. As Rousseau indicates, it was published together with a reprint of the *Discourse:* typically each page of the book is divided into two columns, the left reproducing Rousseau's text, the right bearing the author's point-by-point criticism; an addendum goes on to take issue with Rousseau's "Observations." According to its title page, this *Refutation* was the work of a member of the Dijon Academy who had voted against awarding the prize to Rousseau's entry; but in a statement published in the August 1752 issue of the *Mercure de France,* the Academy categorically denied that the *Refutation* was by one of its own. This prompted Claude-Nicolas Lecat, surgeon in Rouen, the Perpetual Secretary of that city's Academy and a member of numerous other learned societies, to acknowledge that he was the author of the *Refutation,* and to attempt to justify the fact that he had published it as he had.

Rousseau's "Letter" has most recently been reedited by Bouchardy in the Pléiade edition of the *Oeuvres complètes* III: 97–102; and by Launay in the Intégrale edition, *op. cit.,* pp. 173–176, which also reprints Lecat's *Refutation,* the Dijon Academy denial of his membership in that Academy, and Lecat's acknowledgment of his authorship, although it unfortunately does so with unacknowledged omissions (*op. cit.,* pp. 153–173, 176–180). They are reprinted in their integrity by Tente, *Die Polemik, op. cit.,* pp. 210–288, 399f, 402–411.

[5] **the French Academy Prize this year** The topic for the Academy's 1752 competition in eloquence was: "The Love of Letters Inspires the Love of Virtue." Rousseau remarks on the choice of this topic in "Observations" [12]*, p. 33 above.

[8] Jean de **La Fontaine** (1621–1695), Nicolas **Boileau** (1636–

1711), **Molière** (1622–1673), Vincent **Voiture** (1598–1648), Jean François **Regnard** (1655–1709), Jean Baptiste Louis **Gresset** (1709–1777) are poets and playwrights whom Lecat had mentioned. He had further spoken of **Nimrod** as a tyrant and a criminal (*cf. Genesis* 10: 8–10), and had also said that any time thirty **peasants from Picardy** gather for a dance, they will fight and brawl more than will any five hundred people gathered for a ball at the Opera, adding "if you have a farm or a piece of land in those parts of the country, you could not expect much profit."

[9] drawn from Clenard a term used by Cicero Lecat several times charges Rousseau with writing imprecise or unidiomatic French; on one occasion he suggests that the term "investigation," which was unfamiliar in French before its occurrence in the *Discourse* [38], had been adapted by Rousseau from a Latin expression to be found in the *Primer* by Nicolas Clenard, professor of Greek and Hebrew at the University of Louvain. As Rousseau correctly points out in his accompanying note, the Latin *investigatio* may be found in Cicero's *On Duties* (1, iv. 13, vi. 19).

[9]* The Lyon Discourse ... my reply Bordes's *Discourse* and Rousseau's so-called "Last Reply" in response to it, pp. 65–89 above.

[9]** "why should I be denied?"

> *Ego cur, acquirere pauca*
> *Si possum, invideor; cum lingua Catonis et Enni*
> *Sermonem Patrium ditaverit?*
>
> —Horace, *On the Art of Poetry,* 55–57

[10] what their shoulders can carry

> *quid valeant humeri*
> —Horace, *On the Art of Poetry,* 40

[11] I had said In *Discourse* [8]; Rousseau has changed the original wording slightly. **Lulle's pretentious doctrine** Raymon Lulle (1235–1315), the Catalan polymath, claimed to have devised an "art of finding truth" by means of a formal classification of all being and knowledge; Descartes thought it better suited to talking about things we do not know than to discover anything about them: *Discourse on Method* II (Gilson ed., 17: 19f).

PREFACE TO *NARCISSUS*, **pages 96–111**

Rousseau wrote this "Preface" in the winter of 1752–1753, and published it soon thereafter together with the text of the *Narcissus, or The Self-Lover.*

Narcissus is the earliest of several plays he wrote or sketched as a young man (*Confessions* III, *OC* I: 120). None of them was performed at the time. In 1742 or 1743 he showed the *Narcissus* to the great playwright Marivaux (1688–1763), who "touched it up" (*Confessions* VII, *OC* I: 287). Rousseau continued, in later years, to write at least fragments of plays, tales and allegories, and musical entertainments. He composed his best known opera, *Le Devin du village* or *The Village Soothsayer,* early in 1752, at a time when the public debate about the *First Discourse* was still very intense. It was performed before the Court to considerable acclaim in October of that year. The king wanted to reward Rousseau with a pension. Rousseau declined it by not appearing at the ceremony at which it was to be awarded him. The reasons for his action were many and complex, but the fear that, as the beneficiary of royal favors, he might no longer feel perfectly free to speak his mind on the most important issues, or that others might impugn his motives for what he said or did, certainly played an important part in his decision. He had long ago decided to live free and poor, and he remained faithful to that resolve. Diderot and others of his friends remonstrated with him for it (*Confessions* VIII, *OC* I: 374–381).

In the wake of the success enjoyed by the *Devin du village,* the youthful *Narcissus* was brought out of its drawer and produced. The premiere took place on December 18, 1752. Although he apparently did not think much of the play, Rousseau rightly judged the "Preface" which he now wrote for it to be one of his better writings, adding that in it "I began to reveal my principles a little more than I had done up to that time" (*Confessions* VIII, *OC* I: 388). In the immediate sequel he goes on to say that he developed these principles fully in his next major writing, the *Discourse on the Origin of Inequality,* the theme for which was announced that very year, 1753.

This "Preface" is Rousseau's last major published contribution to the controversy most immediately aroused by the *First Discourse.* His next major public statements on the issues which he had first raised in that *Discourse* are the *Letter to d'Alembert* (1758), and the "Prefaces" to the *Nouvelle Héloïse* (1761).

The standard contemporary edition of the "Preface" is that by Jacques Scherer, in the Pléiade *Oeuvres complètes* II: 959–974.

[1] I wrote this Play at the age of eighteen He wrote it in his early twenties: "I lied by a few years" (*Confessions* III, *OC* I: 120).

[3]* the four German sermons of which one begins Rousseau paraphrases almost without parody the beginning of a speech by Johann Friedrich Burscher delivered in 1752 "in defense of learning and the fine arts, against Mr. Rousseau of Geneva" on the occasion of the birthday of the king of Saxony. For the full text of this and the other speeches delivered on that occasion, see Tente, *Die Polemik, op. cit.,* pp. 458–547.

[3]** In the *Mercure* for August 1752 See the introductory editorial note on the "Letter about a new Refutation," p. 322 above.

[9] *glibness enough, not enough wisdom* Satis loquentiae, sapientae parum. According to the Roman grammarian Aulus Gellius (*c.* 165– 123 B.C.), that is how the grammarian Valerius Probus understood Sallust's (86–34 B.C.) remark (in *The Catiline Conspiracy* V: 4) "enough eloquence, too little wisdom," *satis eloquentiae, sapientiae parum* (*Attic Nights* I: 15, 18). I am indebted to my colleague Professor Michael Roberts for this reference.

[15]* *"The Villain"* The play *Le Méchant* by the former Jesuit Jean Baptiste Louis Gresset, written in 1745 and first performed in 1747.

[20] the absurd systems of men like Leucippus Leucippus (fl. 450–420 B.C.) originated the atomic theory. **Diogenes** Called The Cynic (4th century B.C.), he was notorious for the extremes to which he went in leading a life of utter independence. **Pyrrho** of Elis (c. 365–c. 275 B.C.) was the founder of skepticism. **Protagoras** of Abdera (c. 480–411 B.C.), the most famous and successful of the Sophists, best remembered for his dictum "man is the measure of all things." T. **Lucretius** Carus (99–55 B.C.), Roman follower of the materialist and hedonist Epicurus, he was the author of the didactic poem *On the Nature of Things*. Thomas **Hobbes** (1588–1679), the great English political philosopher whose teaching frequently has been and is taken to be strictly materialist and atheist. Bernard **Mandeville** (1670–1733), author of *The Fable of the Bees,* subtitled *Private Vices, Publick Benefits.*

[23]* Here is a modern example. . . . The Republic of Genoa More precisely, the Corsican Academy, or Academy of Bastia, was restored in 1749 by the Marquis de Cursay, commanding general of the French troops charged with pacifying Corsica on behalf of Genoa, and he manifestly did try to revive the Academy for the very reasons Rousseau here mentions. Rousseau wrote his *Discourse on the Virtue most Necessary in Heroes* (*OC* II: 1262–1274) for the Corsican Academy's 1751 prize essay competition; however, he decided not to submit it. He thought it very poor, and never published it.

[24] **"if science, trying to arm us ... seek cover behind it"** Montaigne, "Of Physiognomy," *Essays* III: 12 (*OC* 1016, Frame tr. 795). The adjective "vain" in the last line was added by Rousseau.

[30]* *He is not moved by the people's fasces* ...

> *Illum non populi fasces, non purpura Regum*
> *Flexit, et infidos agitans discordia fratres;*
> *Non res Romanae, perituraque regna. Neque ille*
> *Aut doluit miserans inopem, aut invidit habenti.*
> —Vergil, *Georgics*, 495f, 498f

[32] **He is born to act and to think, not to reflect.** In a striking passage of his next major writing, Rousseau will say "If [Nature] destined us to be healthy then, I almost dare assert, the state of reflection is a state against Nature, and the man who meditates a depraved animal." *Discourse on the Origin of Inequality among Men* I [9], p. 145 above.

[34]* **the two first Kings of Rome** Romulus and Numa. "The name *Rome* which is said to come from *Romulus* is Greek, and means *force;* the name *Numa* is also Greek, and means *Law*. Is it not odd that the first two Kings of that city should in anticipation have borne names so appropriate to what they did?" *Social Contract* IV: 4, n.

[39] **I needed a test** The *Devin du village* had been very successful, and Rousseau later described his feelings of pleasure at its first performance; yet the next day he refused the offer of a royal pension. He may well have exaggerated the lack of success of the *Narcissus* in order to dramatize his equanimity in the face of failure as much as of success.

SECOND LETTER TO BORDES, pages 112–115

Bordes was not satisfied with Rousseau's "Last Reply," and set to work on a renewed, more elaborate criticism of the argument of the *First Discourse*. When Rousseau heard of this project, he wrote his old friend a cordial letter assuring him that their differences of opinion did not alter his fond memories of him, and adding, rather flatteringly, that Bordes was the only one of his critics he took seriously. But he also warned him that he might once again choose to reply in public (May 1753, *CC* II: 218, no. 197). However, after reading Bordes's second rejoinder, he judged it much inferior to the first (*CC* II: 231f, no. 203), and never went beyond drafting the present "Preface" of a reply to it. Besides, by November of 1753 his thoughts and energies became absorbed by what was to become his second *Discourse*.

Bordes read his own *Second Discourse on the Benefits of the Sciences and the Arts* before the Lyon Academy in August 1752; it was published in August 1753. By then, Rousseau's "Preface to *Narcissus*" had appeared, and Bordes appended some comments on it to his own text.

This "Preface" of a second letter to Bordes remained unpublished during Rousseau's lifetime. It was first published by Streckeisen-Moultou in his edition of Rousseau's *Oeuvres et correspondances inédites* (Paris, 1861), pp. 317–322. It is reprinted with notes by Bouchardy in the Pléiade *Oeuvres complètes* III: 103–107; and by Launay in the Intégrale *Oeuvres complètes* II: 190–192; the full text of Bordes's *Second Discourse* is reprinted in Tente, *Die Polemik, op. cit.,* pp. 623–681.

[1] I do not see why Reading *je ne vois pas* with the Intégrale edition and as the sense requires, instead of *je revois pas* with the Pléiade edition.

[4] [my duty] is to tell ... the truth or what I take to be the truth Cf. *Last Reply* [73]; in this spirit, Rousseau took as his motto the phrase *vitam impendere vero,* "to dedicate life to truth"; he discusses that motto most fully in the fourth of the *Reveries of the Solitary Walker.* He always stressed that not everyone has "the sad task of telling people the truth." Emile, for example, explicitly does not (*Emile* V; *OC* IV: 859, tr. 474).

[5] my portrait Maurice Quentin Latour's elegant and frequently reproduced pastel of Rousseau first shown at the summer *Salon* of 1753.

[6] This sad and great System Rousseau had for the first time spoken of his "system" in the "Preface to *Narcissus*" [13]. He now does so five times in the course of this brief text. He may have been prompted to do so again here by the beginning of the Bordes text to which he is here replying: "I had looked upon Mr. Rousseau's first

Discourse as nothing more than a clever paradox, and that was the tone in which I answered him. His last reply has revealed a settled system. . . ."

[7] **most men have degenerated from their primitive goodness** Rousseau had first referred to man's natural goodness in his "Last Reply" [37]*, p. 73 above, also addressed to Bordes; he develops this central theme of his thought most fully in the *Second Discourse*, and in the *Emile*.

SECOND DISCOURSE, pages 117–230

The *Discourse on the Origin and Foundations of Inequality Among Men*, the so-called *Second Discourse*, was again occasioned by a Dijon Academy competition. This time the question was: "What is the Origin of Inequality Among Men, and whether it is authorized by the Natural Law?" In his *Confessions*, immediately after remarking that in the "Preface to *Narcissus*" he had revealed his principles more fully than in any of his previous writings, Rousseau goes on to say: "I soon had the opportunity to unfold them fully in a work of the utmost importance; for it was, I believe, in that same year of 1753 that the program of the Academy of Dijon about the origin of inequality among men was published. I was struck by that great question, and surprised that the Academy had dared to propose it. But since it had had the courage to do so, I could surely have the courage to address it, and that is what I undertook to do." To collect his thoughts, he spent a week walking in the forest of Saint Germain, seeking and finding "the image of the first times." "These meditations resulted in the *Discourse on Inequality,* a work more to Diderot's taste than any of my other writings, and for which his advice was more useful to me, but which in all of Europe found only a very few readers who understood it, and of these none wished to talk about it. It had been written to compete for the prize, so I entered it, convinced though I was in advance that it would not receive it, and well aware that it is not for pieces cut from such cloth that Academy prizes are endowed" (*Confessions* VIII; *OC* I: 388f).

In the event he proved right. The jury did not even read the *Discourse* in its entirety, "because of its length, and its bad tradition, etc."

The topic had been announced in the November 1753 issue of the *Mercure de France;* Rousseau left Paris on June 1, 1754, with the *Discourse* completed, except for the Epistle Dedicatory which he judged it more prudent to sign and date on soil not under either French or Genevan jurisdiction (*Confessions* VIII; *OC* I: 392). Official permission for the book to be sold in France was granted in May 1755.

The circumstances surrounding the 1754 Dijon Academy competition are related, and the other essays submitted for it are reprinted in Roger Tisserand, *Les concurrents de J. J. Rousseau à l'Académie de Dijon pour le prix de 1754* (Paris, 1936).

Jean Morel's pioneering "Recherches sur les sources du Discours de J. J. Rousseau sur l'origine et les fondements de l'inégalité parmi les hommes," in *Annales de la Société Jean-Jacques Rousseau*, 1909, 5: 119–198 (reprinted Lausanne, 1910) remains valuable.

The most important recent editions of the *Discourse* are: C. E. Vaughan, *Jean-Jacques Rousseau: The Political Writings*, 2 vols. (Cambridge, England, 1915; reprinted by Basil Blackwell, 1952), I: 124–220; Jean Starobinski's critical edition in the Pléiade *Oeuvres complètes* III (1964): 109–223; Heinrich Meier, *Diskurs über die Ungleichheit/Discours sur l'inégalité, kritische Ausgabe des integralen Textes, mit sämtlichen Fragmenten und ergänzenden Materialien nach den Originalausgaben und den Handschriften neu ediert, übersetzt und kommentiert* (Schöningh, 1984). Unfortunately this edition appeared as the present volume was going to press, and I could therefore take note only of its corrections of previously published versions of the *Discourse*.

Rousseau's own corrections and additions were first published in the posthumous 1782 Moultou and Du Peyrou edition of the *Collection complète des oeuvres de J. J. Rousseau;* most of them are recorded in the notes that follow.

Fragments and drafts of the *Discourse* were first published by Streckeisen-Moultou (1861); they were edited anew and added to by R. A. Leigh, "Les manuscrits disparus de Jean-Jacques Rousseau," *Annales Jean-Jacques Rousseau* (1956–1958), 34: 39–81, see especially pp. 67–77; reprinted in *OC* III: 224f, 1356–1358; reedited by H. Meier, *Diskurs/Discours,* pp. 386–395, 404–411.

Other fragments, first published by M. Launay, *Revue internationale de philosophie* (1967), 82: 423–428, and reprinted in his Intégrale edition of Rousseau, *Oeuvres complètes* II: 264–267, have most recently been reedited by Meier, *Diskurs/Discours,* pp. 396–403.

I have found two early translations of the *Discourse* helpful: *A Discourse on the Origin and the Foundations of the Inequality among Men,* translated from the French by John Farrington of Clapham, 1756, an unpublished manuscript in possession of the Beinecke Rare Book Library of Yale University; and *A Discourse upon the Origin and*

Foundation of the Inequality among Mankind, printed for R. and J. Dodsley (London, 1761). I also consulted the annotated translations by Roger D. and Judith R. Masters, *Jean-Jacques Rousseau, the First and Second Discourses* (St. Martin's Press, 1964); by Kurt Weigand, *Jean-Jacques Rousseau, Schriften zur Kulturkritik: Die zwei Diskurse von 1750 u. 1755; eingeleitet, übersetzt und herausgegeben,* 2nd ed. (Meiner, 1971); by Moses Mendelssohn, revised and annotated by Henning Ritter in his edition of *J. J. Rousseau: Schriften,* 2 vols. (Hanser, 1978); by Dietrich Leube *et al.,* in *Jean-Jacques Rousseau, Sozialphilosophische und Politische Schriften* (Winkler, 1981), annotations by Eckhart Koch.

The paragraph numbering respects Rousseau's division of the text; in these notes the various sections of the *Second Discourse* are indicated by the following abbreviations:

Epistle Dedicatory: ED; Preface: P; Exordium: E; Part One: I; Part Two: II; Rousseau's notes: N followed by the number of the note, and the number of the paragraph in that note.

Thus, P[5] refers to paragraph 5 of the preface, and N IX[13] to paragraph 13 of Rousseau's note IX.

Discourse See the editorial note on the title of the *First Discourse,* p. 298.

Origin and Foundations The Academy, as Rousseau reminds the reader on p. 137, had asked about the origin of inequality, and whether it is authorized by the natural law. In his answer, he discusses the origins of inequality—that is to say, how it may have come about; but he chooses to discuss how it may be justified in terms of its "foundations," rather than in terms of "natural law." It however does not follow that he rejects either the possibility that inequality might be "authorized," or that there might be a "natural law."

Jean Jacques Rousseau, Citizen Unlike the *First Discourse,* this *Discourse* gives both the author's name and his political identity. It was by now a very famous name; and at the time this *Discourse* was published, Rousseau had been restored to full citizenship.

What is natural The epigraph is given in Latin: *Non in depravatis, sed in his quae bene secundum naturam se habent, considerandum est quid sit naturale* (Aristotle, *Politics* I: 5, 1254a, 36–38). The reference to "Bk. 2" on the title page appears to have been a typographical error, and was corrected in the 1782 edition. The passage is taken from Aristotle's discussion of natural slavery or, more generally, of natural inequality; it was also cited by Hugo Grotius (1583–1645) in his discussion of the two methods by which to establish natural right: from the nature of man, or *a priori;* and from the view held "by all, or at least the most civilized Nations," or *a posteriori.* Grotius chooses the second method, citing this text of Aristotle's among others in support of his choice (Grotius, *The Right of War and Peace* [1625] I: 1, §xii; all references to that work in the following notes shall be to the 1735 English translation which includes "[a]ll the large Notes of Mr. J. Barbeyrac"); Rousseau, citing the same text, chooses the first method.

TO THE REPUBLIC Rousseau as well as the Genevan authorities were fully aware of how unusual it was to dedicate a book to a city. Rousseau acknowledges as much in the opening sentence of this Epistle Dedicatory, and he wrote a long letter to Perdriau to justify his action (28 November 1754, *CC* III: 55–60, no. 258). The *Petit Conseil,* Geneva's ruling body, formally accepted the dedication in June 1755 (*CC* III: 132–134, nos. 299, 300, 301).

Geneva had been repeatedly torn by civil strife between the party of the Citizens and the ruling Patriciate during the preceding half century. The disturbances of 1737, in particular, left an indelible impression on Rousseau (*Confessions* V, *OC* I: 215f), and one of the intentions of this Epistle Dedicatory was to urge the parties to work for a deeper and more lasting reconciliation.

At the same time, Rousseau's description of the **Fatherland** he would have chosen (ED [2]–[13]) corresponds in all particulars to the conditions for a legitimate and good political order he sets down in *Of the Social Contract.*

MAGNIFICENT, MOST HONORED, AND SOVEREIGN LORDS The proper form of address to the citizen body sitting in Council (see *Letters from the Mountain* II: 7; *OC* III: 813f).

ED [5] one national . . . another foreign Chief *I.e.,* the Papacy.

ED [6] the Tarquins' oppression The Tarquins were overthrown, and the first Roman Republic established in 508 B.C.

ED [15] laws lose their vigor The 1782 edition reads "their rigor."

ED [16] MAGNIFICENT AND MOST HONORED LORDS The Magistrates are not sovereign; Rousseau reserves the title "magistrate" for the officers charged with carrying out the sovereign will (*Social Contract* III: 1).

ED [18] the Citizens and even the mere residents The *Citoyens* or Citizens and the *bourgeois* or burghers, together made up the sovereign *Conseil Général* or General Council; two hundred of its members were chosen to make up the *Grand Conseil* or Greater Council; and of these, twenty-five were in turn chosen for life to make up the *Petit Conseil* or Lesser Council; the *habitants,* or residents, were resident aliens.

P [1] inscription on the Temple at Delphi "Know Thyself," and "Everything within Measure"; Rousseau is manifestly thinking of the first. Samuel Pufendorf (1632–1694), *Le droit de la nature et des gens* (II: 4, §v), cites the inscription, and a few lines later quotes the lines from Perseus with which Rousseau closes this preface. Pufendorf's *Right of Nature and of Nations,* translated into French from the original Latin, and copiously annotated by Jean Barbeyrac, has long been recognized as one of Rousseau's main sources for detailed information about the major political doctrines and texts of his own as well as of former times; all references to that work in the following notes are to the second "revised and considerably enlarged" edition of Barbeyrac's translation, published in Amsterdam in 1712, cited hereafter as *Droit;* all references to Pufendorf's own summary of his major work, *The Duties of Man and Citizen,* will be to the fifth edition of Barbeyrac's translation, *Les devoirs de l'homme et du citoyen* (Amsterdam, 1735), cited hereafter as *Devoirs.* **the statue of Glaucus** The fisherman who became a sea god, traditionally depicted in painting and sculpture encrusted with barnacles and covered with seaweed (see Plato, *Republic* X: 611d).

P [3] Physical causes introduced . . . varieties Rousseau is following Buffon, almost half of whose volume *On the Nature of Man*—from which he had quoted in Note II, at the beginning of the preface—surveys the "varieties" of man by summarizing a large body of ethnological literature. Varieties are characterized, Buffon holds, by differences in color, form, shape, and temperament or *naturel;* they are caused by differences in climate, in diet, and in morals or ways of life, that is to say by the "physical causes" Rousseau mentions; and since these varieties result from the steady impact of such general, external causes, varieties may be expected to undergo changes or to disappear with

time and changing circumstances (*De la nature de l'homme,* Michèle
Duchet, ed. [Maspero, 1971], pp. 223, 270f, 319–321; see also Buffon,
Oeuvres philosophiques, Jean Piveteau, ed. [P.U.F., 1954], p. 313,
cited hereafter as *OP.*

All early editions read: "introduced in some species the varieties";
the 1782 edition reads "in some animals the varieties."

P [4] a state which . . . perhaps never did exist   Namely the state
of men living free of whatever is artificial or conventional, or of what
Rousseau also calls the "moral" in contrast to the "physical" aspects
of life. That state does, indeed, not now exist; it may not ever have
existed; and it is most unlikely ever to exist hereafter. For human life
may always involve some admixture of artifice and convention. However,
the state of nature in the general sense of that expression, the state of
men who are not members of one and the same political society,
certainly does, did, and will continue to exist.

P [5] says Mr. Burlamaqui   Rousseau is here quoting from the
Principes du droit naturel (1747), I: 1, ii, by Jean-Jacques Burlamaqui
(1694–1748), professor of natural and civil law at the Academy of
Geneva. The proposition, that the principles of natural right must be
derived from man's nature, is universally accepted, *e.g.,* Pufendorf,
Droit, II: 3, §xiv, Barbeyrac's n. 1, and Montesquieu, *Spirit of Laws,*
I: 2.

P [6] natural Law   Traditionally, what is right and obligatory, by or
according to man's nature; in other words, moral. In addition, the
expression "natural *law,*" especially in contexts where the expression
"natural *right*" also occurs, implies promulgated rules or laws; in other
words, rules or laws properly so called. The most immediate occasion
for Rousseau's here speaking of natural law, and surveying the major
teachings regarding it, is that he is writing in answer to the Academy's
question, whether inequality is "authorized by the natural law." **the
Roman Jurists** *I.e.,* Ulpian (d. 228 A.D.), *Digests* I: 1, and Justinian
(483–565), *Institutes* I: 2, §i, as reported for example in Grotius,
Right I: 1, §xi; in Pufendorf, *Droit* II: 3, §§iif, with Barbeyrac's notes
and his Preface, p. cxiv; in Richard Cumberland, *De legibus naturae*
(London, 1672), Barbeyrac, trans., *Traité philosophique des loix
naturelles* (1744) V: §2. **The Moderns** *I.e.,* Grotius: "Natural Right
is the Rule and Dictate of Right Reason, shewing the Moral Deformity
or Moral Necessity there is in any Act, according to its Suitableness or
Unsuitableness to a reasonable and Sociable Nature," *Right* I: 1, §x;

note that "and Sociable" is Barbeyrac's addition; see also Pufendorf, *Droit* II: 3, §xiii; and Cumberland, *Loix* IV: §4, among others. **So that ... it is impossible to understand the Law of Nature** It should be noted that Rousseau does not always use "law of nature" interchangeably with "natural law," for the reason which he indicates two paragraphs below.

P [9] prior to reason ... without ... sociability Cf. Grotius's definition of natural right cited in the preceding note. Sometimes "sociability" means no more than fellow-feeling; however tradition also distinguishes different forms or kinds of society—*e.g.,* the family, the household, and political or civil society, to which sometimes is added the whole of mankind. In reading Rousseau or his contemporaries one therefore has to ask oneself in which of its various senses "society," and hence "social," and "sociable," is, in any given case, being used; and in particular whether it is or is not interchangeable with "political" in the sense in which Aristotle, for example, speaks of man as a "political animal," namely, as inclined to and perfected in and by political society. It should be noted that the *Encyclopedia*'s article "Sociability" remarks that the term had only recently come to mean "possessed of the qualities of a good citizen"; and its article "Social" remarks that the term is a neologism. **any being like ourselves** *Nos semblables* would normally be rendered "our fellows" or "fellow-human beings"; but since Rousseau brackets fellow-feeling, especially in Part I of this *Discourse,* it seemed more faithful to his intention to avoid all allusions to it wherever he himself is clearly at pains to avoid them.

P [12] *Learn what the God*

> *Quem te Deus esse*
> *Jussit, et humanâ quâ parte locatus es in re, Disce.*
> —Persius (34–62 A.D.), *Satires* III: 71–73

J. G. Herder chose these lines as the epigraph to his *Ideas for a Philosophy of the History of Mankind* (1784).

E [2] two sorts of inequality "Natural or physical" inequalities are independent of man's beliefs or agreements, whereas "moral or political" inequalities are so by virtue of men's beliefs or agreements; the distinction is drawn by Pufendorf, *Devoirs* I: 7, §ii, and developed by Barbeyrac in Pufendorf, *Droit* III: 2, §ii, n. 3. If "moral or political inequality" is understood as Rousseau understands it in this passage, it follows that the quest for its origin and foundations coincides with the quest for the origin and foundations of rule, and in particular of civil or political society.

E [5] The Philosophers ... state of Nature All the philosophers who have examined the foundations of society, *i.e.,* of political or civil society, have indeed inquired into the condition of men outside of, and especially prior to, political or civil society. But for the most part they did not call that condition "state of nature." The expression was for all intents and purposes introduced by Hobbes: "the state of men without civill society (which state we may properly call the state of nature)" (*On the Citizen,* Preface, *op. cit.,* p. 34). It may thus refer to (1) men in a prepolitical or precivil—and hence uncivilized or "savage"—state. But, at least formally, it also refers to (2) the state of men we would call civilized, living outside their own or even any civil society; to (3) the state of men in political societies that have "dissolved" or been destroyed: *e.g.,* Locke, *Treatises* II: 19, §211; and this *Discourse* II [56]; or, finally, to (4) the state of political societies in their relations with one another: *e.g.,* this *Discourse* II [34]. Even if "state of nature" is primarily used as Rousseau for the most part uses it, to refer to (1) men in the prepolitical state, the expression is not entirely univocal. For Rousseau distinguishes at least three stages in the state of nature so understood. **Some ... ascribe ... the Just and the Unjust** For instance Burlamaqui speaks of men's "moral instinct," "the natural tendency or inclination that leads us to approve some things as good and praiseworthy; and to condemn others as bad and blameworthy; independently of any reflection. Or if one wishes to denominate this instinct 'moral sense' as does one Scottish scholar—Mr. Hutcheson— then I would say that it is a faculty of our soul which in certain cases immediately discerns moral good and evil by a kind of sensation and taste, independently of reasoning and reflection" (*Principes du droit naturel* II: 3, §i); accordingly he also speaks of an innate "sentiment or taste of virtue and of justice which in a sense anticipates reason" (*ibid.* II: 3, §iv). **Others ... Natural Right to keep what belongs to him** For instance, Locke speaks of men being naturally in a state of perfect freedom to "dispose of their possessions . . . as they think fit" (*Treatises* II: 2, §4, *cf.* §6). **Others ... the stronger authority over the weaker** *E.g.,* Hobbes: "in the naturall state of men . . . a sure and irresistible power confers the right of dominion and ruling over those that cannot resist" (*On the Citizen* I: 14); or Spinoza, "the greater devour the lesser by sovereign natural right (*summo naturali jure*)" (*Tractatus Theologico-Politicus,* ch. 16). **the Writings of Moses**

Moses is traditionally held to have written down the first five books of the Bible.

E [6] hypothetical and conditional reasonings . . . comparable to those our Physicists For example, Descartes explaining how "certain considerations"—*i.e.,* the condemnation of Galileo—kept him from publishing his cosmology, remarks that "in order to shade these things somewhat and to be able to say more freely what I thought regarding them without having to follow or to refute the opinions of the learned, I even resolved to leave the whole of this world to their disputes, and to speak only of what would happen in a new world if somewhere, in imaginary spaces, God now created enough matter to compose it, and variously and without order shook the various parts of this matter in such a way as to compose as confused a chaos as the poets might feign, and that afterwards he did nothing but to lend nature his ordinary assistance, and let it act according to the laws he had established." *Discourse on Method* V (Gilson ed.), 41f. See also Buffon's statement cited in the editorial note on p. 350 below. **God himself . . . immediately after the creation** The last four words were added in 1782. **the Lyceum** Where Plato's former student, Aristotle, taught; **Xenocrates** (396–314 B.C.), a disciple of Plato, he eventually became head of Plato's Academy.

I [1] Aristotle thinks . . . claws There is no known source for such a claim; however, in his "Reply" to the naturalist Charles-George Le Roy, Rousseau himself adopts a view reminiscent of the view he here attributes to Aristotle; see p. 238 above. **assume that he was always conformed as I see him** Cf.: "But because I did not yet have enough knowledge of them [*i.e.,* of animals and especially of men], to speak about them in the same manner as about the rest [of the universe], namely by proving effects from causes, and by showing from what seeds and in what manner nature must produce them, I contented myself with assuming that God formed the body of a man exactly similar to one of ours in both the external conformation of its limbs and the internal conformation of its organs. . . ." Descartes, *Discourse on Method* V (Gilson ed.), 45f.

I [3] imitate their industry *Industrie* also means, as "industry" used to, activity, enterprise, industriousness.

I [4] Nature . . . as the Law of Sparta Which ordered that defective children be exposed. On nature's allowing only the fit to survive, see *Origin of Languages* 10 [2] and *Emile, OC* IV: 259f, translated as *Emile or On Education* by Allan Bloom (New York: Basic Books,

1979); see p. 147. On our societies' causing children to be killed before birth, and hence indiscriminately, *cf.* also *Second Discourse* NIX [5].

I [5] gather all his machines In the 1782 edition, this became "gather all these machines."

I [6] Hobbes contends "All men in the State of nature have a desire, and will to hurt" (*On the Citizen* I: 4); "this natural proclivity of men, to hurt each other, which they derive from their Passions, but chiefly from a vain esteeme of themselves" (*ibid.,* I: 12). **An illustrious Philosopher** Man in the state of nature "would at first feel only his weakness; his timidity would be extreme: and if the point required empirical confirmation, savage men have been found in forests; everything makes them tremble, everything makes them flee" (Montesquieu, *Spirit of Laws* I: 2). Richard **Cumberland** (1631–1718), bishop of Peterborough, held that fear would incline men to peace more than to war: *De legibus naturae* (London, 1672), French transl. by Barbeyrac, *Traité philosophique des loix naturelles* (1744), ᵗ: §§32, 33. **Pufendorf** A man abandoned to his own resources and living as Rousseau has so far described original man living would be reduced to "trembling at the least noise, at the first sight of another Animal" (*Droit* II: 1, §viii); "afraid at the least object, and filled with wonder at the sight of even the sun" (*Droit* II: 2, §ii).

I [7] These are undoubtedly The entire paragraph was added in 1782. **François Corréal** (1648–1708), *Voyages de François Corréal aux Indes Occidentales;* Rousseau cites almost word for word from the new, revised, corrected, enlarged edition in two volumes (Paris, 1722), I: 8, vol. I, p. 117.

I [9] If . . . [Nature] destined us to be healthy then, I almost dare assert, the state of reflection is a state against Nature Striking as it is, this famous remark is rather guarded: "if," "almost"; in connection with this remark, also consider "Preface to *Narcissus*" [32], as well as Buffon's remark, "This power of reflection has been denied to animals" (*Histoire naturelle* IV [1753]; see *OP,* Piveteau ed., 332 b 42 and 336 a 21). The wording of the last clause, "the man who meditates [is] a depraved animal," echoes—and the thought challenges—the passage from Aristotle which serves as the epigraph of this *Discourse*. **the opinion of Plato** In the *Republic* III: 405d–408c; *cf.* Homer, *Iliad* XI: 637–642; IV: 215–219. **Podalirius and Machaon** The sons of the "flawless healer" Asclepius, and themselves good healers (*Iliad* II:

731f). **And Celsus reports** Added in 1782; A. Cornelius Celsus (*c.* 30 B.C.–30 A.D.) remarks that dietetics became a third branch of medicine at the time of Hippocrates, *i.e.,* about 300 B.C. (*De medicina,* Pref. 3–5).

I [11] The Horse, ... the Bull ... Domesticated ... bastardizing Buffon, once again, using the same examples, sharply contrasts domestic and wild or savage (*sauvages*) animals in the strongest language: "Man changes the natural state of animals by forcing them to obey him, and making them serve his ends; a domestic animal is a slave with which one amuses oneself, which one uses, abuses, alters, displaces and denatures, while the wild animal, obeying only Nature, knows no other laws than those of need and of freedom" (*Histoire naturelle* IV [1753], *OP,* Piveteau ed., 351a 1–9). Rousseau's very next sentence, **As he becomes sociable and a Slave,** would seem further to echo Buffon's text.

I [12] in cold Countries ... appropriate the skins of the beasts "Unto Adam also and to his wife did the Lord God make coats of skin, and clothed them" (*Genesis* 3:21). Barbeyrac, after quoting this verse, comments, "that is to say, in the style of the Hebrews, that he taught them how to do so"; in Pufendorf, *Droit* II: 2, §ii, n. 5.

I [12]* There may be a few exceptions Note added in 1782. The marsupial described by Corréal and Laët is the opossum. Jan **Laët** (1593–1649), Dutch geographer; his account of the West Indies appeared in Latin in 1633, and in a French translation, *L'histoire du Nouveau Monde ou description des Indes Occidentales* (Leyden, 1640).

I [14] Physical ... Metaphysical and Moral The "metaphysical side" here refers to the traditional differentia of man which Rousseau briefly reviews: reason or understanding, and freedom. The "moral side" refers to man as a moral agent, but also, more generally, to needs, passions or feelings, attitudes, beliefs, and conduct insofar as they take others into account.

I [15] or to disturb it Added in 1782.

I [16] Some Philosophers In particular Montaigne, in "Of the Inequality That Is Between Us," *Essays* I: 42 (*OC* 250, tr. 189). Although he may, for rhetorical effect, raise questions about whether the difference between a given man and another is not greater than that between a given man and a beast, Rousseau rejected the underlying philosophical or scientific premise that there is no clear distinction between man and beast; see the early and important letter to de Conzié, 17 January 1742 (*CC* I: 134, no. 43) and this *Second Discourse,* note X [11].

I [17] *perfectibility* Rousseau coined, or at least gave currency to the term on this occasion. **inhabitant of the Banks of the Orinoco** The practice is reported by Corréal, *op. cit.,* I: 260f; Rousseau refers to it again in *Emile* I, *OC* IV: 254, tr. 43; Buffon also calls attention to it in *De la nature de l'homme,* Duchet ed., p. 299.

I [20] **the Sands and Rocks of Attica . . . the fertile Banks of the Eurotas** Athens and Sparta.

I [21] **the sentiment of its present existence** Rousseau will mention that sentiment twice again in the *Second Discourse:* II [2] and [57]. The expression was not uncommon, and Buffon had distinguished at length between what he called a sentiment of one's existence, which he allowed that beasts have, and a consciousness of one's existence, which he attributed to man alone ("Discourse on the Nature of Animals," *Histoire naturelle* IV [1753], *OP,* Piveteau ed., pp. 328b 48-333a 23, cf. 309b 40f, 322a 44f). However, as Rousseau's third and final mention of the sentiment of one's own existence in the present *Discourse* indicates, he comes to endow that sentiment with far greater significance than had his predecessors; it is also central to his argument— his theodicy, really—in the *Letter to Voltaire* (1756) (*OC* IV: 1063f), and to his last discussion of happiness in the fifth of the *Reveries* (*OC* I: 1045–1047, tr. 68 f). For the contrast between "existing" and "living," see *Emile* (*OC* IV: 489, tr. 211), and *Rêveries* X (*OC* I: 1099, tr. 141); and *cf.* the third of the *Letters to Malesherbes* (*OC* I: 1138).

I [25] **the perplexities regarding the origin of Languages** Rousseau knew that in so far as the "perplexities" which he here canvasses arise from an attempt to account for how a being without speech might acquire—discover, devise, or invent—it, they simply cannot be resolved. Such perplexities do not arise in the *Essay on the Origin of Languages* because in that *Essay* he positions himself inside language, so to speak, and attempts to account for the differences between one language or family of languages and another. Etienne Bonnot, **Abbé de Condillac** (1714–1780), and Rousseau had known each other since 1742, when Rousseau was a tutor in the house of Condillac's brother, M. de Mably. They grew close some years later in Paris; at a much later date, Rousseau entrusted him with a copy of his *Dialogues*. Condillac was a Lockean, but held that Locke had failed to recognize the full extent to which what he calls "signs" (and, in particular, language) are the middle term between sensations and ideas, as well as between ideas. Accordingly he devoted half of his first published work, the *Essay on the Origin of Human Knowledge* (1746) to the origin, the growth, and the analysis of language. The *Essay* enjoyed great success. Condillac went on to write extensively on almost all aspects of philosophy. In his speculations about the origin of language, he assumes two children lost or abandoned in a desert place, at first emitting some "natural signs," and gradually associating conventional meanings with these signs; as they grow up and have children of their own, their stock of conventional signs— gestures as well as sounds—gradually grows (*Essay,* Pt. II: ch. 1, §§1– 7; *cf.* Herodotus, *Histories* II: 2–6). As Rousseau says, Condillac assumes "some sort of society already established among the inventors of language."

I [28] present infinitive   "Present" added in 1782.

I [30] general ideas   "Words become general by being made the signs of general ideas; and ideas become general by separating from them the circumstances of time, and place, and any other ideas, that may determine them to this or that particular existence." John Locke (1632–1704), *An Essay Concerning Human Understanding* (1690), III: 3, §6; "the having of general ideas, is that which puts a perfect distinction betwixt man and brutes," *ibid.,* II: 11, §10; *cf.* III: 11, §16; and regarding the general idea of a triangle, see IV: 7, §9. Rousseau appears also to have been acquainted with Bishop Berkeley's criticism of these views, possibly through the *Dialogues,* which were by this time available in a French translation. **archetype** Locke, *Essay,* see especially II: 30, 31; III: *passim;* IV: 4, §§5, 7, 8. Condillac, in contrast to Locke, restricts the term to standards for human action or conduct (*Essay,* I: 3, §§5, 15; I: 5, §12; II: 2, ch. 2, §26). See also Malebranche, *Recherche de la vérité (Search after Truth),* 2, 3, 6.

I [33] we are repeatedly told that nothing would have been as miserable as man   Literally: Pufendorf, *Droit* II: 1, §8; *Devoirs* II: 5, §2; Burlamaqui, *Droit naturel* I: iv, §4; but also, of course, the most famous such remark, "And the life of man solitary, poore, nasty, brutish, and short" (Hobbes, *Leviathan,* ch. 13); *cf. On the Citizen* I: 13; also Spinoza, *Theologico–Political Treatise,* ch. V (near the middle).

I [35] Hobbes very clearly saw the defect of all modern definitions

of Natural right Namely that they define it in terms of man's being rational and sociable—in the sense of political. **his own definition** "the Dictate of right reason,' conversant about those things which are either to be done, or omitted for the constant preservation of Life, and members as much as in us lyes"; where, however, "'[b]y Right Reason in the naturall state of men, I understand not, as many doe, an infallible faculty, but the act of reasoning, that is, the peculiar and true ratiocination of every man concerning those actions of his which may either redound to the dammage, or benefit of his neighbours" (*On the Citizen* II: 1). **A wicked man is, he says** "Unlesse you give Children all they aske for, they are peevish, and cry, aye and strike their Parents sometimes, and all this they have from nature, yet are they free from guilt, neither may we properly call them wicked; first, because they cannot hurt; next, because wanting the free use of reason they are exempted from all duty; these when they come to riper yeares, having acquired power whereby they may doe hurt, if they shall continue to doe the same things, then truly they both begin to be, and are properly accounted wicked; In so much as a wicked man is almost the same thing with a childe growne strong and sturdy, or a man of a childish disposition; and malice the same with a defect of reason in that age, when nature ought to be better governed through good education and experience. Unlesse therefore we will say that men are naturally evill, because they receive not their education and use of reason from nature, we must needs acknowledge that men may derive desire, feare, anger, and other passions from nature, and yet not impute the evill effects of those unto nature. The foundation therefore which I have laid standing firme, I demonstrate in the first place, that the state of men without civill society (which state we may properly call the state of nature) is nothing else but a mere warre of all against all; and in that warre all men have equal right unto all things; Next, that all men as soone as they arrive to understanding of this hateful condition, do desire (even nature it selfe compelling them) to be freed from this misery. But that this cannot be done except by compact, they all quit that right they have to all things" (*On the Citizen,* The Preface to the Reader, pp. 33f; see also I: 10, 11, 12). Rousseau criticizes this passage from the "Preface" again in *Emile* I, *OC* IV: 288, tr. 67. **so much more** *Tantò plus in illis proficit vitiorum ignoratio, quàm in his cognitio virtutis.* Justin (2nd century A.D.) is speaking about the Scythians' ignorance of virtue and the Greeks' knowledge of it (*Histories* II: 2, 15); also quoted by Grotius, *Right of War and Peace* II: 2, §ii (i), n. 6; and by Pufendorf, *Droit* II: 3, §vii, n. 5. **the author of the** *Fable of the Bees*

Bernard de Mandeville (1670–1733); in the context of a discussion of charity in *The Fable of the Bees: or; Private Vices, Publick Benefits* (1714), he writes: "This virtue is often counterfeited by a passion of ours called pity or compassion, which consists in a fellow-feeling and condolence for the misfortunes and calamities of others: all mankind are more or less affected with it; but the weakest minds generally the most. It is raised in us when the sufferings and misery of other creatures make so forcible an impression upon us, as to make us uneasy. . . . Should any one of us be lock'd up in a groundroom, where, in a yard joining to it there was a thriving good humour'd child at play, of two or three years old, so near us, that through the grates of the window we could almost touch it with our hand; and if, whilst we took delight in the harmless diversion, and imperfect prittle-prattle of the innocent babe, a nasty over-grown sow should come in upon the child, set it a screaming, and frighten it out of its wits; it is natural to think that this would make us uneasy, and that with crying out, and making all the menacing noise we could, we should endeavour to drive the sow away. But if this should happen to be an half-starved creature, that, mad with hunger, went roaming about in quest of food, and we should behold the ravenous brute, in spite of our cries, and all the threatening gestures we could think of, and actually lay hold of the helpless infant, destroy and devour it; to see her widely open her destructive jaws, and the poor lamb beat down with greedy haste; to look on the defenceless posture of tender limbs, first trampled on, then tore asunder; to see the filthy snout digging in the yet living intrails, suck up the soaking blood, and now and then to hear the crackling of the bones, and the cruel animal with savage pleasure, grunt over the horrid banquet; to hear and see all this, what tortures would it give the soul beyond expression! Let me see the most shining virtue the moralists have to boast of, so manifest either to the person possessed of it, or those who behold his actions; let me see courage, or the love of one's country, so apparent without any mixture, clear'd and distinct from all other passions. There would be no need of virtue or self-denial to be mov'd to such a scene; and not only a man of humanity, of good morals and commiseration, but likewise an highwayman, an house-breaker, or a murderer, could feel anxieties on such an occasion; how calamitous soever a man's circumstances might be, he would forget his misfortunes for the time, and the most troublesome passion would give way to pity, and not one of the species has a heart so obdurate or engaged, that it would not ake at such a fight, as no language has an epithet to fit it." "An Essay on Charity and Charity-Schools" (3rd and 4th paragraphs), F. B. Kaye ed. (Oxford, 1924), I: 254–256.

I [36] like blood-thirsty Sulla . . . *tender-hearted* This was added in 1782. Lucius Cornelius **Sulla** (139–78 B.C.), Roman general who became a notoriously cruel tyrant (Plutarch, *Sulla* 30:4). **Alexander of Pherae,** as told in Montaigne, "Cowardice, Mother of Cruelty" (*Essays* II: 27; *OC* 671, tr. 523f), drawn from Plutarch (*Pelopidas,* 29:9–11). Rousseau makes the same point with the same examples in the *Letter to d'Alembert* (Fuchs ed., p. 32, Allan Bloom translation [Glencoe, Ill.: Free Press, 1960], pp. 24f), which is quoted in the editorial note to *Essay on the Origin of Languages* 1 [9]*, p. 363 below. ***When nature gave man tears . . .***

> *Molissima corda*
> *Humano generi dare se Natura fatetur*
> *Quae lacrymas dedit.*
> —Juvenal, *Satires* XV: 131–133

I [37] Even if . . . commiseration . . . puts us in the place of him who suffers "Pity is often a sentiment of our own ills in the ills of another," La Rochefoucauld, *Maxims* (1678 ed.), no. 264; see also Aristotle, *Rhetoric* II: 8, 1385b 13–19; Hobbes, *On Man* XII: 10, and *Leviathan* VI; cf. also *Essay on the Origin of Languages* 9 [2].

I [42] the moral and the Physical in . . . love The distinction is drawn by Buffon, who sets all the agreeable aspects of love on the physical and animal side, all its evils on the moral side ("Discourse on the Nature of Animals," *Histoire naturelle* IV [1753], *OP,* Piveteau ed., 341a51–b44); but the distinction is also suggested by Barbeyrac in Pufendorf, *Droit* I: 2, §vi, n. 10 and context, as well as in his discussion of Xenophon's *Education of Cyrus* V (*i.p.*) in Pufendorf, *Droit* I: 4, §vii, n. 5. Regarding the "moral" side of love, also see *Emile* IV, *OC* IV: 493f, tr. 214; and, especially, the whole of the *Nouvelle Héloïse*. **the sex that should obey** According to *Genesis* 3:16. In a striking early fragment, Rousseau wrote: "Let us begin by considering women deprived of their freedom by the tyranny of men, and men the masters of everything . . . everything in their hands, they seized it by I know not what natural right which I could never quite understand, and which may well have no other foundation than main force" (*OC* II: 1254). **a taste which he could not have acquired** In 1782 this reads "a distaste which he could not have acquired."

I [51] have remained in his primitive condition In 1782, this reads "primitive constitution."

II [5] must naturally have engendered In 1782, this reads "must naturally engender."

II [10] various Savage Nations still have today In 1782, this reads "Savage Nations have today." **I cover multitudes** In 1782, a new paragraph opens here.

II [11] a first revolution *Cf.* Lucretius V: 1011–1017; on **families** and fixed **dwellings**, *cf.* Montesquieu, *Spirit of Laws* XIII: 13; on the beginning of this new period or stage, see also *Origin of Languages* 9 [36].

II [14] speech is imperceptibly established In 1782, this reads "speech was imperceptibly established." **Great floods . . . Revolutions of the Globe** *Cf. Origin of Languages* 9 [27], [31], [32], and *Fragments politiques, OC* III: 533; Lucretius V: 380–415; in his *Histoire et théorie de la terre* (1749), Buffon speaks of the especially frequent early revolutions the earth must have undergone (*OP*, Piveteau ed., pp. 49–55).

II [17] Locke ". . . *no injury . . . no property*" What Locke had said is: "Where there is no property, there is no injustice, is a proposition as certain as any demonstration in Euclid" (*Essay* IV: 3, §18); De Coste's French translation reads "Where there is no property, there can be no injustice"; which Barbeyrac quotes and discusses in his preface to Pufendorf, *Droit,* (p. xx). By substituting "injury" for "injustice," Rousseau substitutes the more for the less comprehensive term; "[the brute beasts] cannot distinguish between *injury* and *harme;* Thence it happens that as long as it is well with them, they blame not their fellowes: But those men are of most trouble to the Republique, who have most leasure to be idle; for they use not to contend for publique places before they have gotten the victory over hunger, and cold." Hobbes, *On the Citizen* V, v; see *ibid.* I, x note; similarly, Pufendorf refers to all voluntary hurt as "injury or wrong" [*injure ou tort*], *Droit* I: 7, §§xiii–xvii, and see *ibid.* II: 3, §iii, esp. note 10; on harm and injury, see also this *Discourse* I [39].

II [18] the true youth of the World Lucretius speaks of the "youth of the world" to describe the first state of the world and of man (*On the Nature of Things* V: 780, 818, 943, *cf.* 330); Rousseau borrows the expression, but thinks it correctly describes a later state in the history of man and the world.

II [20] For the Poet it is gold and silver Ovid's fourth age—Rousseau's third stage in the state of nature—introduces gold as well as iron, together with *amor sceleratus habendi,* "evil concupiscence" (*Metamorphoses* I: 127–150); *cf.* Locke, *Treatises* II: 8, §111; Rousseau's account of this stage culminates with another Ovidian indictment of gold (II [29]). **both [metallurgy and agriculture] were unknown to the Savages of America** So, too, Locke, *Essay* IV: 12, §11.

II [24] to render to each his own A traditional formula for justice: Ulpian, *Digest* I: 1; Justinian, *Institutes* I: 1; it may be traced to Simonides (556–468 B.C.) (Plato, *Republic* I: 331e; see also *Republic* IV: 433e–434a). **nascent property . . . manual labor** The remark echoes and fully agrees with Locke: "The *Labour* of his Body and the *work* of his Hands, we may say, are properly his. Whatsoever then he removes out of the State that Nature hath provided, and left it in, he hath mixed his *Labour* with, and joined to it something that is his own, and thereby makes it his *Property*" (*Treatises* II: 5, §27); on the origin of property, see also *Emile* II, *OC* IV: 330–333, tr. 98f. **the Ancients, says Grotius** In *Right* II: 2, §2(5), quoting Servius's (fl. *c.* 400 A.D.) commentary on Vergil (*Aeneid* IV: 58). Pufendorf quotes the same text, *Droit* IV: 4, §xiii. **Ceres** The Romans' goddess of the fruits of the earth.

II [27] instills in all men In 1782, this reads "instill."

II [29] *Shocked by the novelty* . . .

> *Attonitus novitate mali, divesque miserque*
> *Effugere optat opes, et quae modò voverat, odit.*
> —Ovid, *Metamorphoses* XI: 127f

The poet Rousseau had cited to introduce this stage is now cited to mark its climax with his description of King Midas's condition when he was granted his wish to have everything he touches turn to gold. The passage is also quoted by Montaigne, "Apology of Raymond Sebond" (*Essays* II: 12, *OC* 560, tr. 434).

II [33] in a few great Cosmopolitan Souls In the copy of the *Discourse* which Rousseau gave his English friend and host Richard Davenport, and which is now in the Morgan Library, New York, he by hand changed the remainder of this sentence to read: "worthy of crossing the imaginary barriers that separate Peoples, and embracing the whole of mankind in their benevolence on the model of the supreme being that created it."

II [35] **I know . . . other origins to Political Societies . . . conquests by the more powerful** Possibly Hobbes, *On the Citizen* VIII: 1, or Barbeyrac in Pufendorf, *Droit* VII: 1, §vii, note 1. **or the union of the weak** *E.g.,* Glaucon in Plato, *Republic* II: 358e–359a, or d'Alembert, "Preliminary Discourse of the *Encyclopedia*."

II [36] **begin by purging the threshing floor** *Cf. Luke* 3:17. **as Lycurgus did in Sparta** "The second law that Lycurgus made, and the boldest and hardest he ever took in hand, was the making of a new division of their lands. For he saw so great a disorder and unequality among the inhabitants, as well of the country, as of the city Lacedaemon, by reason some (and the greatest number of them) were so poor, that they had not a handful of ground, and other some being least in number were very rich, that had all: he thought with himself to banish out of the city all insolency, envy, covetousness, and deliciousness, and also all riches and poverty, which he took the greatest, and the most continual plagues of a city, or common-weal." Plutarch, *Lives,* "Lycurgus," 8, North trans.; see also *Social Contract* II: 8, and III: 10, n. 1.

II [37] **protect their goods, their freedoms and their lives** The remark echoes Locke's assertion that men unite "for the mutual *Preservation* of their Lives, Liberties, and Estates" (*Treatises* II: 9, §123, and 15, §171). *If we have a Prince* Pliny the Younger (61–c. 113), *Panegyric of Trajan* LV: 7.

II [38] **Politicians . . . Philosophers** The 1782 edition reads "Our Politicians . . . our Philosophers"; "Politicians" here translates *politiques,* which can also mean "political thinker." **Brasidas to a Satrap** Rousseau attributes to the Spartan general Brasidas (d. 422 B.C.) the answer which Herodotus (*Histories* VII: 133–136) attributes to the Spartans Sperchias and Bulis when the Persian Satrap Hydarnes asked them why they did not choose to become subjects of the King of Persia (Starobinski).

II [39] *they call . . . servitude peace* *Miserrimam servitutem pacem appellant;* Rousseau took this very slightly paraphrased citation from Tacitus's *Histories* (IV: 17) from Algernon Sidney's (1622–1683) *Discourses Concerning Government* (II: §15) (Starobinski).

II [40] **Paternal authority . . . absolute Government** *E.g.,* Sir

Robert Filmer (1588–1653), *Patriarcha* (1640, publ. 1680); Jacques Bénigne, Bishop Bossuet (1627–1704), *Politique tirée des propres paroles de l'Ecriture Sainte* (1709) II: 1, prop. 3. **Locke's or Sidney's proofs** Locke's *First Treatise of Government* (1680/1681, publ. 1689/1690), and Algernon Sidney's *Discourses Concerning Government* (1683, publ. 1698) are both detailed criticisms of Filmer. On paternal and political authority, see also *Political Economy, OC* III: 241–244, tr. [2]–[7]; *Social Contract* I: 2. **Despotism** In Rousseau's technical vocabulary, the despot usurps the sovereign power and places himself above the laws, whereas the tyrant usurps the royal or ruling authority and exercises it according to the laws; see *Social Contract* III: 10.

II [41] examine the facts in terms of Right In contrast to holding that whatever is or happens to be the case, is right or just, as Rousseau charges Aristotle and Grotius with doing in respect to slavery (*Social Contract* I: 2); as Locke remarks in the context of a discussion of the same problems which Rousseau is here considering, "an Argument from what has been, to what should of right be, has no great force . . ." (*Treatises* II: 8, §103); consider, also, the epigraph to this *Discourse;* and the argument of the "Letter to Philopolis," pp. 231–237 above. **a famous Text published in 1667** Namely *Traité des droits de la Reine très chrétienne sur divers états de la monarchie d'Espagne;* the passage was cited without reference by A. Sidney, *Discourses Concerning Government* II: 30 (Laslett ed., p. 235). The fact is noted and the reference identified by Barbeyrac in Pufendorf, *Droit* VII: 6, §x, n 1. As a number of previous editors have noted, in context the passage has a very different effect: Rousseau's citation ends with the remark that Princes are subject to the law; the text goes on, in the very next sentence, to say that they are also its authors. **I shall ignore . . . of which one is not master.** This sentence was added in 1782. Jean Baptiste **Barbeyrac** (1674–1744), so frequently mentioned in these notes, the French translator and learned annotator of Grotius, Pufendorf, and Cumberland, was a strong partisan of Locke's political teaching. Rousseau is here quoting his comment in Pufendorf, *Droit* VII: 8, §vi, n. 2, based on Locke, *Treatises* II: 4, §23, and/or II: 15, §172.

II [42] Pufendorf says In his chapter "On the Origin and Foundations of Sovereignty": "For as one transfers one's goods to another by conventions and contracts, so one can, by a voluntary submission, yield to someone who accepts the renunciation, one's right to dispose of one's freedom and natural forces. Thus a man who commits himself to be my slave, genuinely confers on me the Authority to be his Master; and it is crass ignorance to object to this, as some do, the common— and, in other respects, true—maxim, that *one cannot relinquish what one does not have*" (*Droit* VII: 3, §i). **And the Jurists who have gravely pronounced** Both Grotius (*Right* II: 5, §xxix) and Pufendorf (*Droit* VI: 3, §ix; and *Devoirs* II: 4, §vi) allow that the child of a slave may be born a slave, although they do so with some qualifications.

II [44] Without at present entering into The "common opinion" which Rousseau here briefly summarizes is the so-called double-contract doctrine. By the first contract or convention, independent individuals agree, each with all the rest, to combine wills and strengths or forces to form a permanent union for the sake of their common security and welfare, and issue an ordinance regarding the form of the government. This much provides "the beginnings and rudiments of a State." By the second contract or convention, this beginning state or people and those it has chosen or accepted to govern it, mutually obligate themselves to fulfill their respective responsibilities toward one another. As Pufendorf points out, this second contract is scarcely evident in democracies, where the same persons are at different times or in different respects both sovereign and subject. The primary focus of this doctrine is the second contract, which was seen as a way of placing restrictions on a Hobbesian sovereign (Pufendorf, *Droit* VII: 2, §§vii–xix, *Devoirs* II, 6 §§vii–ix, adopted by Burlamaqui, *Droit politique* I: 1, 4, §15, and also by Diderot in his *Encyclopedia* article "*Autorité politique*," *Oeuvres complètes* [J. Assezat ed.] XIII: 392–400). In the immediately following two paragraphs of the *Discourse*, II [45] and [46], Rousseau indicates that the double contract does not succeed in solving the problem it sets out to solve: it does not provide for a common superior capable of insuring or enforcing the parties' adherence to the contract. In other words, "the common opinion" is untenable. He explicitly and fully spells out his criticism of the double contract in the *Social Contract;* see III: 16; I: 7; III: 1.

II [48] Gerontes ... Senate ... *Seigneur* The root of all three is "elder"; the Spartan Gerontes were the city's supreme legislative council, as the Senate was in Rome. In the present context, *Seigneur* is best translated "Sir"; see also *Social Contract* III: 5. **equals of the Gods and Kings of Kings** As, respectively, the Roman Emperors and the Kings of Persia were called.

II [49] the progress of inequality As in the state of nature, so in the civil state; Rousseau distinguishes three stages, separated by "revolutions."

II [52] even without the Government's intervention Added in 1782.

II [53] *If you order me*

> *Pectore si fratris gladium juguloque parentis*
> *Condere me jubeas, gravidaeque in viscera partu*
> *Conjugis, invitâ peragam tamen omnia dextrâ.*
> —Lucan (39–65), *Pharsalia* I: 376–378

As quoted and very slightly paraphrased by Sidney, *Discourses* II: 19; see context.

II [55] where honesty offers no hope *Cui ex honesto nulla est spes,* in Tacitus, *Annals* V: 3 (Meier); again, as very slightly paraphrased by Sidney, *Discourses* II: 20.

II [57] Diogenes did not find a man Diogenes the Cynic (fl. 370 B.C.) went about by day with a lantern, explaining, "I am looking for a man" (Diogenes Laertius, *Lives* VI: 41). **the Stoic's ataraxia,** i.e. imperturbability, or repose of soul or mind, more originally and typically the aim of the Epicurean and of the Pyrrhonist wise man (Diogenes Laertius, *Lives* X: 136; IX: 107); on Pyrrhonist ataraxia see also Montaigne, "Apology of Raymond Sebond" (*Essays* II: 12, *OC* 562, tr. 435f).

II [58] that a child command Montaigne puts these words in the mouth of his "Cannibals": "They said that in the first place they thought it very strange that so many grown men, bearded, armed, and strong, who were around the king . . . should submit to obey a child, and that one of them was not chosen to command instead. Second (they have a way in their language of speaking of men as halves of one another) they had noticed that there were among us men full and gorged with all sorts of good things, and that their other halves were beggars at their doors, emaciated with hunger and poverty; and they thought it strange that these needy halves could endure such an injustice, and did not take the others by the throat, or set fire to their houses." "Of Cannibals," *Essays* I: 31, *OC* 212f, tr. 159.

N I Herodotus relates In *Histories* III: 83; the restriction placed on this privilege was that Otanes and his descendants not transgress the laws of the realm; Otanes, too, suffered from a genital disorder (Herodotus III: 149).

N II [2] *de la Nat[ure] de l'homme* Buffon's *Of the Nature of Man* (1749), *OP,* Piveteau ed., p. 293a, Duchet ed., p. 39. Georges-Louis Leclerc (1707–1788), who early assumed the name Buffon, began publishing his monumental and influential *Natural History* in 1749. The first volume dealt with *The History and Theory of the Earth.* It was immediately censured by the ecclesiastical authorities as "containing principles and maxims not in conformity with those of Religion" (Piveteau ed., pp. 106f). Buffon thereupon issued a public statement, the first article of which reads: "I declare that (1) I had no intention of contradicting the text of Scripture, and I very firmly believe what is related regarding Creation, both with respect to the order of time and to the factual circumstances; and that I renounce everything in my book that pertains to the formation of the earth, and in general everything that might be contrary to the narration of Moses, as I presented my hypothesis about the formation of the planets only as a pure philosophical suggestion" (*ibid.,* p. 108).

Rousseau's note II quotes the opening paragraph of the third volume of Buffon's *Natural History, Of the Nature of Man,* a work which in many particulars influenced this *Discourse.* However, Buffon did not agree with all of Rousseau's arguments and conclusions: the "Observations" forwarded to Rousseau in Le Roy's name (p. 238 above), were presumably Buffon's own; and in subsequent volumes of the *Natural History,* especially in his discussion of the "Nomenclature of Monkeys" (vol. xiv, 1765), he challenges features of Rousseau's account of the "pure" state of nature.

N III [1] the Child found in 1344 The episode is reported by Barbeyrac in Pufendorf, *Droit* II: 2, §ii, n. 1, where he also tells of another feral child found in 1661. **the Child found in 1694** The episode is, as Rousseau says, reported by Condillac, *Essay* I: IV, ch. II, §23; Rousseau quotes from that report in N. X [7]. **The little Savage of Hanover** Known as "Peter"; about whom see James Burnett, Lord Montboddo, *Ancient Metaphysics* (London, 1784), III: Bk. II, ch. 1; and Joh. Fr. Blumenbach, *The Anthropological Treatises* (London: Th. Bendyshe tr., 1865), pp. 329–340. **in 1719 two more . . . in the Pyrenees** It is not clear to which cases Rousseau is here referring; see, however, regarding them, F. Tinland, *L'homme sauvage* (Paris, 1968), pp. 65f; Tinland also very fully and illuminatingly reviews the known cases of feral children as well as the issues of comparative anatomy which Rousseau raises, especially in the Notes to this *Discourse*. In connection with Rousseau's argument in this Note, it might be pointed out that Linnaeus had classified man as a quadruped; Rousseau, instead, accepts the traditional view that the upright posture is natural to man: see, for example, Socrates in Xenophon, *Memorabilia* I: 4, ix; and in Plato, *Cratylus,* 399 b–c; and Aristotle in *History of Animals* I: 15, 494a 27–35; *Parts of Animals* IV: 10, 686a 26–35.

N IV [1] the following passage   Again taken from Buffon: "Preuves de la théorie de la Terre," art. VII, in *Histoire naturelle* (1749), I: 242f.

N IV [2] Arabia Petraea   The northwestern section of the Arabian peninsula, and extending beyond it to include Sinai.

N V Dicaearchus   (fl. 300 B.C.), disciple of Aristotle's. **St. Jerome** (348–420), the Church Father best remembered for his Latin or Vulgate translation of the Bible; the passage from his *Against Jovianus* II: §13, which Rousseau here cites, is quoted by Barbeyrac in his edition of Grotius's *Right* II: 2, §ii, n. 13; Rousseau however omits Dicaearchus's equation of the age of Saturn with the golden age. The sentence immediately following the quote, **This opinion . . .** , was added in the 1782 edition. The reference is to **François Corréal,** *Voyage aux Indes Occidentales* I: 2. **the Lucayes** are the Bahamas.

N VI [3] "The Hottentots," says Kolben   In the digest of his book in the *Histoire des Voyages* (1746–1781), a twenty-volume collection of travelers' reports, begun under the editorship of the Abbé Prévost; P. Kolben's *Description du Cap de Bonne Espérance* (3 volumes, Amsterdam, 1741; German original, 1719) is summarized in volume V; Rousseau is quoting somewhat freely from chapter 3, pp. 155f.

N VI [6] Father du Tertre   The Dominican Jean-Baptiste du Tertre (1610–1687), *Histoire générale des Isles de Saint Christophe* (Paris, 1654), Pt. V, ch. 1, §4.

N VI [7] In the year 1746, an Indian   The episode is, as Rousseau remarks, reported in Jacques Gautier d'Agoty's (1710–1785) periodical *Observations sur l'histoire naturelle, la physique et la peinture,* published in Paris between 1752 and 1758 (I: 262). The 1782 edition of the *Discourse* has the Indian's proposal addressed to the Government instead of to the Governor.

N VII "The Life-span of Horses," says M. de Buffon   In *Histoire*

Naturelle (1753), IV: 226f; this volume also contains the important article "Donkey," in which Buffon sets forth his influential definition of "species": "a constant succession of individuals that are similar [*semblables*] and reproduce" (Piveteau ed., 756a 52–54).

N IX [1] A famous Author Probably Pierre Louis Moreau de Maupertuis (1698–1759), *Essai de philosophie morale* (Berlin, 1749), ch. 2. In this important Note Rousseau traces some of the connections between the First and Second *Discourses;* he discusses many of the issues which he here raises at greater length in his *Letter to Voltaire* of 1756, occasioned by Voltaire's poem about the Lisbon earthquake (*OC* IV: 1059–1075).

N IX [2] not a single commercial house ... dishonest debtor "Dishonest" added in 1782. **London fire** In 1666, which is said to have destroyed as much as four-fifths of the city; Mandeville makes much the same point, using the London fire and other instances which Rousseau also adduces in this indictment of society ("A Search into the Nature of Society," Kaye ed., I: 359). **Montaigne blames** "One Man's Profit Is Another's Harm," in *Essays* I: 22, *OC* 105, tr. 76f. **Demades** Atheneian orator, executed in 319 B.C.

N IX [4] poisonous Utensils Rousseau shared the widely held view that copper pots are noxious; see his letter to Raynal, published in the *Mercure de France,* July 1753, pp. 5–13 (*CC* II: 221–227, no. 200).

N IX [6] But are there not This paragraph and the first sentence of the next paragraph were added in 1782.

N IX [8] Realgar Arsenic monosulfide, a poisonous red-orange pigment used to enhance the color of gold and gilding; see Rousseau's *Institutions chymiques,* in *Annales de la société Jean-Jacques Rousseau* (1918/ 19) 12: 1–164; (1920/21) 13: 1–178, see 166–170.

N IX [14] What, then? Must Societies be destroyed Rousseau added this concluding paragraph while the book was in page proof (letter to his publisher Rey, 23 February 1755, *CC* III: 103, no. 279). **a precept indifferent in itself** In all likelihood refers to the precept or warning not to eat of the tree of knowledge of good and evil (*Genesis* 2:17, 3:5, 3:22, 23). Rousseau discusses that precept and the failure to heed it—in other words the Fall—in an important note of the *Lettre à M. de Beaumont,* Archbishop of Paris, which he wrote in response to that prelate's condemnation of *Emile.* "To demur against a useless and arbitrary prohibition is a natural inclination, but which, far from being in itself vicious, conforms to the order of things and to man's good constitution; since he would be unable to attend to his preservation if he had not a very lively love for himself and for the conservation of all his rights and privileges, as he received them from nature. He who could do anything would wish nothing but what would be useful to him; but a feeble Being, whose power is further limited and restrained by law, loses a part of himself, and in his heart he reclaims what he is being deprived of. To impute this to him as a crime, is to impute to him as a crime that he is what he is and not some other being; it would be to wish at one and the same time that he be and not be. For this reason, the command infringed by Adam appears to me to have been not so much a true prohibition as a paternal advice; a warning to abstain from a pernicious and deadly fruit. Surely this idea conforms better to the idea one should have regarding God's goodness, and even to the text of *Genesis*, than do the ideas which Divines are pleased to prescribe to us; for with regard to the threat of the twofold death, it has been shown that the expression *morte morieris* has not the emphatic meaning which they attach to it, and is only an hebraism that is [also] used elsewhere [in Scripture], where such an emphasis would have no place" (*OC* IV: 939f, n). The Vulgate's *morte morieris,* King James's "thou shalt surely die" (*Genesis* 2:17 and 3:4), attempts to render faithfully the Hebrew cognate accusative "dying you will die"; for the same construction, see for example, *Genesis* 1:11, *Joel* 2:22; on these texts, see Robert Sacks, "The Lion and the Ass," *Interpretation* (1980), 8: 54. **they will love their kind** *Ils aimeront leurs semblables,* brings to mind, especially in the present context, the biblical precept to love one's neighbor, *Leviticus* 19:18 (cf. *Mark* 12:28–34, *Luke* 10:25–28, *Matthew* 22:34–40); but also recalls the reference at the beginning of this long and difficult sentence to the "men like myself," or "men of my kind," the *hommes semblables à moi.*

N X [1] Nations of men of gigantic size   Traditionally, the Patagonians, about whom see Note X [11]; about giants, see also *Origin of Languages* 3 [3] and Editorial Note. **Pygmies** Homer, *Iliad* III: 6; Aristotle, *History of Animals* VIII: 12, 597a 6–10; Edward Tyson, *Orang-outang, Sive Homo Sylvestris, or the anatomie of the Pygmie compared with that of a monkey, an ape, and a man; to which is added a Philological Essay concerning the Cynocephali, the satyrs and sphinges of the ancients, wherein it will appear that they are all, either apes or monkeys, and not men as formerly pretended* (London, 1699). In spite of his title, Tyson evidently studied a chimpanzee (see Franck Tinland, *L'Homme sauvage, op. cit.,* pp. 104–119). **Laplanders . . . Greenlanders . . . Peoples with tails** Buffon, *De l'homme,* ed *cit.,* pp. 223–226, 242–244. **Ctesias** (fl. *c.* 400 B.C.) Physician at the court of King Artaxerxes II of Persia, he wrote a work on Persia and another on India, only fragments of which survive.

N X [2] the Kingdom of the Congo The present Zaire. **the translator of the Hist[oire] des Voyages** Samuel Purchas (1577–1626) in *Purchas, His Pilgrimage; or Relations of the World and the Religion observed in all ages* (London, 1613 and 1625). *Orangoutangs* are, of course, not found in Africa, but only in Borneo and Sumatra. Andrew **Battel** An English merchant (*c.* 1565–1645) whose adventure-filled accounts of Brazil and Angola Purchas recorded. **Mayomba** Mountain in central Congo or Zaire. **Kingdom of Loango** North of the mouth of the Congo River. *Pongos* Gorillas. *Enjokos* As Purchas remarks at the end of the next paragraph, Battel did not describe these "monsters."

N X [4] Olfert **Dapper** Dutch physician and geographer (d. 1690), whose *Description de l'Afrique* Purchas summarized. **Prince Frederick-Henry of Orange** (1684–1747) If, as it appears, the animal sent to him is the same as that described by Nicholas Tulp, it in all likelihood was a chimpanzee (see Tinland, *op. cit.,* pp. 103f). Jerome **Merolla** (*c.* 1650–*c.* 1710), whose account of the Congo, where he spent ten years as a Franciscan missionary, appeared in 1692.

N X [5] These . . . Anthropomorphic animals . . . in the third volume Rousseau evidently erred; the descriptions are found in volume IV of the *Histoire des Voyages* (Starobinski). *Beggos* and *Mandrills* Respectively, the natives' and the Europeans' name for what here probably is either a chimpanzee or a gorilla. **monsters . . . yet . . . reproduce** In the vocabulary of the time, "monster" still commonly refers to an animal or plant that cannot reproduce; see Rousseau's *Letters on Botany* VII, *OC* IV: 1188; *cf.* Lucretius V, 845–848. **Pongos . . . fire** *Cf. Origin of Languages* 9 [29*]. Throughout Rousseau's discussion in this and subsequent notes, it must be kept in mind that any twentieth-century reader will have seen and read about more varieties of monkeys and apes than had the most intrepid and learned scholars of Rousseau's time. However, Rousseau and all his contemporaries knew (see N X [4]) that "orang-outang" means "man of the woods" in Malay, and hence in Latin *homo sylvestris;* which is what, for example, Lucretius called the first men (V: 967, 970); thus the name alone tended to prejudge the question at issue, especially for all those who had never so much as seen a single great ape; and the learned and careful Tyson thought he had dissected an orang when he had spent his labors on a chimpanzee.

N X [6] that they are neither beasts nor gods, but men Added in 1782.

N X [7] What would have been . . . Child found in 1694 Mentioned in Rousseau's N III [1]. **gave no sign . . . Cradle** is a direct quote from Condillac, *Essay,* Pt. 1, sec. IV, ch. II, §23. Immediately after **If, unfortunately for him,** Rousseau inserted by hand "or fortunately" in the copy of the *Discourse* which he presented to Davenport.

N X [9] the Platos, the Thales, and the Pythagorases All three philosophers traveled extensively.

N X [11] Charles Marie de **La Condamine** (1701–1774) participated in an expedition to the equator in 1736 and published an absorbing *Relation abrègée du voyage fait à l'intérieur de l'Amérique méridionale* (Paris, 1745), reprinted as *Voyage sur l'Amazone,* H. Minguet ed. (Paris: Maspero, 1981). This book clearly influenced Rousseau in many particulars, but especially in its discussion of the growth of language: "All the *South-American* languages with which I had any acquaintance, are extremely poor; some are energetic and can be elegant, but all lack terms to express abstract and universal ideas; a clear proof of the little progress made by these people. *Time, duration, space, being, substance, matter, body;* all these and many other words are without equivalent in their languages: not only the names of metaphysical beings, but those of moral beings can be rendered among them only imperfectly and only with the help of elaborate circumlocutions. There is no proper term corresponding to the terms *virtue, justice, freedom, gratitude, ingratitude*" (pp. 53f; reprint, pp. 62f). In the *Emile,* Rousseau quotes La Condamine's report (*op. cit.,* pp. 56f; reprint, p. 68f) about a people that could count only up to three, although, as Rousseau adds, they had of course seen the five fingers on their hand (*OC* IV: 572n, tr. 271n). Pierre Louis Moreau de **Maupertuis** (1698–1759) led a scientific expedition to Lapland and reported on that journey in his *Relation d'un voyage au fond de la Laponie.* Jean **Chardin** (1643–1713), who journeyed through Persia as far as India between 1671 and 1681, afterwards settled in London, was created baronet by Charles II, and became the British chargé d'affaires and agent of the East Indias Company in Holland; he published a widely read *Travels in Persia and the East Indies* (1686). Engelbert **Kaempfer** (1651–1716), German physician who spent some years in the Far East, from whose papers a posthumous *History of Japan and Siam* was compiled (London 1728; French translation, expanded, Amsterdam, 1729). Charles Pinot **Duclos** (1704–1772), member of the French Academy, whose commentary on the *Port Royal Grammar* at least in part inspired the *Essay on the Origin of Languages,* was to prove one of Rousseau's steadiest friends; Rousseau dedicated his opera *The Village Soothsayer* to him. **Malabar** Province of southwestern India, now part of Kerala. **Pegu** Formerly a kingdom, and now a province north of Rangoon. **Ava** City, southwest of Mandalay, which for four hundred years was the capital of what is now Burma. **Tucumán** Province of northern Argentina.

N XII [1] Locke's Civil Government Or *Second Treatise of Government,* ch. 7, "Of Civil or Political Society," §§79, 80. We have translated the text Rousseau published; it departs only slightly from the French version which he used:

where the original reads	Rousseau writes
to feed on grass	*to graze the grass*
is de facto commonly with child	*is commonly with child*
the wisdom of the great creator	*the wisdom of the creator*

All other divergences between Locke's original and Rousseau's version are due to the published French translation available to Rousseau; a number of them are noteworthy, and the reader may wish to compare the text published here with Locke's text.

N XII [5] the Horse ... the Stag, or all other Quadrupeds In 1782, this reads "Quadruped animals." **live exclusively off grass** In 1782, this reads "off grasses."

N XIII "Nor would the happiness ..." *Nec quidquam felicitati humani generis decederet, si, pulsâ tot linguarum peste et confusione, unam artem callerent mortales, et signis, motibus, gestibusque licitum foret quidvis explicare. Nunc vero ita comparatum est, ut animalium quae vulgò bruta creduntur, melior longè quam nostra hâc in parte videatur conditio, ut pote quae promptiùs et forsan feliciùs, sensus et cogitationes suas sine interprete significent, quàm ulli queant mortales, preasertim si peregrino utantur sermone.* Is[aac] Vossius [1618–1689], *de Poëma[tum] Cant[u] et Viribus Rythmi* (Oxford, 1673), pp. 65f; where Rousseau wrote *motibus,* "movements,"

Vossius had written *nutibus,* "clues."

N XIV Plato, showing In the *Republic* VII: 522d. **Palamedes** was one of the Greek leaders in the Trojan War; in the *Essay on . . . Languages* 5[11], Rousseau refers to the tradition that credits him with also having added some letters to the alphabet. In connection with the issue raised in N XIV, see also the passages from La Condamine cited on p. 355 above.

N XV [1] *Amour propre* **and** *amour de soi-même* Rousseau here for the first time, and succinctly, formulates the contrast between the two forms of love of self that is so basic to his entire moral psychology. He develops and illustrates it in all of his subsequent writings, even when he does not explicitly refer to either passion by name. Partly for that reason, it is difficult to single out specific passages for special notice; still, see, among others: *Emile* IV, *OC* IV: 494 and context, and 547f, tr. 214f, 252f; *Dialogues, OC* I: 669f, 789f, 805–807; *Political Economy, OC* III: 255, 259ff, Sherover tr. [30], [36]; *Corsica, OC* III: 937f; and this *Discourse,* II [52].

N XVI [3] the Greenlanders The story is told by Isaac de La Peyrère, *Relation du Groenland,* Paris, 1647 (Starobinski), pp. 169–184.

N XVI [4] "All the efforts of the Dutch Missionaries . . ." The story is told by Peter Kolbe, and may, as Rousseau indicates, be found in the *Histoire des voyages.*

N XVIII Marshal de V*** Louis-Hector, Duke of Villars (1653–1734), Marshal of France (Starobinski).

N XIX Distributive justice Distributes, as Rousseau indicates, honors and rewards in proportion to contributions to the polity: Aristotle's classic statement of the issues (*Nicomachean Ethics* V. 2.1130b 30–33, V. 3.1131a 23–28; and *Politics* III: 13) is reported by Pufendorf (*Droit* I: 7, §12 and *Devoirs* I: 2, §14); Pufendorf further discusses distributive justice at length in *Droit* (I: 7, §§9–13), and in the course of that discussion (I: 7, §11, n. 4) he quotes the passage from **Isocrates** (*Aeropagetica* 21f), which Rousseau also quotes in this note. Regarding the role of Roman **Censors,** *cf. Social Contract* IV: 7. **rigorous right,** or right strictly and narrowly so called, is right or justice that may appropriately be legislated and enforced, in contrast to what virtue and equity might require: this distinction between distributive justice and rigorous right is introduced by Grotius, *Right,* Proleg. viii–x and I: 1, v–viii, followed by Hobbes, *On the Citizen* III: 6 and XIV: 6, f; see also Pufendorf, *Droit* I: 2, §8; Burlamaqui, *Droit naturel* I: 11, §11; and Rousseau's *Letter to d'Alembert* (Fuchs ed., p. 89, Bloom tr. p. 66).

The issue briefly raised in this note, the relation between morals and law, is central to both *Discourses,* but also to the *Essay on the Origin of Languages,* and indeed to the whole of Rousseau's moral and political thought.

LETTER TO PHILOPOLIS, pages 231–237

This letter replies to the main points raised in a quite thoughtful criticism of the *Discourse on Inequality* published in the October 1755 issue of the *Mercure de France* over the signature "Philopolis," or Patriot. The pseudonym had been chosen for the occasion by Charles Bonnet (1720–1793), a well-known naturalist, scion of a patrician Geneva family, and himself for many years a member of his city's ruling council, the Two Hundred. Bonnet disapproved of Rousseau's views from the first, and he eventually played an active part in having the *Social Contract* and the *Emile* condemned by Geneva. He at that time also urged his fellow-scientist Albrecht von Haller, of Berne, to get that city to expel Rousseau after he had taken refuge in its territory. Rousseau later described Bonnet as a man who, "though a materialist, is of a most intolerant orthodoxy wherever I am concerned" (*Confessions* XII, *OC* I: 632).

Rousseau clearly thought of this "Letter" as an authoritative statement of his views. Although he did not publish it, he did make a clean copy of it, and a letter of Bonnet's in 1763 indicates that he had learned of the existence and of the tone, if not of the contents, of Rousseau's reply to him.

The "Letter to Philopolis" has most recently been edited by Vaughan, in *The Political Writings of Jean-Jacques Rousseau* I: 221–227; by Starobinski in Rousseau, *Oeuvres complètes* (Pléiade ed.) III: 230–236; by Launay in Rousseau, *Oeuvres complètes* (Intégrale ed.) II: 272–275; by Leigh in Rousseau, *CC* III: 185–193, no. 328; and by H. Meier, *Diskurs/Discours,* 450–477. The last four also reprint Bonnet's letter.

[10] the Leibnizian ... Philosophy Bonnet had read Gottfried Wilhelm Leibniz's (1646–1716) *Theodicy* (1710) some years earlier, and in his *Mémoires autobiographiques* he tells of the lasting impression it had made on him.

[11] According to Leibniz Who argued that this is the best of all

possible worlds—*e.g., Theodicy* §§195, 416. **and to Pope** Alexander
Pope (1688–1744), who held "Whatever is, is right" (*Essay on Man,*
Epistle I, line 294).

[12] Algonquins   Indian nation of northeastern America. **Chickasaws**
Indians of the Muskhogean tribe in Louisiana.

[14] the monkey ... the Orang-outang   See *Second Discourse,*
note X, especially the first half of that long note.

[15] very powerful reasons for not choosing that kind of life   See
especially the replies to criticisms of the *First Discourse,* and *Second
Discourse* N IX [14].

[16] *to be saints*   Rousseau had, of course, written *sains* or "healthy,"
and not *saints* or "saintly," and Bonnet had clearly understood him
correctly. It is to be hoped that Rousseau would not have let stand this
gratuitous remark if he had revised the text for publication; the passage
in question occurs in *Second Discourse* I [9], p. 145 above.

[18] *never known pain ... pity*   Cf. *Emile, OC* IV: 313f, 504–506,
tr. 87, 221–223, and especially *Origin of Languages* 9 [2]–[4].

[19] *the Populace, to which M. Rousseau attributes*   Cf. *Second
Discourse* I [37], p. 162 above. **Seide murder his Father** In Voltaire's
tragedy *Fanaticism, or Mohammed the Prophet.* **Thyestes drink his
son's blood** Thyestes caused his brother Atreus to kill his own son; in
revenge Atreus killed Thyestes's sons and, at a banquet, placed their
flesh before their father.

[20] I had said so   In the *Second Discourse* I [25].

REPLY TO LE ROY, page 238

Rousseau jotted down this reply at the bottom of the pages of a note
by Charles-Georges Le Roy (1723–1789), Master of the King's Hunt,
and the author of several entries in the *Encyclopedia.* Le Roy's note
had been forwarded to him by Condillac who, in a covering letter,
indicated that Buffon agreed with these objections if, indeed, he was
not their author (*CC* IV: 98f, 7 September 1756, no. 434). The
objections are aimed at Rousseau's suggestion that man may not by
nature be carnivorous.

Le Roy's first comment is that if men originally roamed without
settled abode and if, as in Note V Rousseau speculates, they originally

lived entirely off vegetation, then they would have starved half the year.

He goes on to take issue with the argument in note VIII, that carnivorous species typically have larger litters than do species that live off vegetation, and that this is as it must be because carnivores need less time than do herbivores to provide for themselves and for their young. Yet, so his critic points out, some herbivorous species, for example rabbits and hares, also have large litters. He accordingly concludes: "It is always assumed that everything in nature is well ordered. Make sure of your facts, and perhaps you will find that it is not the case that everything is well ordered."

Finally, he maintains that Locke, in the passage from the *Second Treatise* which Rousseau quotes in note XII, is right when he asserts that the male and female wolf stay together until the young no longer need their help, and he concludes that these aspects of behavior appear not to be directly correlated with whether a species is carnivorous or not. As Vaughan remarks, "On this Rousseau makes no comment."

These criticisms and Rousseau's replies to them were first published by Vaughan, under the title "Reply to a Naturalist," *op. cit.,* I: appendix 1, pp. 512f. R. Leigh identified the writer of the criticisms, and he includes a full critical edition of the relevant texts in *CC* IV: appendix A 172, pp. 423-425; as does H. Meier, *Diskurs/Discours,* pp. 450-477.

Rousseau's reply has also been edited by Starobinski, in Rousseau, *Oeuvres complètes* (Pléiade ed.) III: 237; and by Launay, in Rousseau, *Oeuvres complètes* (Intégrale ed.) II: 275.

ESSAY ON THE ORIGIN OF LANGUAGES, pages 239-295

The *Essay on the Origin of Languages* remained unpublished during Rousseau's lifetime, although he had at one time planned to bring it out in a volume that was also to contain a short essay, *On Theatrical Imitation,* which for the most part summarizes and paraphrases Plato's discussions of imitation in the *Republic* and the *Laws,* and a prose poem, *The Levite of Ephraim,* inspired by the story told at the end of the book of *Judges.* In a surviving draft of the preface for this proposed volume, Rousseau says that what became the present *Essay* had initially been "but a fragment of the *Discourse* on inequality," which he decided to omit from the final version of the *Discourse* because it "was too long and out of place." He was at least in part prompted to expand and recast it by Rameau's attacks on the articles on musical subjects which he had written for the *Encyclopedia,* and he may well have reworked the text on several occasions. It is certainly one of his most carefully wrought writings.

Scholars have been divided over whether what he says about pity in this *Essay* and what he had said about it in the *Second Discourse* indicates a change in his views, or whether, as seems more natural and convincing, these differences are best understood in the light of differences in perspective and intention between the two works. In any event, the central problem which he explores throughout the *Essay,* as he had throughout the *Discourses,* is the problem of the relations between what he frequently refers to as the *physical* and the *moral,* or nature and art or convention.

The *Essay* is scheduled for inclusion in the as yet unpublished volume V of the Pléiade *Oeuvres complètes.* The current standard edition of the text is Jean-Jacques Rousseau, *Essai sur l'origine des langues, où il est parlé de la mélodie et de l'imitation musicale,* édition, introduction et notes de Charles Porset (Ducros, 1970). This excellent edition will certainly remain indispensable. I have also consulted Antonio Verri's Italian translation in his *Origine delle lingue e civiltà in Rousseau* (Longo, 1970), pp. 150–274, and the German translation in E. Koch *et al., Rousseau, Sozialphilosophische und Politische Schriften* (Winkler, 1981), pp. 162–221.

The numerals preceding the following notes indicate the chapter, and the bracketed numerals the paragraph in which the passage under consideration may be found.

1 [2] **As soon as one man . . . instinct suggested**   Parallels Condillac, *Essay on the Origin of Human Knowledge,* Pt. II, sect. 1, ch. 1, §2. **men dispersed** See this *Essay,* 9 [1]*, p. 260 above.

1 [3] **Love . . . inventor of drawing . . . invented speech**   Pliny the Elder (23–79 A.D.), in *Natural History* XXXV: 43, 12, mentions the tradition that drawing was "invented" by a girl tracing the outline of her lover's face (Porset); in 9 [35] below, Rousseau traces much of the early development of language to love.

1 [5] **the art of pantomime**   Or of conveying attitudes, feelings, and passions by means of gestures and movements alone; hence an enacted picture, pure spectacle. See Rousseau's article "Pantomime" in his *Dictionnaire de musique; cf.* Condillac, *Essay,* Pt. II, sect. 1, ch. 1, §11. **grammars** The prevailing view of grammar is well conveyed in the opening sentences of the so-called *Port Royal Grammar:* "Grammar

is the Art of speaking. To speak is to explain one's thoughts by means
of signs which men invented to that end. The most convenient such
signs have been found to be sounds and words [*voix*]. But because
sounds are transient, other signs were invented to make them lasting
and visible, and these are the written characters which the Greek call
grammata, from which came the word *Grammar*": *Grammaire générale
et raisonnée* (*General and Rational Grammar*) by Antoine Arnauld
and Claude Lancelot, first edition 1660, third revised and expanded
edition 1676, reissued by R. E. Breckle (Frommann, 1966), p. 5;
Rousseau worked with the 1754 edition, which included the Commentary by his friend Charles Pinot Duclos. **the symbols of the Egyptians**
Egyptian hieroglyphs are "allegorical figures" (see this *Essay,* 5[2]).
The Rosetta stone, with writing in Greek and in Egyptian hieroglyphs,
was found in 1799, and by the time of his early death, J. F. Champollion
(1790–1832) had laid the foundation for deciphering the hieroglyphs.

1 [6] Consult ancient history   Sextus, son of Lucius Tarquin, surnamed
"Superbus," tyrant of Rome (530–510 B.C.), sent to his father for
advice on how to subdue the Gabii. **Tarquin** walked through a field
with the messenger, lopping off the heads of the flowers that stood out
above the others, and so conveyed to his son that he should decimate
the first families (Livy, *Histories* I: 54; Ovid, *Fasti* II: 701–710). Much
the same story is told of **Thrasybulus,** tyrant of Miletus, who, when
he was asked by Periander (625–585 B.C.), tyrant of Corinth, how best,
most beautifully, and most safely to rule, took Periander's messenger
for a walk in a field and, while they talked of others things, lopped off
the tallest and best grown, the most beautiful ears of corn (Herodotus,
Histories V: 92; Aristotle reverses the roles of the two tyrants, *Politics*
III: 13. 1284a 25–32, *cf.* V: 11. 1313a 38–41; see also Shakespeare,
King Richard II, III: iv. 33–36). **Alexander** the Great (356–323),
reading his mother's latest plea that he curb his largess toward friends
and associates, realized that his friend Hephaestion happened also to
have read her letter. Alexander put his seal ring over his friend's lips
to indicate that he was not to tell anyone that his mother thought his
generosity excessive (Plutarch, *Life of Alexander,* 39). **Diogenes** the
Cynic (fl. 360 B.C.) upon hearing someone deny the reality of motion,
got up and walked away (Diogenes Laertius, *Lives* VI: 39). **Zeno** (fl.
450 B.C.), the Eleatic philosopher, challenged the common-sense belief
in the reality of motion; his best-known paradox is that fleet-footed
Achilles cannot overtake a turtle that has a headstart on him (Aristotle,
Physics VI: 9, 239b 14). When **Darius** (c. 558–485), king of Persia,
invaded the land of the Scythians in 512, a Scythian messenger brought

him the gifts which Rousseau mentions. Darius took them as a sign that
the Scythians were ready to surrender; his adviser Gobrias took them
to say: Unless you Persians fly away like birds, or burrow underground
like mice, or jump into the water like frogs, you will never get home,
but will be shot here by our arrows. Darius accepted Gobrias's interpretation and, as Rousseau says, hastened to leave Scythia for home
(Herodotus, *Histories* IV, 131f). Rousseau makes the same point, citing
the same examples in *Emile* (Bk. IV, *OC* 647 f, tr. 332 f).

1 [7] **Levite of Ephraim**   *Judges* 19, 20; Rousseau wrote a prose
poem recounting this episode, which he had intended to publish
together with this *Essay on the Origin of Languages*. **King Saul**
I Samuel 11:7; the story in many particulars parallels that of the Levite
of Ephraim. **Phryne acquitted** "Hyperides, while defending Phrynê
. . . caused her to be brought where all could see her; tearing off her
undervests he laid bare her bosom and broke into such piteous
lamentation . . . that he caused the judges to feel superstitious fear of
this handmaid and ministrant of Aphrodite. . . ." Athenaeus (*c.* 230
A.D.), *The Deipnosophists* XIII: 590e (Ch. B. Gulick, tr.).

1 [8] **Horace's judgment**   *Ut pictura poesis,* "as is painting, so is
poetry" (*Art of Poetry,* l. 361).

1 [9]* **I have said elsewhere**   "I hear it said that tragedy leads to
pity through fear; so be it; but what is this pity? A fleeting and vain
emotion that lasts no longer than the illusion which produced it; a
vestige of natural sentiment soon stifled by the passions; a sterile pity
which feeds on a few tears and which has never produced the slightest
act of humanity. Thus the sanguinary Sulla cried at the account of evils
he had not himself committed. Thus the tyrant of Pherae hid at the
theatre for fear of being seen to moan with Andromache and Priam
while he heard without emotion the cries of so many unfortunates slain
daily by his orders. Tacitus reports that Valerius Asiaticus, falsely
accused by the order of Messalina, who wanted him to perish, defended
himself before the Emperor in a way that touched this prince very
deeply and drew tears from Messalina herself. She went into the next
room to regain her composure after having, in the midst of her tears,
whispered a warning to Vitellius not to let the accused escape. I never
see one of those weeping ladies in the boxes at the theatre, so proud
of their tears, without thinking of the tears of Messalina for poor
Valerius Asiaticus." *Lettre à M. d'Alembert sur les spectacles* (Fuchs
ed., p. 32; Bloom tr. [slightly altered], pp. 24f; see also *Second
Discourse* I, [36]).

1 [10] Mr. Pereyre Giacobbo Rodriguez Pereira's (1715–1780) dramatic success in teaching the deaf to sign, but also to speak and to read and write, was widely admired; Buffon speaks of it at the end of his discussion of hearing in *Of Man* (*De l'homme,* 1754, Duchet ed., pp. 201f).

1 [11] Chardin says In *Voyages,* partially reprinted as *De Paris à Ispahan,* Yerasimos ed. (Paris: Maspero, 1953), vol. 2, p. 208.

1 [13] Animals have a structure more than adequate So, too, Locke, *Essay,* Bk. 2, ch. 11, §11; Descartes, *Discourse on Method* V (penultimate paragraph), and Letter to Morus, 5 February 1649 (antepenultimate paragraph); and *cf. Second Discourse,* N X [5]. **They say that it can be explained** For example, the materialist Julien Offroy de la Mettrie (1709–1751) in his *L'homme machine* (*Man a Machine,* 1748); A. Vartanian ed. (Princeton University Press, 1960), pp. 160f (Porset).

2 [1] utterings [*voix*] *Voix* of course means "voice"; but it is difficult to find a single idiomatic English equivalent for Rousseau's use of the term; here, and frequently throughout the *Essay, voix* means "voiced sound," "utterance," "vocalization," or even "phonation"; he however does not here explicitly draw the distinction he draws in *Emile* between (1) the speaking or articulate voice, (2) the singing or melodic voice, and (3) the passionate or accented voice (*OC* IV: 404f, tr. 148f). Number (1) corresponds to the traditional meaning of "voice" as "the voiced letters," or the vowels (see, *e.g., Port Royal Grammar* I: 1), and to its traditional meaning as "word": thus the Latin *vox* is sometimes interchangeable with *verbum* (*e.g.,* Quintilian, *Institutes* I: 5, §1), and Montaigne writes, "*Il y a le nom et la chose: le nom c'est une voix qui remarque et signifie la chose*" ("Of Glory," *Essays* II: 16, *OC* 601, tr. 468), where *voix* means "word" or "name," but also suggests "mere breath," as it does in the parallel passage in Shakespeare: "What is that honor? air" (Falstaff, in *King Henry IV* [Part I], V: 1, ll. 143f). Regarding (2), the singing or melodic voice, see *Dictionnaire de musique,* "Voix." And (3) the passionate or accented voice is most fully discussed in the present *Essay.* See also p. 253 above.

2 [2] It is claimed that men invented speech in order to express their needs For example, by Condillac, *Essay,* Pt. II, sect. 1, ch. 1, §1, and ch. 10, §103. Rousseau spells out his criticism of this view more fully in *Second Discourse* I [25].

3 [1] ... Tropes. Figurative language Rousseau here uses "trope," "figure," and "figurative language" interchangeably, to refer, as he goes on to explain, to transpositions of the "literal," "proper," or "true" meaning of a word or expression, as, for example, when we speak of the arm of a chair.

3 [3] *Giants* See *Genesis* 6:4; *Numbers* 13:32, 33; *Deuteronomy* 2: 20, 21; *I Samuel* 17:4; the references to men of gigantic size and to the Patagonians "true or false," *Second Discourse,* N X [1] and [11]; the references to the Cyclopes, *Essay* 9 [7]; Hesiod, *Theogony,* 185 (and context); and *cf.* Vico, *New Science,* §§121, 243, 338.

4 [1] Father Lamy Bernard Lamy (1640–1715), *La Rhétorique, ou l'art de parler;* Rousseau had studied Fr. Lamy's scientific and mathematical works as a young man (*Confessions* VI, *OC* I: 232, 238). **meter or quantity** "In music as well as in prosody this term refers not to the number of notes or of syllables, but to their relative duration. Quantity produces rhythm, just as accent produces intonations: from rhythm and intonation result melody" (*Dictionary of Music,* "Quantity").

4 [3] many synonyms *cf. Second Discourse* I [29] and [31]. **persuade without convincing** In the sense in which to persuade is to move to action, and to convince is to prove or demonstrate. Persuasion is properly the province of rhetoric, while proof is that of philosophy and science (*e.g.,* Aristotle, *Rhetoric* I: 2, 1355b, 26f); *cf.* this *Essay* 19 [2]: "In cultivating the art of convincing [men], the art of moving [them] was lost." **Plato's *Cratylus*** In which Socrates, at times playfully, explores the question of whether names are natural or conventional.

5 [3] a twofold convention One regarding the relation between words or sentences and their objects: this animal is called "dog"; and another regarding the relation between words or sentences and their written representations: "dog" is written d-o-g.

5 [5] savage ... barbarian ... and ... civilized peoples The same distinction as in the *Second Discourse* II [20]; it is enlarged upon in this *Essay* 9 [19]. Rousseau planned to organize a "History of Morals" in terms of it (*Fragments politiques, OC* III: 560, §24); it is based on Montesquieu's distinction between "savages" as small, scattered nations, and "barbarians" as small, united nations; savage and barbarian peoples live by *moeurs* or morals, customs, and traditions, whereas civilized peoples, *i.e.,* peoples in civil societies, live by laws (*Of the Spirit of Laws* XVIII: 11).

5 [7] Tchelminar   or Chihil-Minar, the ancient name of Persepolis. **Chardin** *Voyages du Chevalier Chardin en Perse et Autres Lieux de l'Orient* (Amsterdam, 1735, enlarged ed.), II: 167f. The cuneiform writing Chardin here describes was not fully deciphered until 1846. The **Parsees** Chardin mentions in the second note to this paragraph are the descendants of the ancient Persians who, even after the Muslim conquest of the 7th century, continued to adhere to the Zoroastrian religion: they eat no meat (*Emile* II, *OC* IV: 411n, tr. 153n).

5 [9] Cadmus   For the story that Cadmus and the Phoenicians who came with him introduced the alphabet as well as much other knowledge to the Greeks, see Herodotus, *Histories* V: 58; Pliny, *Natural History* VII: 192.

5 [10]** See Pausanias, *Arcad*[*ia*]   Rousseau's reference is in error; Pausanias speaks of this form of writing in his section on Eleia (*Travels* VIII: 17, vi). **Marius Victorinus** (fl. 350 A.D.), celebrated Roman grammarian and rhetorician, and teacher of St. Jerome. Rousseau's reference is to his *ars grammatica,* Bk. I (Heinrich Keil, ed., *Grammatici Latini,* 7 vols. [Leipzig: Teubner, 1855–1880], VI [1874]: 55f). The Latin *versus* translates the Greek *boustrophedon;* Rousseau proposed to have this way of writing reintroduced in music (see his "Letter to Dr. Burney," October 1777, #2 and #3; see *CC* XL: 148–150).

5 [11] Palamedes   One of the Greek leaders in the Trojan War; **Simonides** (556–468 B.C.), Greek lyric poet and philosopher or sophist; the tradition of their contributions to the Greek alphabet is reported by Pliny the Elder (*Natural Histories* VII: 56, 192); by Isidore of Seville (*c.* 570–636 A.D.) (*Origins* I: 3, 9); by Marius Victorinus (*de arte grammatica,* in *Grammatici Latini* [Keil ed.] VI: 194). **lustra** or lusters, the five-year periods separating the purification of the entire Roman people after each census.

5 [12] the Gentlemen of Port Royal   Antoine Arnauld and Claude Lancelot, the authors of the *General and Rational Grammar,* commonly known as the *Port Royal Grammar.* Duclos's discussion and list of the vowels is found in Pt. I, ch. 1 of his Commentary to that *Grammar.*

5 [12]* Greek records   *Vocales quas Graece septem, Romulus sex, usus posterior quinque commemorat* y *valut Graeca rejecta.* **Mart[ianus] Capel[la]** (fl. early 5th century); Rousseau here quotes from his *De Nuptiis Philologiae et Mercurii* (Porset), a work edited by the young Hugo Grotius.

6 [1] Bellerophon Proitos wanted to see Bellerophon dead; however "[h]e shrank from killing him, since his heart was awed by such action . . . but sent him away to Lykia, and handed him murderous symbols which he inscribed in a folded tablet, enough to destroy his life, and told him to show it to his wife's father, that he might perish" (Homer, *Iliad* VI: 167–170, Lattimore tr.). **Father** Jean **Hardouin** (1646–1729), a learned Jesuit, among whose "paradoxes" were the claims that most ancient Greek and Roman texts were medieval forgeries, and that the New Testament had originally been written in Latin. Torquato **Tasso** (1544–1595), author of the heroic epic *Jerusalem Delivered.* Rousseau translated portions of the poem, and he quotes from it in a discussion of lying (*Reveries* IV, *OC* I: 1038, tr. 56).

6 [2] compiled . . . rather late By Peisistratos in the second half of the 6th century B.C.

7 Prosody From the Greek word for "accent", prosody is the study of the elements and structures involved in the rhythmic aspects of speech and is traditionally a branch of grammar (see *Dictionary of Music,* "Accent").

7 [1]* Some scholars claim Porset points out that this note is specifically directed against the views of du Marsais, first set forth in his *Encyclopedia* article "Accent." **from Cicero's . . . *On the Orator*** *Hanc diligentiam subsequitur modus etiam et forma verborum, quod iam vereor ne huic Catulo videatur esse puerile. Versus enim veteres illi in hac saluta oratione propemodum, hoc est numeros quosdam nobis esse adhibendos putaverunt; interspirationes enim, non defatigationes nostrae neque librariorum notis, sed verborum et sententiarum modo interpunctas clausulas in orationibus esse voluerunt; idque princeps Isocrates instituisse fertur, ut inconditam antiquorum dicendi consuetudinem delectationis atque aurium causa, quem ad modum scribit discipulus eius Naucrates, numeris adstringeret. Namque haec duo musici, qui erant quondam idem poëtae, machinati ad voluptatem sunt, versum atque cantum, ut et verborum numero et vocum modo delectatione vincerent aurium satietatem. Haec igitur duo, vocis dico moderationem et verborum conclusionem, quoad orationis severitas pati posset, a poëtica ad eloquentiam traducenda duxerunt* (III: xliv, 173f). **from Isidore's Origins** *Praeterea quaedam sententiarum notae apud celeberrimos* *auctores fuerunt, quasque antiqui ad distinctionem scripturarum carminibus et historiis apposuerunt. Nota est figura propria in litterae modum posita ad demonstrandum unamquamque verbis sententiarumque ac versuum rationem. Notae autem versibus apponuntur numero XXVI quae sunt nominibus infra scriptis, etc.* (Isidore, *Etymologiarum sive originum* [Oxford, 1911; W. M. Lindsay ed.], ch. XXI, 1).

7 [2] *à* **[to] used as an article**   Presumably in the dative of the article, as in *à la; à le* and *à les* by contraction yield *au* and *aux*.

7 [2]** Buonmattei   Benedetto Buonmattei (1581–1647), Italian grammarian.

7 [8] The ancient Hebrews   The problems of biblical interpretation which this raises are discussed by Spinoza in *Theologico-Political Treatise,* ch. 7 (in the middle).

9 [6] Everyone, it is said, considered himself to be master   *Cf.* Hobbes, *On the Citizen* I: 10, 11; Spinoza, *Theologico-Political Treatise,* ch. 16 (beginning) and n. 26; *cf.* also *Second Discourse* I [35].

9 [7] the Cyclops   The race of giant shepherds with one eye in the middle of their foreheads—hence their name—whose leader Polyphemus kept Odysseus and his companions prisoners in his cave by blocking its entrance with a huge boulder. He had devoured some of the men when Odysseus blinded him and, by a ruse, succeeded in escaping together with his surviving companions (Homer, *Odyssey* IX: 112–115); on the primitive existence of the Cyclopes, see Plato, *Laws* III: 680 a–c; Aristotle, *Politics* I: 2, 1252b, 17ff, and *Nicomachean Ethics* X: 9, 1180a 25–32; Strabo, *Geography* XIII: 1, 24f. On the life of Odysseus and his companions among the Cyclopes as the image of life under despotic rule, see *Of the Social Contract* I: 4 [3]; and Locke, *Treatises* II: 19, §228.

9 [8] Cain was a tiller   *Genesis* 4:3. **Noah planted a vineyard** *Genesis* 9:20. **Cain became a fugitive** *Genesis* 4:12. **the wandering life of Noah's descendants** *Genesis* 10, 11. **the Scythians in their wagons** Herodotus, *Histories* IV: 46.

9 [9] lived solely off acorns   Which Pelasgos taught them to eat (see Pausanias, *Travels* VIII, "Arkadia," I: vi); later Triptolemos taught agriculture to King Arkos—for whom the Pelasgians were now named Arkadians (*ibid.* IV: i; *cf.* Plato, *Laws* III: 782b) on the introduction of agriculture, see the *Second Discourse* II [20]–[23].

9 [10] Abraham served a calf *Genesis* 18:7. **Eumaeus** served Ulysses piglets, not kids (Homer, *Odyssey* XIV: 72–80). **Rebecca did the same** or, more precisely, she instructed her youngest son, Jacob, to do so after overhearing her husband, Isaac, promise their older son, Esau, to bless him if he brought him some meat (*Genesis* 27:9).

9 [11] first cake . . . the communion of mankind This striking remark refers to the transition from nomadic to settled life described in *Second Discourse* II [22]; its biblical echoes—*Genesis* 18:6, cf. *Genesis* 19:3—amplify the reference to the Abraham story in the preceding paragraph. **Passover** *Exodus* 12:39, 13:3–10; *Deuteronomy* 16:8.

9 [12] Job's wealth . . . the Sabeans carried them off *Job* 1:3, 14, 15.

9 [13] Scripture lists ten generations Ten generations separate Noah's children and Abraham (*Genesis* 10:1, 11:10–29).

9 [14] Adam spoke *Genesis* 2:19–20, 3:10, 3:12. **Noah spoke** *Genesis* 9:25–27. **the common language perished** *Genesis* 11:1, 11:6. **even if there had never been a tower of Babel** As, indeed, the biblical account suggests (*Genesis* 10:5, 10:20, 10:31–32).

9 [15] born of the earth The earth-born giants, in Hesiod (*Theogony* 185); Pelasgos, in Pausanias (*Travels* VIII: 1.4); Deucalion's earth-born generation, in Ovid (*Metamorphoses* I, 384–413); Cadmus's (*ibid.* III, 106–115); see also Plato (*Republic* III: 414d–e, cf. *Menexenus* 237d–238a) and Isocrates (*Panegyricus* 24); Lucretius (V: 821–823, 1402, 1411); consider also Hobbes, *On the Citizen* VIII: 1, and this *Essay* 9 [22]: "assume men issuing from the hands of nature," and 9 [36]: "were men born of the earth before that time?"

9 [18] the ark and the tabernacle of Moses *Exodus* 26:14, *Numbers* 4:25. **Moses . . . appears to have disapproved of agriculture** Moses is traditionally said to have written down the first five books of the Bible. **God reject his offerings** *Genesis* 4:2–7.

9 [20] the earliest morals "Earliest" here translates *premier(s)*, which has elsewhere consistently been translated "first," as in "first ages" or "first men"; in the present context *moeurs*, which has been translated "morals" throughout, is best understood as "ways of life."

9 [22] **Assume perpetual spring** As, Pufendorf says, did the pagan poets, not knowing of the earthly paradise (*Droit* II: 2, §2); indeed, he borrowed the expression "perpetual spring" from Ovid's description of it (*Metamorphoses* I: 107).

9 [23] **He who willed . . . inclined the globe's axis** Which makes for the cycle of the seasons. Rousseau's reflections on the subject are developed further in an important fragment, *OC* III: 529–533.

9 [25] **Chaldea** The province of southern Babylonia situated between the lower Euphrates, the head of the Persian Gulf, and the Arabian Desert. **Phoenicia** The mountainous strip along the eastern shore of the Mediterranean Sea; the Phoenicians were great travelers and traders.

9 [26] **It is said to be natural** By Montesquieu, *Of the Spirit of Laws* XVIII: 3; Rousseau's discussion of the influence of terrain on modes of life takes up many of the points, examples, and even expressions in this book *Of the Spirit of Laws*. **Magna Graecia** The Greek mainland cities together with their far-flung colonies. **the Attic people . . . called themselves Autochthonous** For example, Isocrates, in *Panegyricus* 24; the Athenians alone withstood the invasions by the Doric tribes from the North. **the factory of mankind** In light of the end of the preceding paragraph, probably Switzerland.

9 [27] **The traditions about natural disasters** *E.g.*, *Genesis* 7:10–8:14; Plato, *Statesman* 269a–274e, *Timaeus* 22a–25d, *Critias* 112a, *Laws* III 677a–d; Aristotle, *Metaphysics* XII: 8, 1074a 10–14, *Politics* VII: 10, 1329b 25–30; Lucretius, *Of the Nature of Things* V: 380–415; Ovid, *Metamorphoses* I: 253–312.

9 [30]* **the well of the Oath** or Beersheba, in *Genesis* 21:25–33.

9 [31] **The chaos which the Poets feigned among the elements** See Hesiod, *Theogony* 116; Ovid, *Metamorphoses* I: 5–31; *cf.* Lucretius, *Of the Nature of Things* II: 118–122. Descartes uses the very same expression—"a chaos as confused as the poets might feign"—to describe the starting point of his own cosmology, in *Discourse on Method* V (Gilson ed.), 42: 23f. **did prevail among its productions** Lucretius, *op. cit.*, V: 243f, 380f; and for Rousseau's argument in this paragraph and the next, consider *ibid.*, V: 380–415.

9 [33]* **It is claimed** by Buffon in "Le Boeuf" ("The Ox"), *OP*, Piveteau ed., 359b 6–359a 15; "Les animaux carnivores" ("The Carnivorous Animals"), *ibid.*, 366b 25–367a 10, 373a 32–377a 44; and "Le Lièvre" ("The Hare"), *ibid.*, 363–365.

9 [34] How many arid lands   The issue was discussed frequently in the seventeenth and eighteenth centuries; Montesquieu points out how much human industry contributed to the fertility of Persia, China, the Lowlands, and Egypt—the four instances Rousseau cites (*Of the Spirit of Laws* XVIII: 6, 7). However, whereas Montesquieu's point is that where human industry is needed, the laws have to foster it, Rousseau's point is that laws and government will arise first where human industry and collaborative efforts are needed.

9 [36]* The first men . . . marry their sisters   After canvassing this traditional problem at length, Pufendorf concludes that such marriages cannot be held to violate either natural right or the biblical account of the beginnings (*Droit* VI: 1, §34); so, too, Grotius, *Right* II: 5, §18, ¶¶5, 6, 7; and even Cumberland, *Loix* VIII, §9; *cf.* Plato, *Republic* V: 460e–461e, with *Laws* VIII: 838a–c.

12 [1] Around the fountains which I have mentioned   In this *Essay* 9 [34]–[35].

12 [2] The first stories . . . in verse   For example, Plutarch: "There was a time when people used for the currency of speech, verses and tunes and songs, converting into music and poetry, all history, all philosophy, every passion, and to speak generally, every circumstance that required more dignified utterance. For things that nowadays few people listen to, everybody then used to hear, and took pleasure in their being sung; 'ploughmen and fowlers too,' as Pindar hath it." (*On the Pythian Responses* [C. W. King tr.], 24f). **says Strabo** (63 B.C.– 24 A.D.), in *Geography* I: 2.6.

12 [2]* Archytas and Aristoxenus   *Archytas atque Aristoxenus etiam subjectam grammaticen musicae putaverunt, et eosdem utriusque rei praeceptores fuisse. . . . Tum Eupolis, apud quem Prodamus et musicen et litteras docet, et Maricas, qui est Hyperbolus, nihil se ex musicis scire nisi litteras confitetur,* in M. Fabius Quintilian (*c.* 35–*c.* 100 A.D.), *Institutes* I: 10, 17f. Rousseau's transcription of this passage contains an uncharacteristically large number of errors: *Architas* instead of *Archytas; Aristoxenes* instead of *Aristoxenus; grammaticem* instead of *grammaticen; musicem* instead of *musicen; docet. Et* instead of *docet, et.* However Rousseau's most striking departure from Quintilian's text is that he speaks of Archytas and Aristoxenos, where Quintilian speaks of Archytas and Evenus. Archytas (*fl.* ca. 400 B.C.), Pythagorean philosopher and statesman who helped Plato escape from the court of Dionysius, tyrant of Syracuse (Plato, *Seventh Letter,*

350 a-b); Evenus (*fl* ca. 400 B.C.), poet, sophist, and rhetorician who taught "the virtue of man and citizen" for a mere 5 minae (Plato, *Apology of Socrates,* 20 b, cf. *Phaedo* 60 d); Aristoxenos (*fl.* ca 318 B.C.), Aristotelian philosopher who held that judgment of musical intervals rests on what we perceive, and not, as the Pythagoreans maintained, on mathematical ratios; on *le jugement de l'oreille* rather than on *le calcul* is how Rousseau put it in the article "Aristoxéniens" of his *Dictionary of Music;* see also "Intervalle" and "Pythagoréciens." The disagreement between Rousseau and Rameau in many respects parallels that ancient quarrel between the Aristoxenians and the Pythagoreans. **Prodamus** and **Maricas** are dramatic characters in comedies by **Eupolis** (ca. 445–411 B.C.); and, as Quintilian points out, the character called Maricas represents the fifth-century Athenian demagogue **Hyperbolus.**

12 [4]   Pierré-Jean **Burette**   (1665–1747), the physician and antiquary who wrote extensively on the music of the ancients, translated and commented on Plutarch's dialogue *Of Music,* to which Rousseau refers in chapter 19 of this *Essay.*

12 [4]* Abbé Jean **Terrasson**   (1670–1750), in *Dissertation critique sur l'Iliade d'Homère* (Porset). **Amphion** Son of Zeus and Antiope, whose music was said to have caused the stones to move into place by themselves and form the wall protecting Thebes; *e.g.,* Pausanias, *Travels* IX: 5. iv. **Orpheus** The legendary pre-Homeric singer and founder of mystery cults concerned with afterlife, whose lyre playing was said to tame wild beasts, and move trees and rocks; *e.g.,* Pausanias, *Travels* IX: 30. iii.

12 [5] such very different instruments   In the sense in which a singer's voice is his "instrument."

13 [1] a touching painting ... an etching   Before photography, etchings provided the only means for reproductions of the image. "Paintings are all fated to perish. Cold, heat, air, and worms have already destroyed many. It is up to etching to preserve what can be saved" (Diderot, "Salon de 1765," in *Salons* II [Oxford, 1979; Jean Seznec ed.], p. 227).

13 [5] the experiment with the prism   Newton first reported his experiments analyzing natural light into its component colors in 1672. His full discussion appeared in the *Opticks, or a Treatise of the Reflections, Refractions, Inflections, and Colours of Light* (1704).

14 [2] Regarding harmony properly so called   Rousseau develops the point at greater length in his *Examen de deux principes avancés par M. Rameau: Oeuvres complètes* (Paris: Alexandre Houssiaux, 1853), III: 549–552.

14 [4] M. Rameau contends   Jean Philippe Rameau (1683–1764), in *Traité de l'harmonie* (1722), and in many subsequent writings; the disagreement between Rousseau and Rameau was long-standing, and it led to sometimes acrimonious exchanges, not only between the principals, but also between their partisans and mediators. It was certainly embittered by personal pique and antipathy. But that should not obscure the fact that it involves fundamental issues in the theory of music and of the fine arts in general.

15 [3] Tarantula bites   The bite of these poisonous spiders was said to cause sluggishness and melancholy which could be dispelled only by vigorous movements or dancing; hence the tarantella. Nicolas **Bernier's** (1664–1734) **Cantatas**   Some of which Rousseau recalls studying and learning by heart in his early twenties (*Confessions* V, *OC* I: 184).

15 [5] one sense ... without ... moral component   In writing this sharp criticism of gluttony, Rousseau may have remembered that the materialist La Mettrie had died in 1751 from overeating.

16 [1] The analysis of sound ... the analysis of light   Newton himself repeatedly called attention to possible correspondences between them: "May not the harmony and discord of Colours arise from the proportions of the Vibrations propagated through the Fibres of the optick Nerves into the Brain, as the harmony and discord of sound arise from the proportions of the Vibrations of the Air? For some Colours, if they be view'd together, are agreeable to one another, as those of Gold and Indigo, and others disagree" (*Opticks* III: Pt. I, qu. 14; see also I: II, prop. III, prob. I; II: I, ob. 14; II: III, prop. XVI). **the famous clavichord**   By the Jesuit Louis Bertrand Castel (1688–1757), teacher of mathematics and physics, who in a work entitled *Optique des couleurs* (1740) suggested matching tones to colors and so to "play" pictures. He built a prototype of such an "ocular clavichord" and exhibited it in Paris in 1739, but he never succeeded in making it play properly. Rousseau had known Castel when he first came to Paris (*Confessions* VII, *OC* I: 283, 288f, 326). Castel published a criticism of Rousseau's *Letter on French Music,* and another of the *Second Discourse,* entitled *L'Homme moral opposé à l'homme physique de M. R**** (Toulouse, 1756).

16 [3] not the mechanical flutist ... but the engineer Jacques de Vaucanson (1709–1782) built and, in 1737, exhibited a widely admired mechanical toy flutist. Voltaire compared its maker to Prometheus; so did La Mettrie, who thought the device proved the possibility of a talking machine and hence of his materialist understanding of man (in *L'homme machine, op. cit.,* p. 190). Rousseau had met Vaucanson: see his letter to de Conzié of 17 January 1742 (*CC* I: 139, no. 41).

16 [6] harmony of the heavenly spheres The Pythagorean view that in their revolutions the heavenly spheres cause a music which we cannot hear because the noise of the world drowns it out; for a summary and criticism, see Aristotle, *On the Heavens* (II: 9, 290b12–291a22), and *cf. Metaphysics* (I: 5, 985b23–986a7); Quintilian, *Institutes* I, x, 12. Rameau appealed to the Pythagorean tradition in support of his claim that harmony, as he understands it, is "natural"; see, *e.g., Demonstration du principe de l'harmonie* (1750) in *Complete Theoretical Writings* (E. R. Jacobi ed.), III: 157f, and *Nouvelles réflexions sur le principe sonore, ibid.,* IV: 213.

18 [1] songs of American savages Some of which Rousseau included in his *Dictionary of Music* under the heading "Songs of Canadian Savages."

18 [3] they would have called the second *do re* a consonance Because *re* forms a perfect consonance with the unsounded *sol.* I am indebted to Mr. Robert Burns for this note.

18 [4] pathetic forms "Dramatic and theatrical musical form which tends to depict and to arouse great passions, especially suffering and sadness. . . . True *pathos* resides in a passionate accent which is not determined by rules but which genius finds and the heart feels without its being possible for art to formulate any law regarding it" (*Dictionary of Music,* "Pathétique").

19 [2] Melanippides ... Plutarch In the dialogue *Of Music* traditionally attributed—and now believed to have been misattributed—to Plutarch (*c.* 46–*c.* 120 A.D.), the 5th century B.C. poet Melanippides and the early 4th century B.C. poet **Philoxenus** are said to have broken with traditional musical practice. Indeed, Philoxenus's play *Cyclopes* evidently created a sensation by calling for a sung solo by the Cyclops. The dialogue goes on to quote a speech from **Pherecrates's** (fl. 440–420 B.C.) *Chiron,* in which Music tells the story of her fall from being literature and music united, to being music "alone" (*De musica* 30:

1141c–1142a). Condillac, in contrast to Rousseau, speaking about this and similar texts, derides such an attachment to old ways (*Essay* II: I, ch. 8, §73, pp. 229f). **Plato, jealous of Homer and Euripides** Plato's Socrates, speaking of the traditional quarrel between poetry and philosophy, prefaces a criticism of Homer with the remark that while he has honored him since boyhood, he honors truth more (*Republic* X: 595 b–c); he had Socrates criticize Euripides (480–408 B.C.) by name earlier in the dialogue (*Republic* VIII: 568 a–b); according to tradition, Plato himself began by writing tragedies (Diogenes Laertius, *Lives* III: 5).

19 [4] The Emperor Julian, surnamed the Apostate (332–363), had been a general in Gaul.

19 [7] did not know the principle of an effect which they knew Namely, why they found pleasant the chords which they did find pleasant. **verbiage in Jean de Muris** or Jehan des Murs (*c.* 1300–*c.* 1350); the encyclopedic compendium of medieval musical knowledge, the *Speculum musicae,* traditionally attributed to him, is now attributed to his somewhat older contemporary, Jacques de Liège (*c.* 1260–*c.* 1330). Giovanni Andrea Angelini, known as **Bontempi** (*c.* 1624–1705), composer, poet, musicologist, author of an *Historia musicae* (Perugia, 1695), which Rousseau read in 1737 and which first aroused his interest in the history and theory of music (*Confessions* VI, *OC* I: 246).

19 [7]* M. Tartini has confirmed Giuseppe Tartini (1692–1770), composer, violinist, and musical theorist whose works on harmony greatly influenced Rousseau.

19 [9] doubly the voice of nature *I.e.,* the appropriate or "natural" imitation of the spontaneous or natural sounds and utterings; see especially *Essay* 14 [7].

20 [3] Among the ancients . . . in a public square So, too, Condillac, *Essay,* II: ch. 3, §§28f; by contrast, Aristotle, discussing the proper size for a polis, remarks that if it is too large, "who can give it orders unless he has Stentor's voice?" (*Politics* VIII: iv, 1326b 6f, *cf.* V: v, 1305a 8–15). **M. d'Alembert** published an *Elements of Music . . . according to the Principles of M. Rameau* in 1752.

INDEX

The index should be used in conjunction with the Editor's Notes, where names and concepts are commonly identified the first time Rousseau mentions them. The occasional references to those Notes in the index are italicized; an asterisk (*) indicates a footnote of Rousseau's.

orang-outang, 215–18, 235, *353, 354–55*
origin of: things, 139, 259; knowledge, 14; man, 141; differences among men, 130; inequality, 117, 129, 131; moral inequality, 133, 168, 195, 199; passions, 150; languages, 152, 154, 158, 235–95, *339;* human institutions, 260; instituted signs, 153; rules of justice, 179; society and laws, 183; political societies, 185; societies and languages, 271; the arts, **266**; music, 276–78
original: constitution, 129; state, 130, 199, 216; condition, 149; man, 133, 198; happiness, 149; simplicity, 213; and artificial, 130
Orpheus, 277**
Otanes, 200
Ovid, quoted, 1, 182; 8, 177, *298–99, 301–2, 345, 362, 369, 370*
Ozymandias, 58

Palamedes, 225, 252
paradox, 16, 35, 39, 54, 139, 225, 231, 232, 254, 257
Parsees, 250**
passion, 6, 27, 32, **37–38, 51,** 76, 91, 98, 103, 106*, 107*, 113, 129, 143, 145, **149–50,** 158, **160,** 163–65, 166, 175, 181, 193–94, 195, 196, 197, **198,** 224, 231, 242–43, 245–49 *passim,* 266*, 273–74, 276, 278–79, 281–82; silence of, 27; calm of, 160; indolent, 265; idleness feeds, labor represses, 273; vocal signs of, 282; passionate language, 246, 249; accent, 282
Pausanias, 252*, *368, 369, 372*
Peisistratos, *303, 367*
Pelasgos, *368, 369*
people (the), 65*, 107, 119, 121, 122, 126, 139, 194, 212, 242, 255
people(s), 106*, 108*; the first, 271; true cradles of, 271; of the North and the South, 150, 212–13, 259–76; savage, 250; most savage, known to us, 176, 263; comparative study of, 69; free, 33, 120, 125, 187; with morals, 107; corrupted, 108; mixtures of, 101*, 212–13, 214; popular languages, 272, 294
Pereyre, Giaccobo R., 243

perfectibility, 149, 156, 168, 216
Periander, *362*
Pericles, 61, 78*
Persia, Persians, 9, 16–17, 21*, 86–87, 263, 271
Persius Flaccus, Aulus, quoted, 134
Petty, Sir William, *306*
Pharisees, 40
Phidias, 18
Philip of Macedon, 8, 82, 96*
Philo, called Judaeus, 40
philosophaster, 219
philosopher, 2, 5, 10, 12, 15, 23, 24, 26, 35, 36, 38, 40, 41, 42, 58, 65*, 68, 69*, 70, 72, 74, 76, 87, 91, 93, 102, **104,** 106*, 129, 130, 131, 139, 143, 148, 152, 153, 154, 157, 162, 177, 187, 195, 197, 200, 211, 218, 220, 221, 224, 225, 233, 268*, 291; true, 33, 65*, 75, 102, 235; half, 106; the first, 102; ancient, 81, 131; our, 152, 157, 195, 220; Christian, 139; Chinese, *313*
philosophic, 5, 9, 225, 226, 277*, 295; peoples, 69
philosophize, 48*, 87, 219, 235, 259, 279, 284
philosophy, 5, 7, 9, 14, 16, 23, 43, 76, **102–8,** 129, 130, 150–51, 162, 169, 185, 199, 218, 233, 285, 290; genuine, 5, 27; the new, 285; one people's, 218
Phoenecia, 252, 267
Phryne, 242
physical: good and evil, 143; man, 147; needs, **88,** 150, 220, 243, 273; impulsions, 288; inequality, 138, 199; aspect of love, 164; sense of "virtue" and "vice," 159; causes, 130, 274, 279; impressions, 288; aspects of art, 280; effects, 280, 283; nouns, 157; and moral, 361
physicist, 15*, 22, 139, 203
physics, 14, 36, 56, 60, 148, **222,** 292*
Pierre, Jean-Baptiste-Marie, 18, *305, 307*
Pigalle, Jean-Baptiste, 18
Pindar, 278
pity, **160–63,** 176, 181, 226, 236, 243*, 245, **261,** *342, 361, 363;* natural, 161, 176, 181. *See also* commiseration
Plato, 17*, 21*, 43, 45, 57, 74, 86, **140,** 145, 189, 219, 220, 225,

EDITORS, TRANSLATORS, AND ANNOTATORS